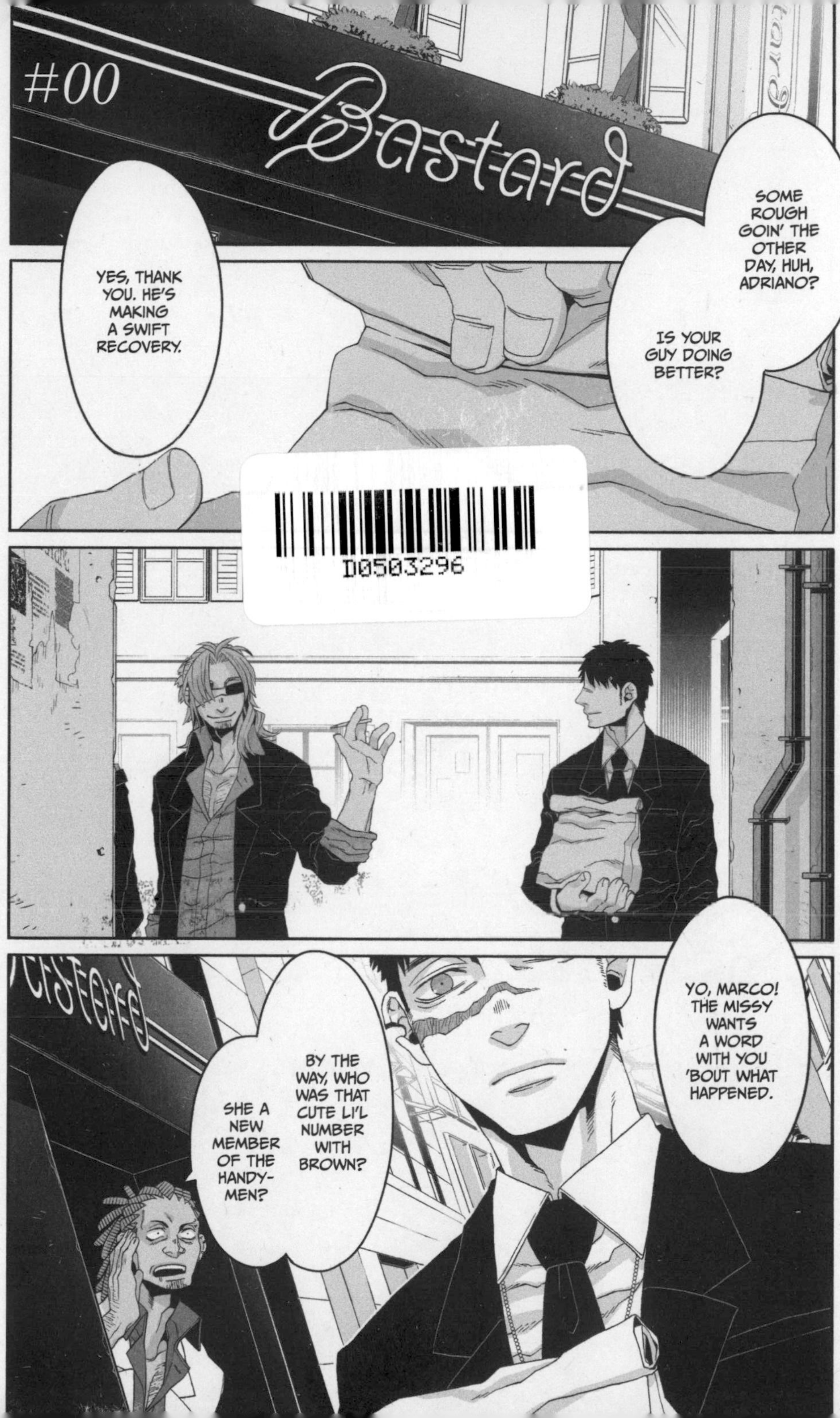
#00
Bastard
SOME ROUGH GOIN' THE OTHER DAY, HUH, ADRIANO?
IS YOUR GUY DOING BETTER?
YES, THANK YOU. HE'S MAKING A SWIFT RECOVERY.
YO, MARCO! THE MISSY WANTS A WORD WITH YOU 'BOUT WHAT HAPPENED.
BY THE WAY, WHO WAS THAT CUTE LI'L NUMBER WITH BROWN?
SHE A NEW MEMBER OF THE HANDY-MEN?

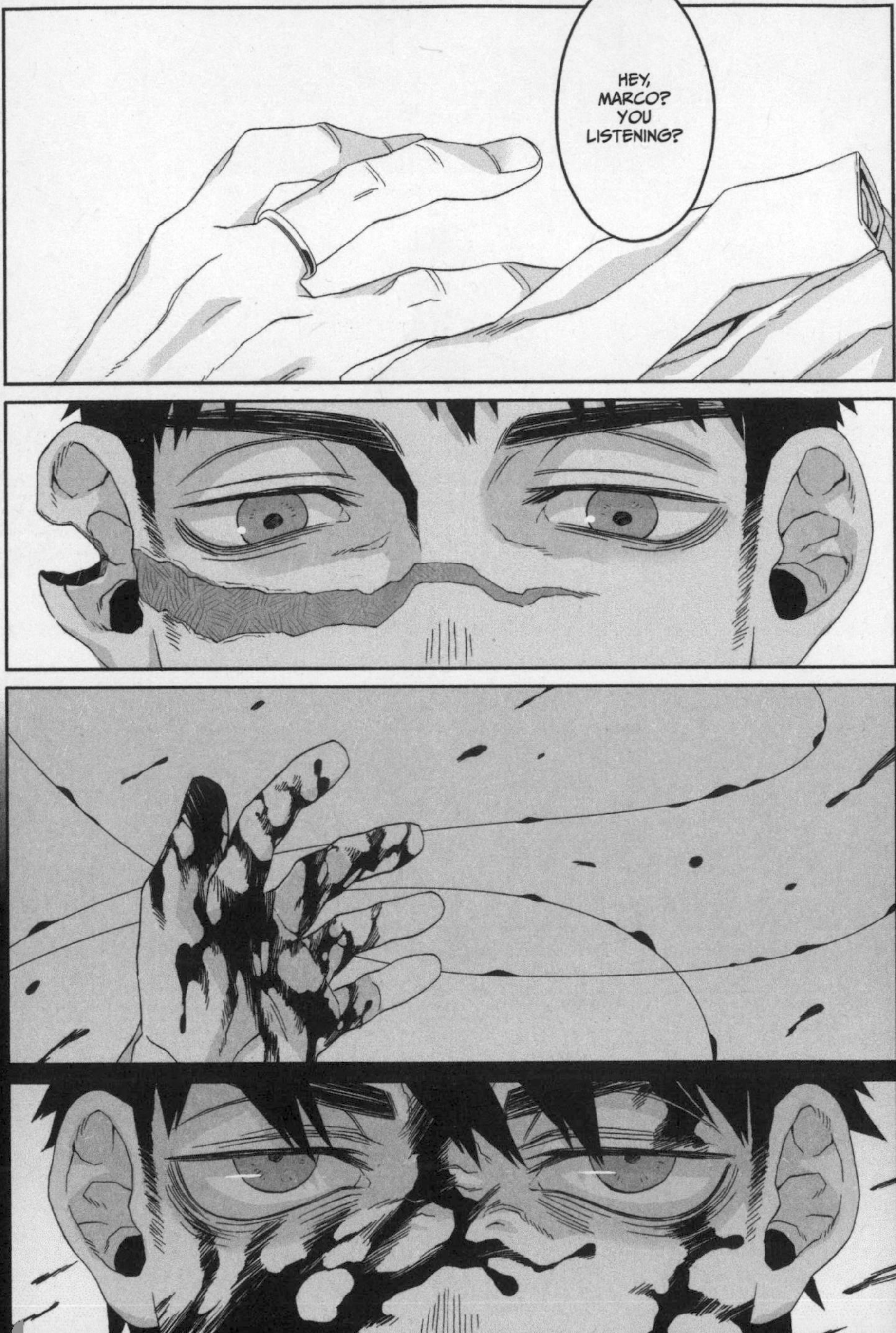
HEY, MARCO? YOU LISTENING?

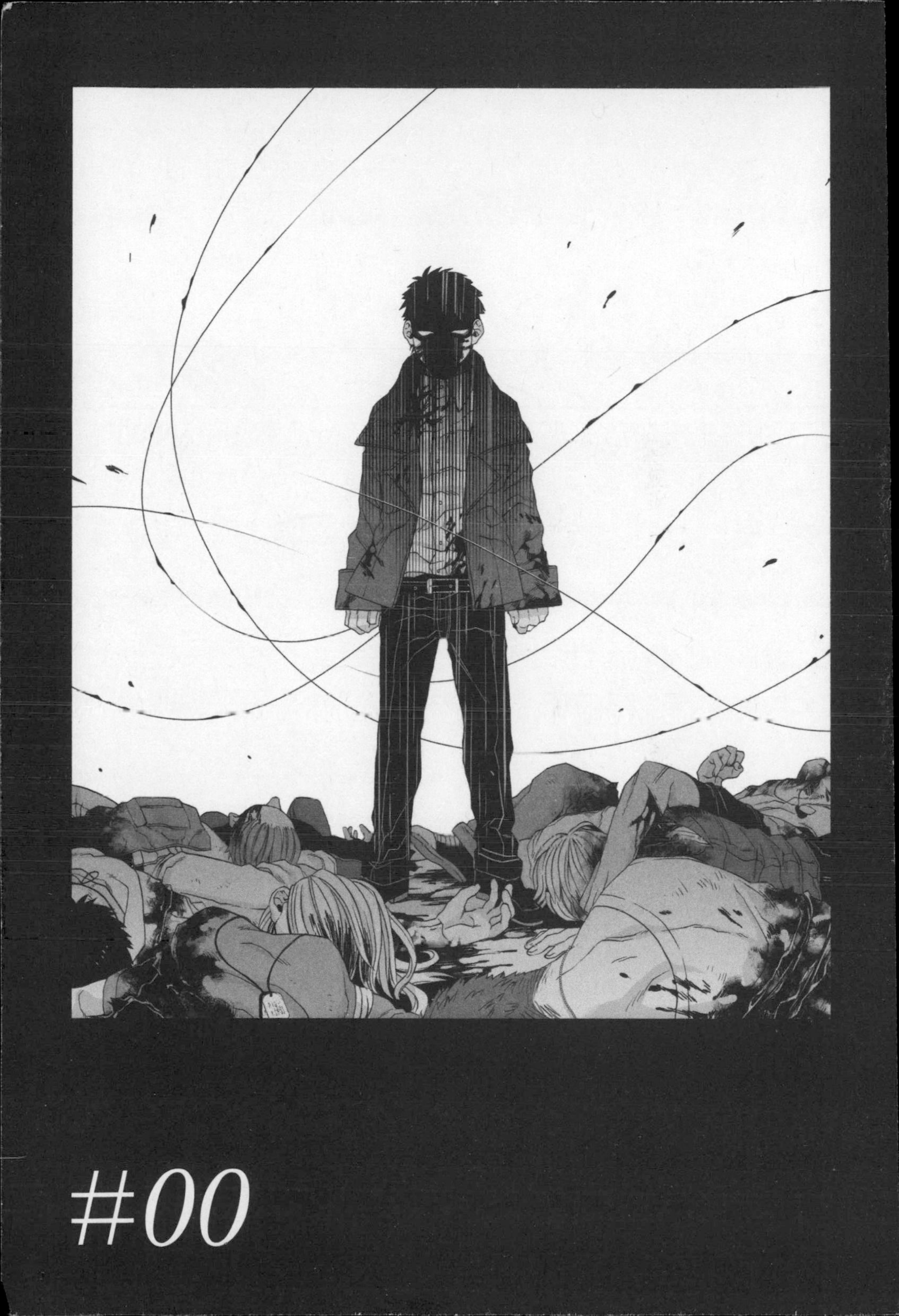

#00

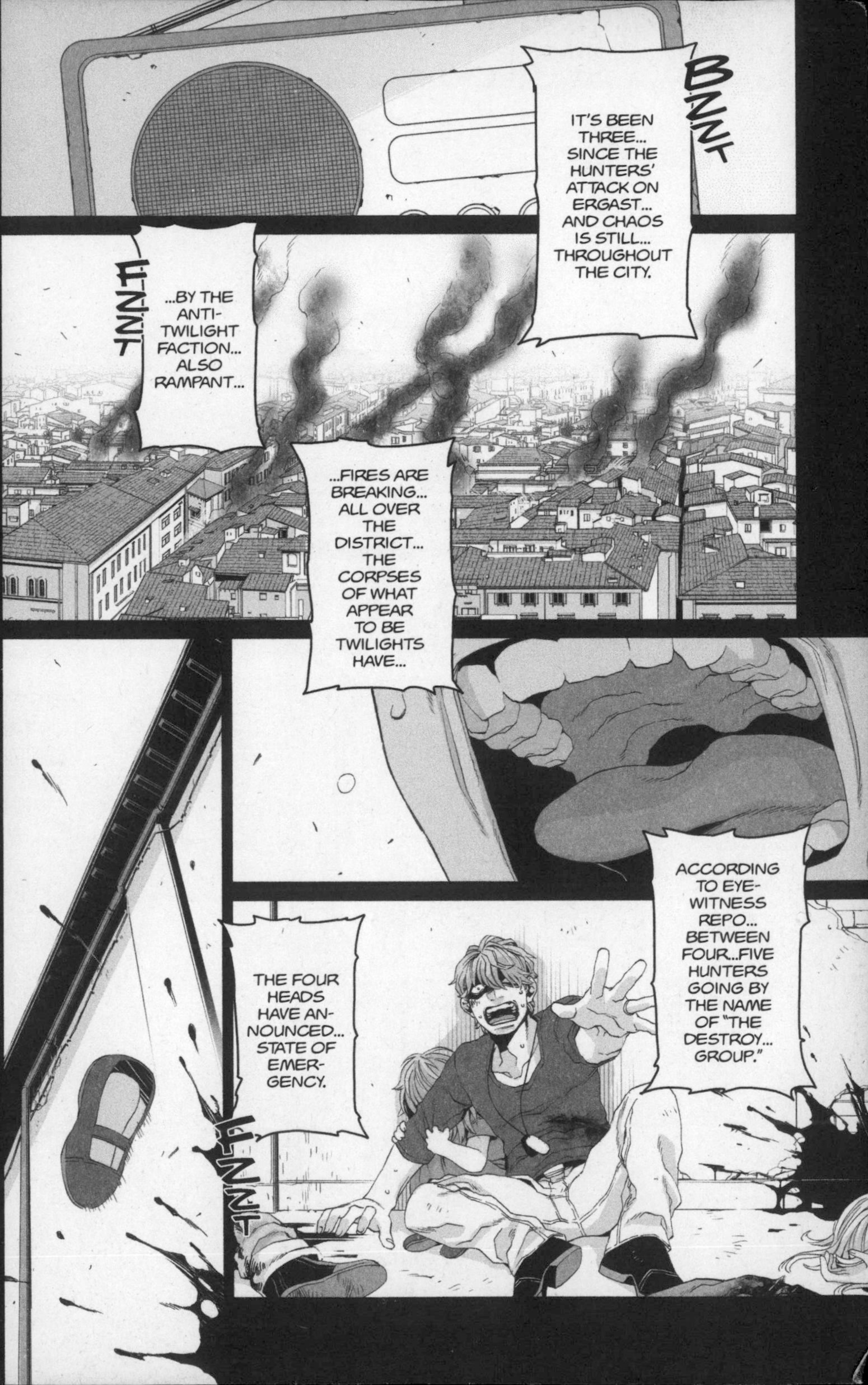
BZZT
IT'S BEEN THREE... SINCE THE HUNTERS' ATTACK ON ERGAST... AND CHAOS IS STILL... THROUGHOUT THE CITY.
FZZT
...BY THE ANTI-TWILIGHT FACTION... ALSO RAMPANT...
...FIRES ARE BREAKING... ALL OVER THE DISTRICT... THE CORPSES OF WHAT APPEAR TO BE TWILIGHTS HAVE...
ACCORDING TO EYE-WITNESS REPO... BETWEEN FOUR...FIVE HUNTERS GOING BY THE NAME OF "THE DESTROY... GROUP."
THE FOUR HEADS HAVE AN-NOUNCED... STATE OF EMER-GENCY.
FZZT

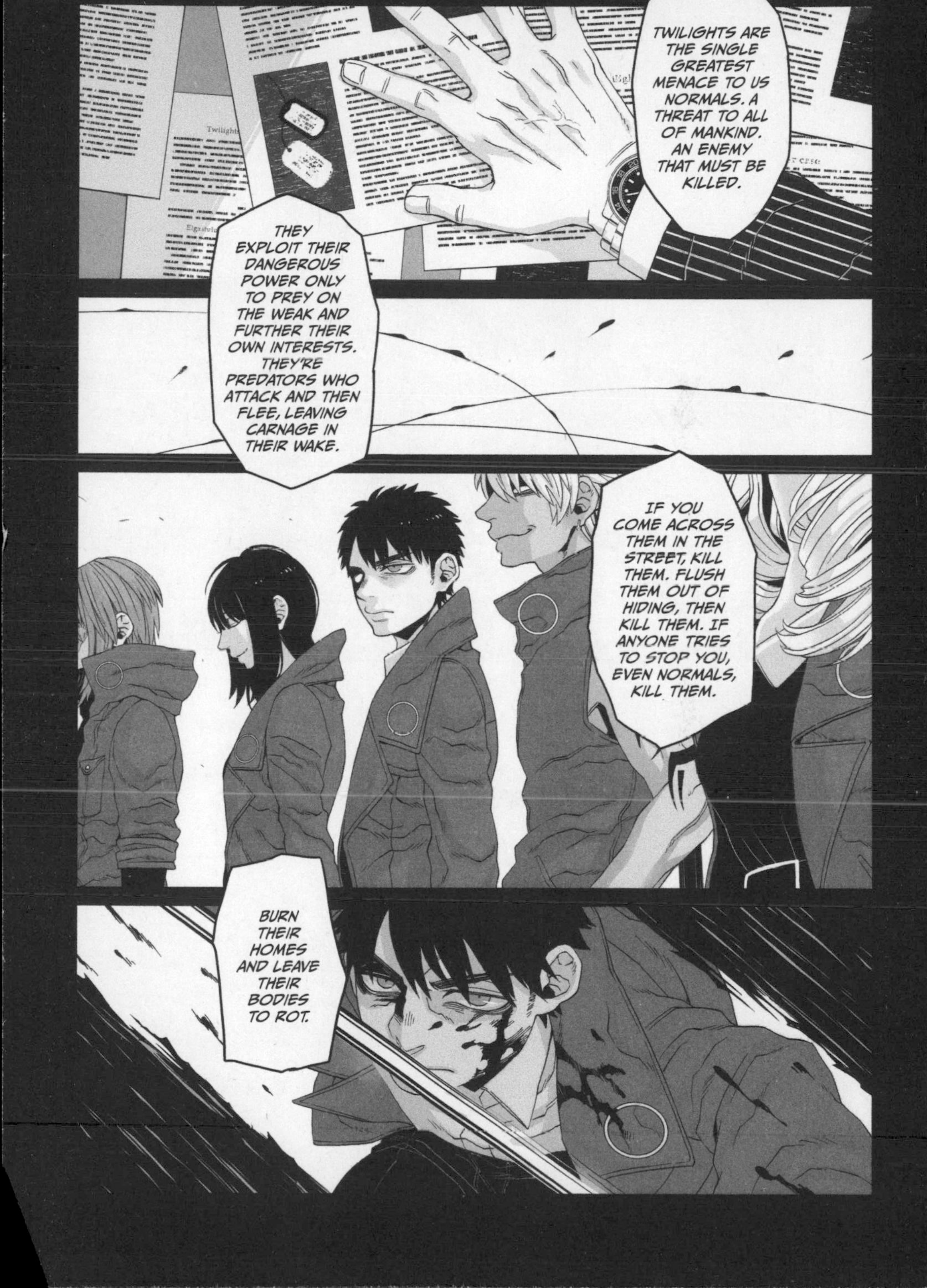
TWILIGHTS ARE THE SINGLE GREATEST MENACE TO US NORMALS. A THREAT TO ALL OF MANKIND. AN ENEMY THAT MUST BE KILLED.
THEY EXPLOIT THEIR DANGEROUS POWER ONLY TO PREY ON THE WEAK AND FURTHER THEIR OWN INTERESTS. THEY'RE PREDATORS WHO ATTACK AND THEN FLEE, LEAVING CARNAGE IN THEIR WAKE.
IF YOU COME ACROSS THEM IN THE STREET, KILL THEM. FLUSH THEM OUT OF HIDING, THEN KILL THEM. IF ANYONE TRIES TO STOP YOU, EVEN NORMALS, KILL THEM.
BURN THEIR HOMES AND LEAVE THEIR BODIES TO ROT.

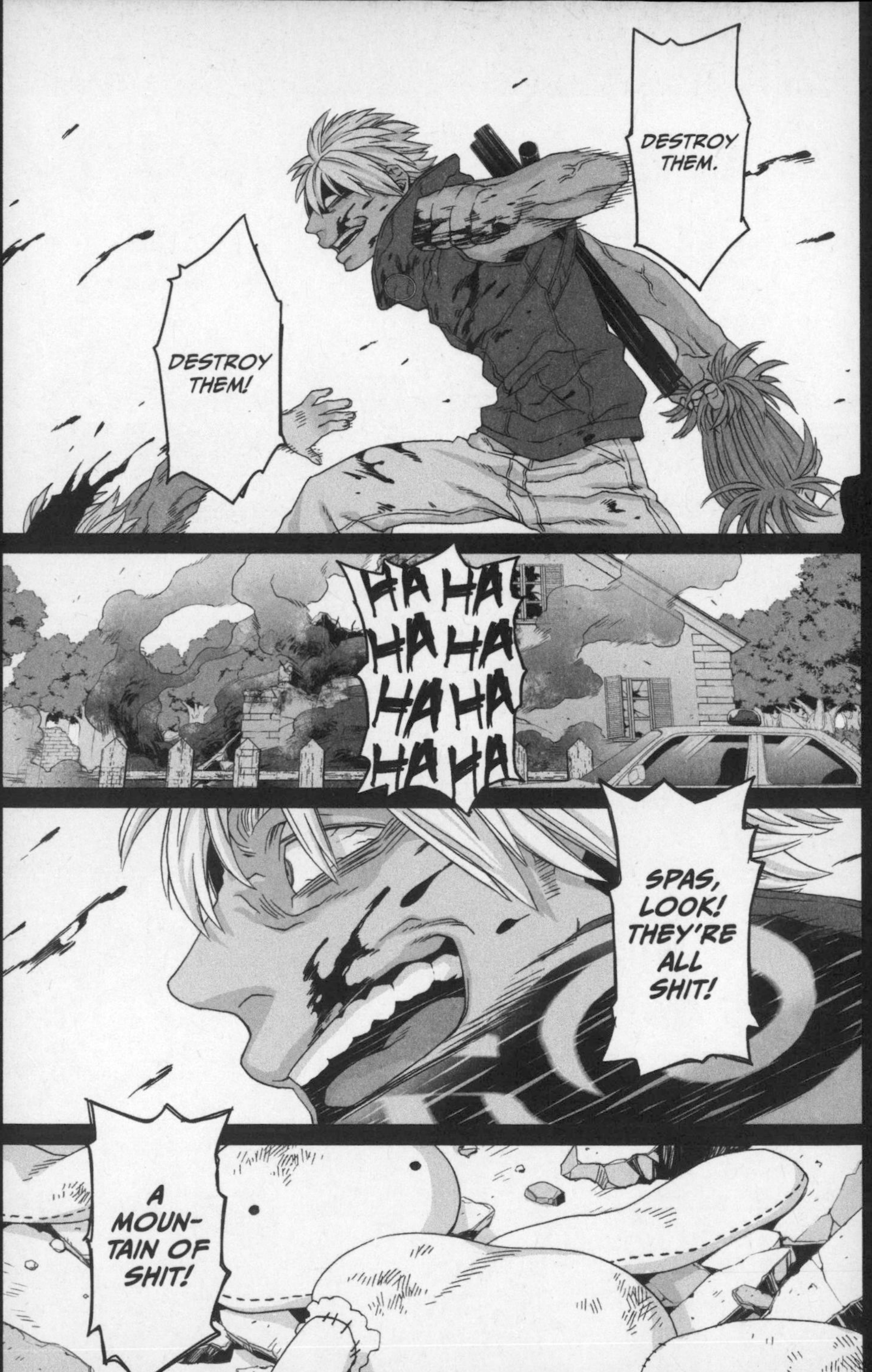
DESTROY THEM.
DESTROY THEM!
HA HA HA HA HA HA HA HA
SPAS, LOOK! THEY'RE ALL SHIT!
A MOUN-TAIN OF SHIT!

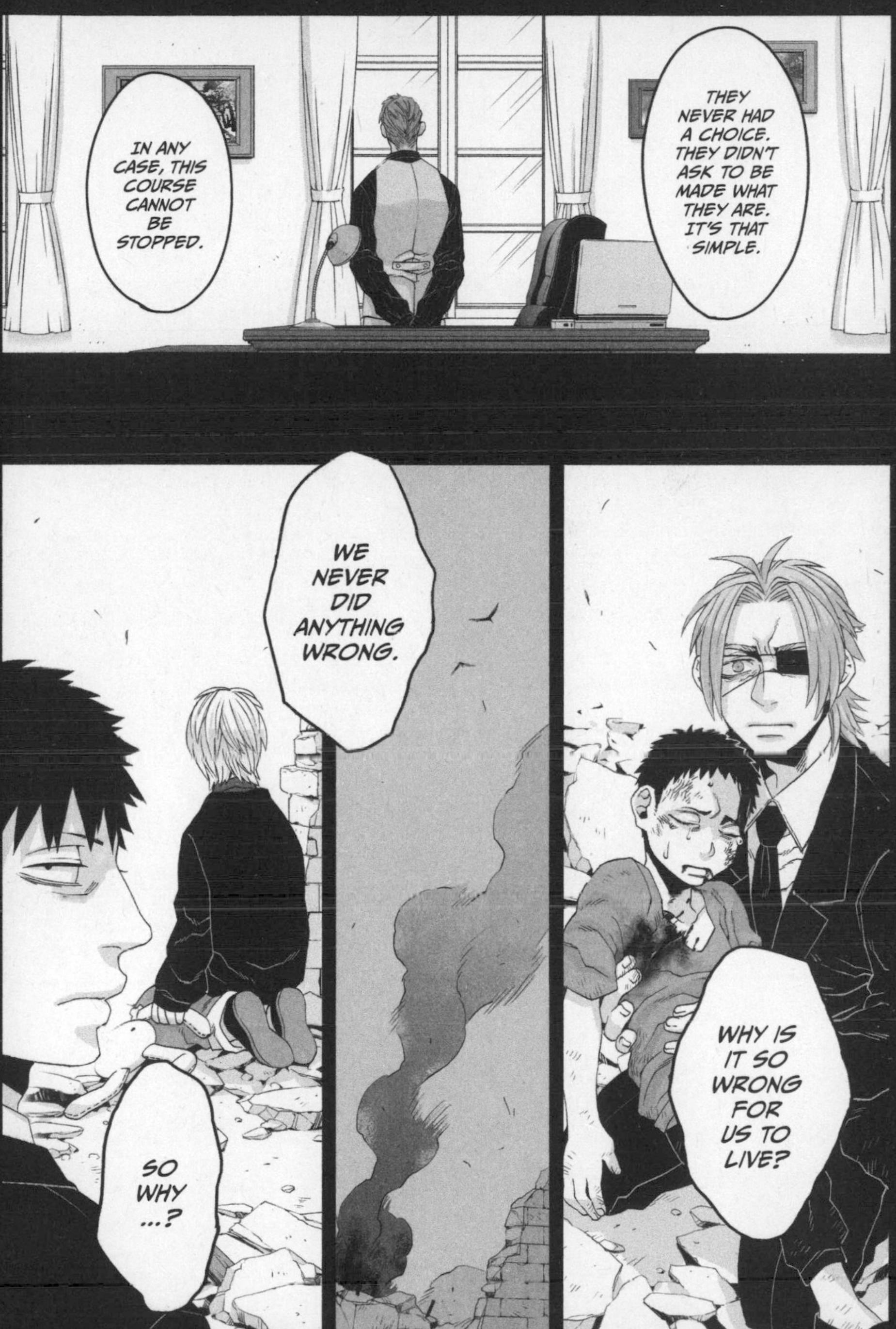
THEY NEVER HAD A CHOICE. THEY DIDN'T ASK TO BE MADE WHAT THEY ARE. IT'S THAT SIMPLE.
IN ANY CASE, THIS COURSE CANNOT BE STOPPED.
WHY IS IT SO WRONG FOR US TO LIVE?
WE NEVER DID ANYTHING WRONG.
SO WHY ...?

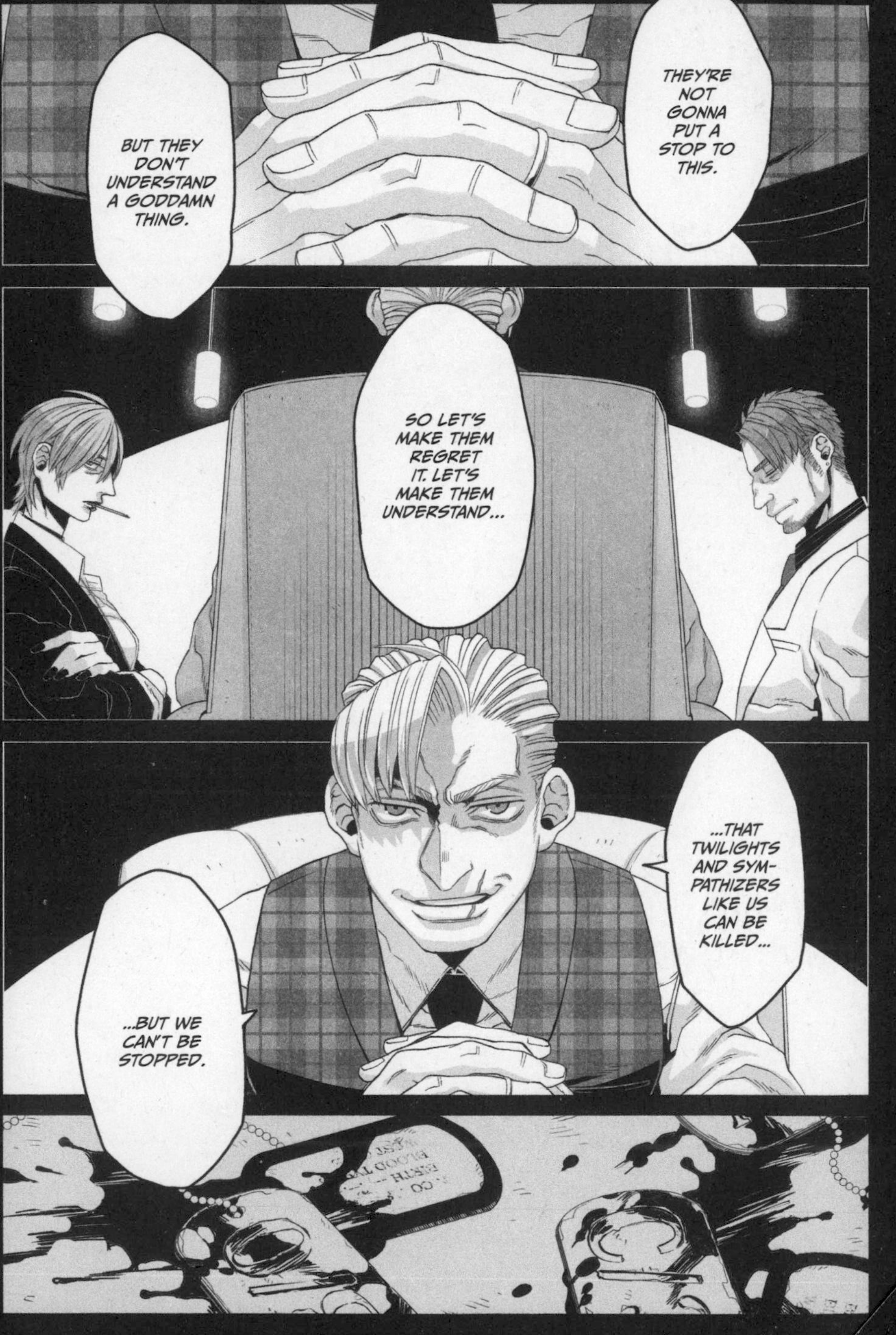
THEY'RE NOT GONNA PUT A STOP TO THIS.
BUT THEY DON'T UNDERSTAND A GODDAMN THING.
SO LET'S MAKE THEM REGRET IT. LET'S MAKE THEM UNDERSTAND...
...THAT TWILIGHTS AND SYM-PATHIZERS LIKE US CAN BE KILLED...
...BUT WE CAN'T BE STOPPED.

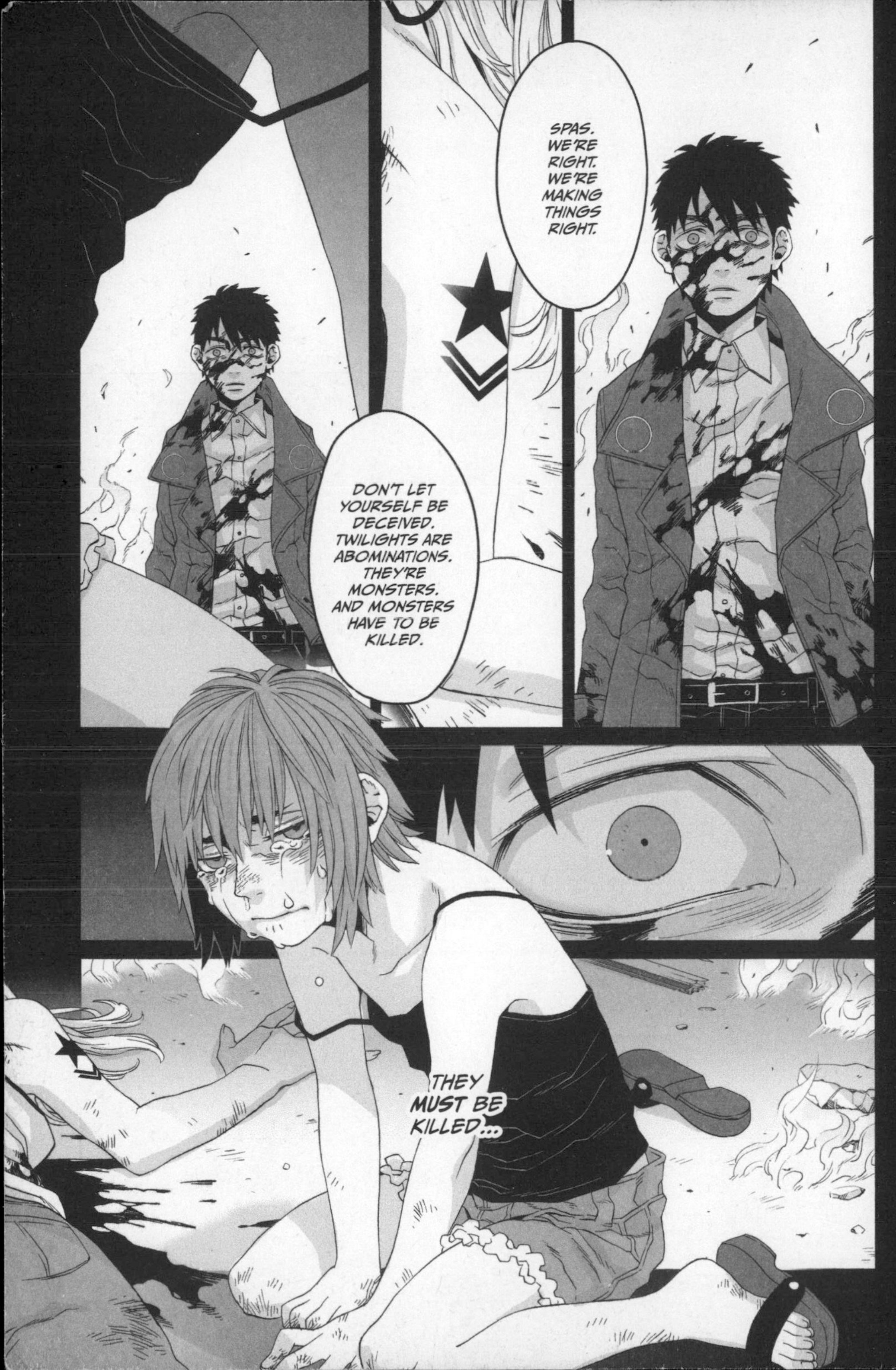
SPAS. WE'RE RIGHT. WE'RE MAKING THINGS RIGHT.
DON'T LET YOURSELF BE DECEIVED. TWILIGHTS ARE ABOMINATIONS. THEY'RE MONSTERS. AND MONSTERS HAVE TO BE KILLED.
THEY MUST BE KILLED...

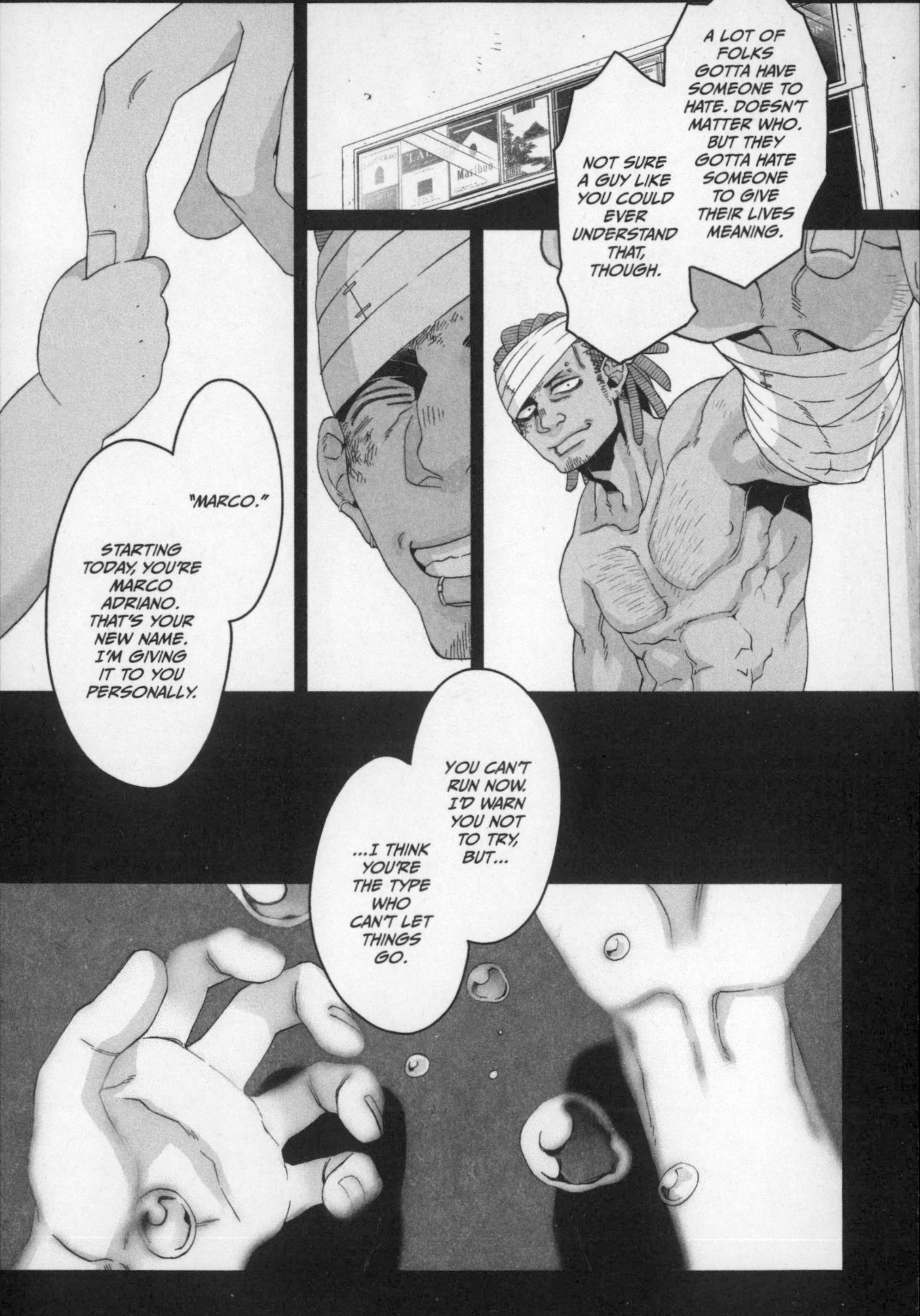
A LOT OF FOLKS GOTTA HAVE SOMEONE TO HATE. DOESN'T MATTER WHO. BUT THEY GOTTA HATE SOMEONE TO GIVE THEIR LIVES MEANING.
NOT SURE A GUY LIKE YOU COULD EVER UNDERSTAND THAT, THOUGH.
"MARCO."
STARTING TODAY, YOU'RE MARCO ADRIANO. THAT'S YOUR NEW NAME. I'M GIVING IT TO YOU PERSONALLY.
YOU CAN'T RUN NOW. I'D WARN YOU NOT TO TRY, BUT...
...I THINK YOU'RE THE TYPE WHO CAN'T LET THINGS GO.

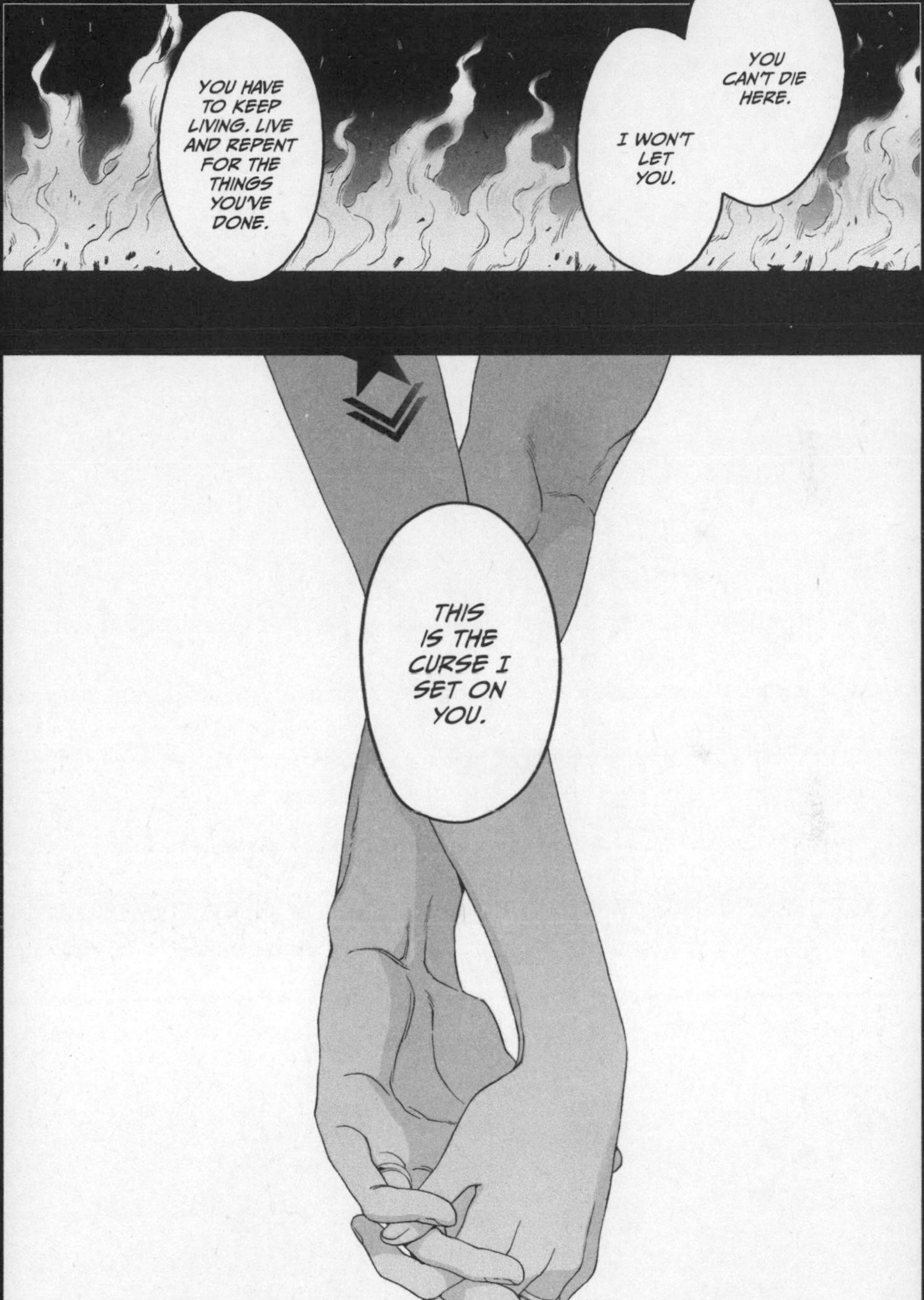
YOU CAN'T DIE HERE.
I WON'T LET YOU.
YOU HAVE TO KEEP LIVING. LIVE AND REPENT FOR THE THINGS YOU'VE DONE.
THIS IS THE CURSE I SET ON YOU.

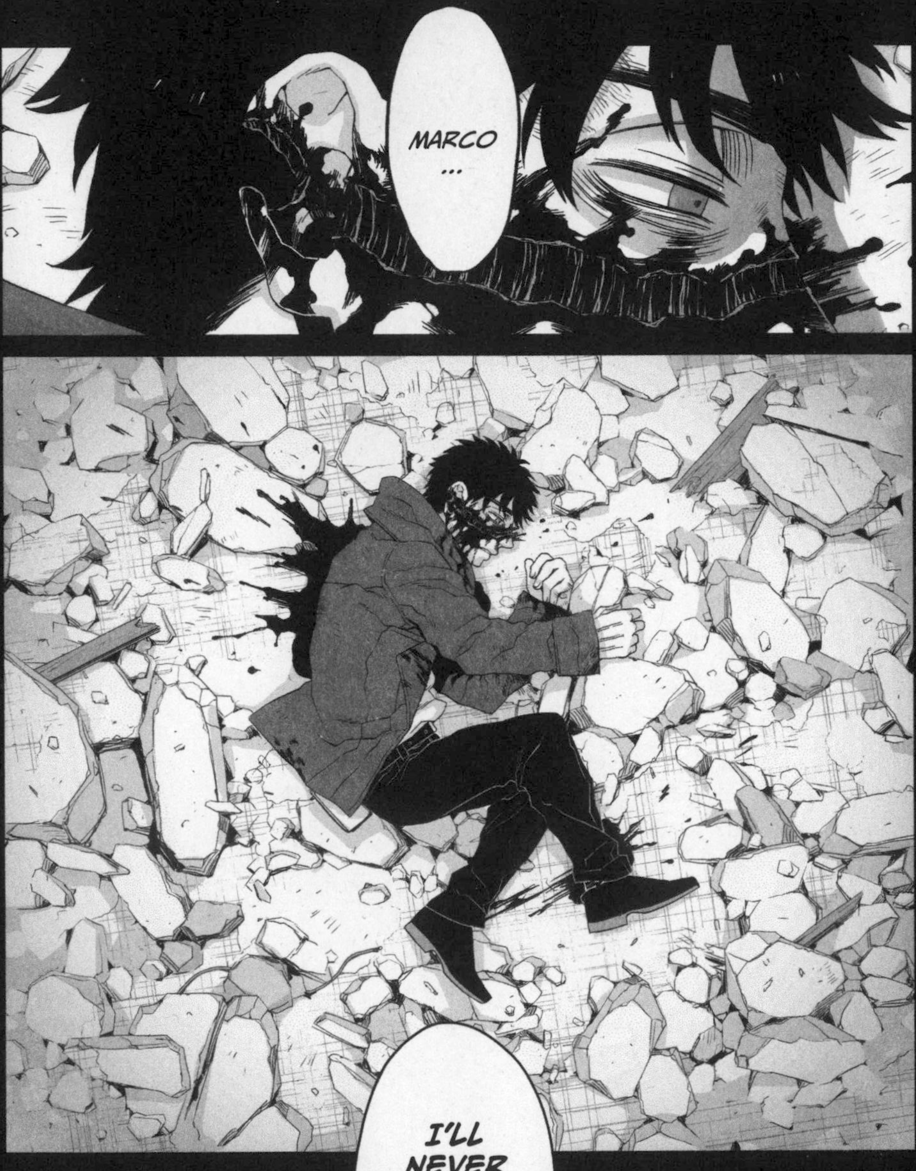
MARCO ...
I'LL NEVER LET YOU GO.

#00 END

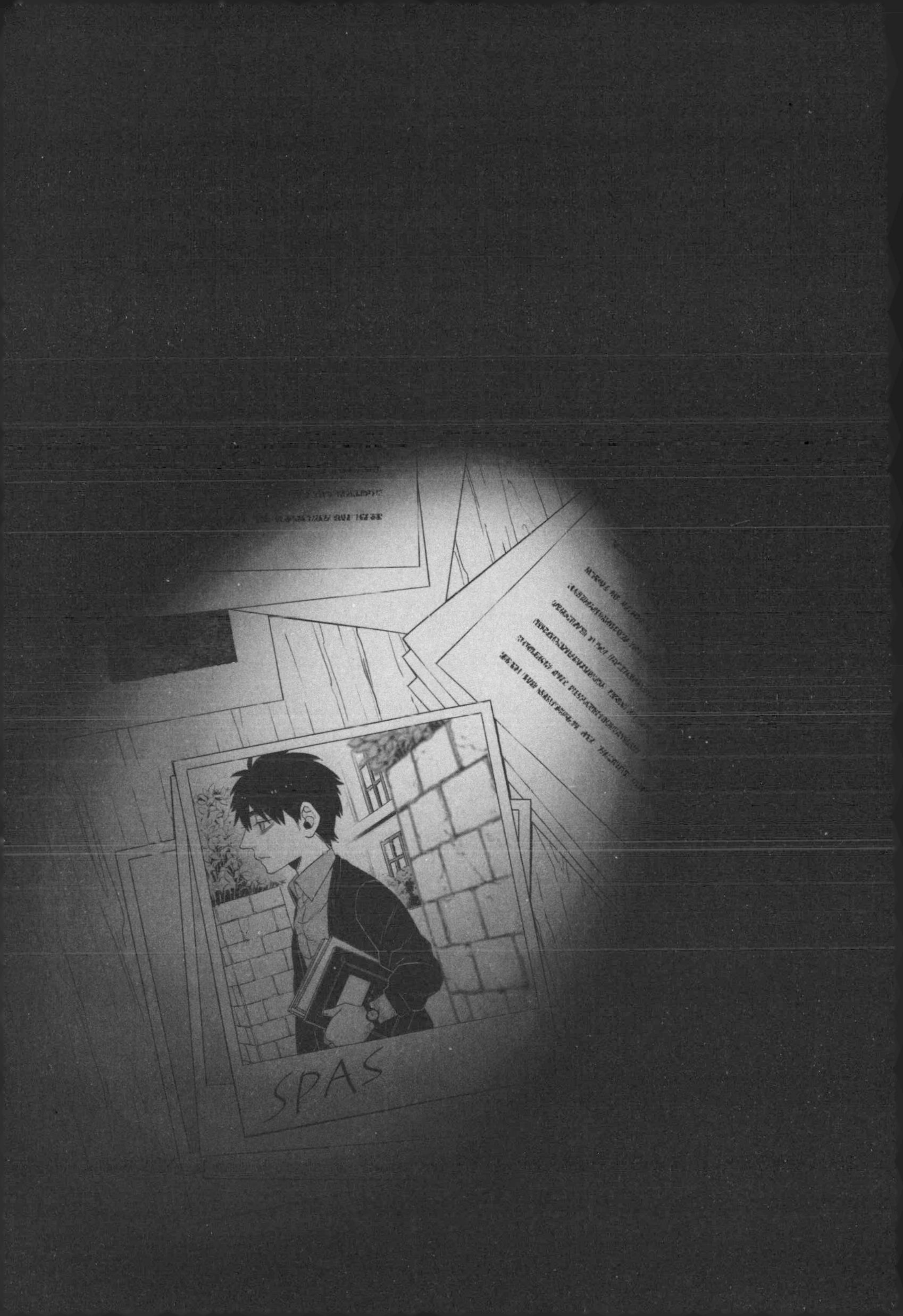
SPAS

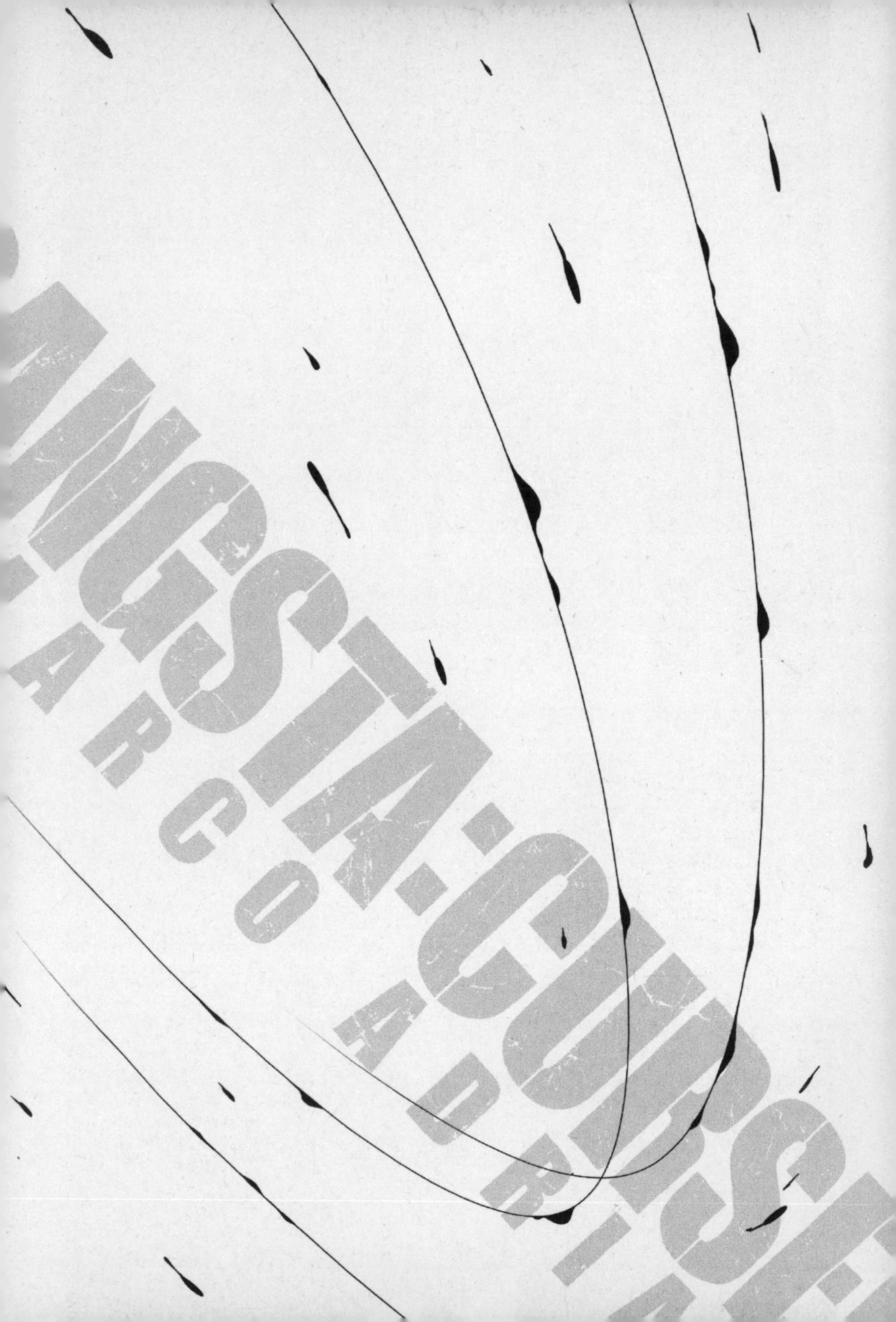
NGSTA:CURS
ARCO ADRI

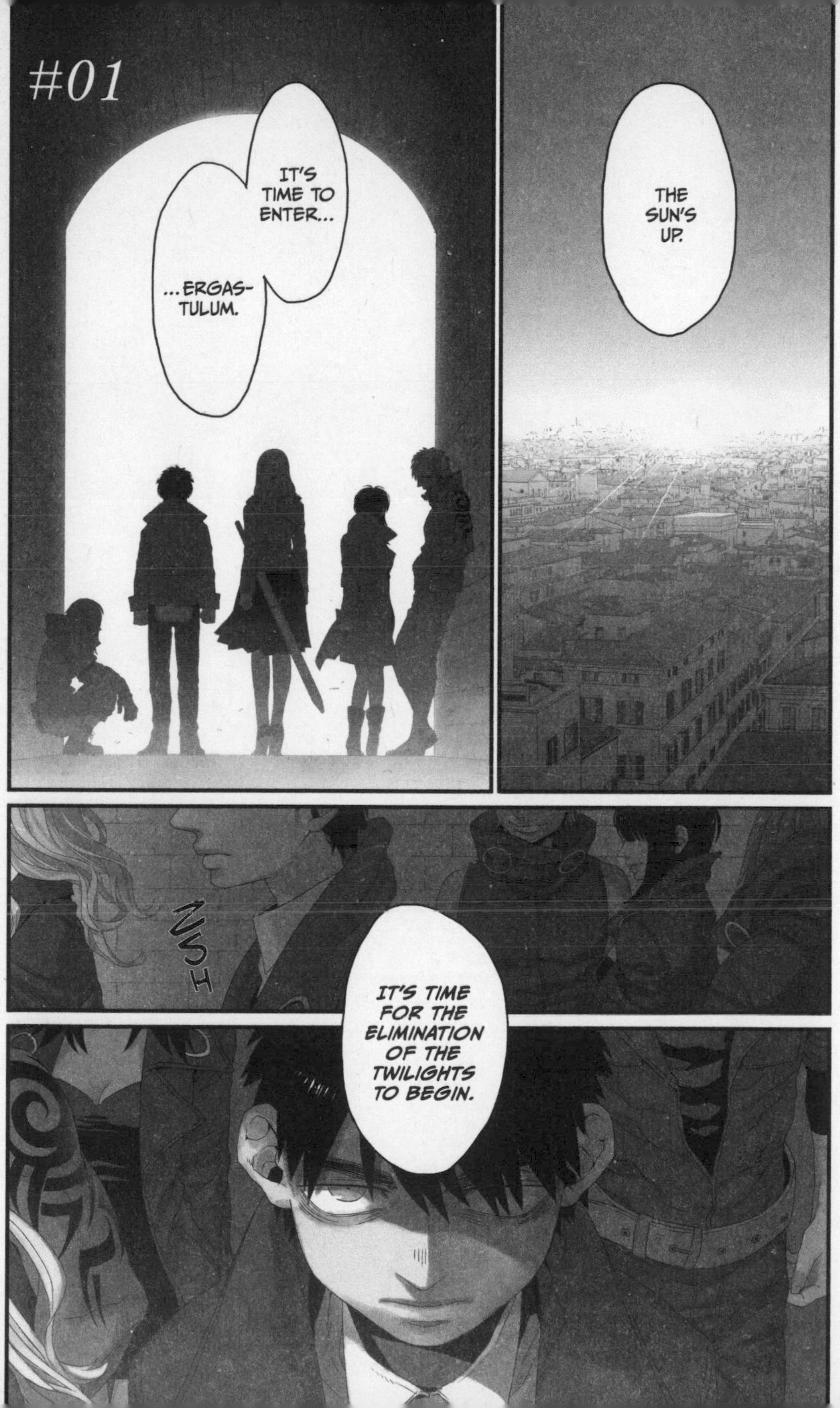
THE SUN'S UP.
#01
IT'S TIME TO ENTER...
...ERGASTULUM.
WSH
IT'S TIME FOR THE ELIMINATION OF THE TWILIGHTS TO BEGIN.

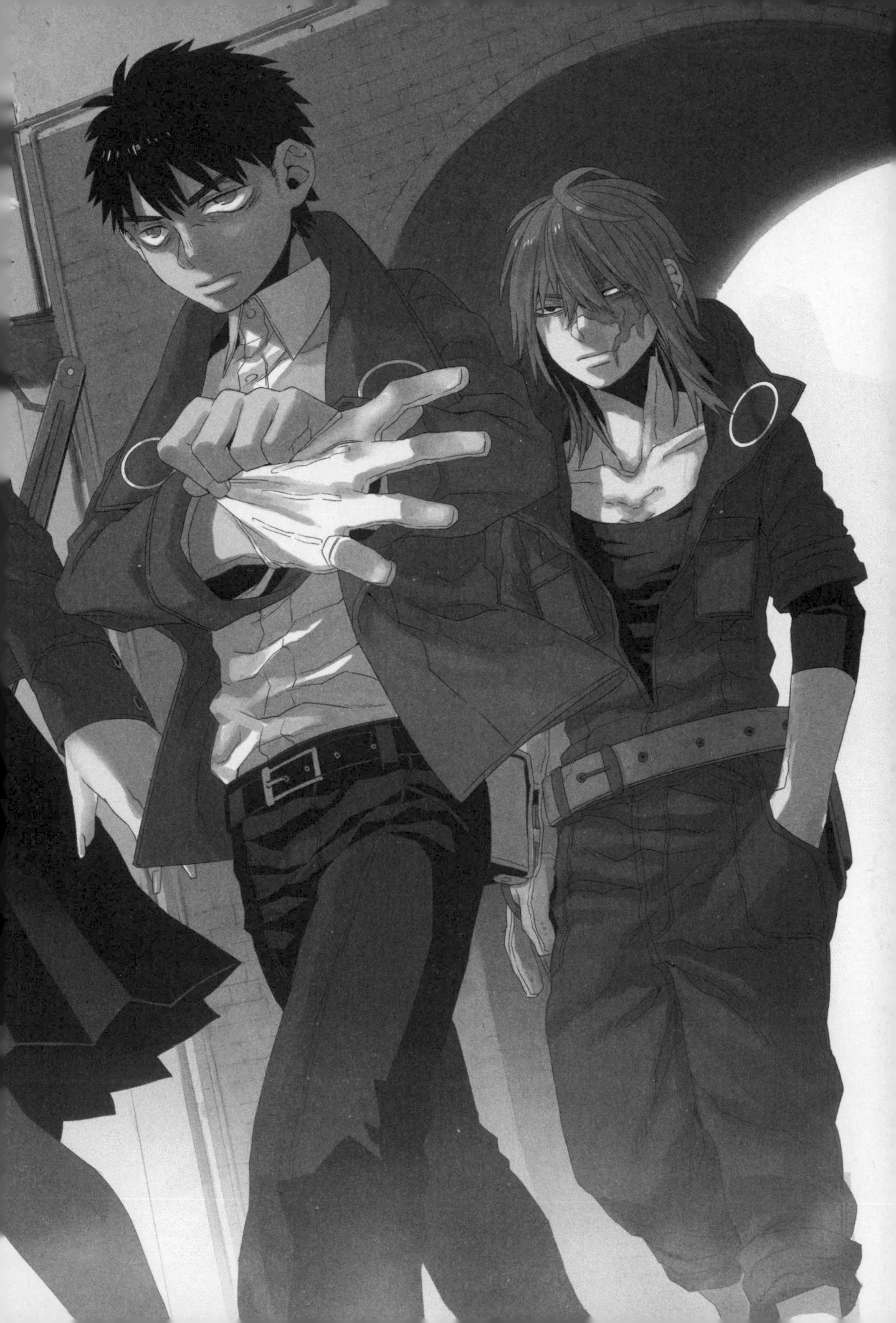

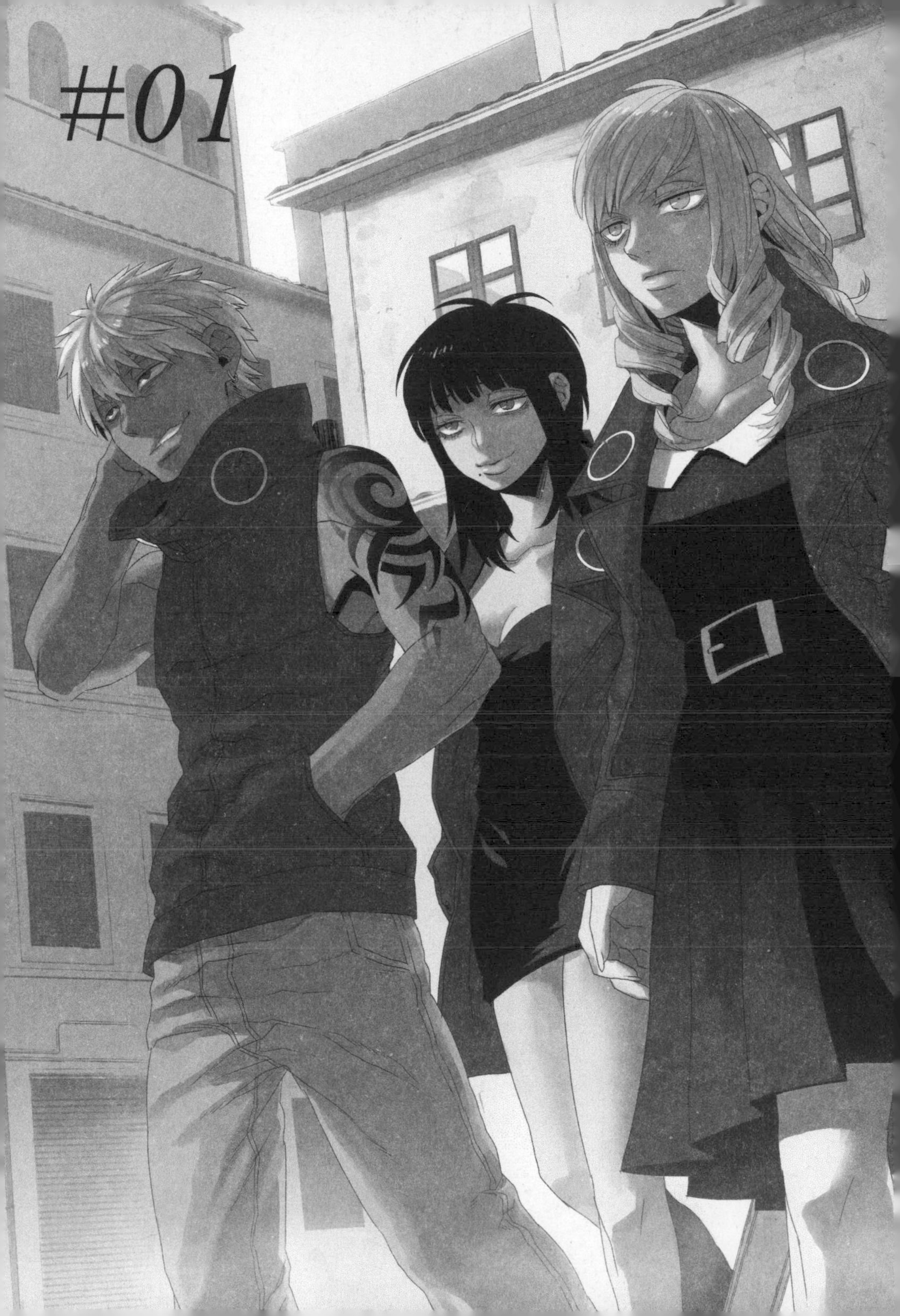
#01

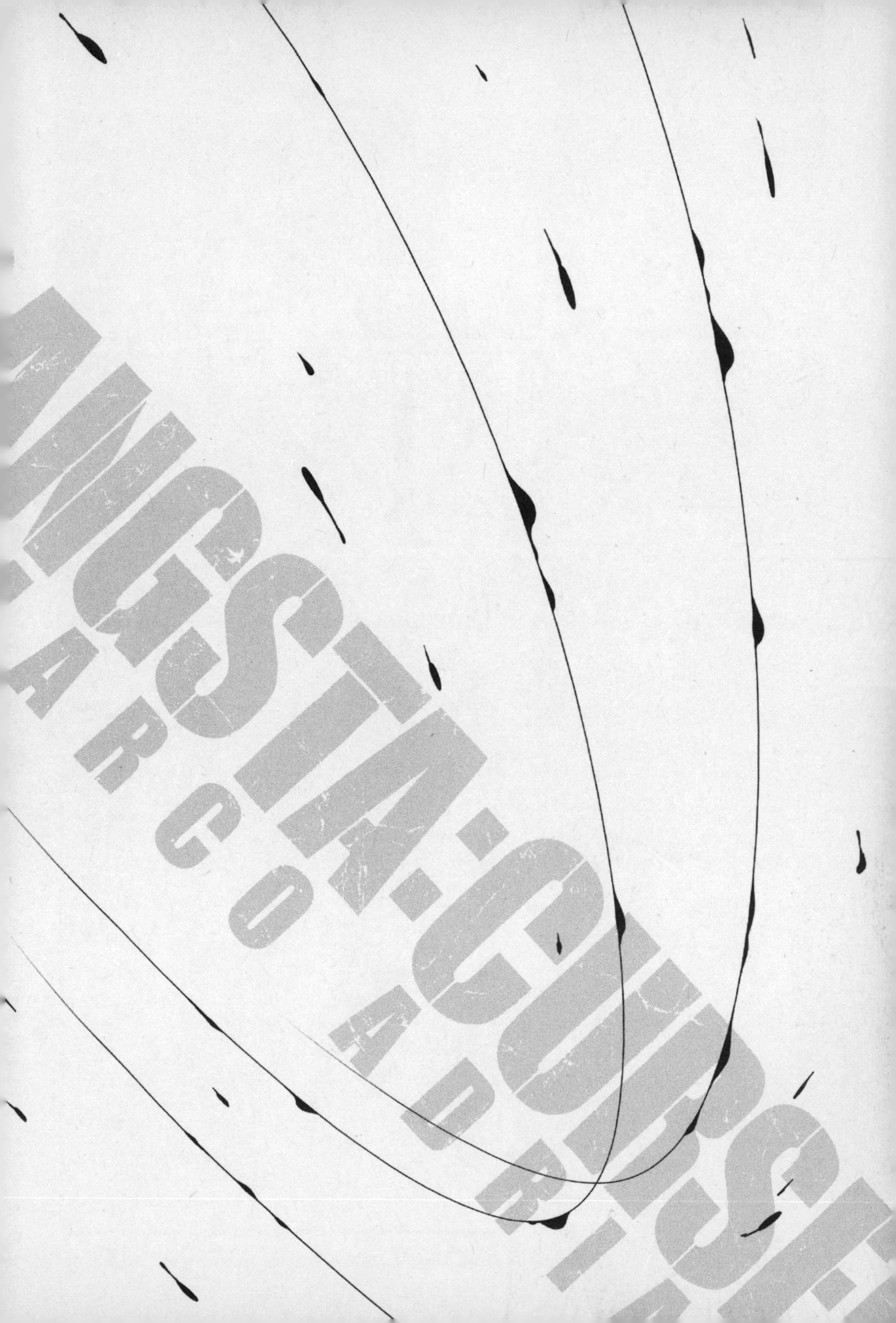

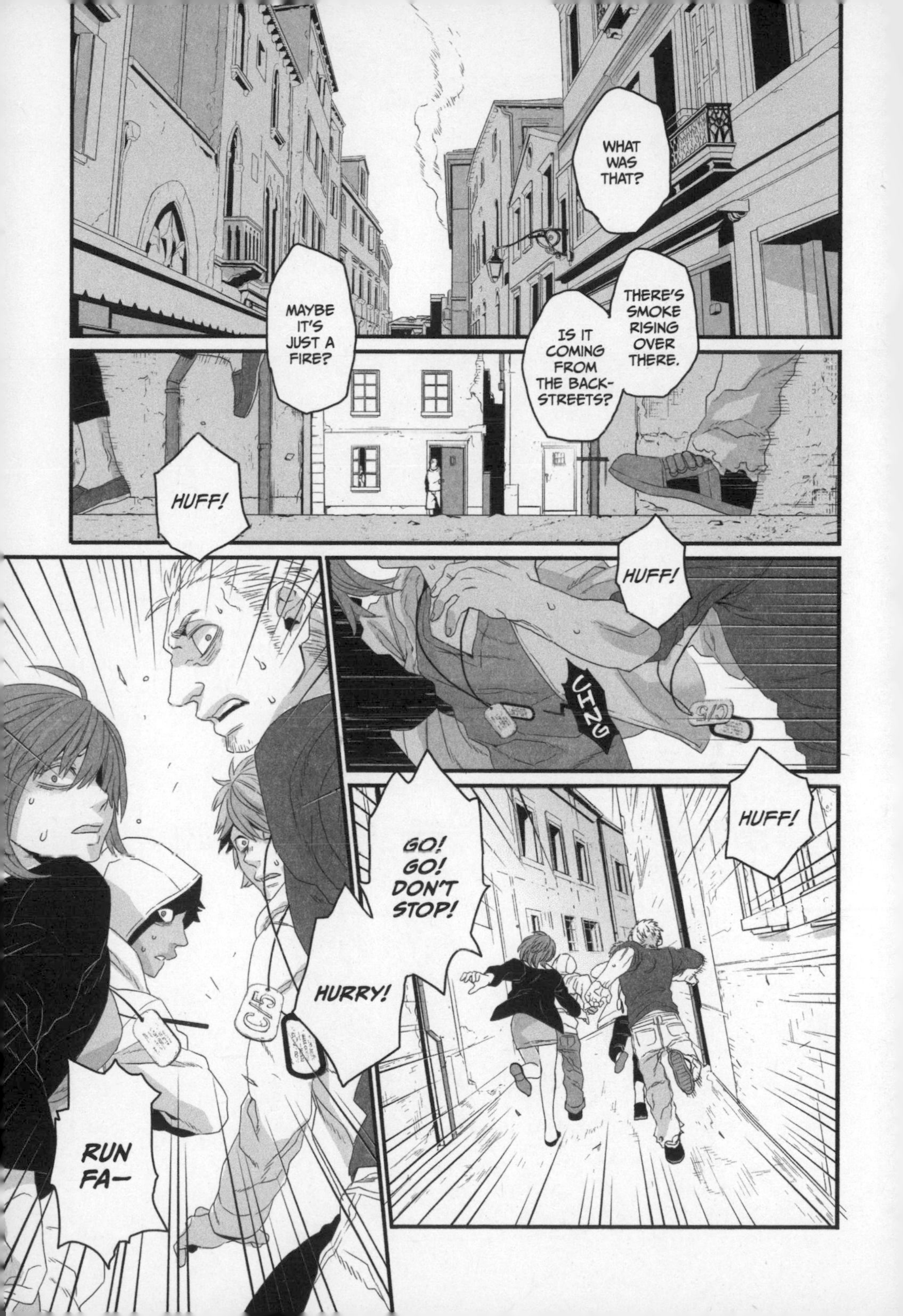
WHAT WAS THAT?
THERE'S SMOKE RISING OVER THERE.
IS IT COMING FROM THE BACK-STREETS?
MAYBE IT'S JUST A FIRE?
HUFF!
HUFF!
UHNG
HUFF!
GO! GO! DON'T STOP!
HURRY!
RUN FA—

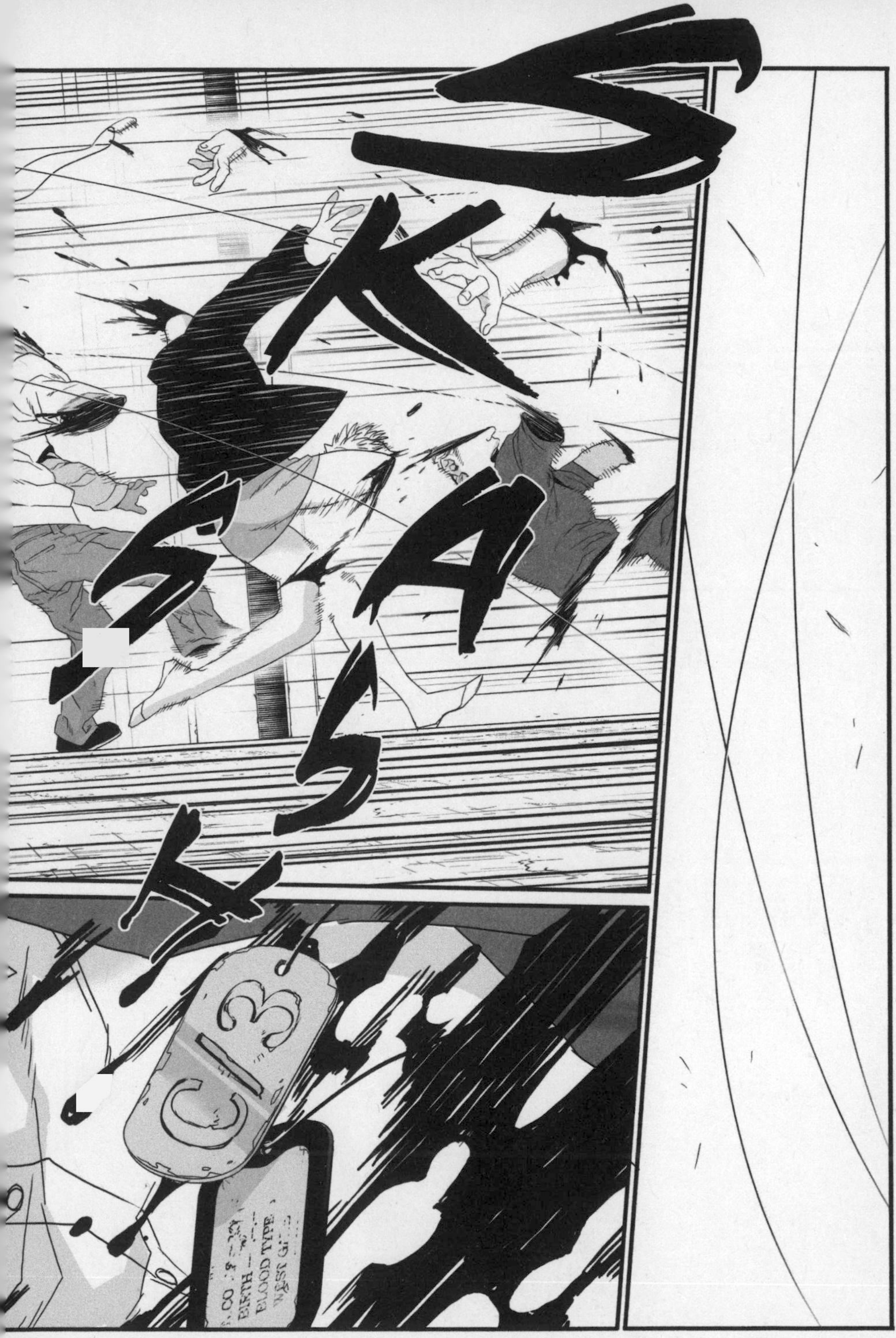
SKASSSH
C–3
BIRTH
BLOOD TYPE

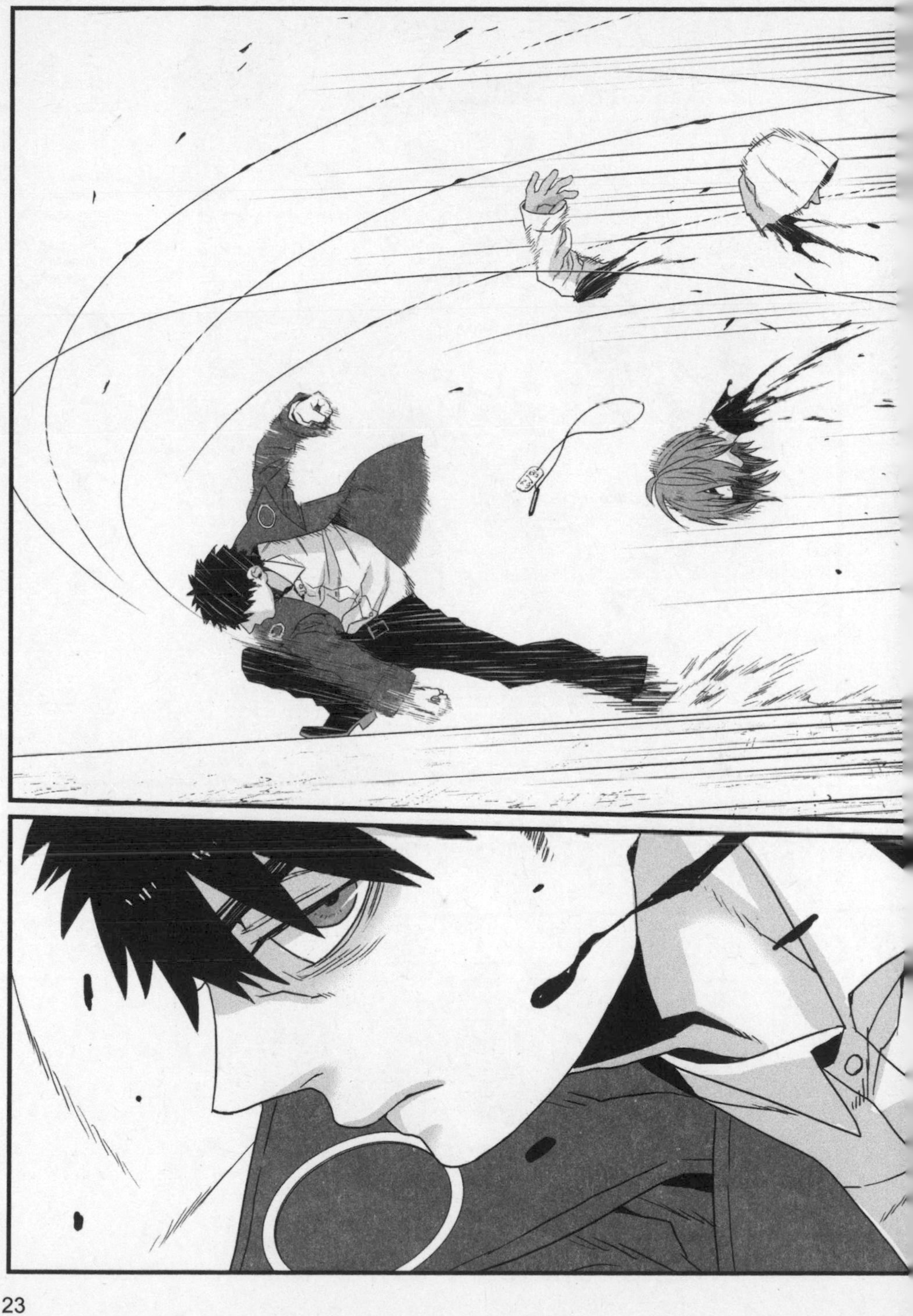

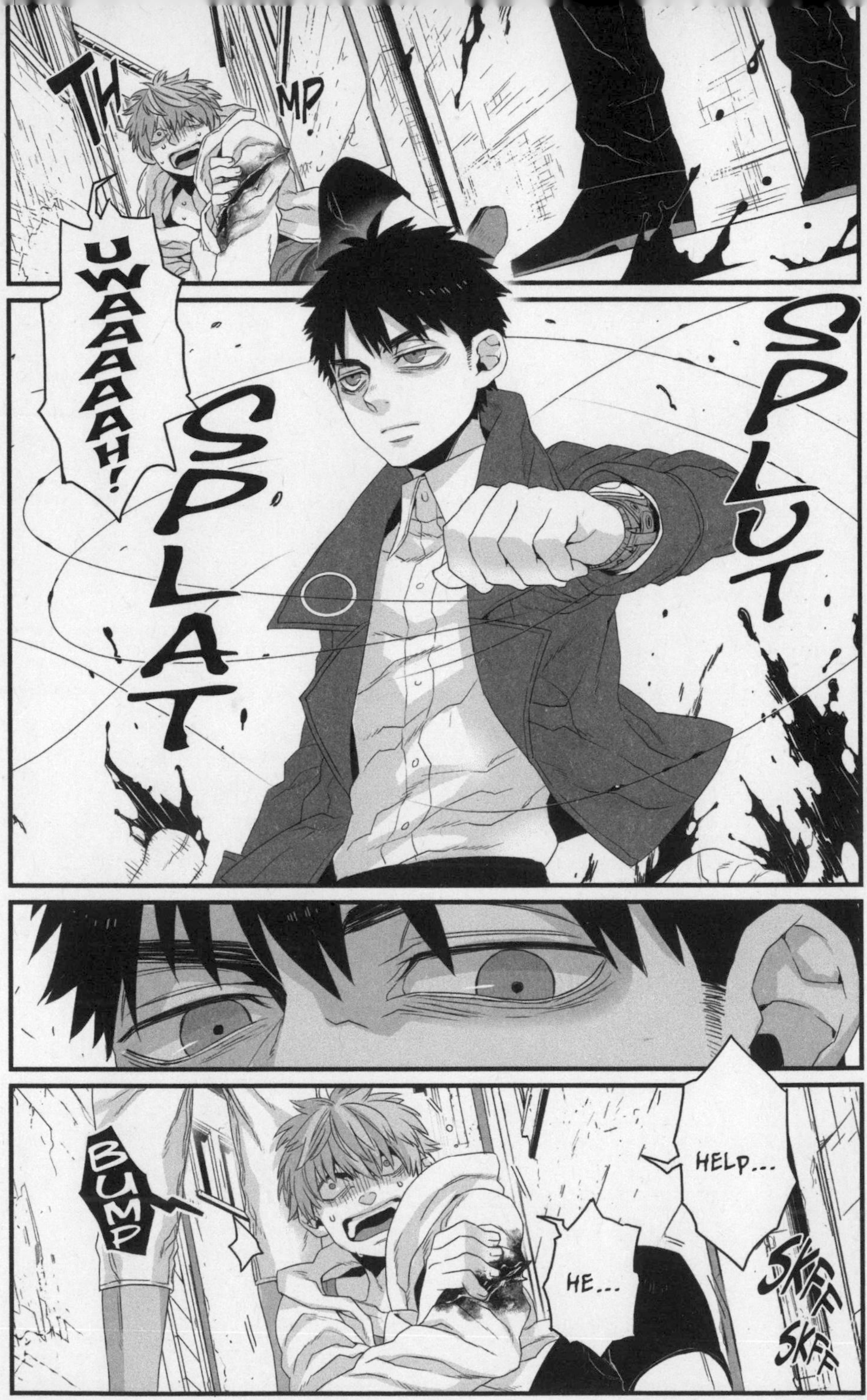
THMP
UWAAAAAH!
SPLUT
SPLAT
HELP...
SKFF
SKFF
HE...
BUMP

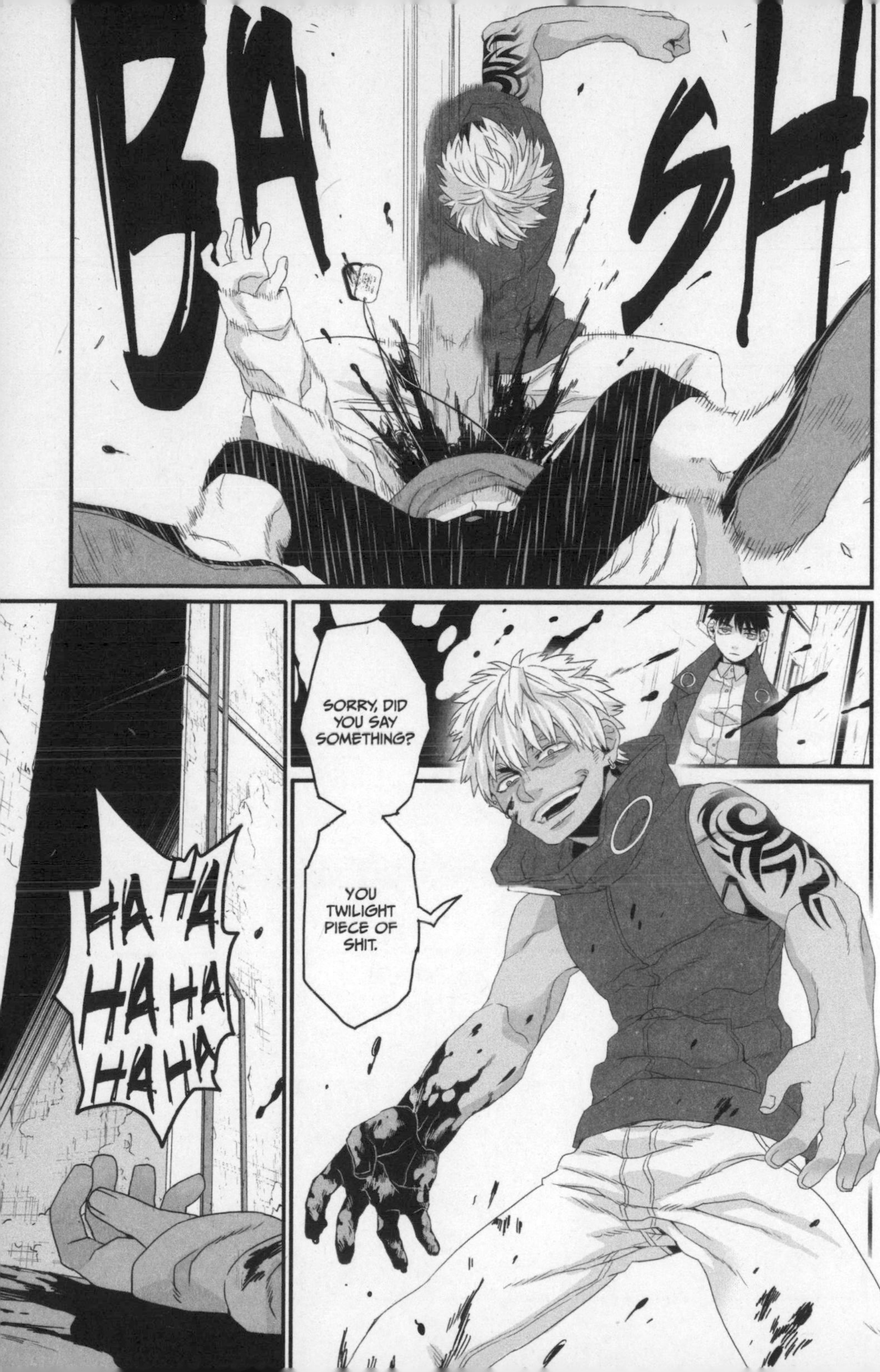
BASH
SORRY, DID YOU SAY SOMETHING?
YOU TWILIGHT PIECE OF SHIT.
HA HA HA HA HA HA

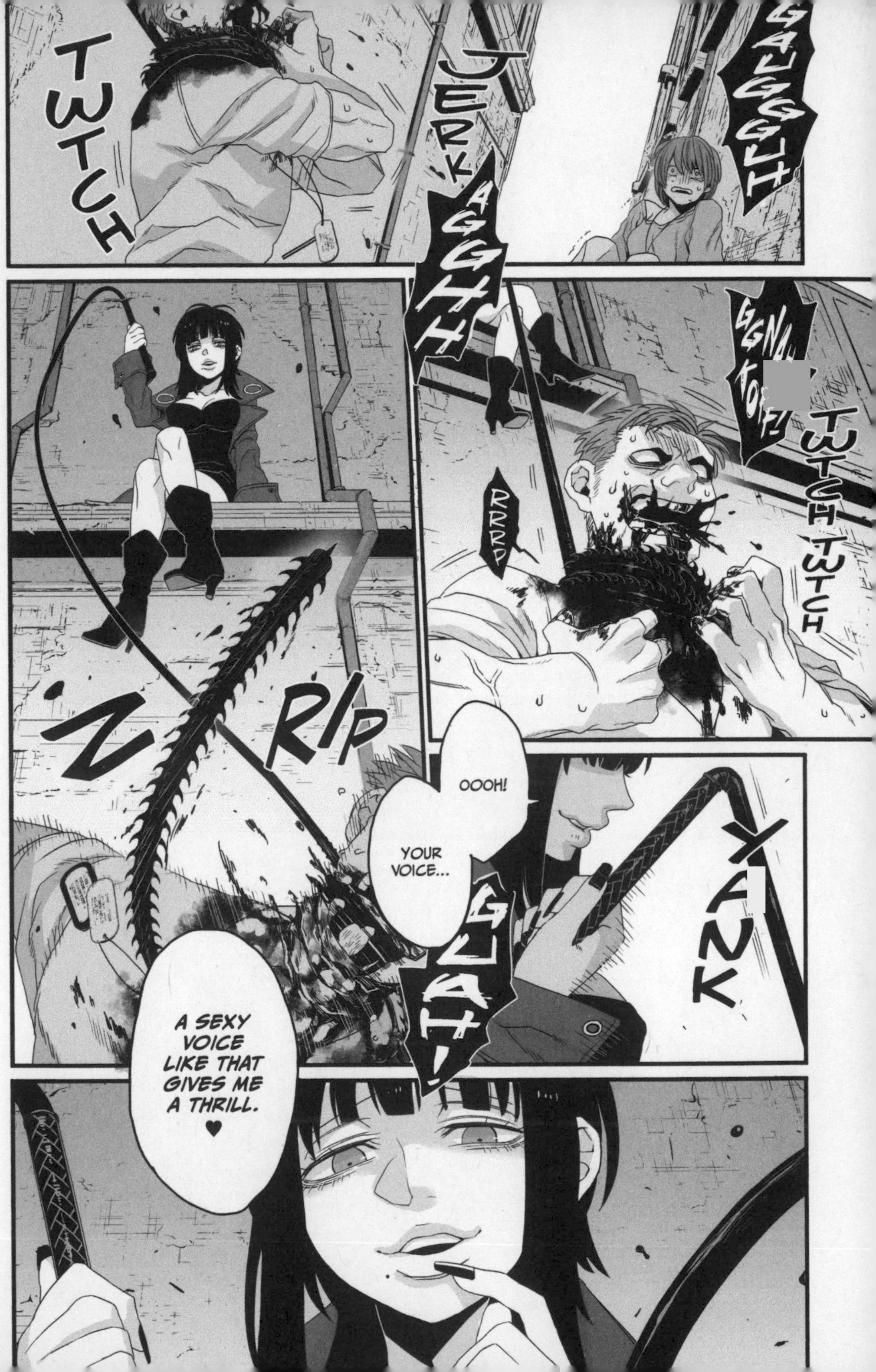
GAUGGGUH
JERK
TWTCH
GGNA KOFF!
TWTCH TWTCH
RRRP
AGGHHH
ZZRIP
YANK
OOOH!
YOUR VOICE...
AGGUAH!
A SEXY VOICE LIKE THAT GIVES ME A THRILL. ♥

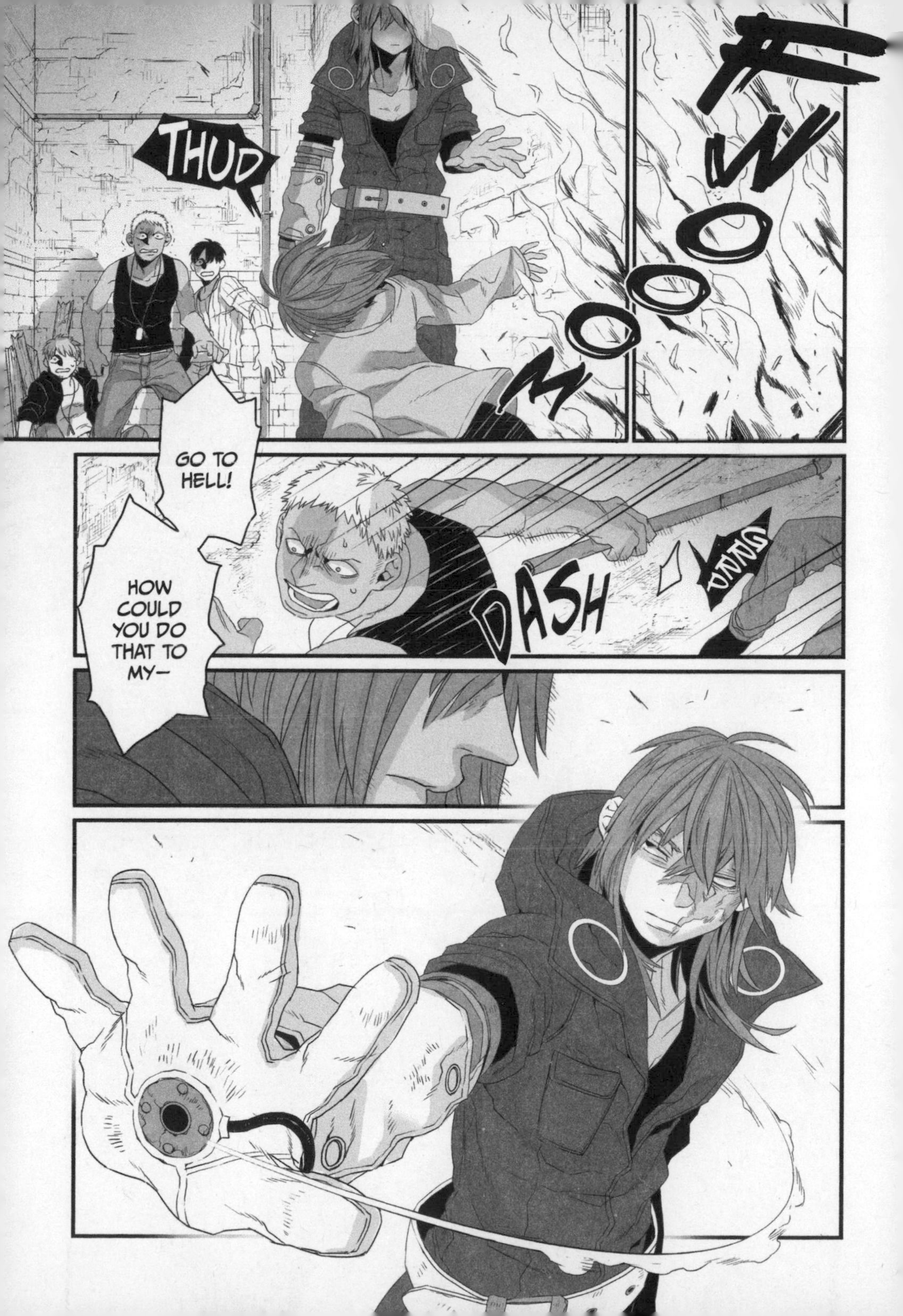
FWOOOOM
THUD
GO TO HELL!
HOW COULD YOU DO THAT TO MY—
DASH

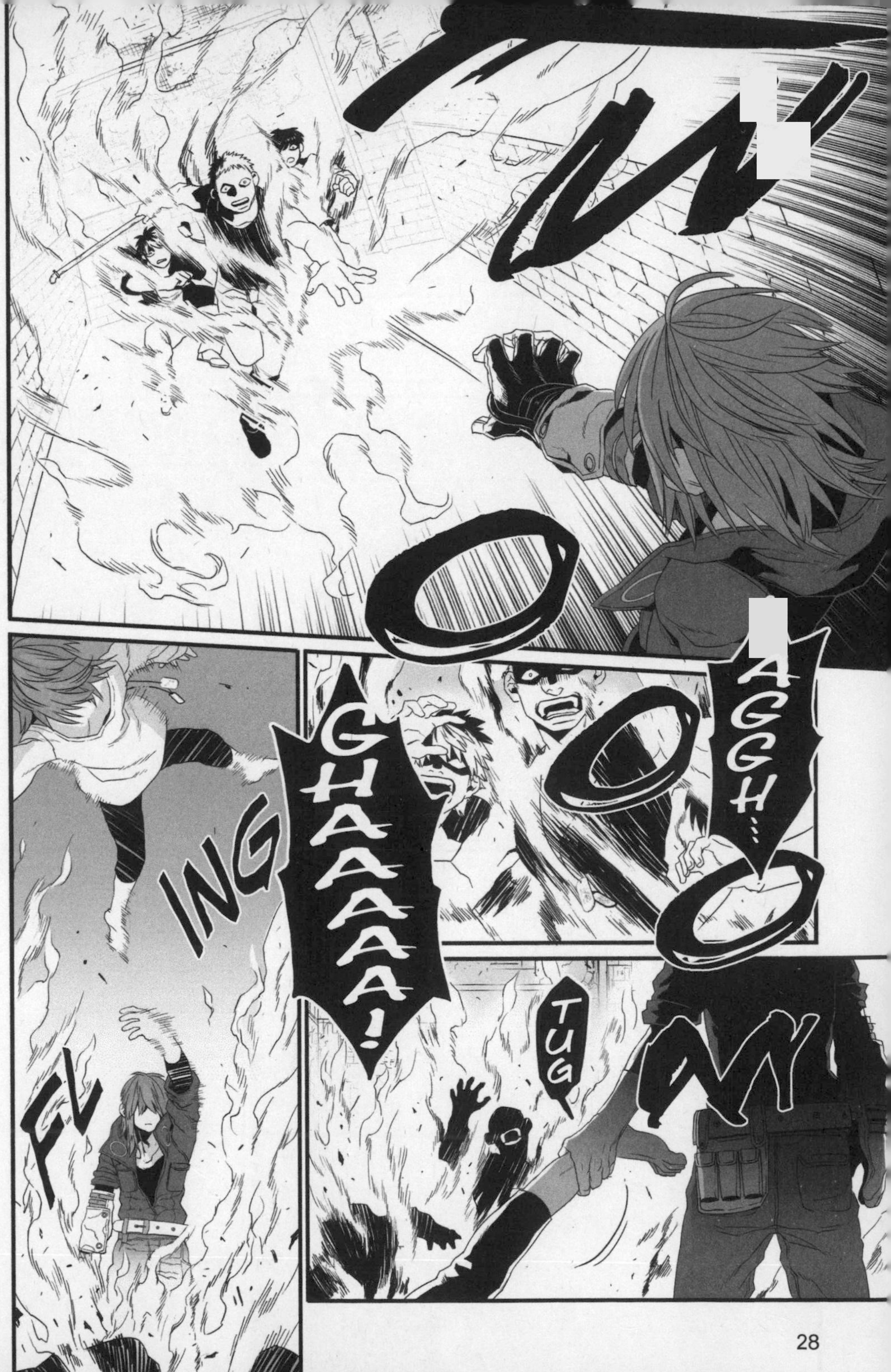
AGGH...
GHAAAAA!
TUG
FL
ING

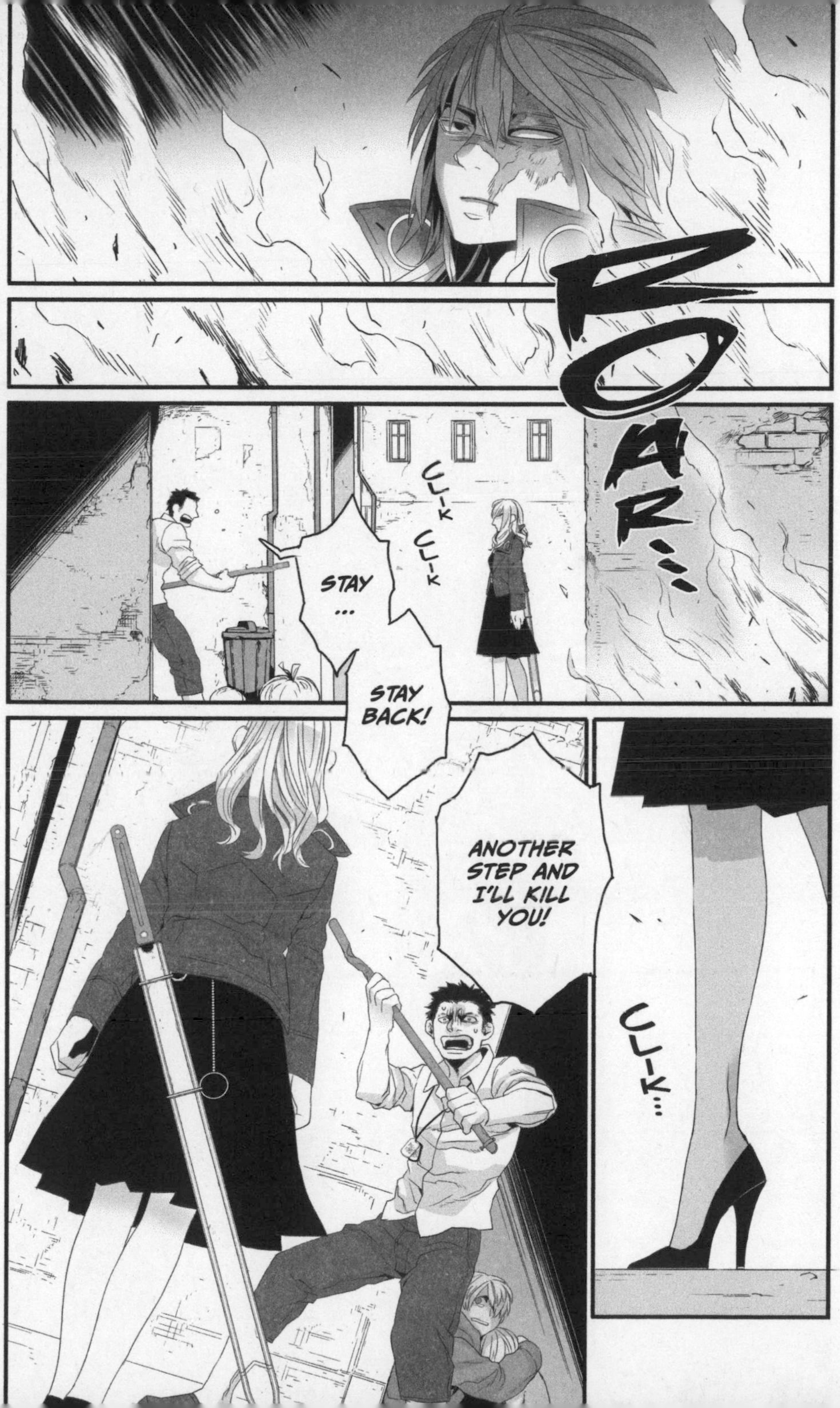
ROAR...
CLIK
CLIK
STAY ...
STAY BACK!
CLIK...
ANOTHER STEP AND I'LL KILL YOU!

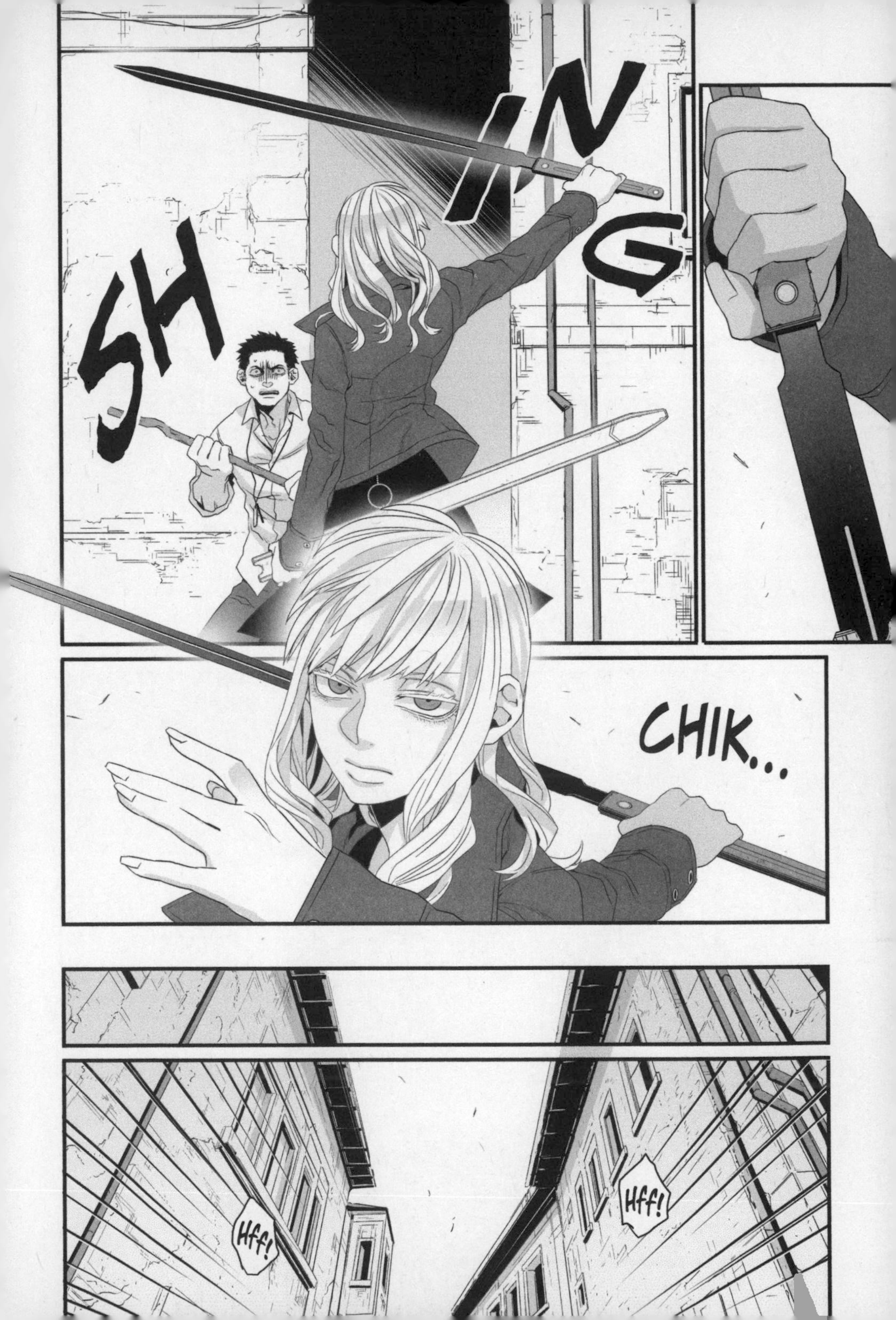
SH
ING
CHIK...
Hff!
Hff!

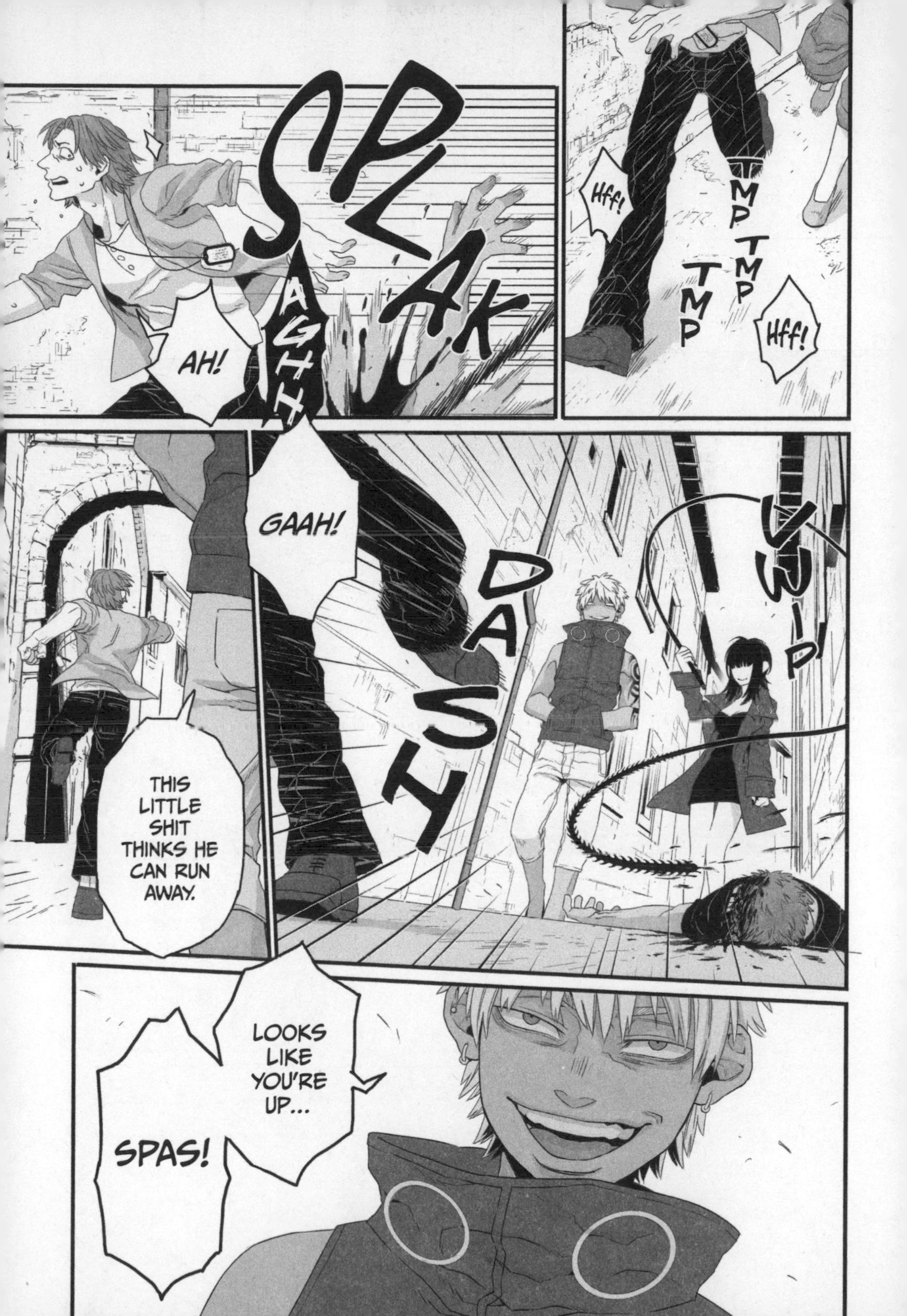
Hff!
TMP TMP TMP
Hff!
SPLAK
AH!
AGHH
WHIP
GAAH!
DASH
THIS LITTLE SHIT THINKS HE CAN RUN AWAY.
LOOKS LIKE YOU'RE UP...
SPAS!

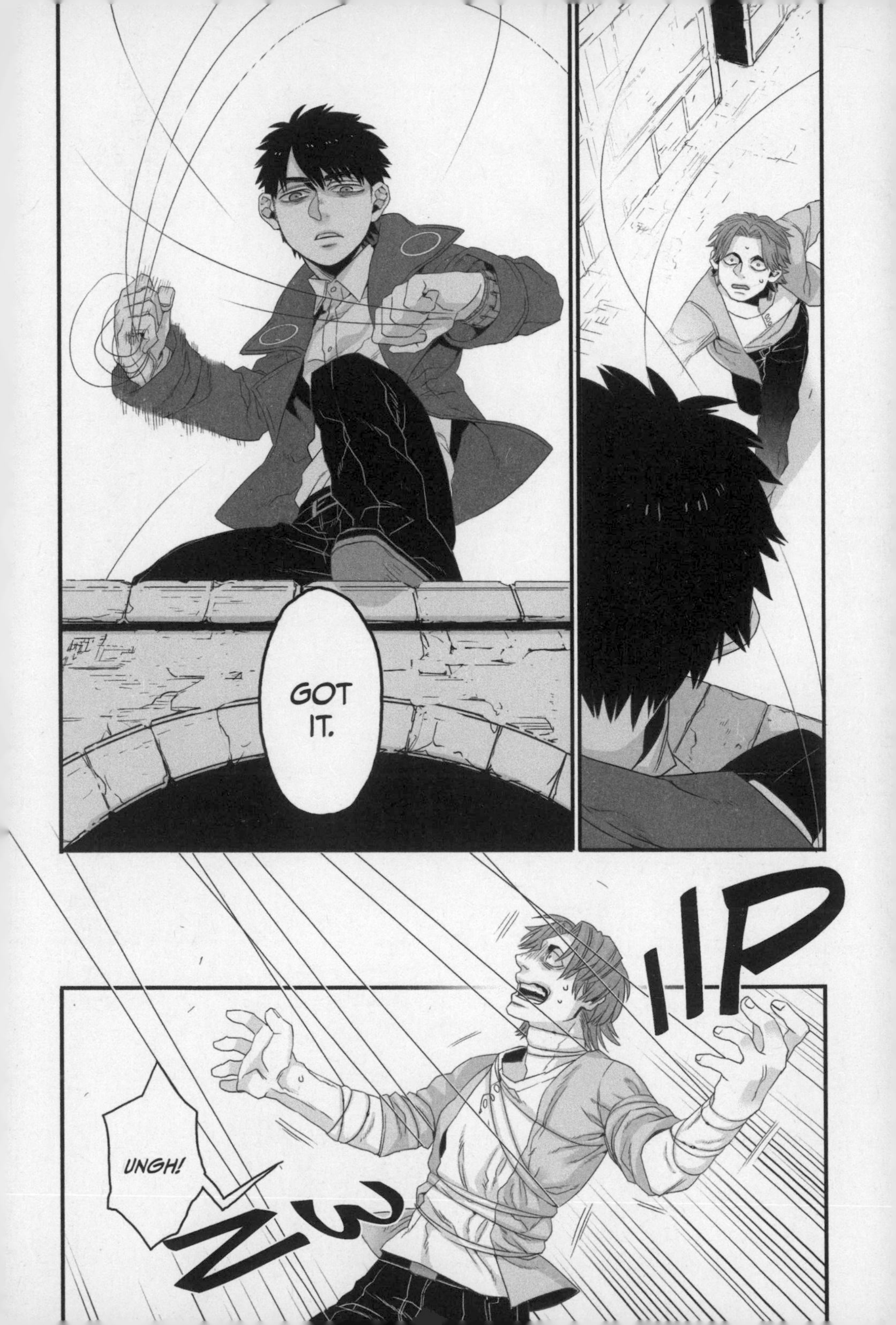
GOT IT.
RIP
UNGH!
ZING

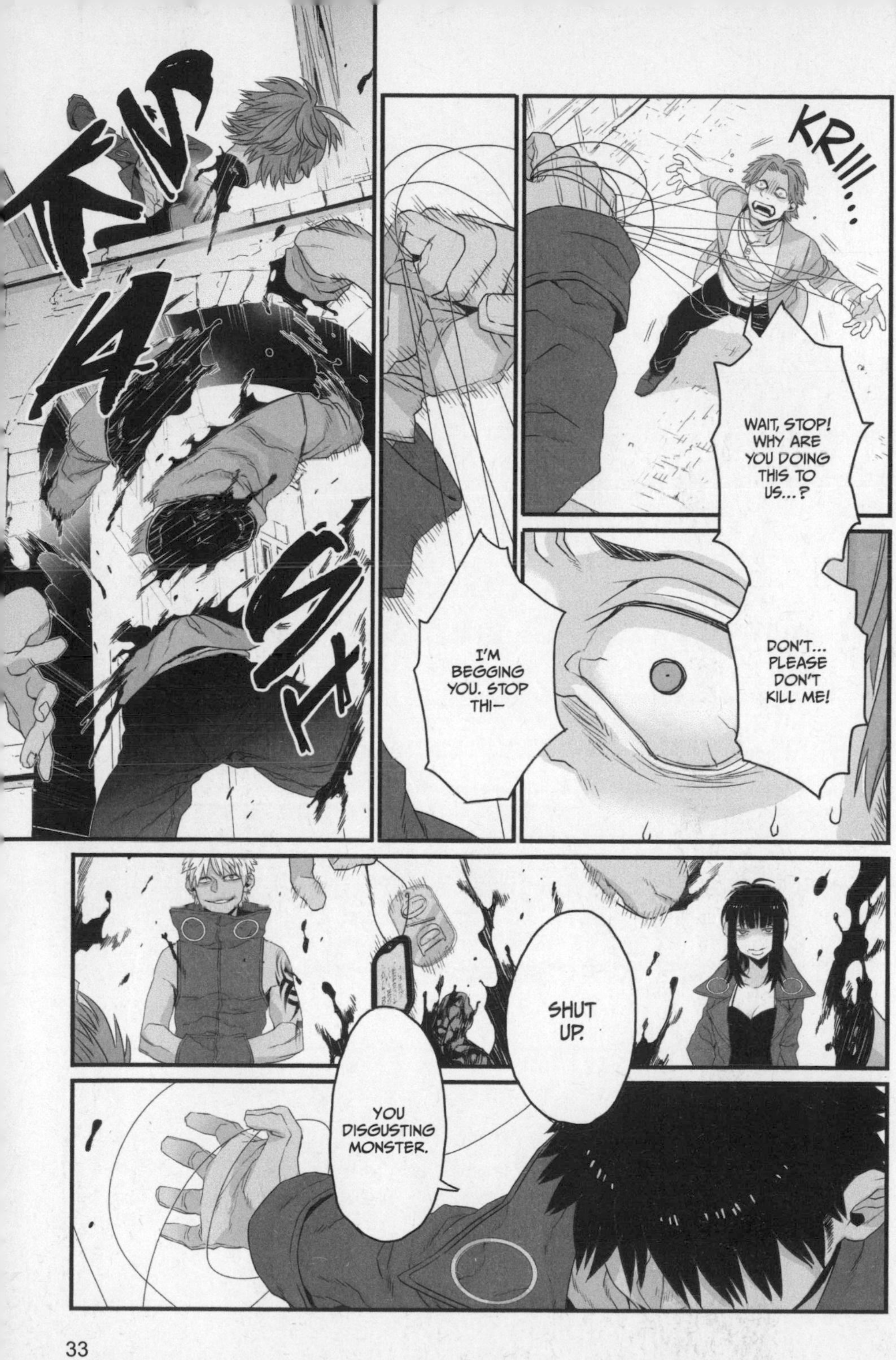
KRIII...
WAIT, STOP! WHY ARE YOU DOING THIS TO US...?
DON'T... PLEASE DON'T KILL ME!
I'M BEGGING YOU. STOP THI—
KASH
SHUT UP.
YOU DISGUSTING MONSTER.

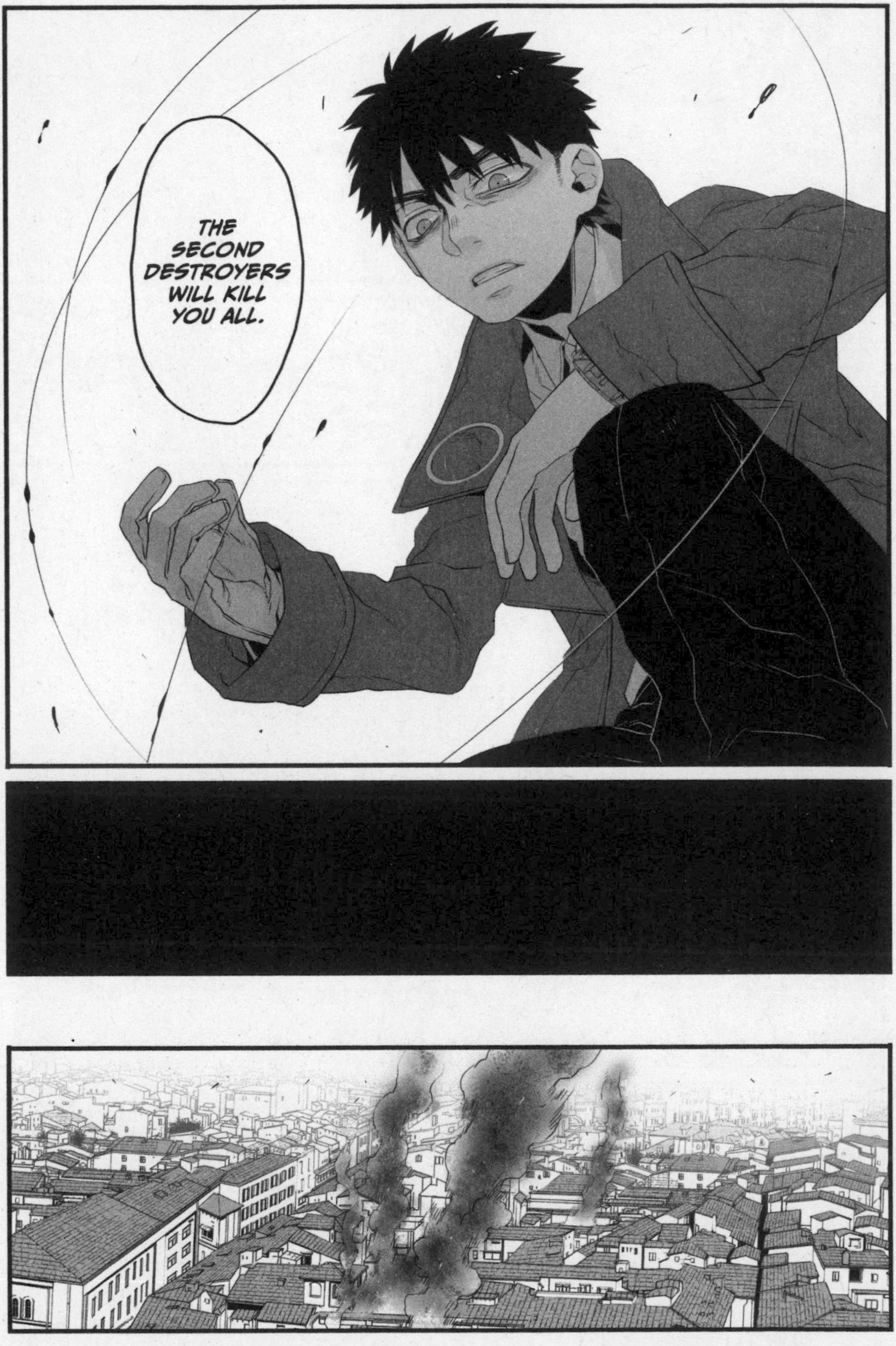
THE SECOND DESTROYERS WILL KILL YOU ALL.

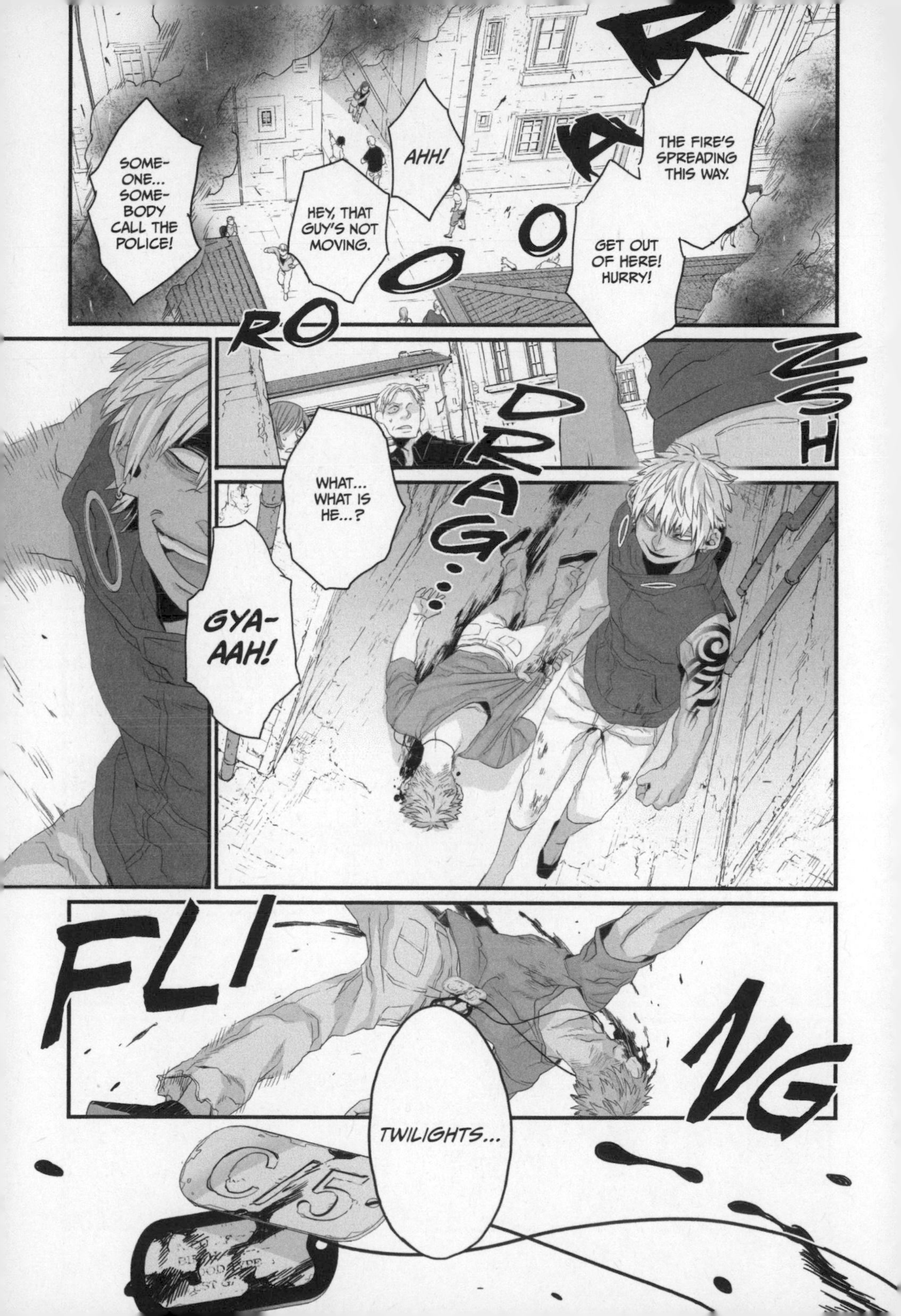
ROOOAR
THE FIRE'S SPREADING THIS WAY.
GET OUT OF HERE! HURRY!
AHH!
HEY, THAT GUY'S NOT MOVING.
SOME-ONE... SOME-BODY CALL THE POLICE!
ZSH
WHAT... WHAT IS HE...?
DRAG...
GYA-AAH!
FLING
TWILIGHTS...
C/5

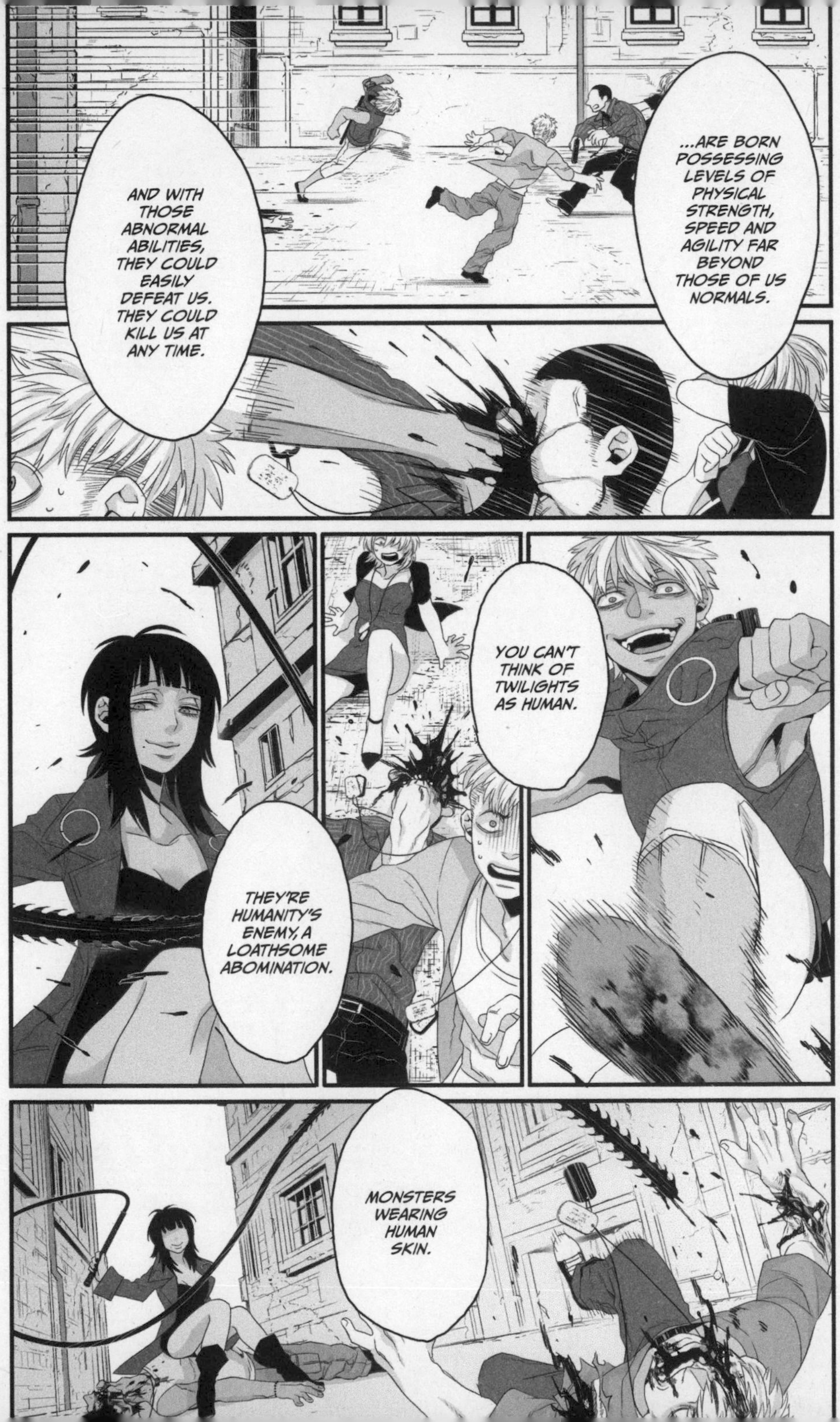
...ARE BORN POSSESSING LEVELS OF PHYSICAL STRENGTH, SPEED AND AGILITY FAR BEYOND THOSE OF US NORMALS.
AND WITH THOSE ABNORMAL ABILITIES, THEY COULD EASILY DEFEAT US. THEY COULD KILL US AT ANY TIME.
YOU CAN'T THINK OF TWILIGHTS AS HUMAN.
THEY'RE HUMANITY'S ENEMY, A LOATHSOME ABOMINATION.
MONSTERS WEARING HUMAN SKIN.

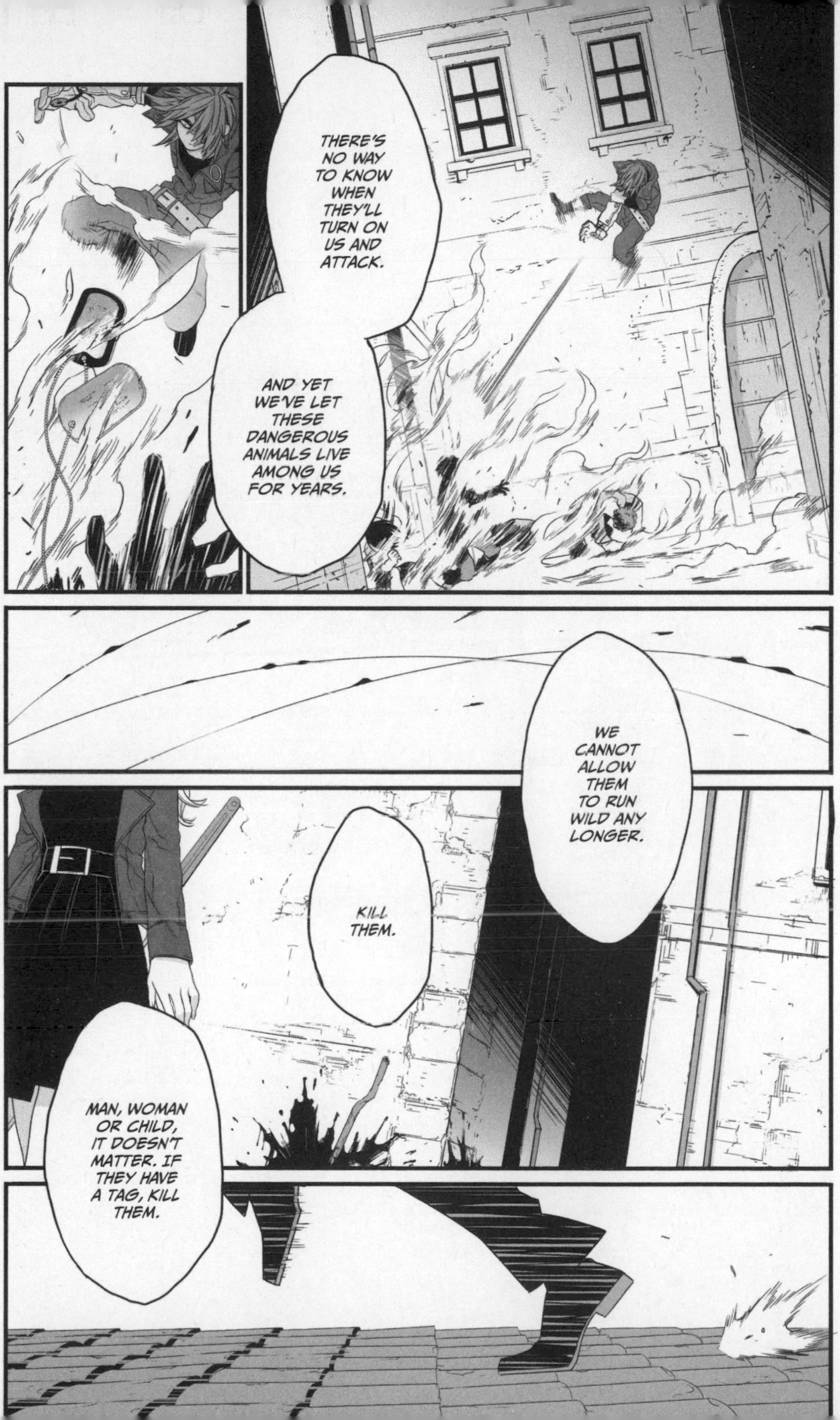
THERE'S NO WAY TO KNOW WHEN THEY'LL TURN ON US AND ATTACK.
AND YET WE'VE LET THESE DANGEROUS ANIMALS LIVE AMONG US FOR YEARS.
WE CANNOT ALLOW THEM TO RUN WILD ANY LONGER.
KILL THEM.
MAN, WOMAN OR CHILD, IT DOESN'T MATTER. IF THEY HAVE A TAG, KILL THEM.

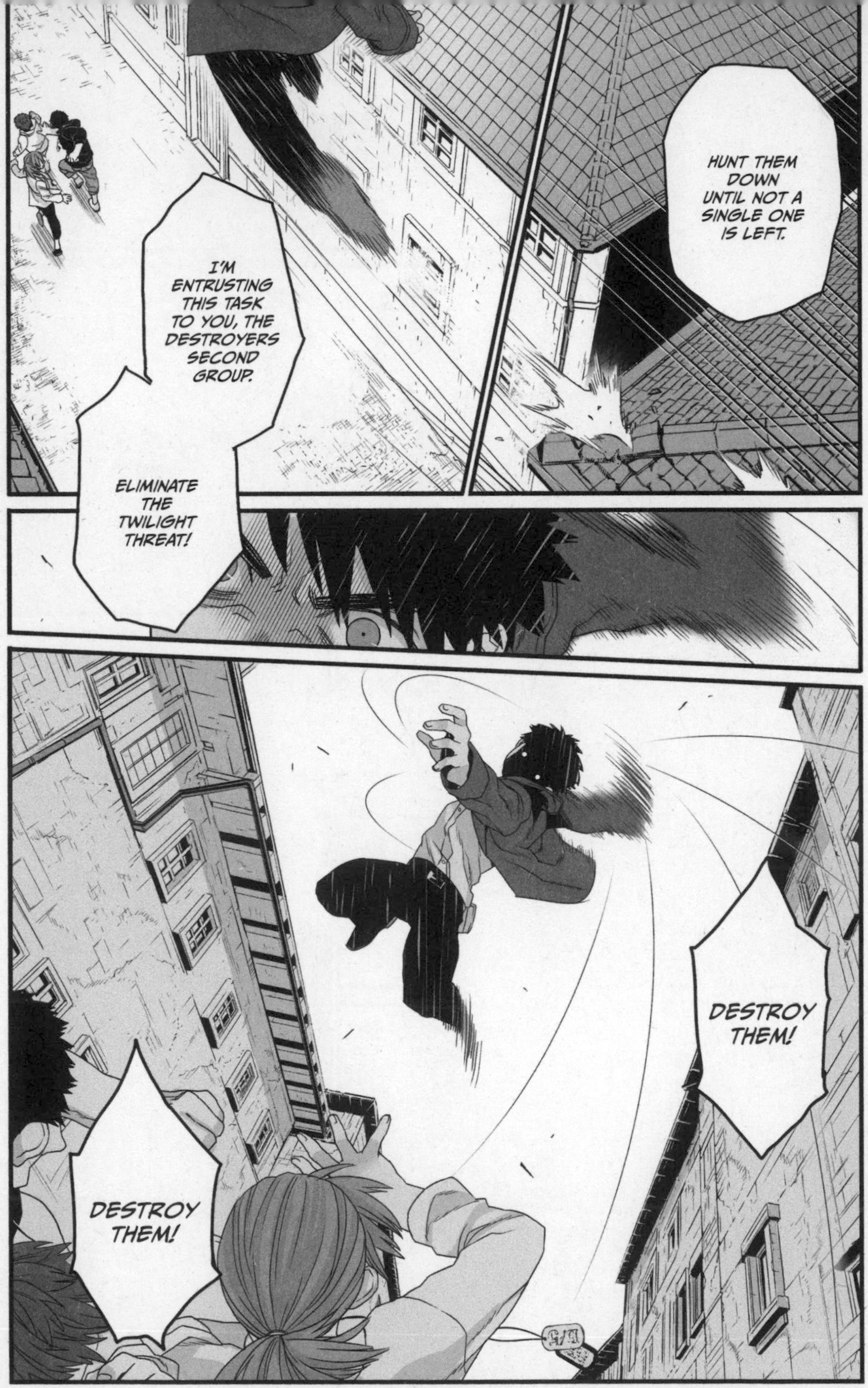
HUNT THEM DOWN UNTIL NOT A SINGLE ONE IS LEFT.
I'M ENTRUSTING THIS TASK TO YOU, THE DESTROYERS SECOND GROUP.
ELIMINATE THE TWILIGHT THREAT!
DESTROY THEM!
DESTROY THEM!

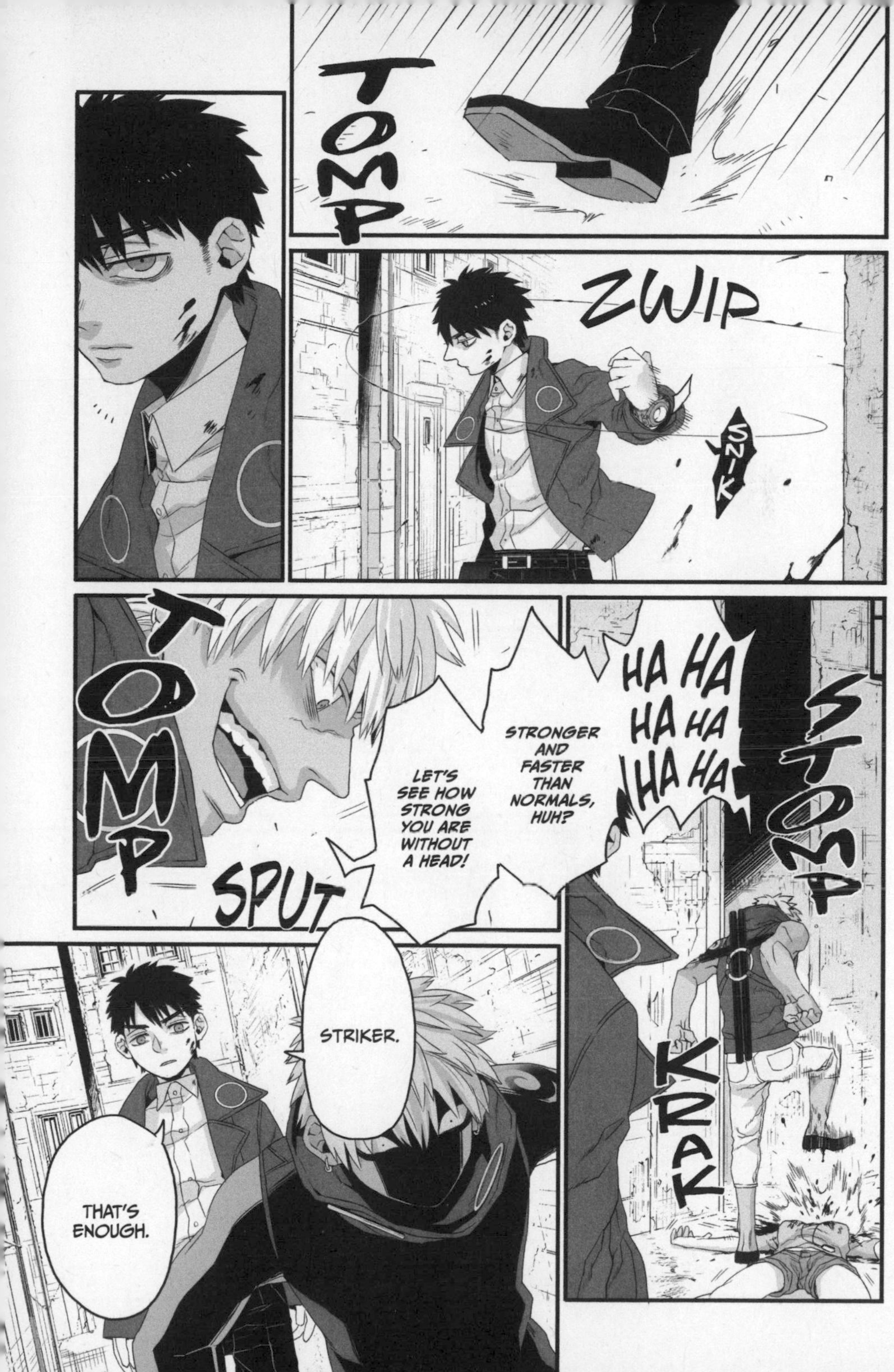

TOMP
ZWIP
SNIK
HA HA HA HA HA HA
STOMP
KRAK
STRONGER AND FASTER THAN NORMALS, HUH?
LET'S SEE HOW STRONG YOU ARE WITHOUT A HEAD!
TOMP
SPUT
STRIKER.
THAT'S ENOUGH.

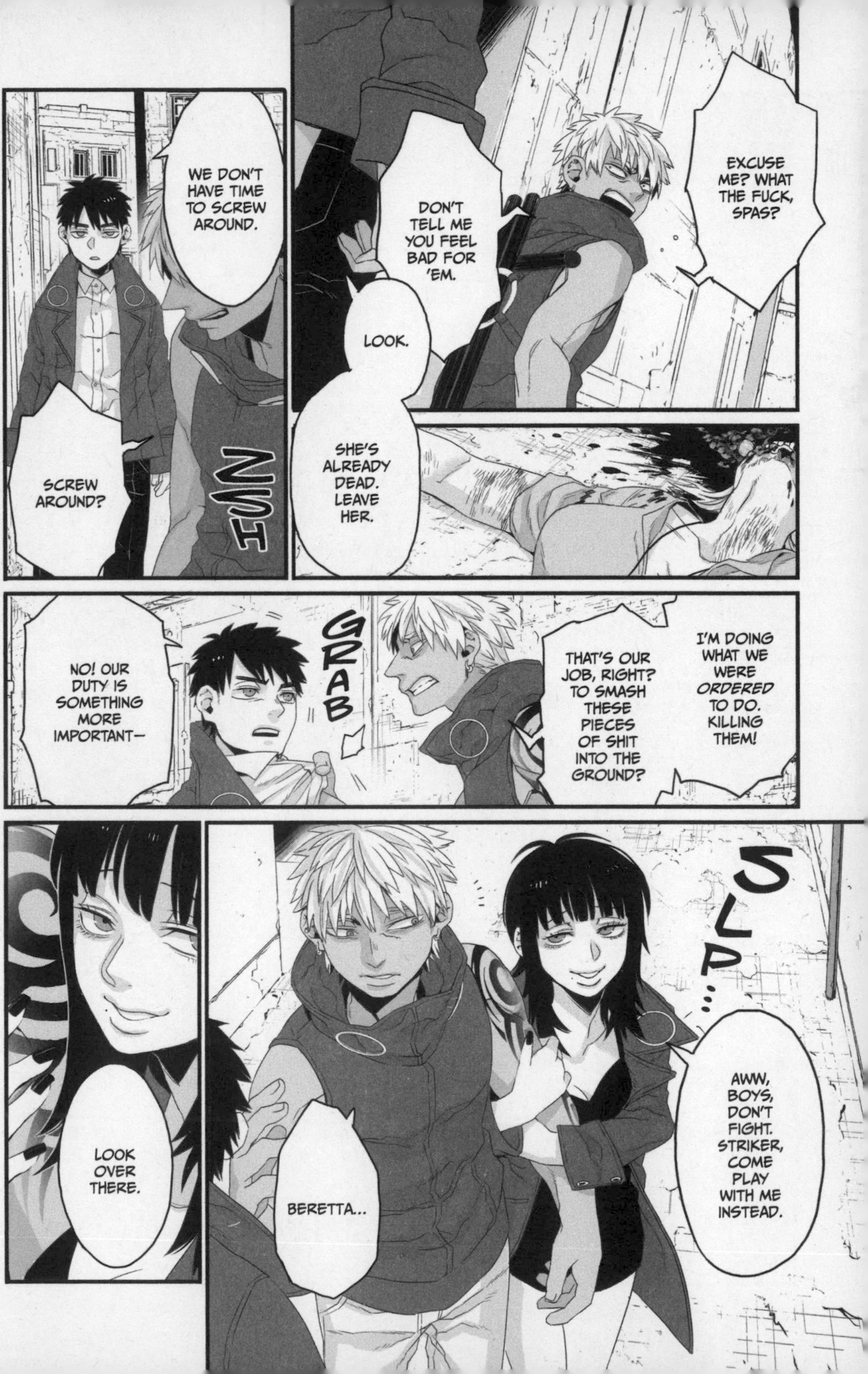
EXCUSE ME? WHAT THE FUCK, SPAS?
DON'T TELL ME YOU FEEL BAD FOR 'EM.
LOOK.
SHE'S ALREADY DEAD. LEAVE HER.
WE DON'T HAVE TIME TO SCREW AROUND.
ZSH
SCREW AROUND?
I'M DOING WHAT WE WERE *ORDERED* TO DO. KILLING THEM!
THAT'S OUR JOB, RIGHT? TO SMASH THESE PIECES OF SHIT INTO THE GROUND?
GRAB
NO! OUR DUTY IS SOMETHING MORE IMPORTANT—
SLP...
AWW, BOYS, DON'T FIGHT. STRIKER, COME PLAY WITH ME INSTEAD.
BERETTA...
LOOK OVER THERE.

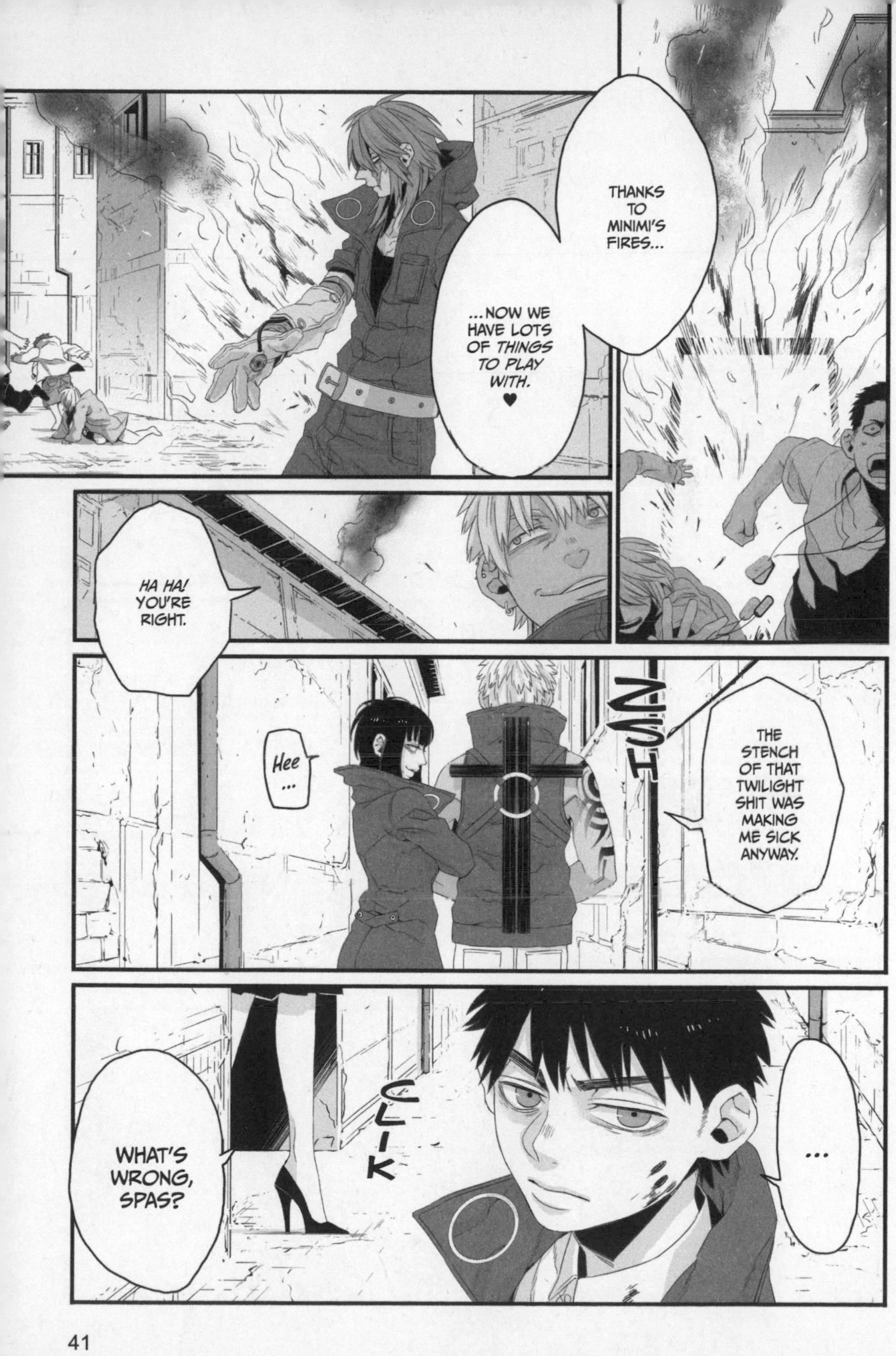
THANKS TO MINIMI'S FIRES...
...NOW WE HAVE LOTS OF *THINGS* TO PLAY WITH. ♥
HA HA! YOU'RE RIGHT.
THE STENCH OF THAT TWILIGHT SHIT WAS MAKING ME SICK ANYWAY.
Hee...
...
CLIK
WHAT'S WRONG, SPAS?

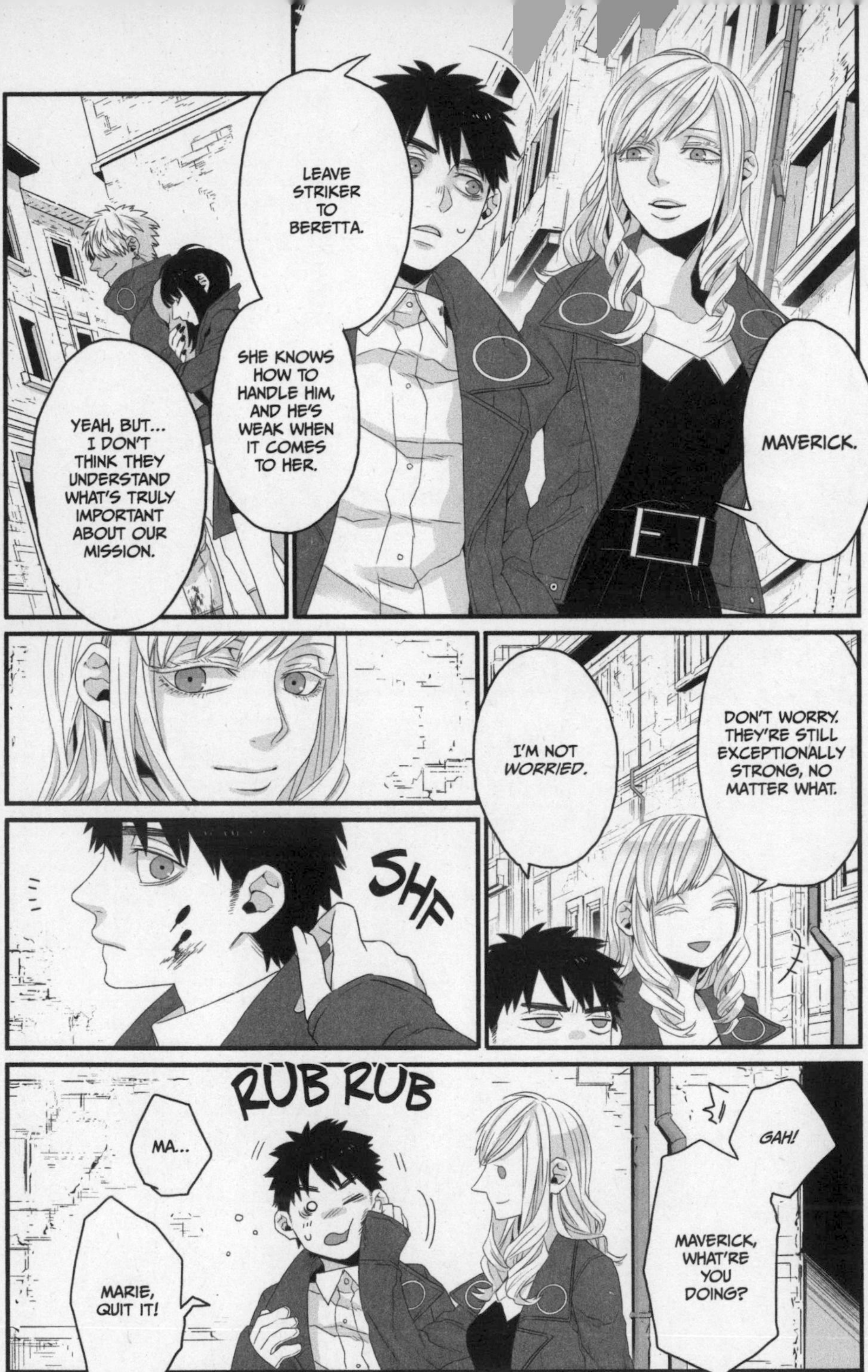
MAVERICK.
LEAVE STRIKER TO BERETTA.
SHE KNOWS HOW TO HANDLE HIM, AND HE'S WEAK WHEN IT COMES TO HER.
YEAH, BUT... I DON'T THINK THEY UNDERSTAND WHAT'S TRULY IMPORTANT ABOUT OUR MISSION.
DON'T WORRY. THEY'RE STILL EXCEPTIONALLY STRONG, NO MATTER WHAT.
I'M NOT WORRIED.
SHF
GAH!
MAVERICK, WHAT'RE YOU DOING?
RUB RUB
MA...
MARIE, QUIT IT!

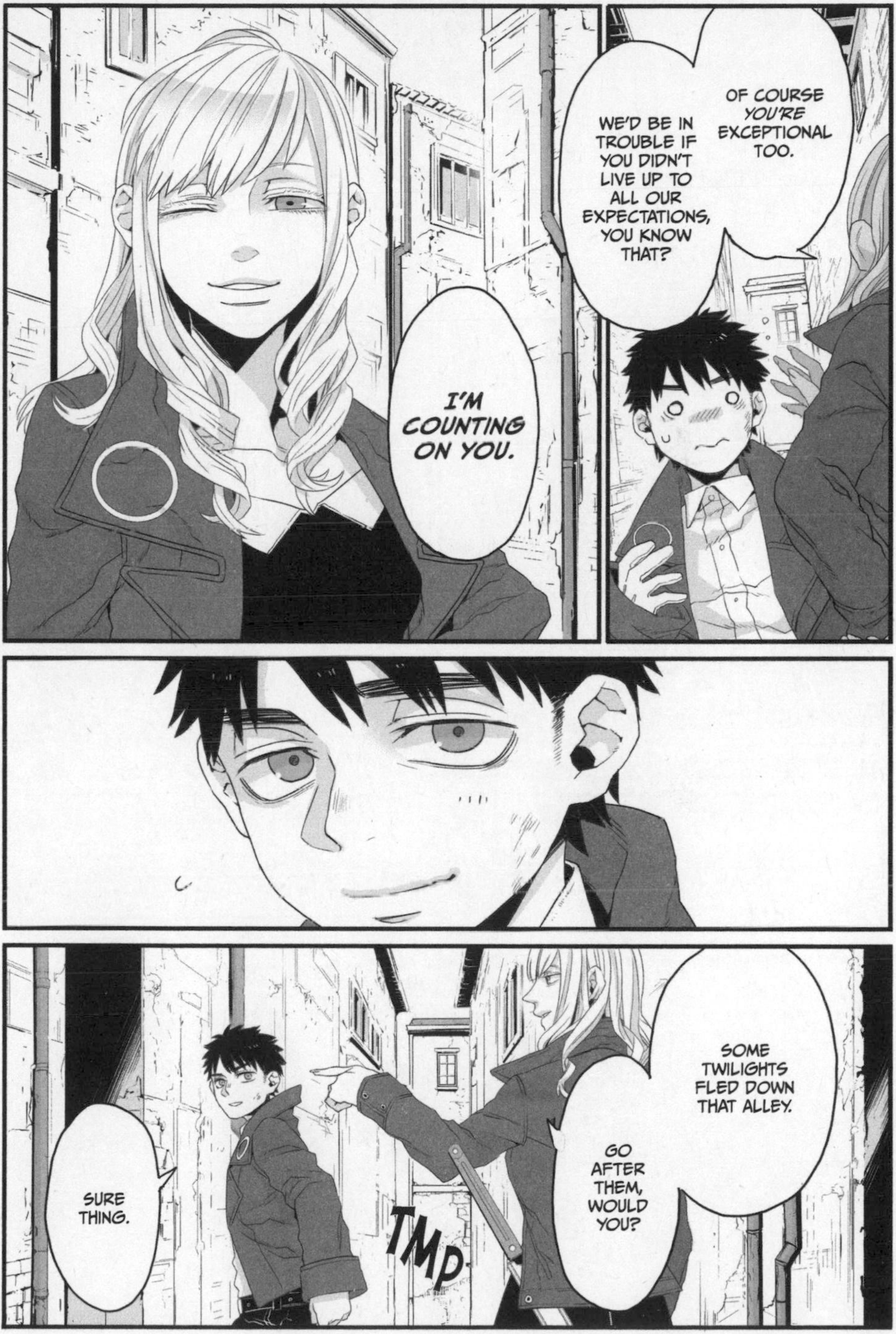
OF COURSE YOU'RE EXCEPTIONAL TOO.
WE'D BE IN TROUBLE IF YOU DIDN'T LIVE UP TO ALL OUR EXPECTATIONS, YOU KNOW THAT?
I'M COUNTING ON YOU.
SOME TWILIGHTS FLED DOWN THAT ALLEY.
GO AFTER THEM, WOULD YOU?
TMP
SURE THING.

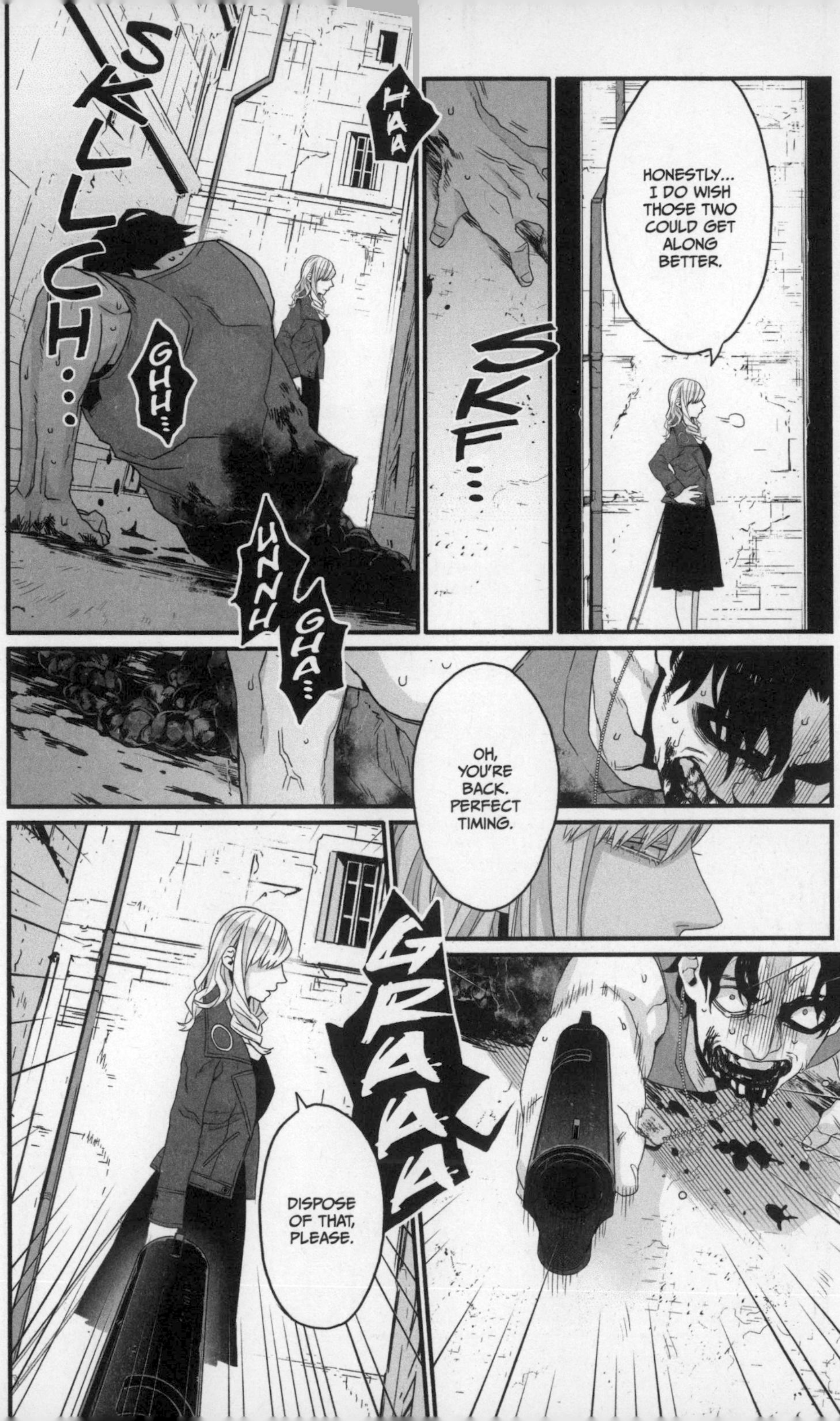
HONESTLY... I DO WISH THOSE TWO COULD GET ALONG BETTER.
SKF...
HAA
SKLLCH...
GHH...
UNNH
GHA...
OH, YOU'RE BACK. PERFECT TIMING.
GRAAA
DISPOSE OF THAT, PLEASE.

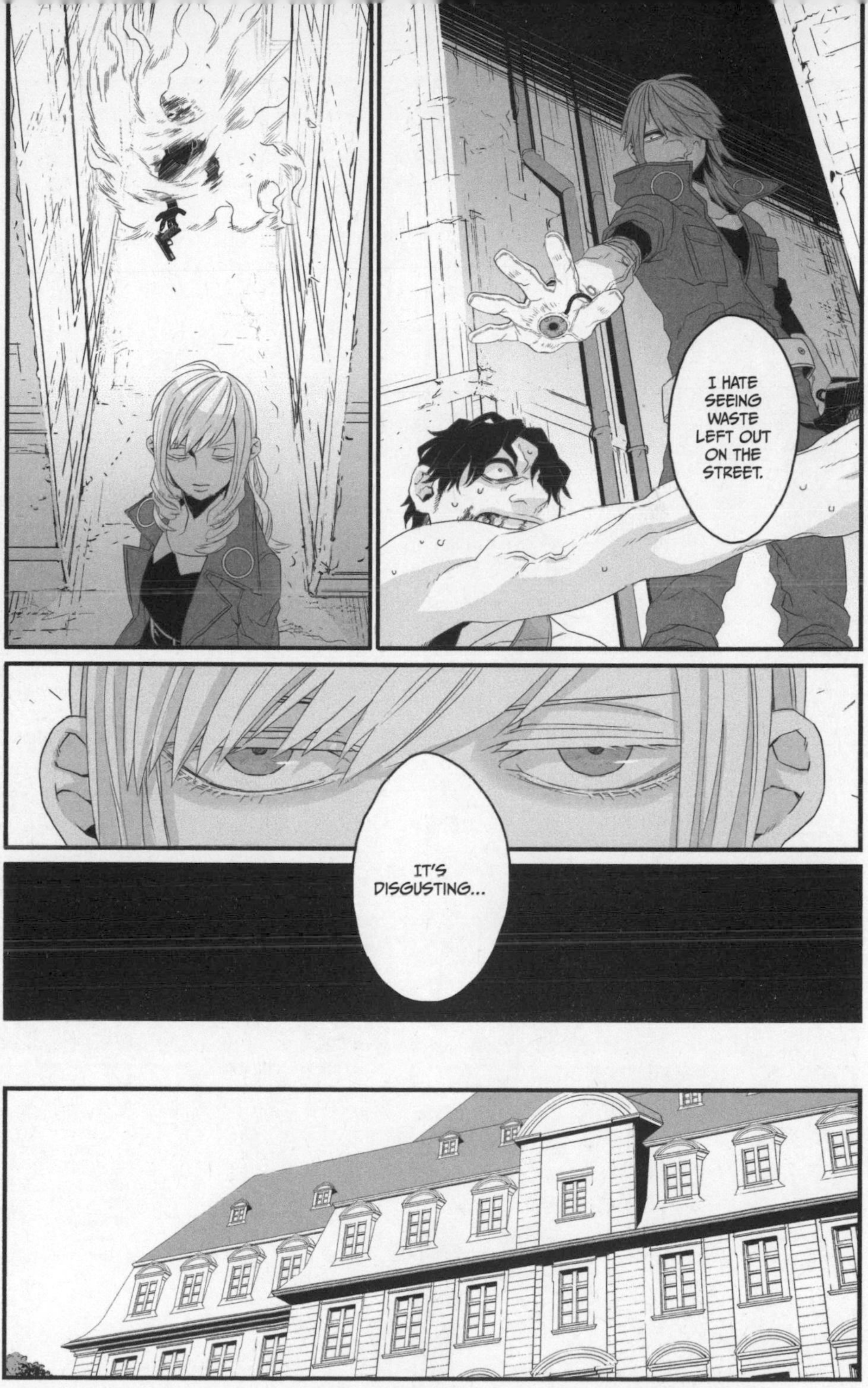
I HATE SEEING WASTE LEFT OUT ON THE STREET.
IT'S DISGUSTING...

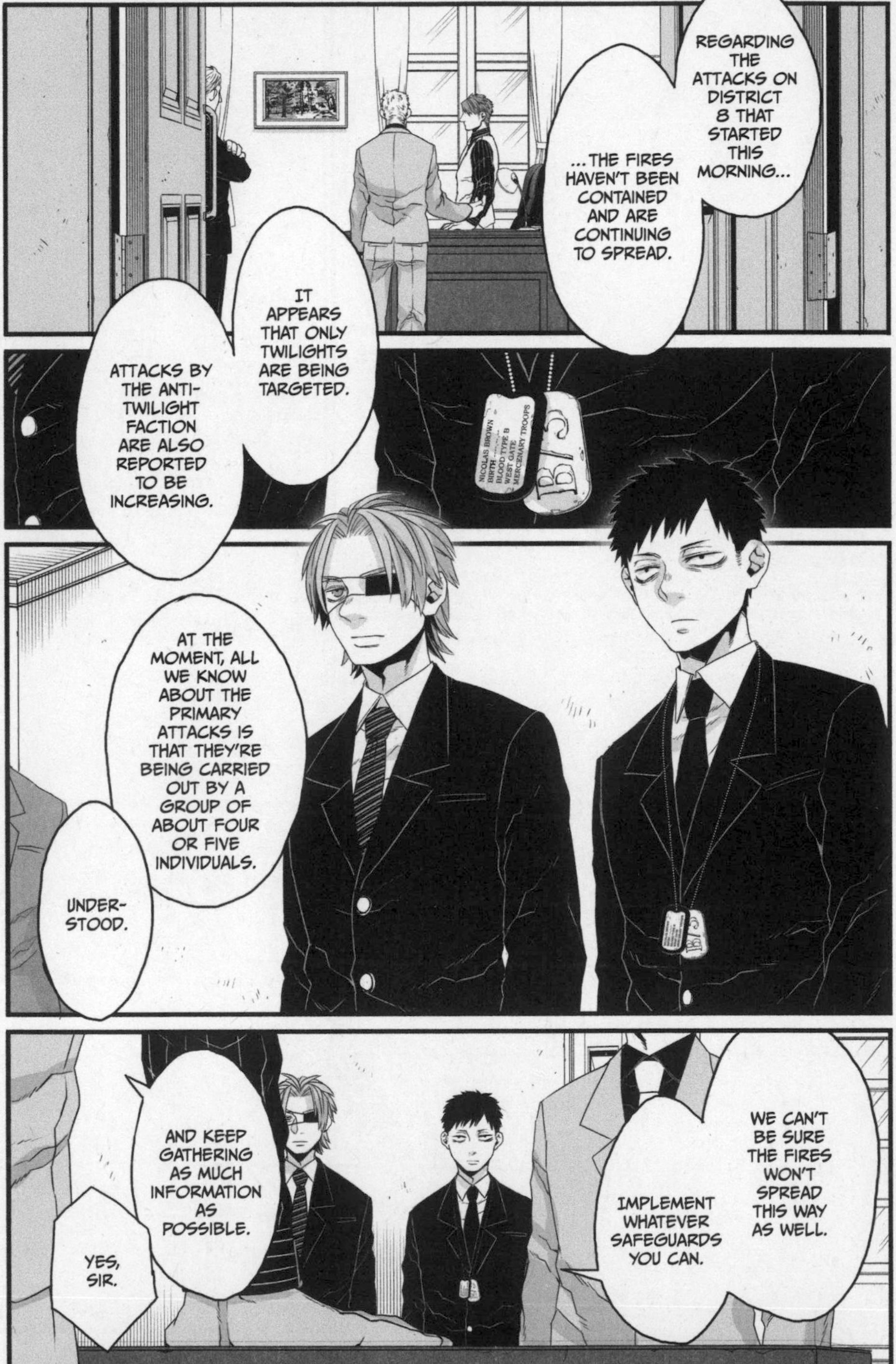
REGARDING THE ATTACKS ON DISTRICT 8 THAT STARTED THIS MORNING...
...THE FIRES HAVEN'T BEEN CONTAINED AND ARE CONTINUING TO SPREAD.
IT APPEARS THAT ONLY TWILIGHTS ARE BEING TARGETED.
ATTACKS BY THE ANTI-TWILIGHT FACTION ARE ALSO REPORTED TO BE INCREASING.
NICOLAS BROWN
BIRTH
BLOOD TYPE B
WEST GATE
MERCENARY TROOPS
AT THE MOMENT, ALL WE KNOW ABOUT THE PRIMARY ATTACKS IS THAT THEY'RE BEING CARRIED OUT BY A GROUP OF ABOUT FOUR OR FIVE INDIVIDUALS.
UNDER-STOOD.
WE CAN'T BE SURE THE FIRES WON'T SPREAD THIS WAY AS WELL.
IMPLEMENT WHATEVER SAFEGUARDS YOU CAN.
AND KEEP GATHERING AS MUCH INFORMATION AS POSSIBLE.
YES, SIR.

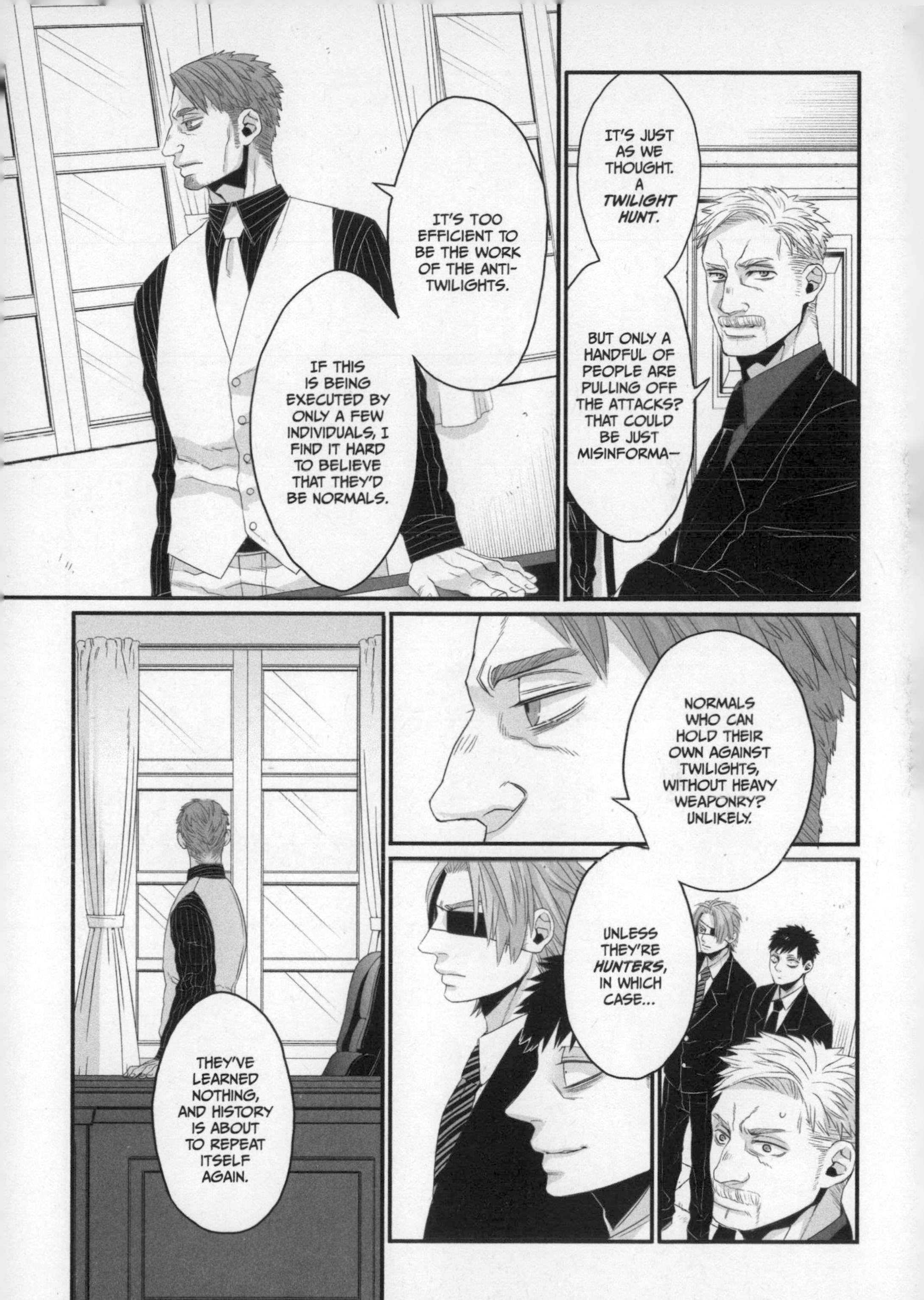
IT'S JUST AS WE THOUGHT. A *TWILIGHT HUNT*.
BUT ONLY A HANDFUL OF PEOPLE ARE PULLING OFF THE ATTACKS? THAT COULD BE JUST MISINFORMA—
IT'S TOO EFFICIENT TO BE THE WORK OF THE ANTI-TWILIGHTS.
IF THIS IS BEING EXECUTED BY ONLY A FEW INDIVIDUALS, I FIND IT HARD TO BELIEVE THAT THEY'D BE NORMALS.
NORMALS WHO CAN HOLD THEIR OWN AGAINST TWILIGHTS, WITHOUT HEAVY WEAPONRY? UNLIKELY.
UNLESS THEY'RE *HUNTERS*, IN WHICH CASE...
THEY'VE LEARNED NOTHING, AND HISTORY IS ABOUT TO REPEAT ITSELF AGAIN.

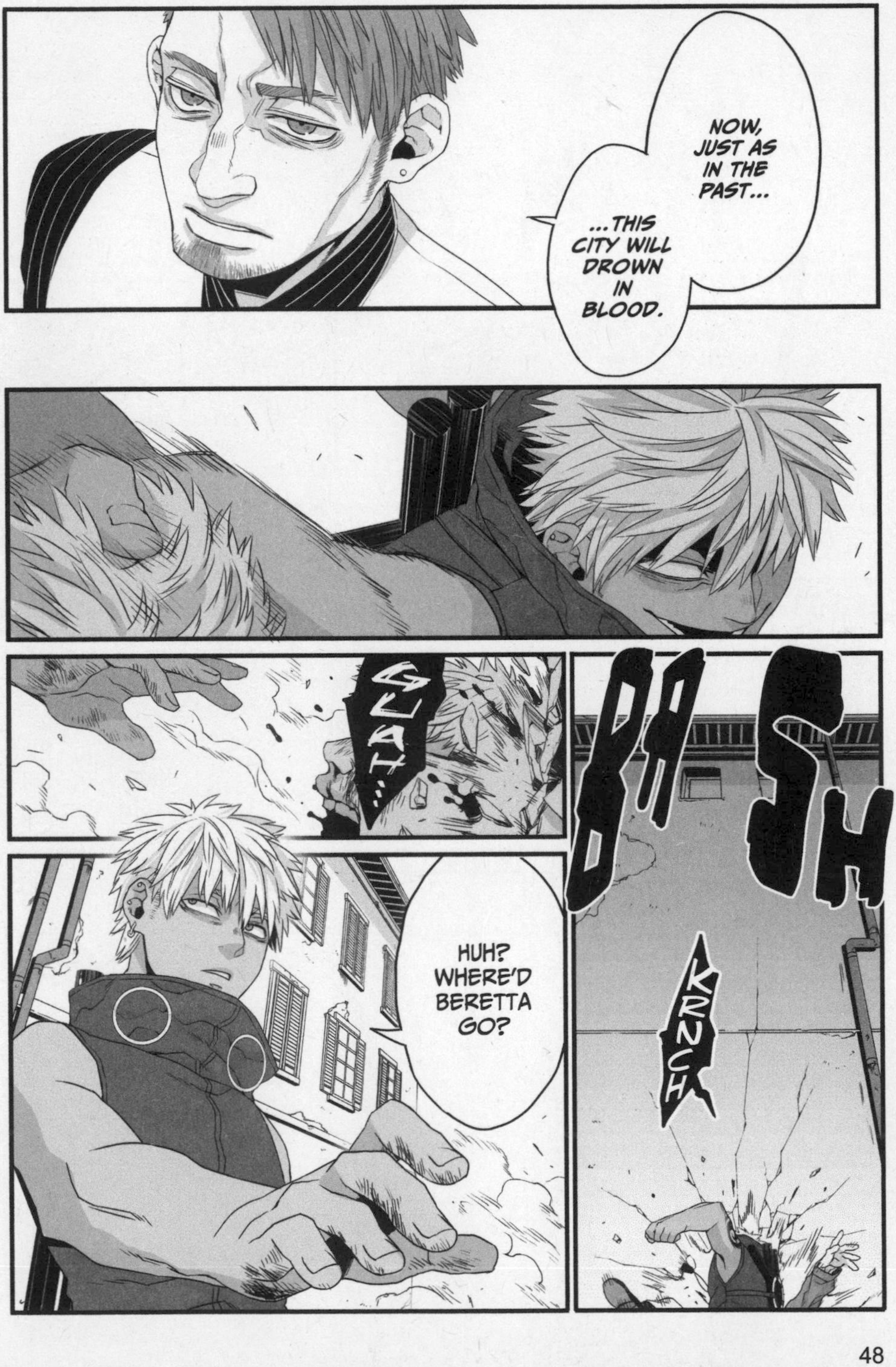
NOW, JUST AS IN THE PAST...
...THIS CITY WILL DROWN IN BLOOD.
BASH
KRNCH
GUAH...
HUH? WHERE'D BERETTA GO?

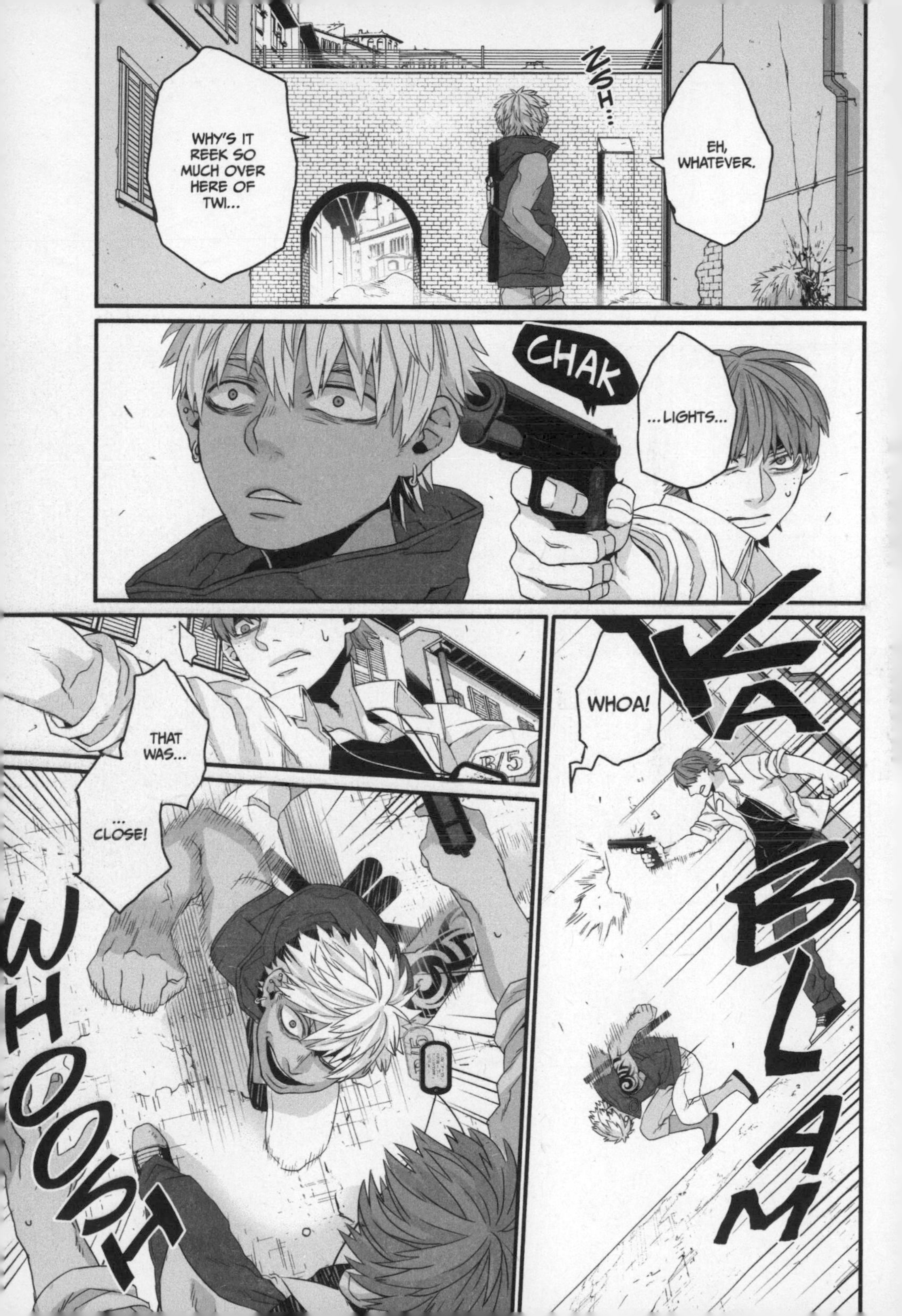
ZSH...
EH, WHATEVER.
WHY'S IT REEK SO MUCH OVER HERE OF TWI...
CHAK
...LIGHTS...
KABLAM
WHOA!
THAT WAS...
...CLOSE!
WHOOSH

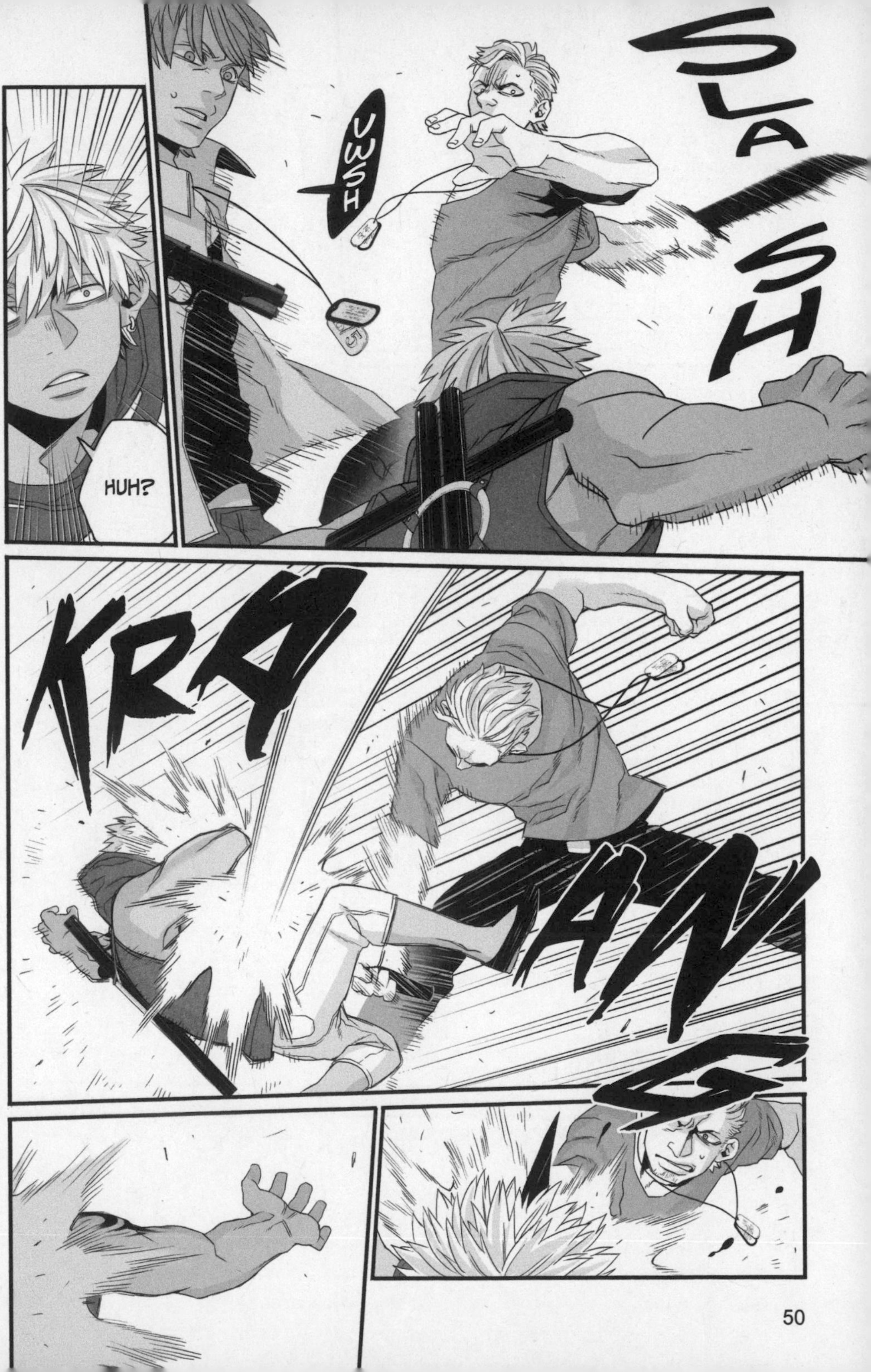
SLASH
VWSH
HUH?
KRA

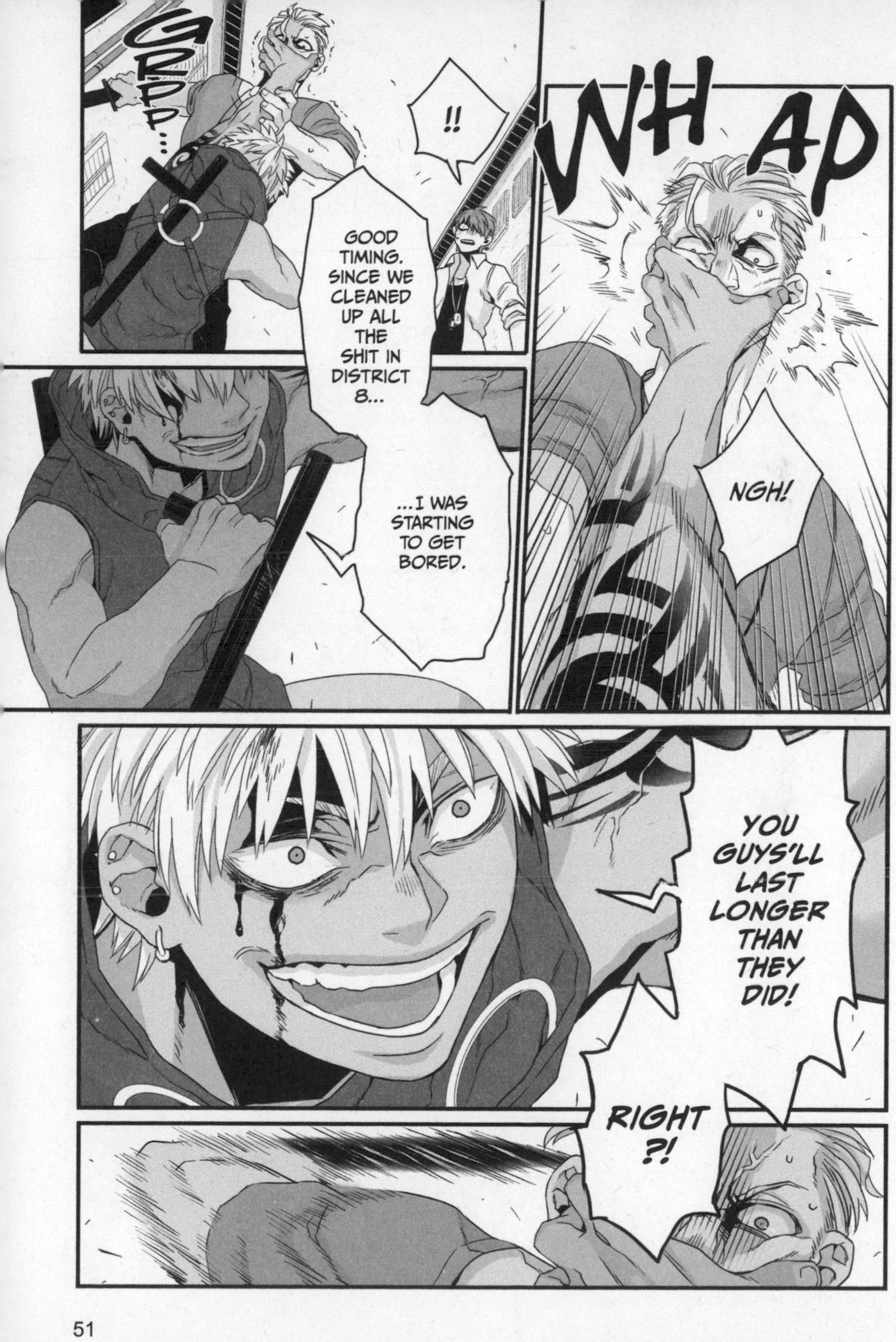
WH AP
NGH!
GRPP...
!!
GOOD TIMING. SINCE WE CLEANED UP ALL THE SHIT IN DISTRICT 8...
...I WAS STARTING TO GET BORED.
YOU GUYS'LL LAST LONGER THAN THEY DID!
RIGHT?!

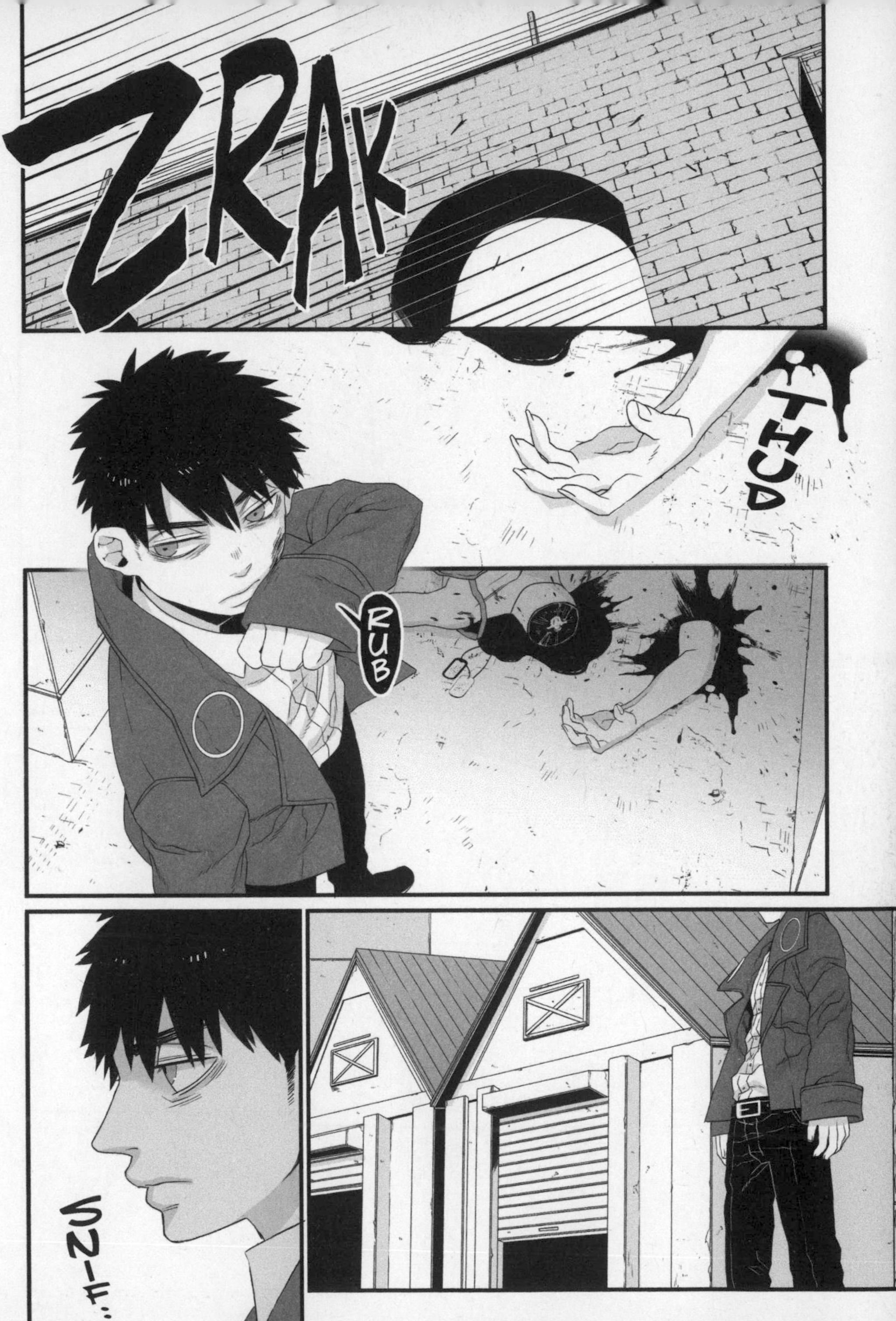
ZRAK
THUD
RUB
SNIF...

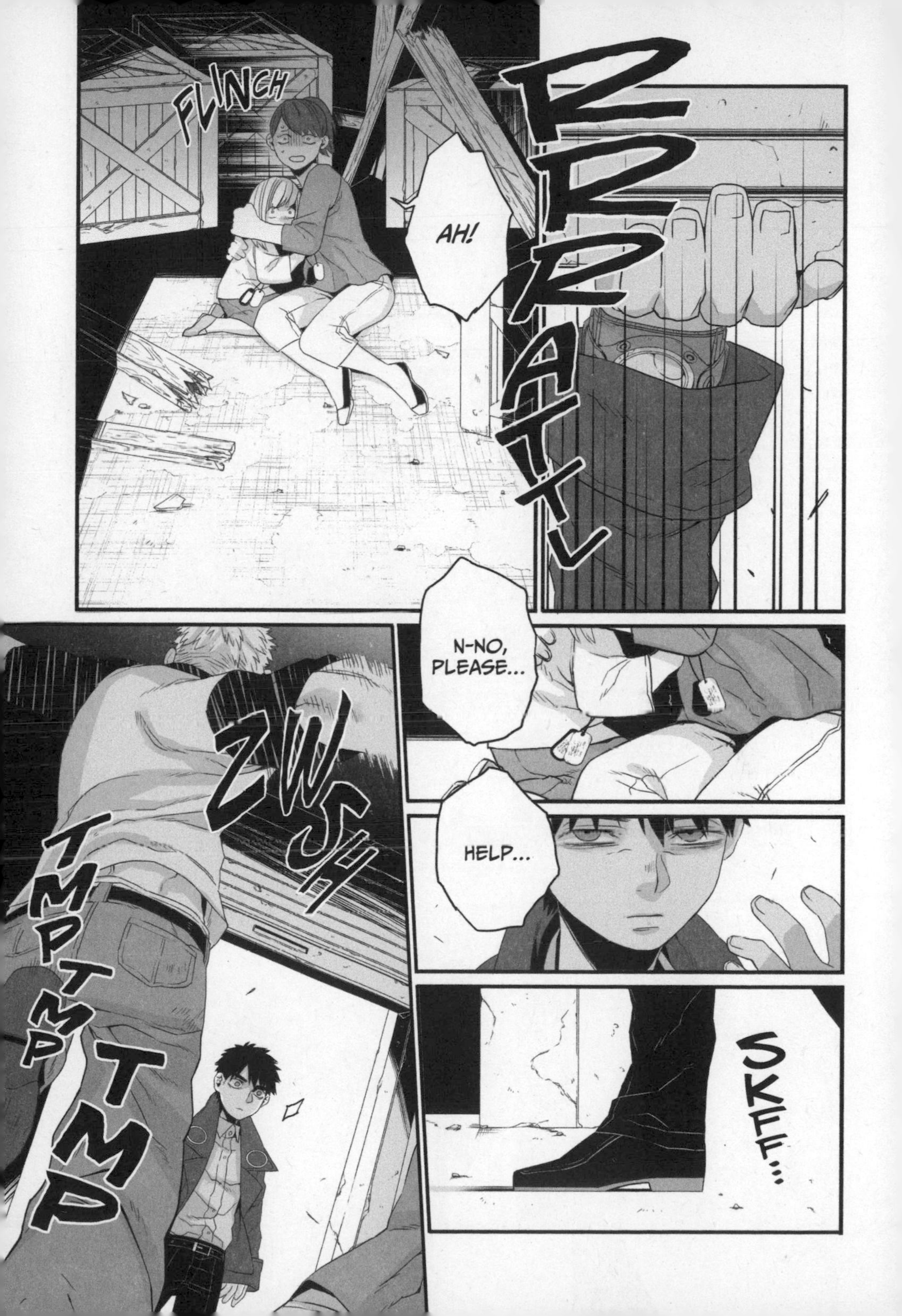
RRRATTL
AH!
FLINCH
N-NO, PLEASE...
HELP...
SKFF...
ZWSH
TMP
TMP
TMP

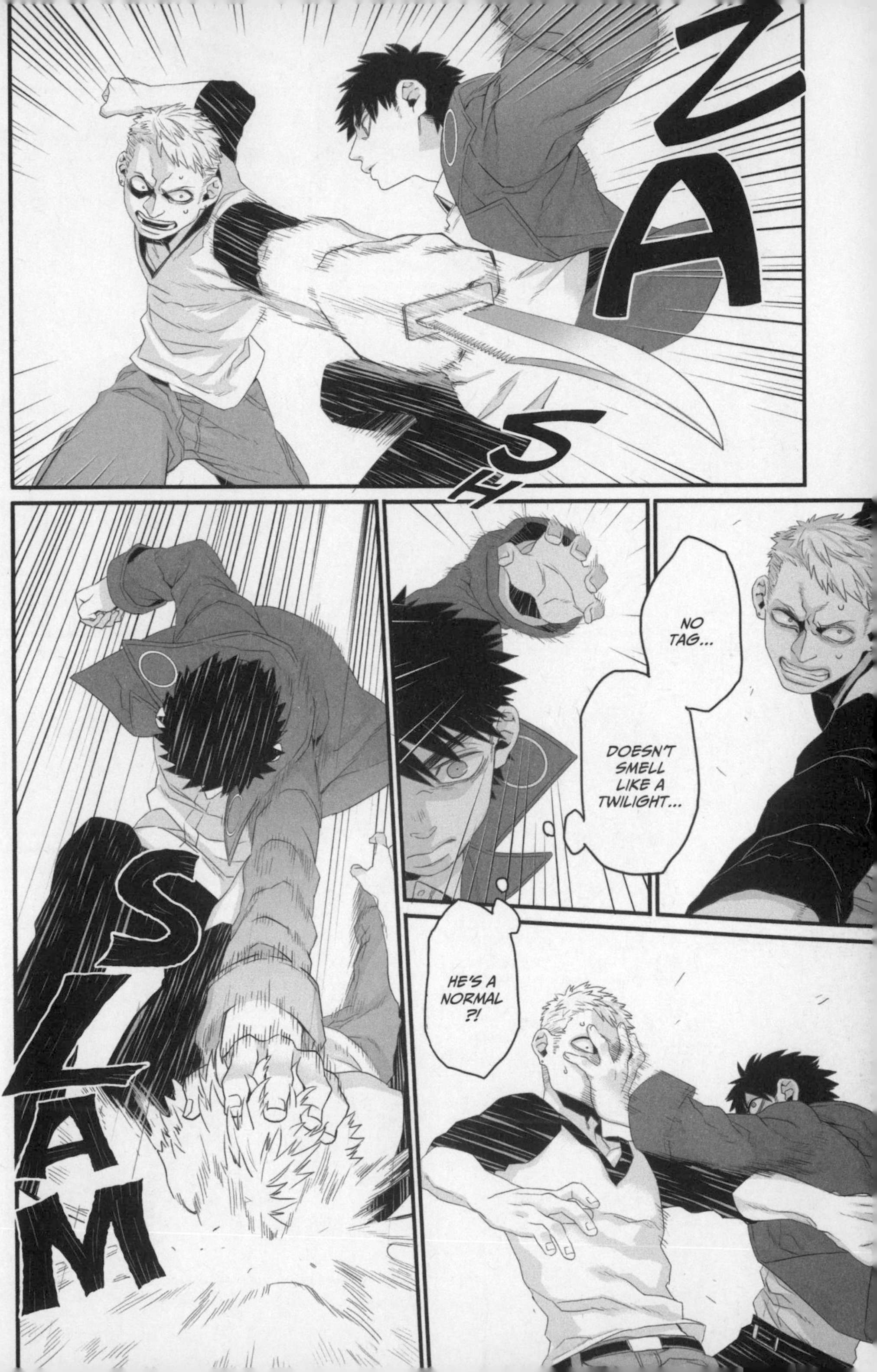
ZA
SH
NO TAG...
DOESN'T SMELL LIKE A TWILIGHT...
HE'S A NORMAL ?!
SLAM

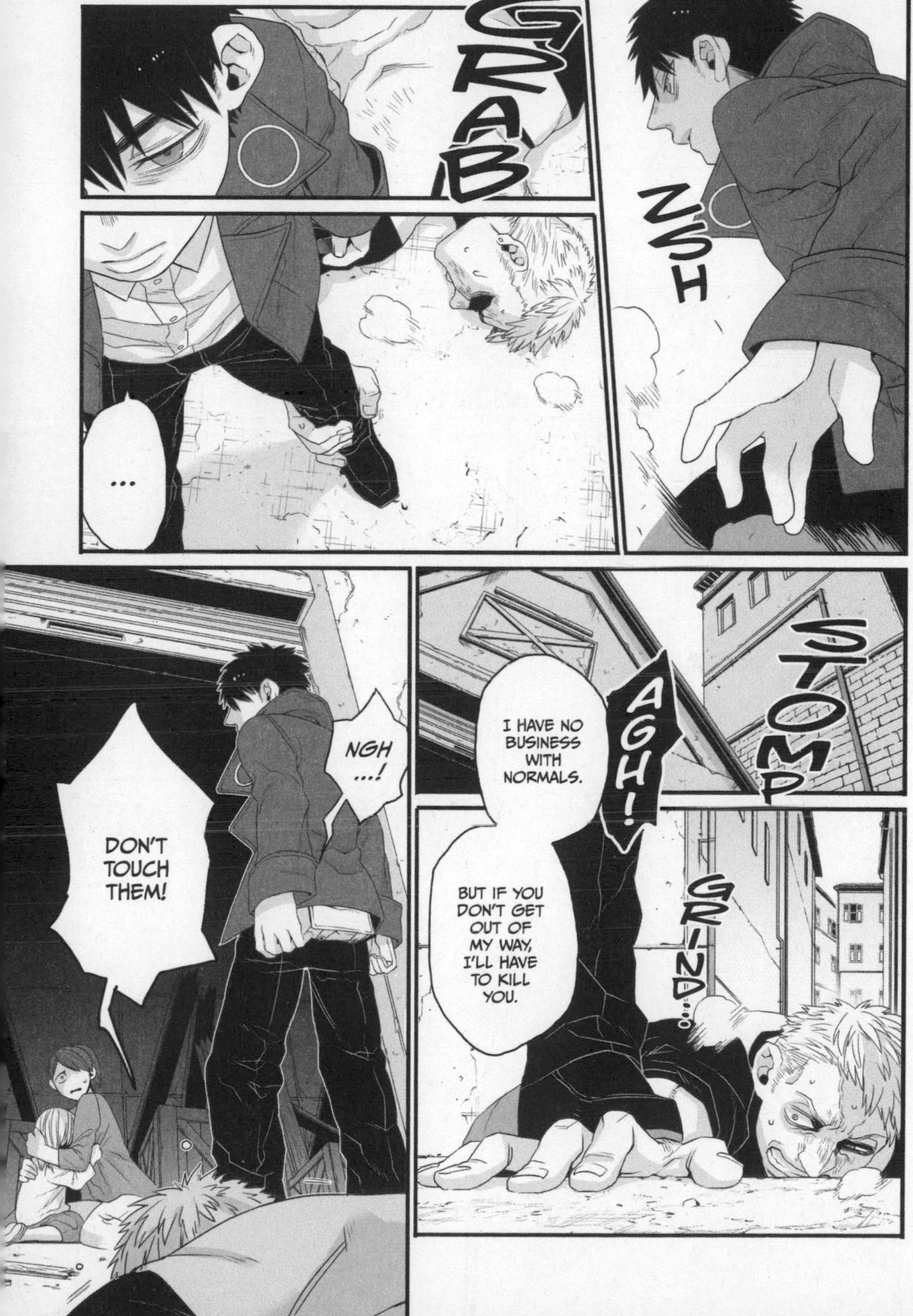
ZSH
GRAB
...
STOMP
AGH!
I HAVE NO BUSINESS WITH NORMALS.
BUT IF YOU DON'T GET OUT OF MY WAY, I'LL HAVE TO KILL YOU.
GRIND...
NGH...!
DON'T TOUCH THEM!

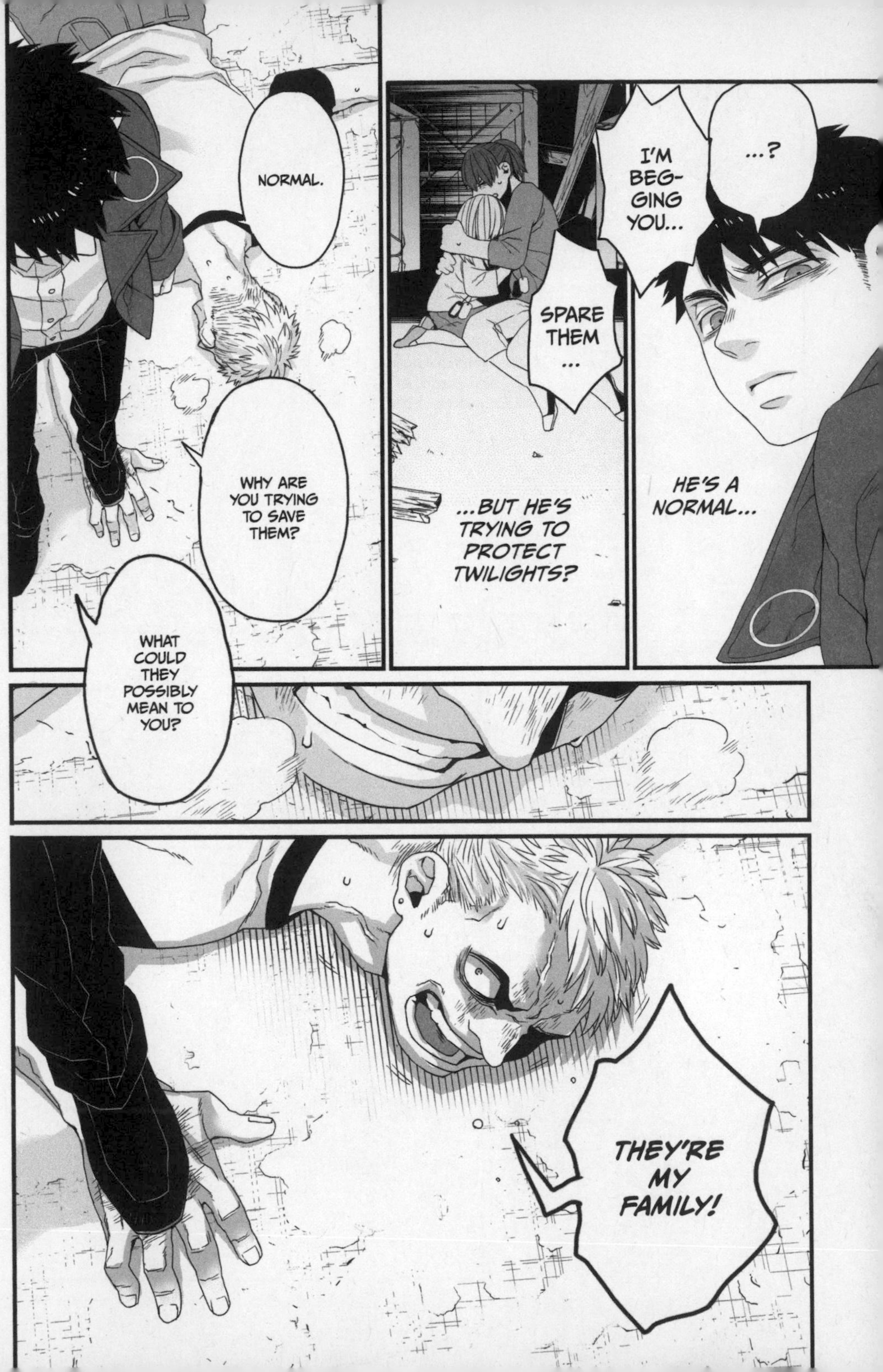
I'M BEG-GING YOU...
SPARE THEM ...
...?
HE'S A NORMAL...
...BUT HE'S TRYING TO PROTECT TWILIGHTS?
NORMAL.
WHY ARE YOU TRYING TO SAVE THEM?
WHAT COULD THEY POSSIBLY MEAN TO YOU?
THEY'RE MY FAMILY!

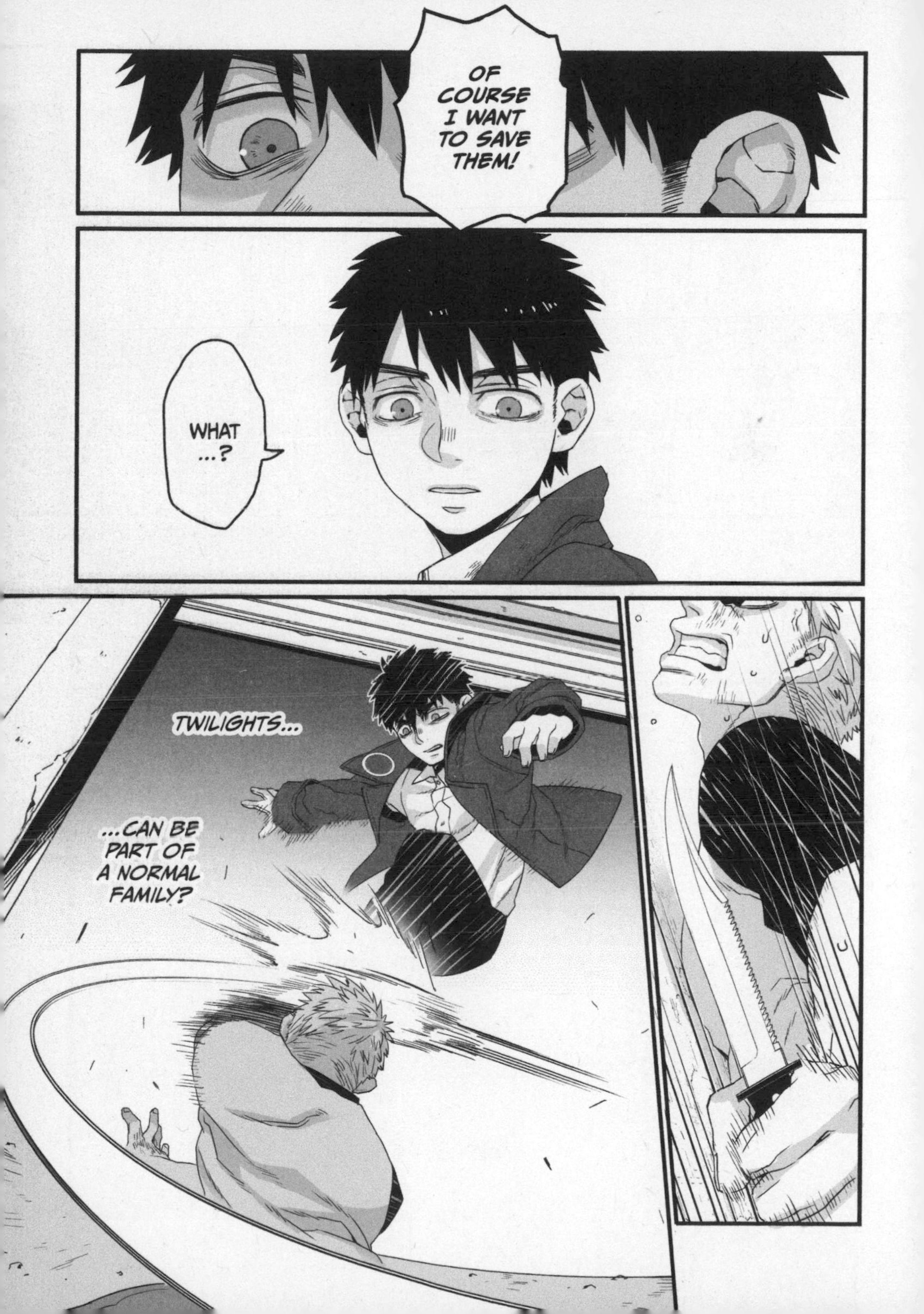
OF COURSE I WANT TO SAVE THEM!
WHAT ...?
TWILIGHTS...
...CAN BE PART OF A NORMAL FAMILY?

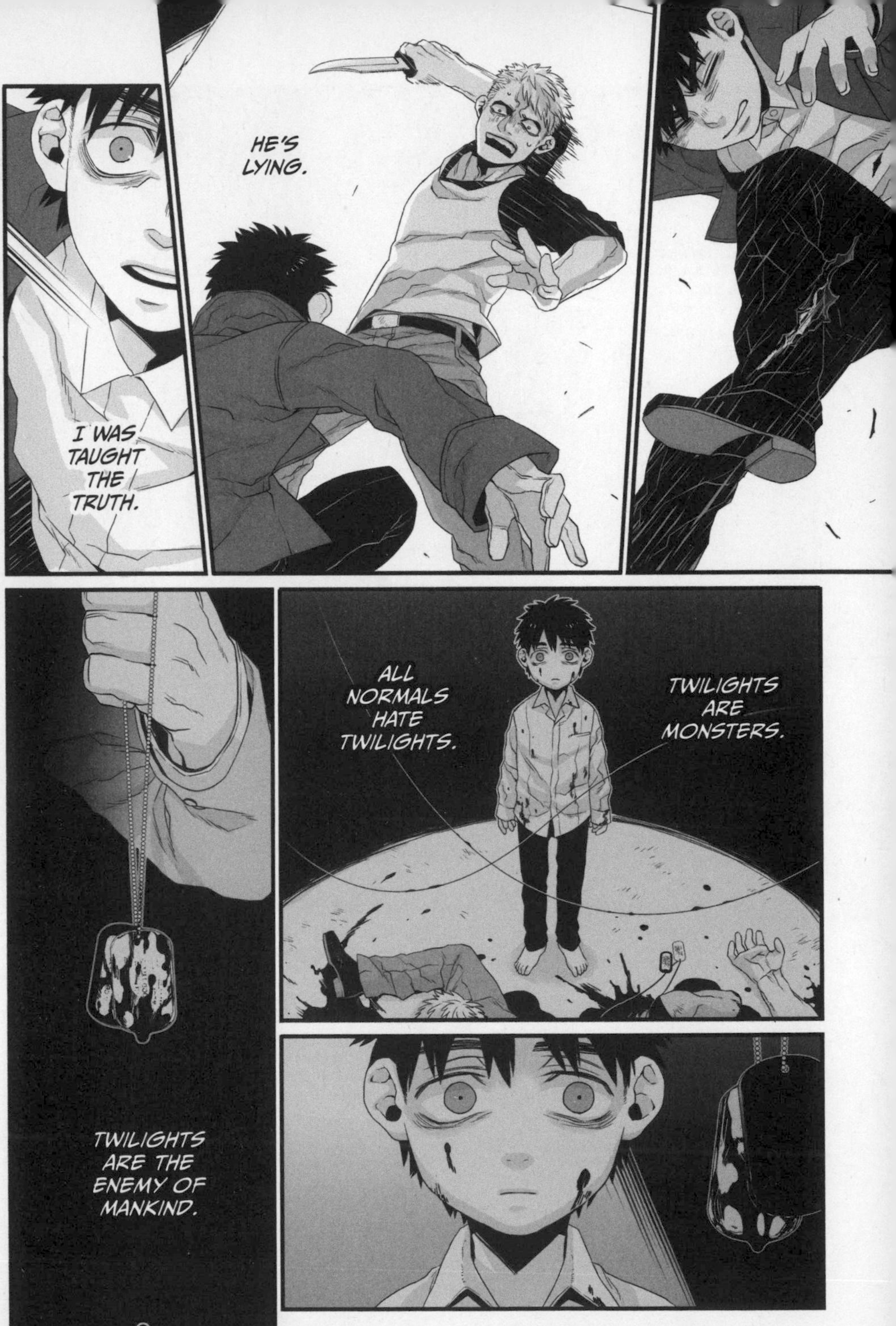
HE'S LYING.
I WAS TAUGHT THE TRUTH.
TWILIGHTS ARE MONSTERS.
ALL NORMALS HATE TWILIGHTS.
TWILIGHTS ARE THE ENEMY OF MANKIND.

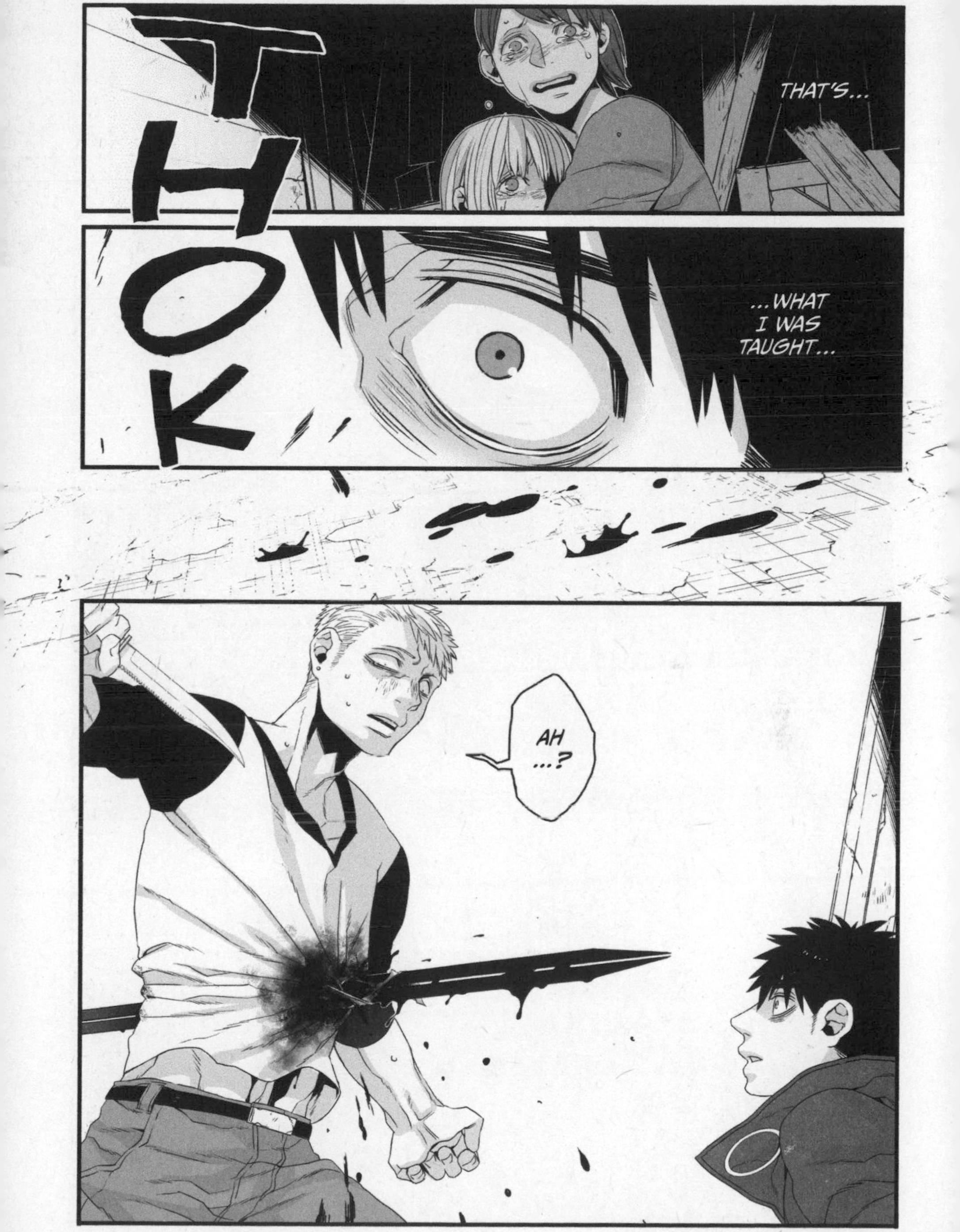
THOK
THAT'S...
...WHAT I WAS TAUGHT...
AH ...?

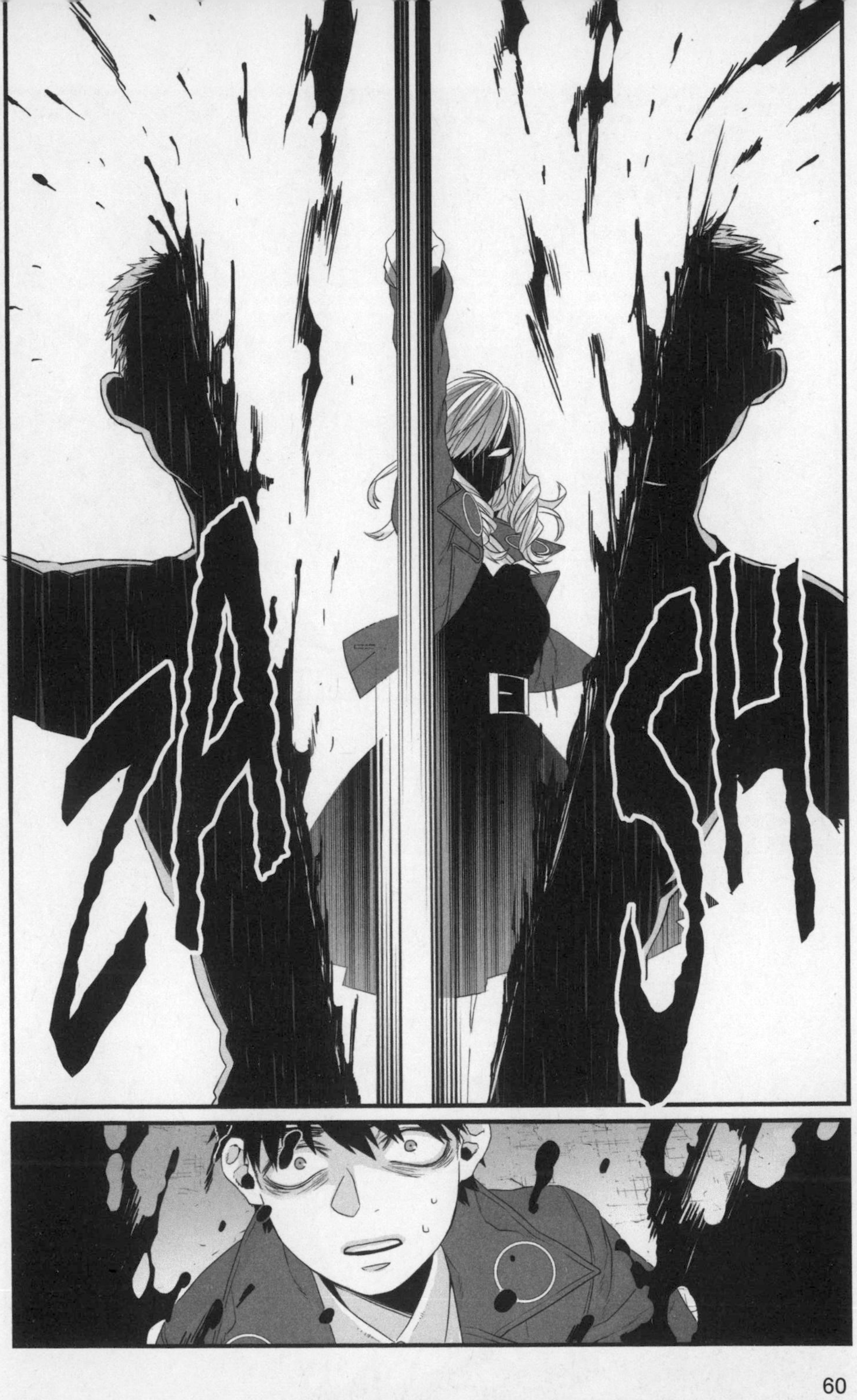
ZASH

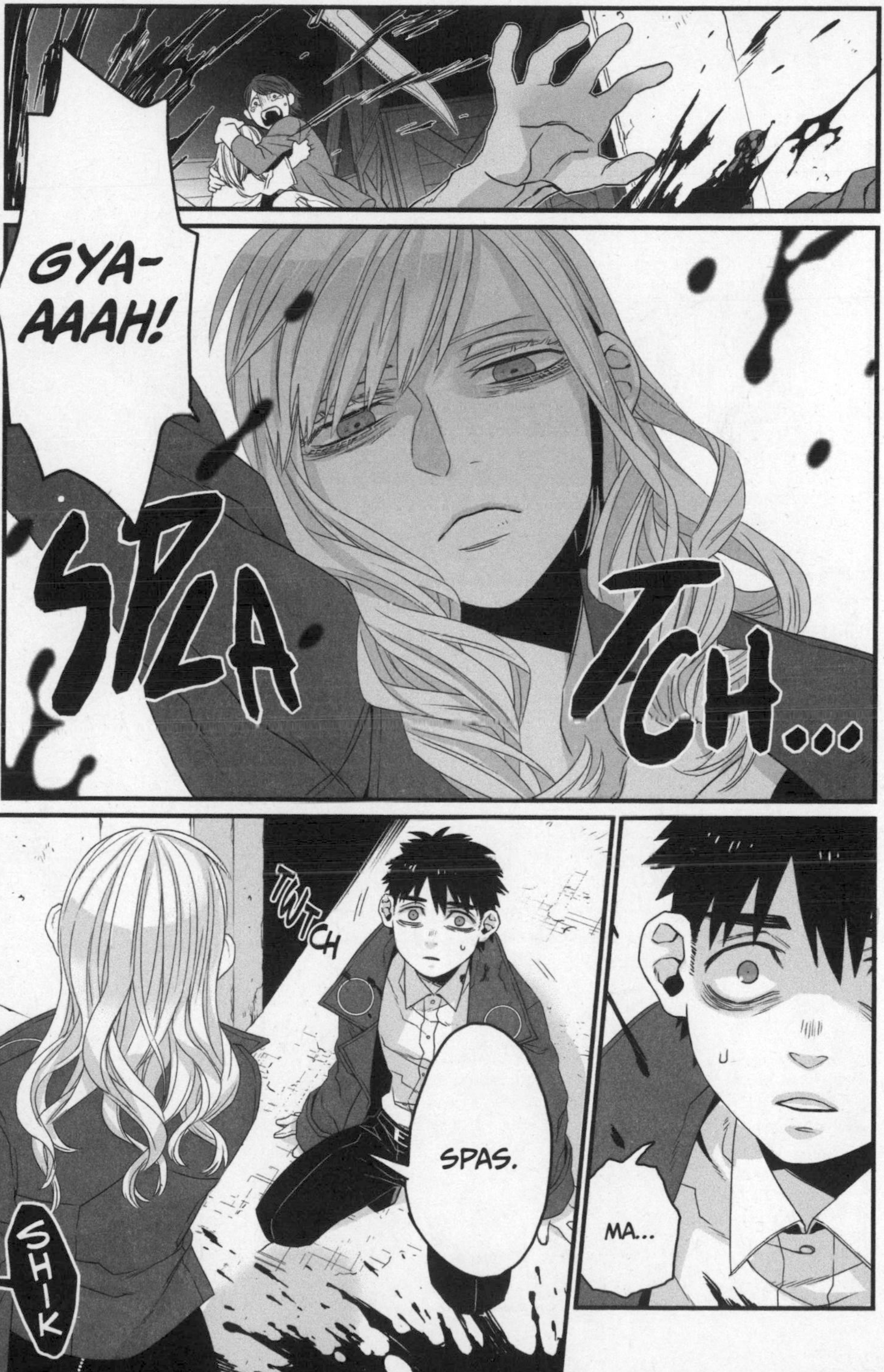
GYA-AAAH!
SPLATCH...
MA...
TWITCH
SPAS.
SHIK

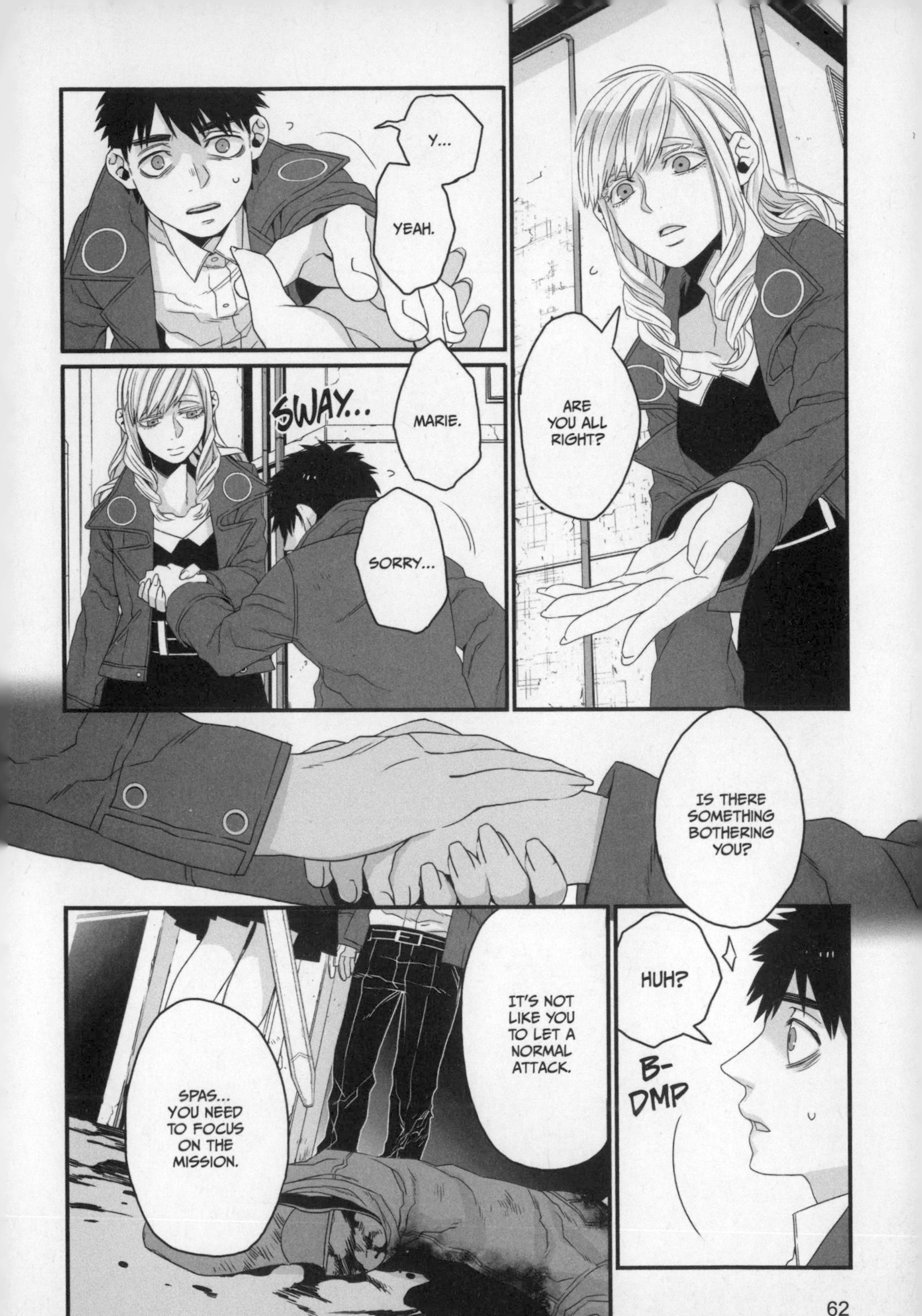
ARE YOU ALL RIGHT?
Y...
YEAH.
MARIE.
SWAY...
SORRY...
IS THERE SOMETHING BOTHERING YOU?
HUH?
B-DMP
IT'S NOT LIKE YOU TO LET A NORMAL ATTACK.
SPAS... YOU NEED TO FOCUS ON THE MISSION.

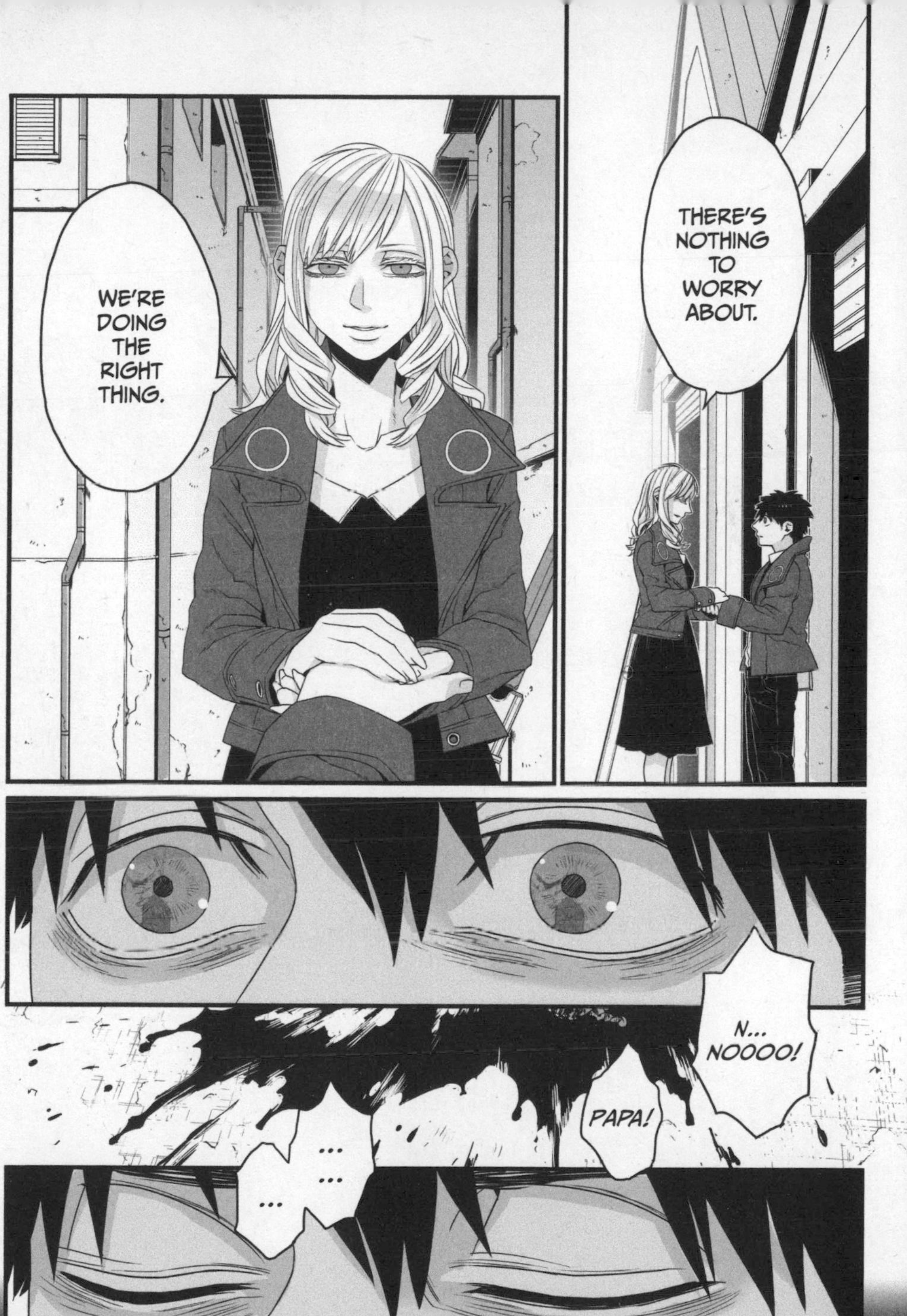
THERE'S NOTHING TO WORRY ABOUT.
WE'RE DOING THE RIGHT THING.
N... NOOOO!
PAPA!
...
...
...

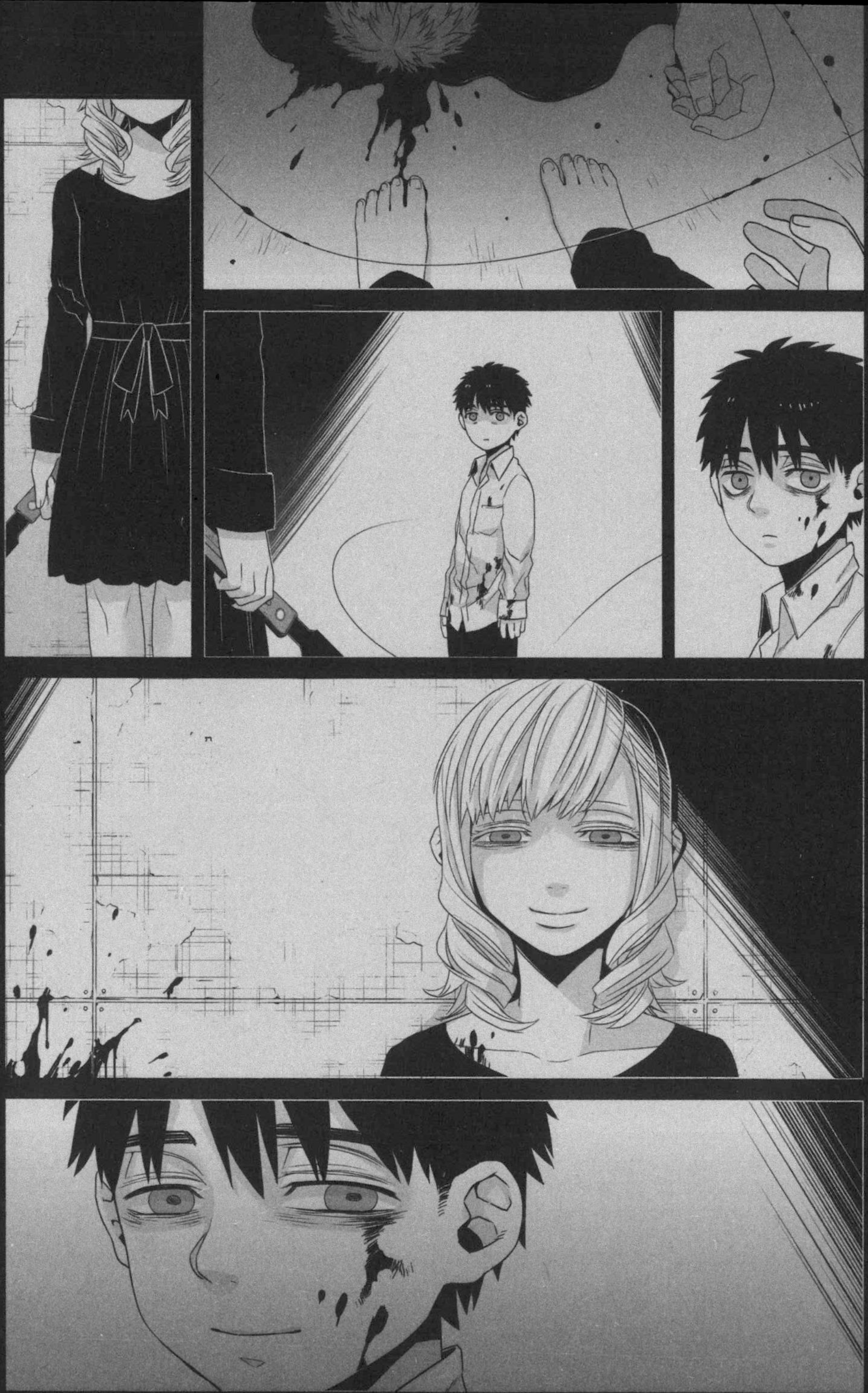

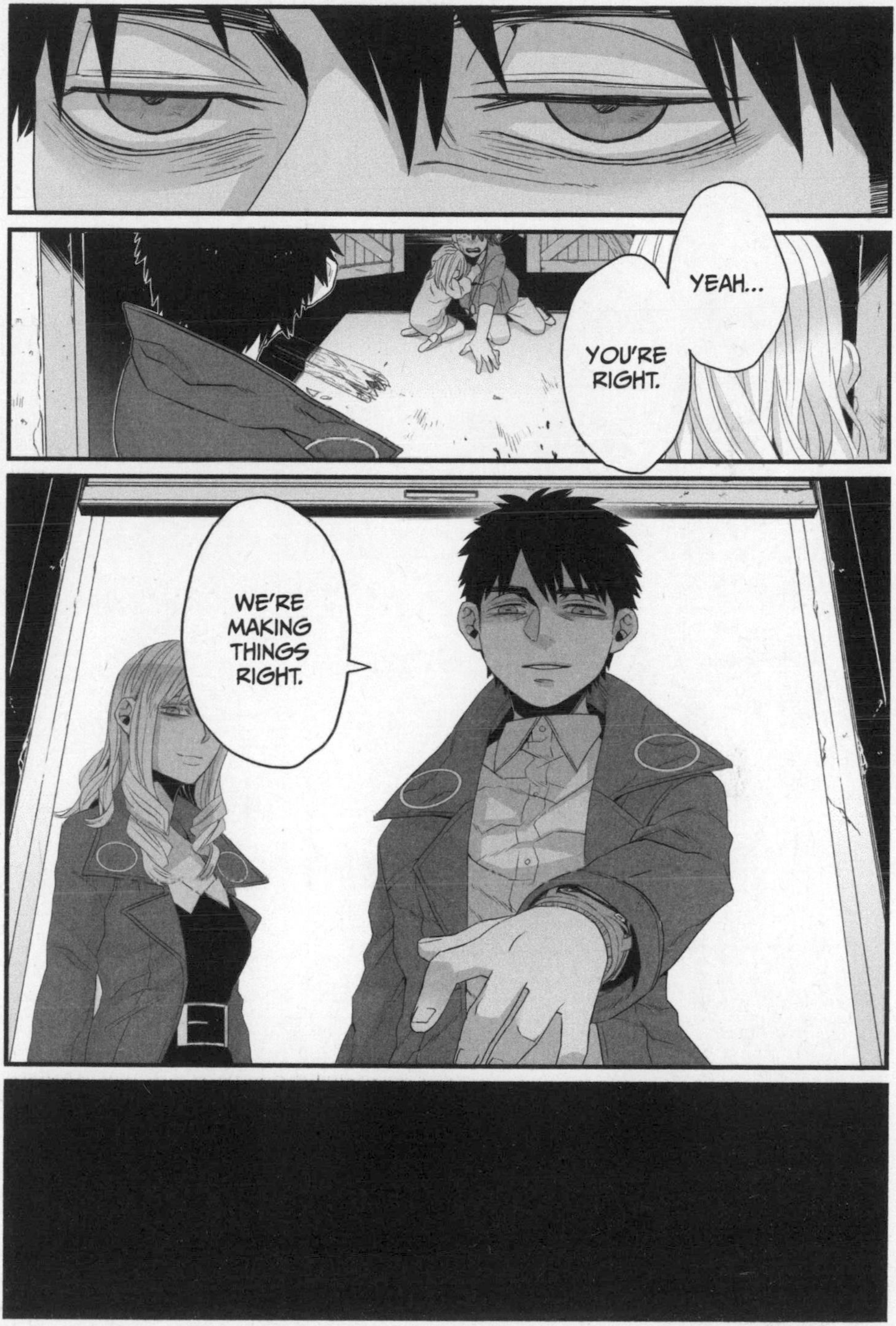
YEAH...
YOU'RE RIGHT.
WE'RE MAKING THINGS RIGHT.

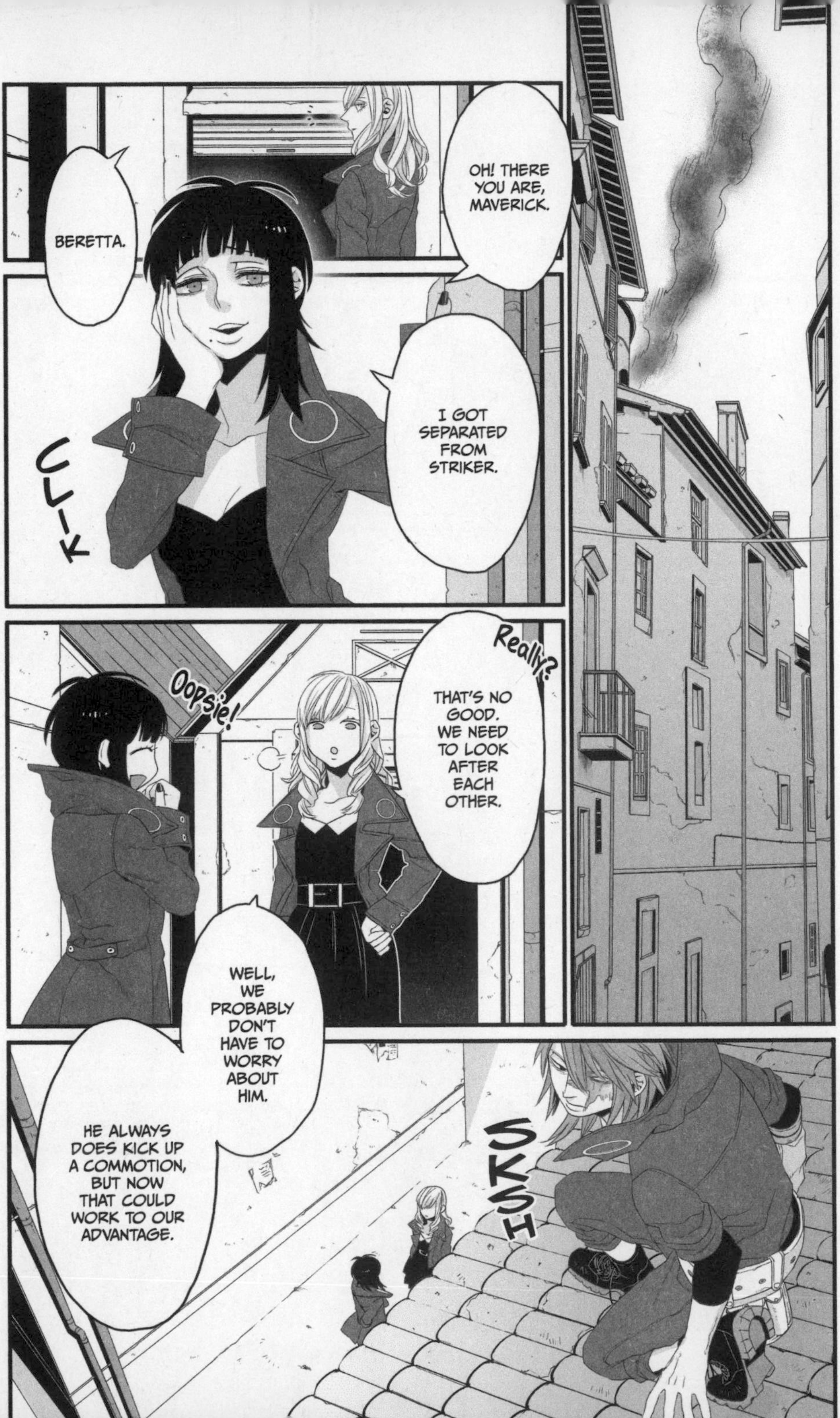
OH! THERE YOU ARE, MAVERICK.
BERETTA.
I GOT SEPARATED FROM STRIKER.
CLIK
Really?
THAT'S NO GOOD. WE NEED TO LOOK AFTER EACH OTHER.
Oopsie!
WELL, WE PROBABLY DON'T HAVE TO WORRY ABOUT HIM.
HE ALWAYS DOES KICK UP A COMMOTION, BUT NOW THAT COULD WORK TO OUR ADVANTAGE.
SKSH

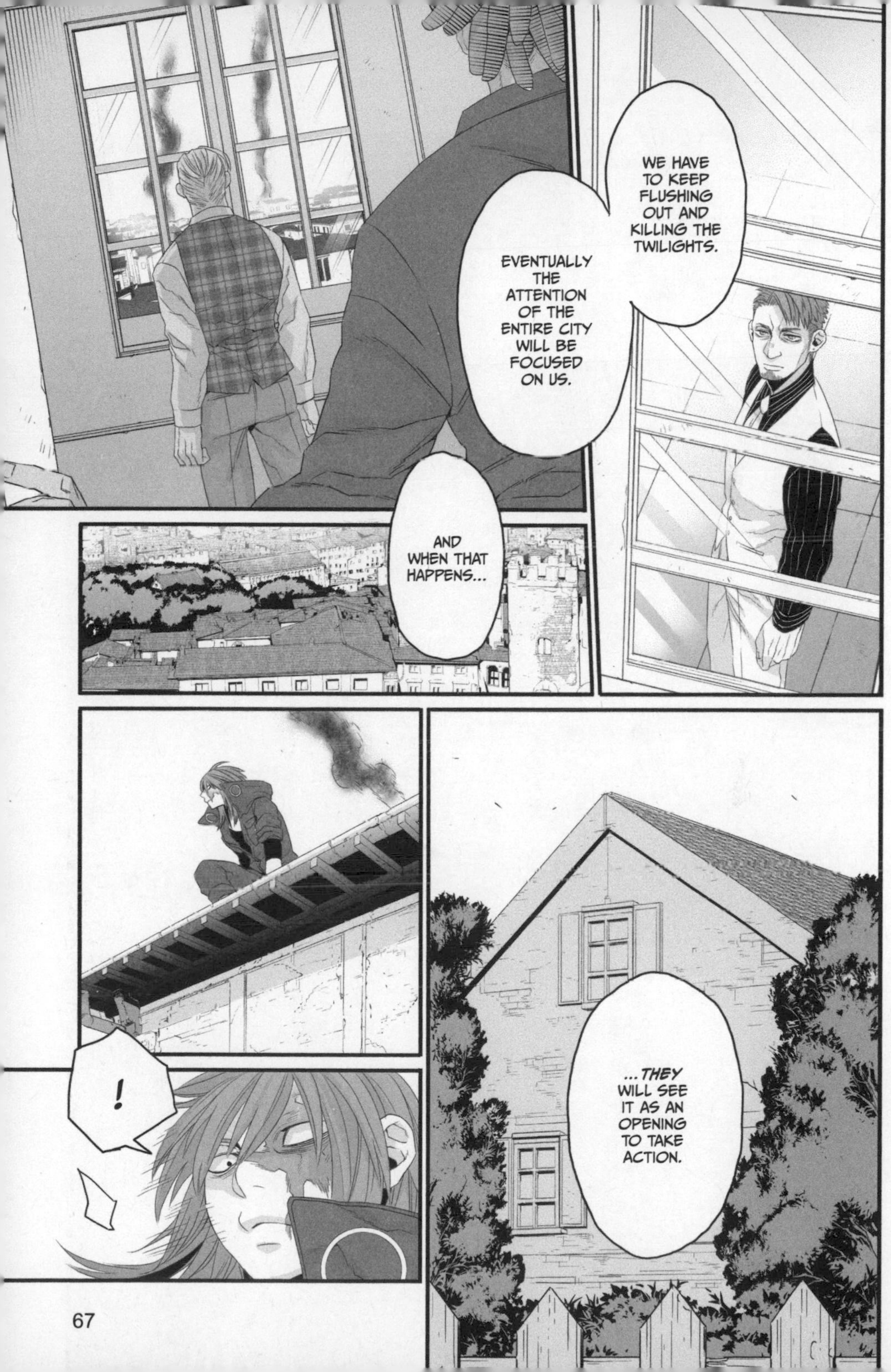
WE HAVE TO KEEP FLUSHING OUT AND KILLING THE TWILIGHTS.
EVENTUALLY THE ATTENTION OF THE ENTIRE CITY WILL BE FOCUSED ON US.
AND WHEN THAT HAPPENS...
...*THEY* WILL SEE IT AS AN OPENING TO TAKE ACTION.
!

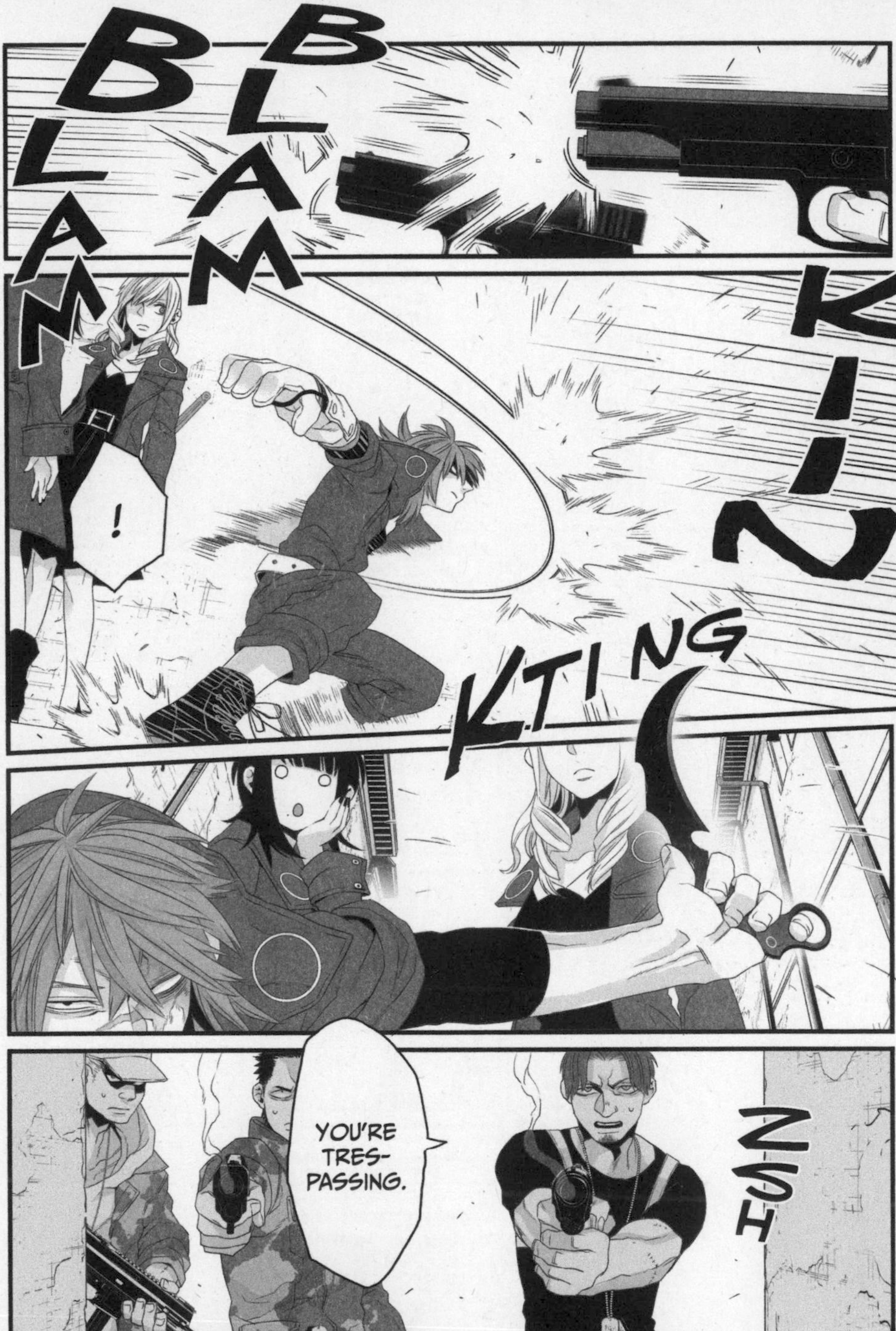
BLAM
BLAM
KIN
!
KTING
ZSH
YOU'RE TRES-PASSING.

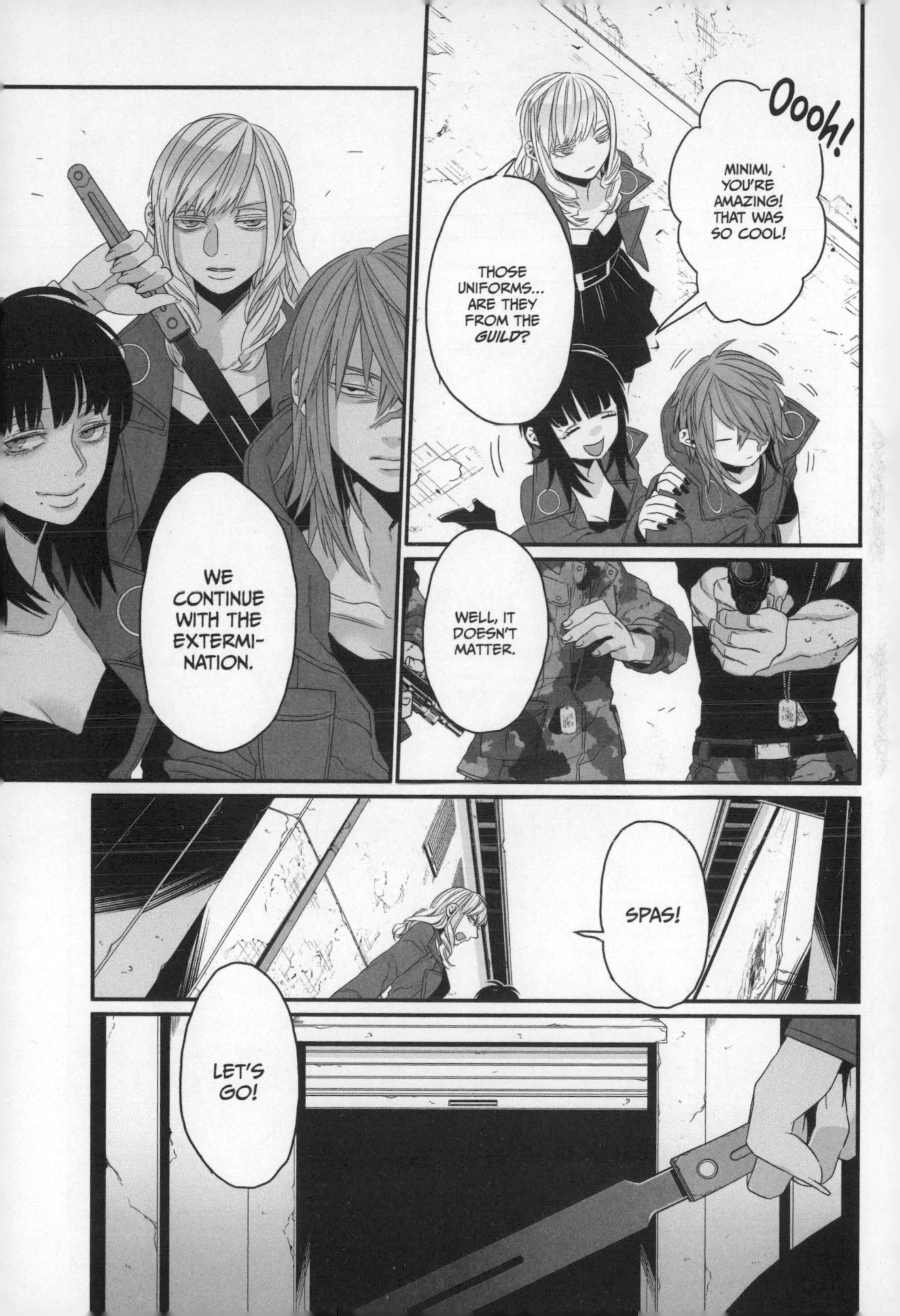
Oooh!
MINIMI, YOU'RE AMAZING! THAT WAS SO COOL!
THOSE UNIFORMS... ARE THEY FROM THE *GUILD*?
WELL, IT DOESN'T MATTER.
WE CONTINUE WITH THE EXTERMI-NATION.
SPAS!
LET'S GO!

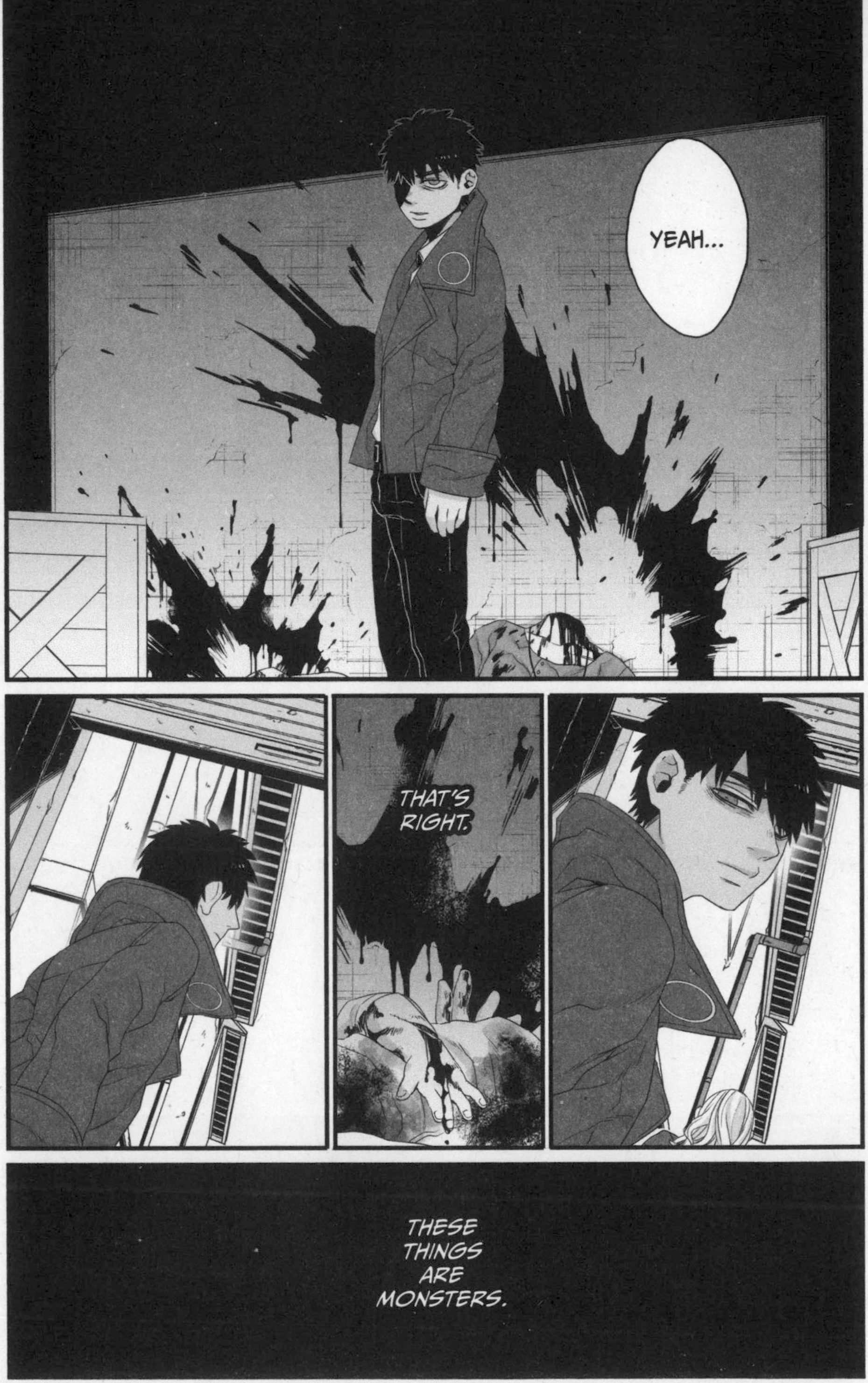
YEAH...
THAT'S RIGHT.
THESE THINGS ARE MONSTERS.

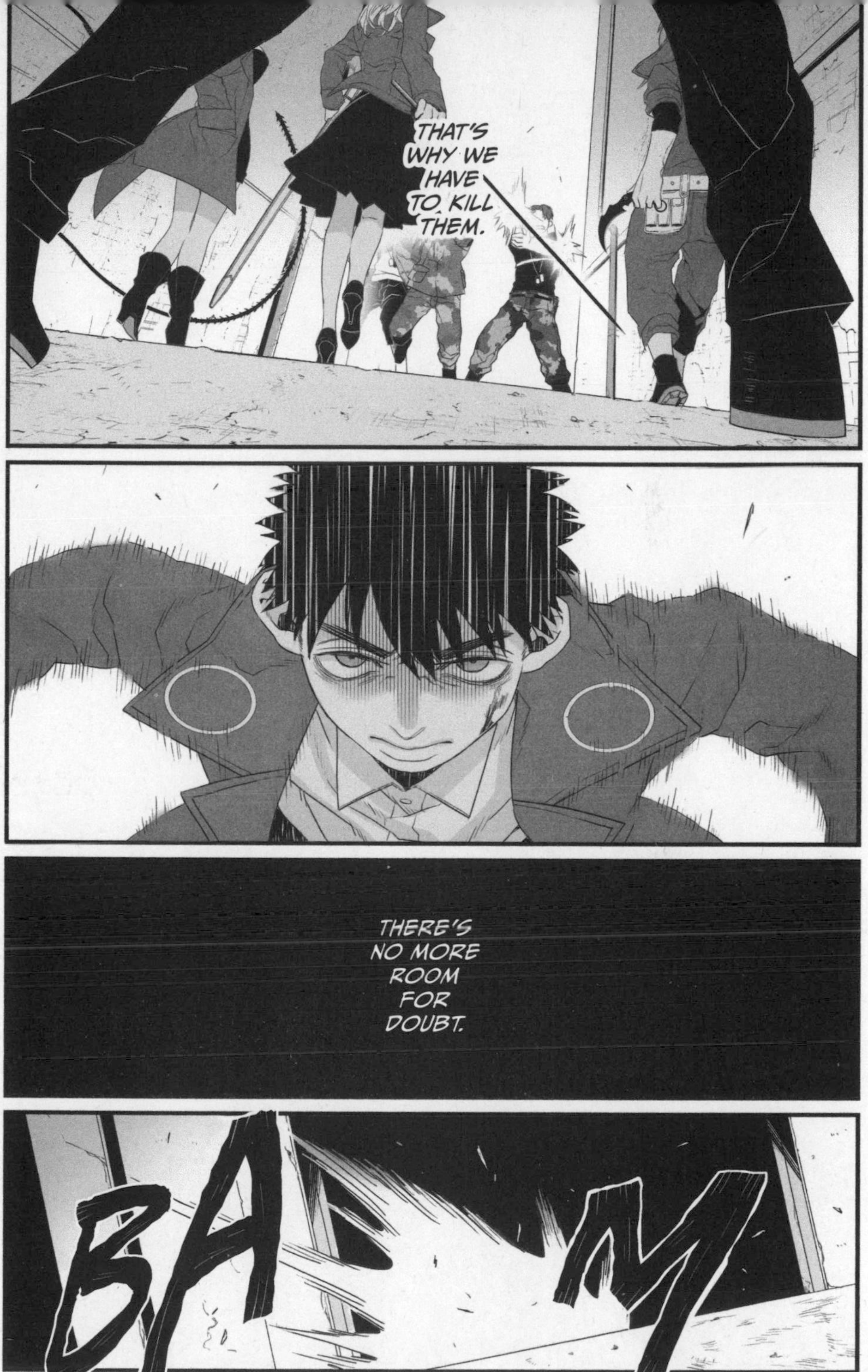
THAT'S WHY WE HAVE TO KILL THEM.
THERE'S NO MORE ROOM FOR DOUBT.
BAM

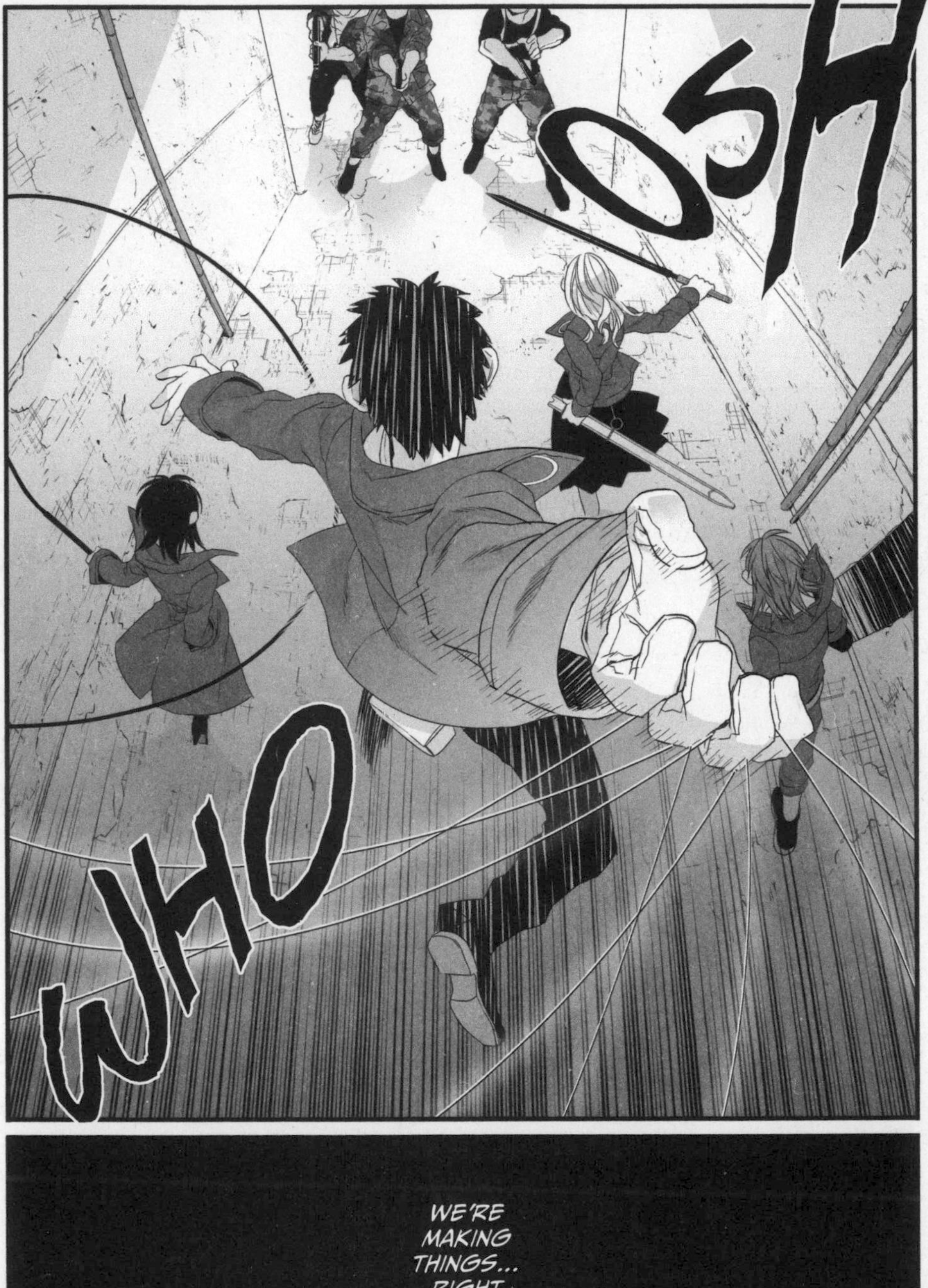
WHOOSH
WE'RE MAKING THINGS... RIGHT.

#01 END

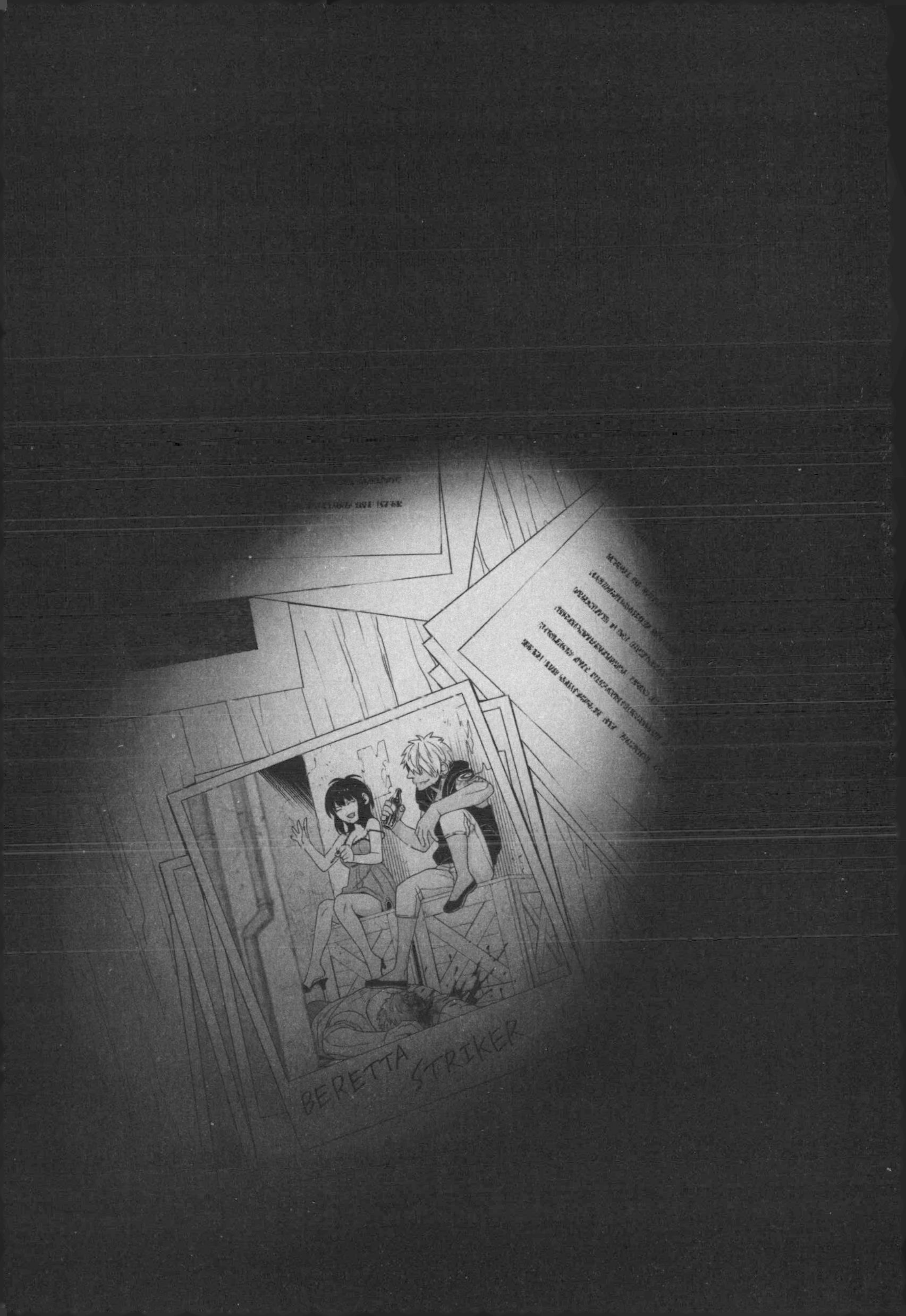
BERETTA
STRIKER

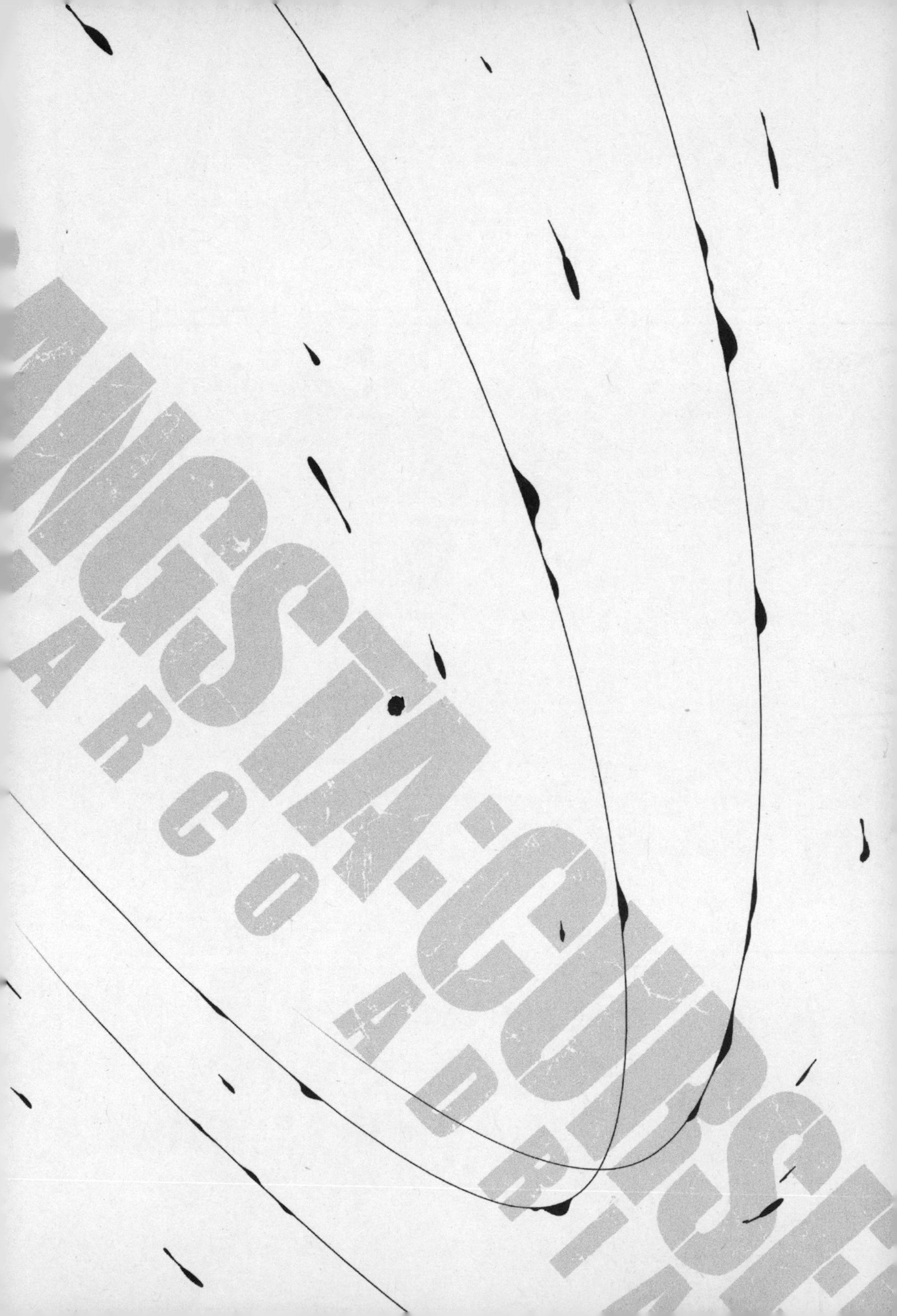

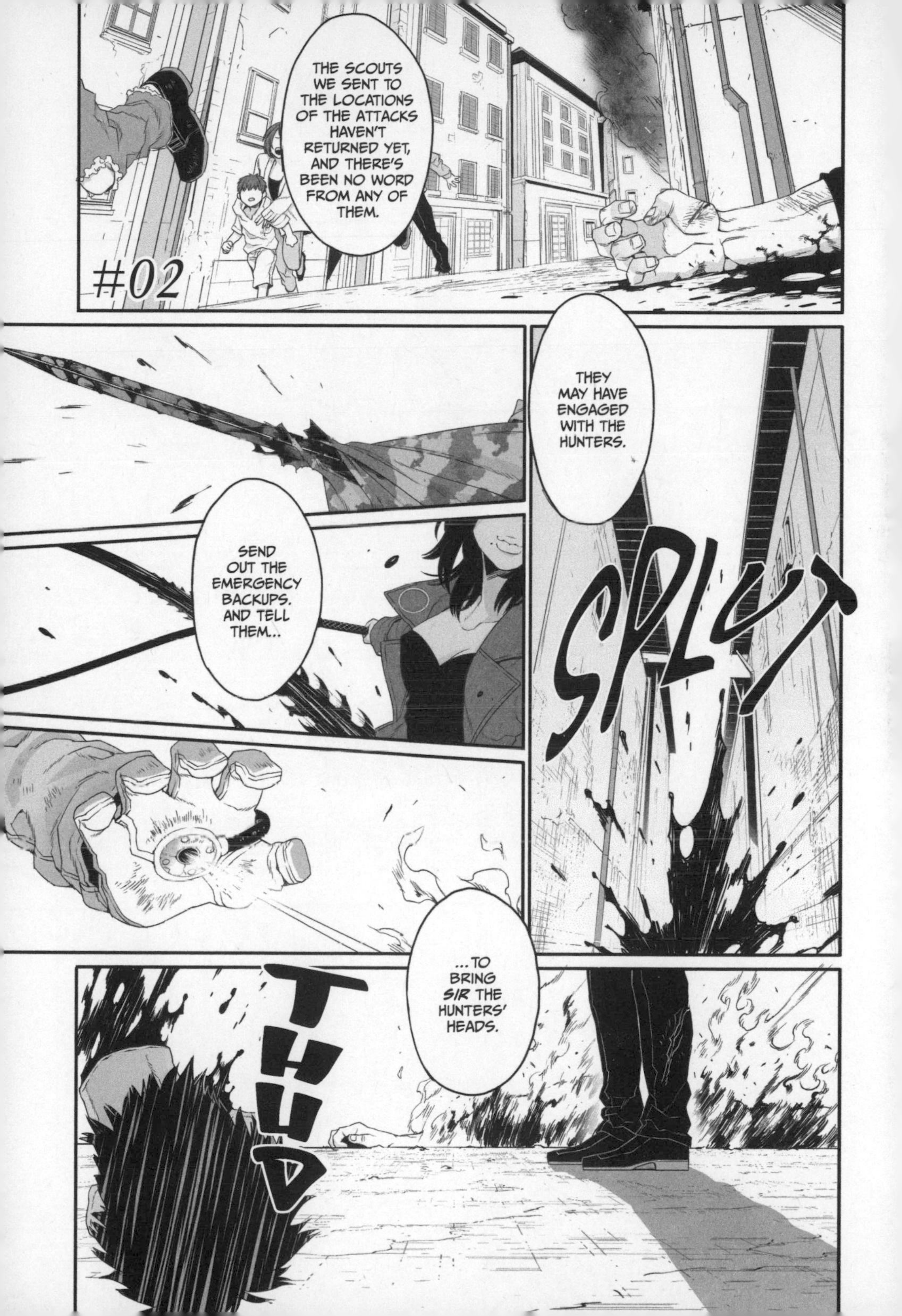
#02
THE SCOUTS WE SENT TO THE LOCATIONS OF THE ATTACKS HAVEN'T RETURNED YET, AND THERE'S BEEN NO WORD FROM ANY OF THEM.
THEY MAY HAVE ENGAGED WITH THE HUNTERS.
SPLUT
SEND OUT THE EMERGENCY BACKUPS. AND TELL THEM...
...TO BRING *SIR* THE HUNTERS' HEADS.
THUD

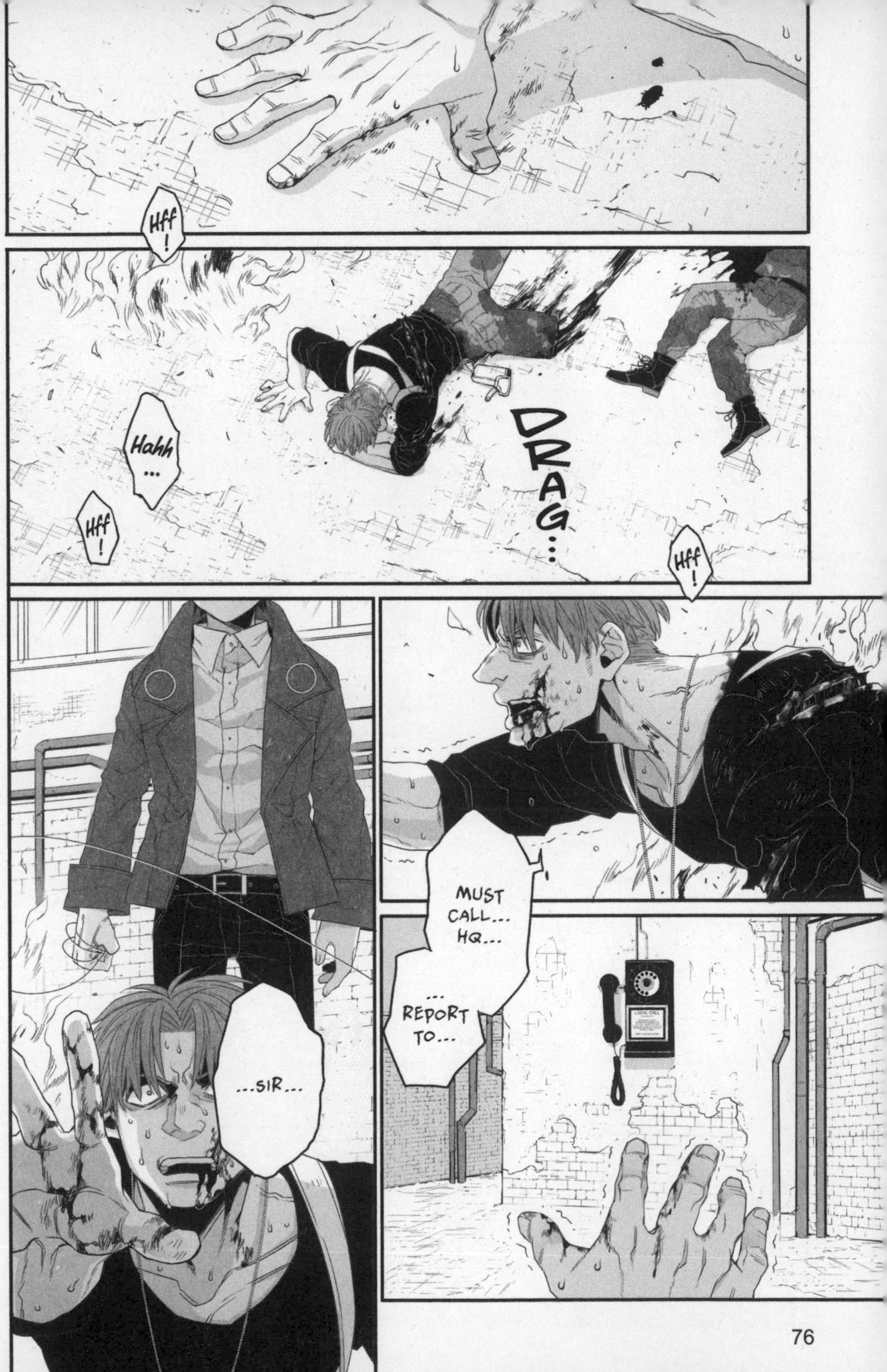

Hff!
DRAG...
Hff!
Hahh...
Hff!
MUST CALL... HQ...
...REPORT TO...
...SIR...

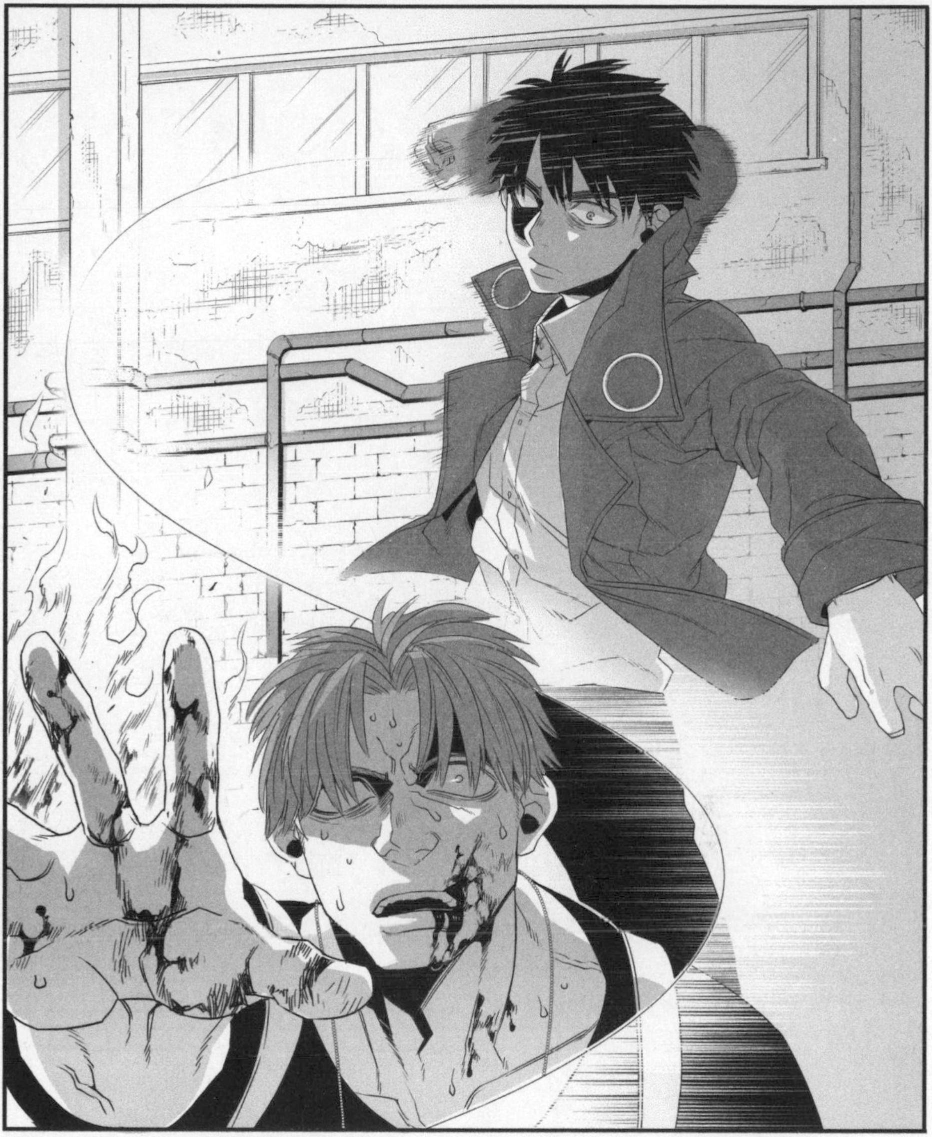

#02

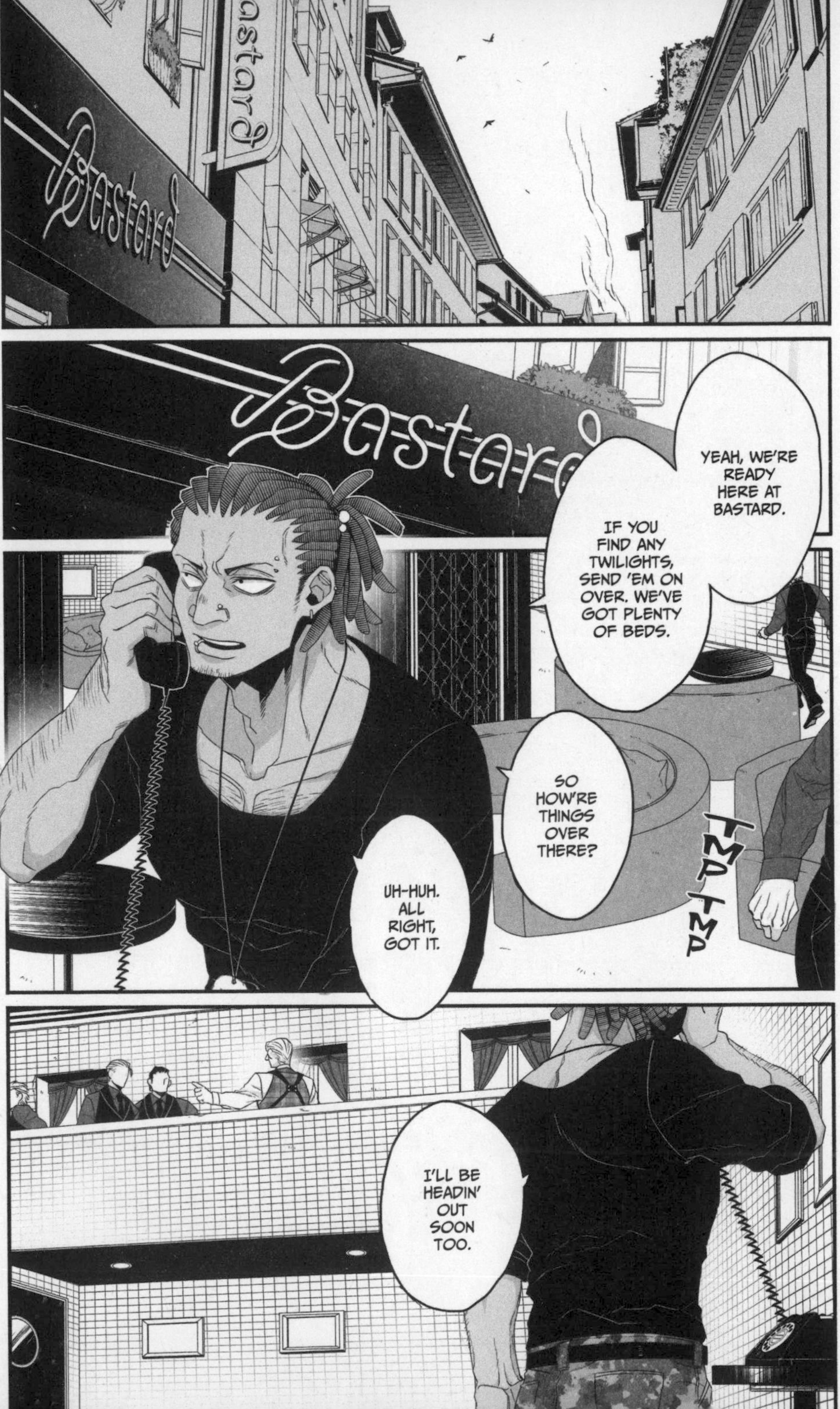
Bastard
Bastard
YEAH, WE'RE READY HERE AT BASTARD.
IF YOU FIND ANY TWILIGHTS, SEND 'EM ON OVER. WE'VE GOT PLENTY OF BEDS.
SO HOW'RE THINGS OVER THERE?
TMP TMP
UH-HUH. ALL RIGHT, GOT IT.
I'LL BE HEADIN' OUT SOON TOO.

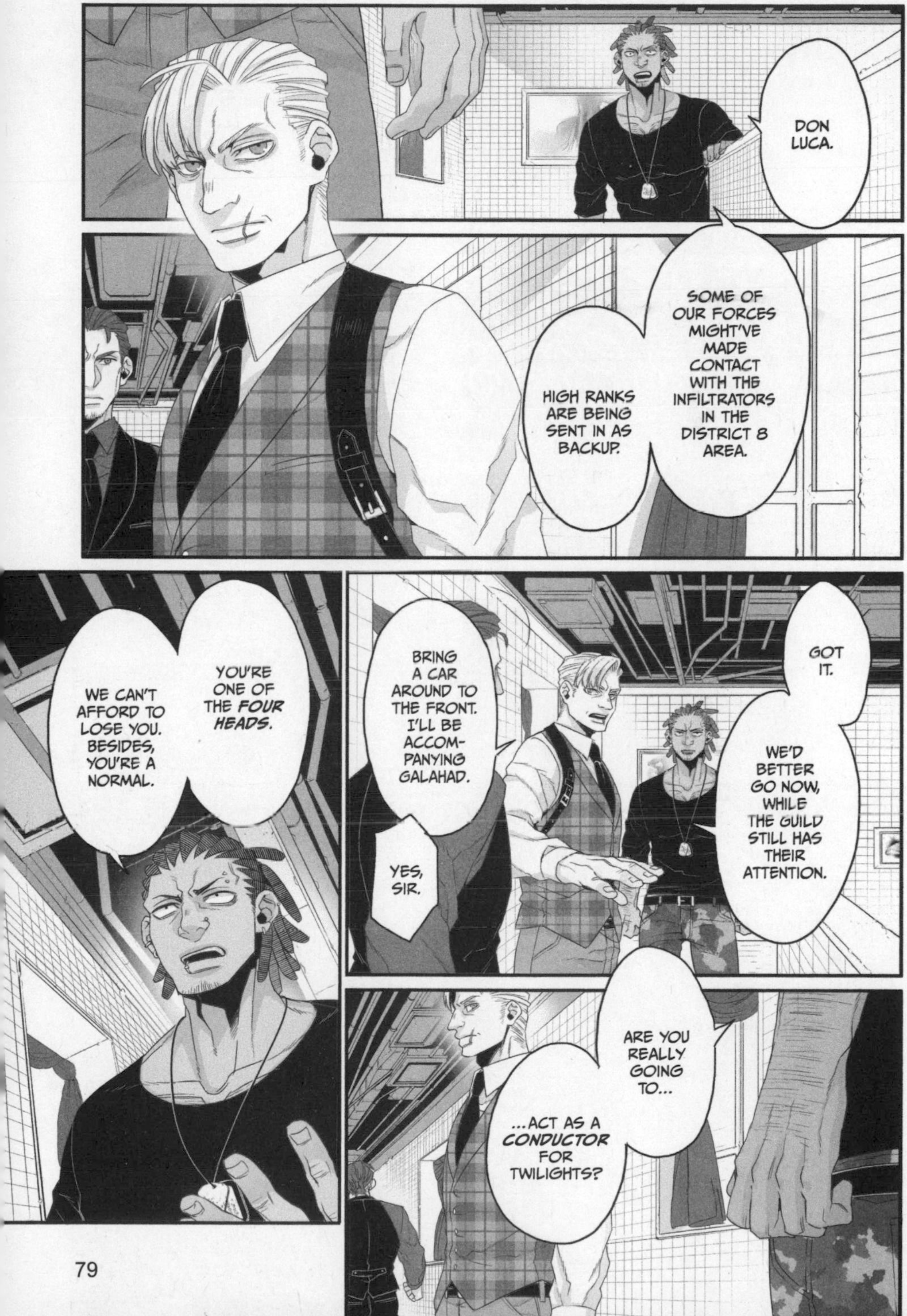
DON LUCA.
SOME OF OUR FORCES MIGHT'VE MADE CONTACT WITH THE INFILTRATORS IN THE DISTRICT 8 AREA.
HIGH RANKS ARE BEING SENT IN AS BACKUP.
GOT IT.
WE'D BETTER GO NOW, WHILE THE GUILD STILL HAS THEIR ATTENTION.
BRING A CAR AROUND TO THE FRONT. I'LL BE ACCOMPANYING GALAHAD.
YES, SIR.
ARE YOU REALLY GOING TO...
...ACT AS A *CONDUCTOR* FOR TWILIGHTS?
YOU'RE ONE OF THE *FOUR HEADS*.
WE CAN'T AFFORD TO LOSE YOU. BESIDES, YOU'RE A NORMAL.

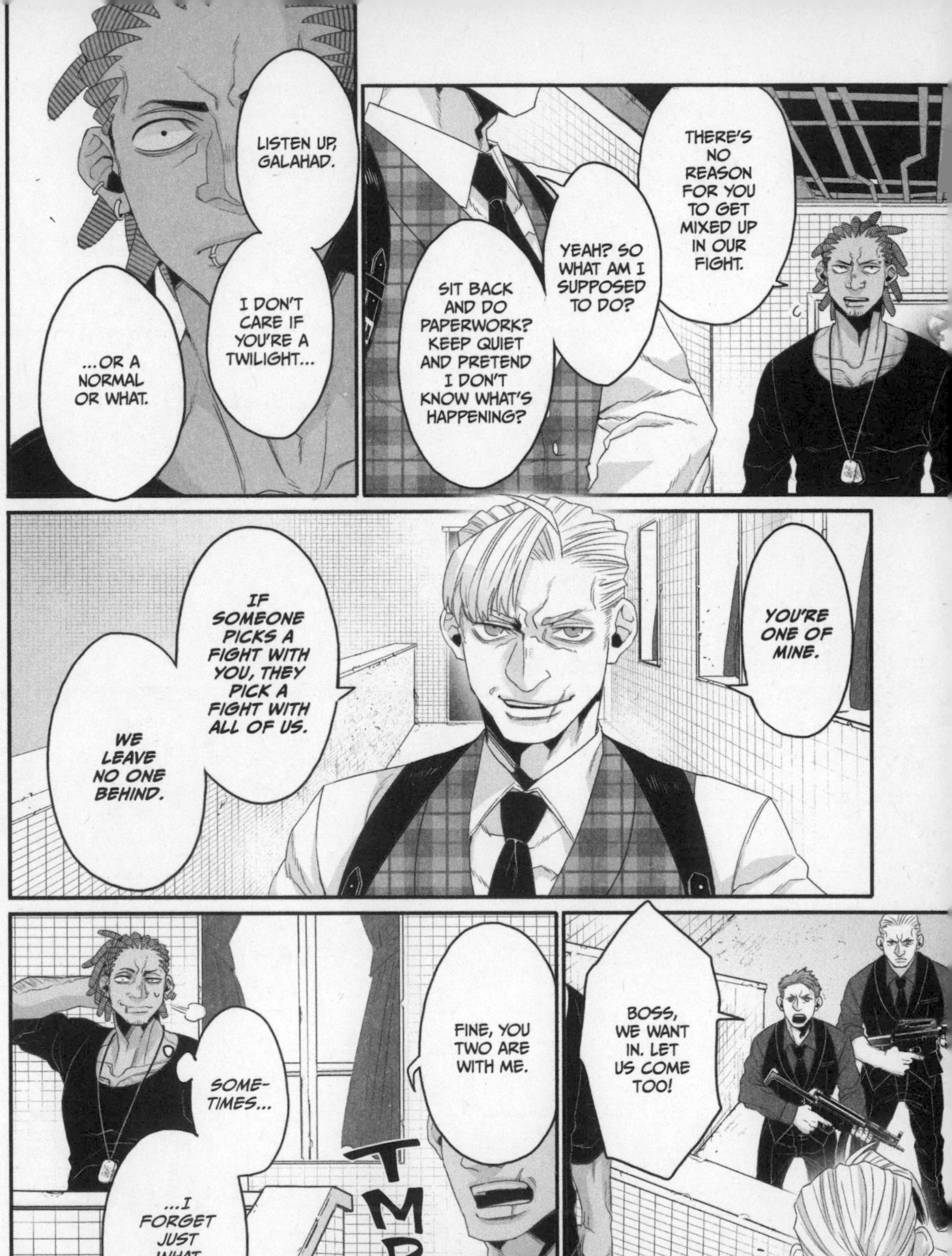
THERE'S NO REASON FOR YOU TO GET MIXED UP IN OUR FIGHT.
YEAH? SO WHAT AM I SUPPOSED TO DO?
SIT BACK AND DO PAPERWORK? KEEP QUIET AND PRETEND I DON'T KNOW WHAT'S HAPPENING?
LISTEN UP, GALAHAD.
I DON'T CARE IF YOU'RE A TWILIGHT...
...OR A NORMAL OR WHAT.
YOU'RE ONE OF MINE.
IF SOMEONE PICKS A FIGHT WITH YOU, THEY PICK A FIGHT WITH ALL OF US.
WE LEAVE NO ONE BEHIND.
BOSS, WE WANT IN. LET US COME TOO!
FINE, YOU TWO ARE WITH ME.
TMP TMP
SOME-TIMES...
...I FORGET JUST WHAT KINDA MAN HE IS.

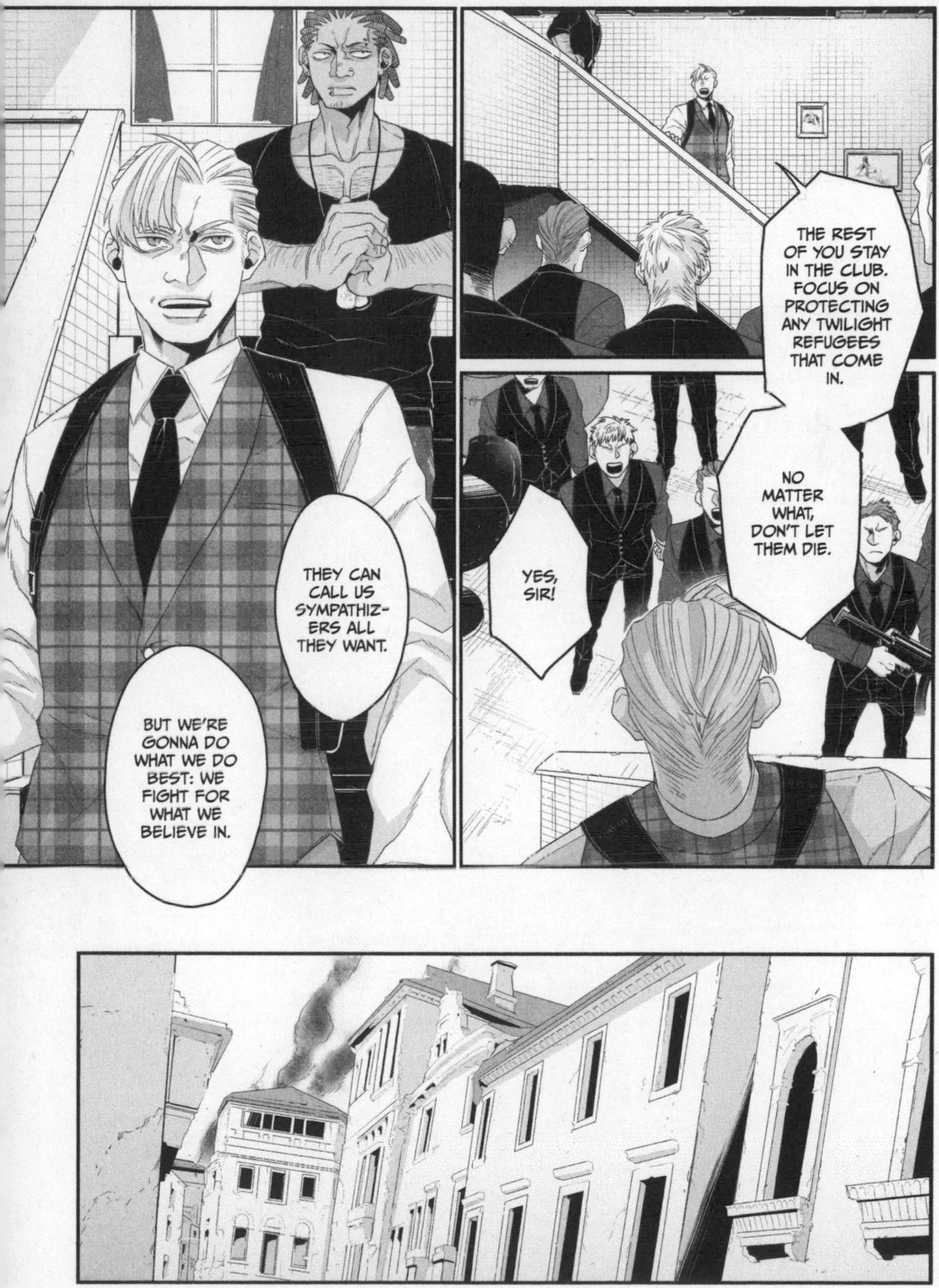
THE REST OF YOU STAY IN THE CLUB. FOCUS ON PROTECTING ANY TWILIGHT REFUGEES THAT COME IN.
NO MATTER WHAT, DON'T LET THEM DIE.
YES, SIR!
THEY CAN CALL US SYMPATHIZERS ALL THEY WANT.
BUT WE'RE GONNA DO WHAT WE DO BEST: WE FIGHT FOR WHAT WE BELIEVE IN.

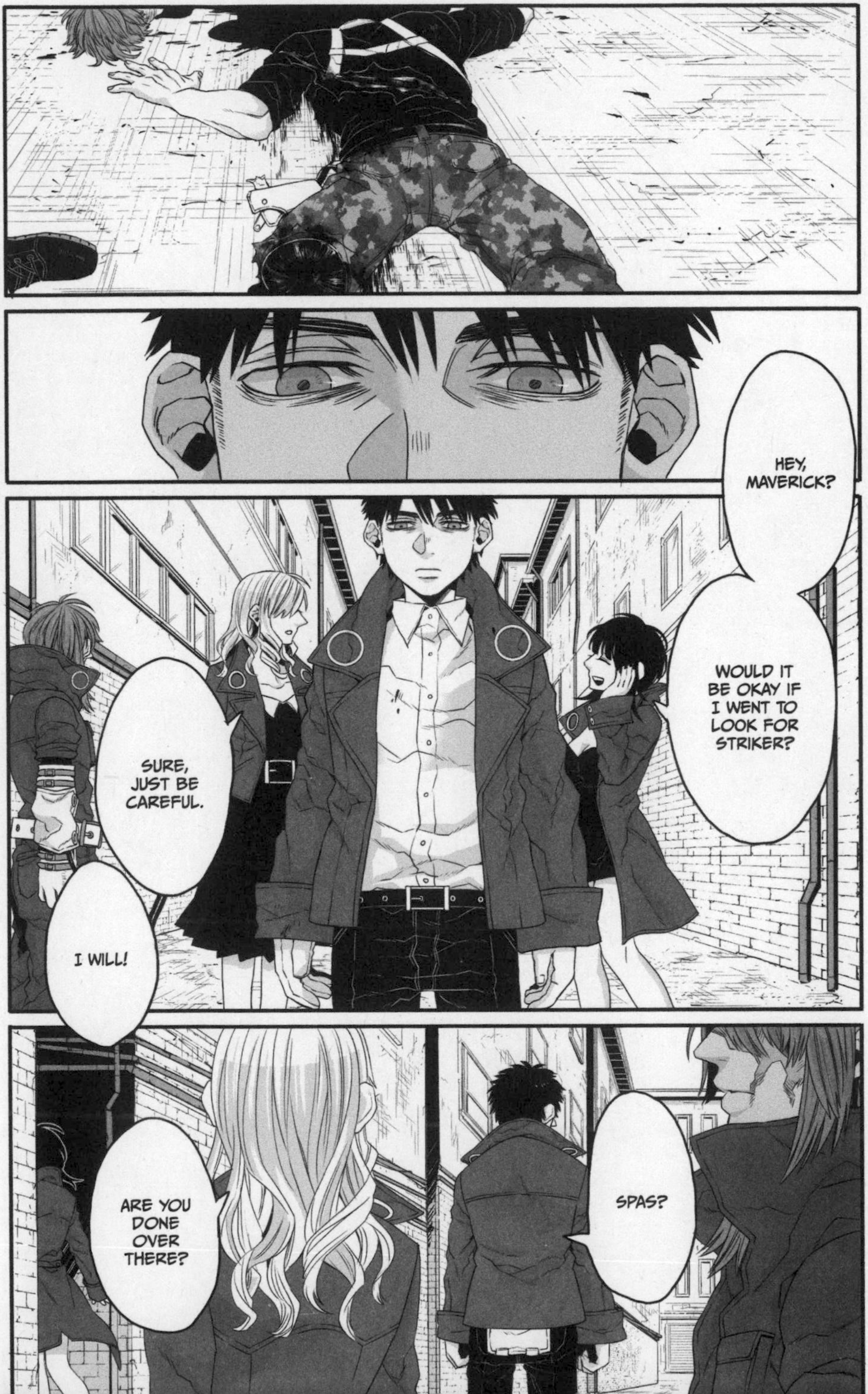
HEY, MAVERICK?
WOULD IT BE OKAY IF I WENT TO LOOK FOR STRIKER?
SURE, JUST BE CAREFUL.
I WILL!
SPAS?
ARE YOU DONE OVER THERE?

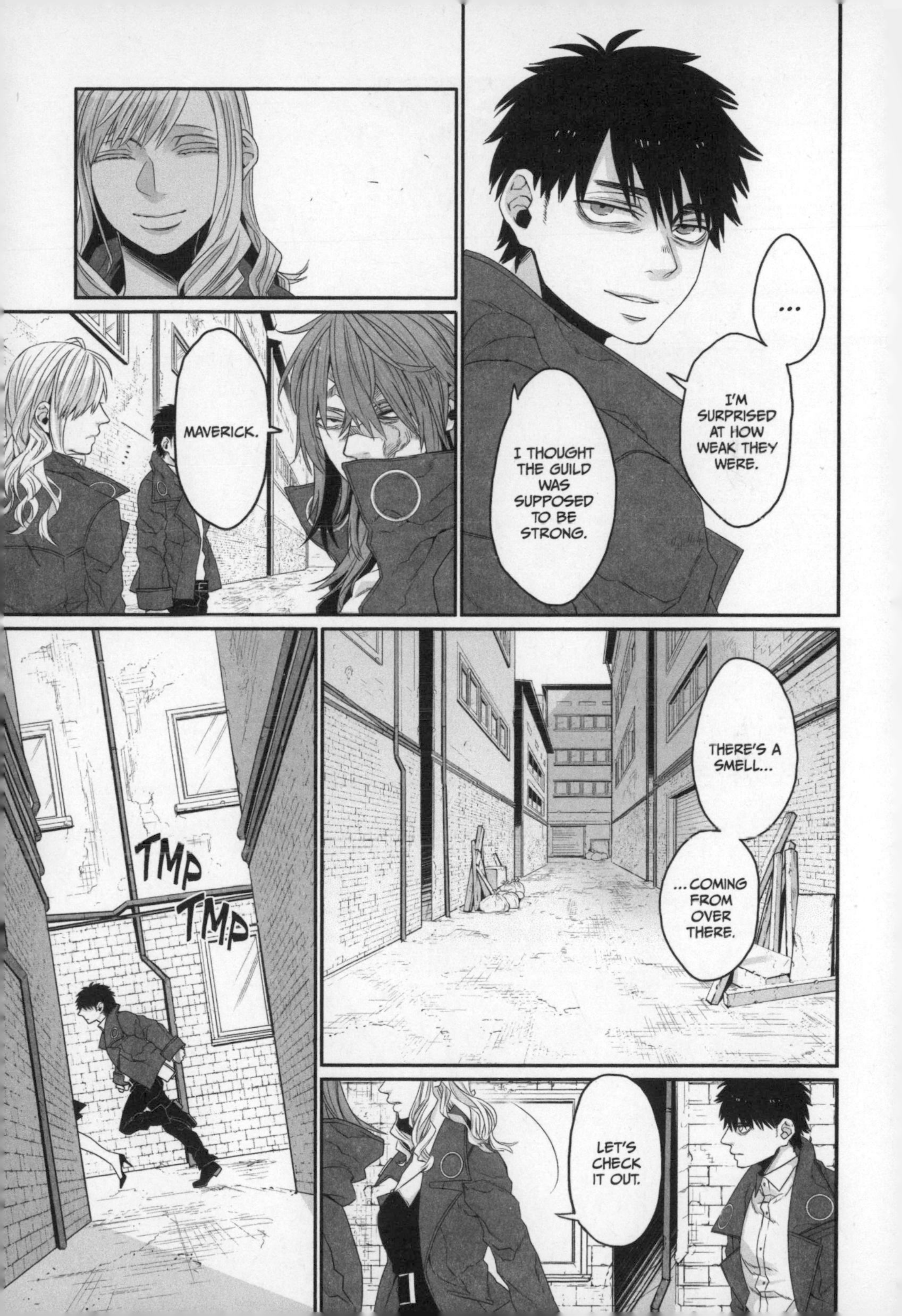
...
I'M SURPRISED AT HOW WEAK THEY WERE.
I THOUGHT THE GUILD WAS SUPPOSED TO BE STRONG.
MAVERICK.
...
THERE'S A SMELL...
...COMING FROM OVER THERE.
LET'S CHECK IT OUT.
TMP
TMP

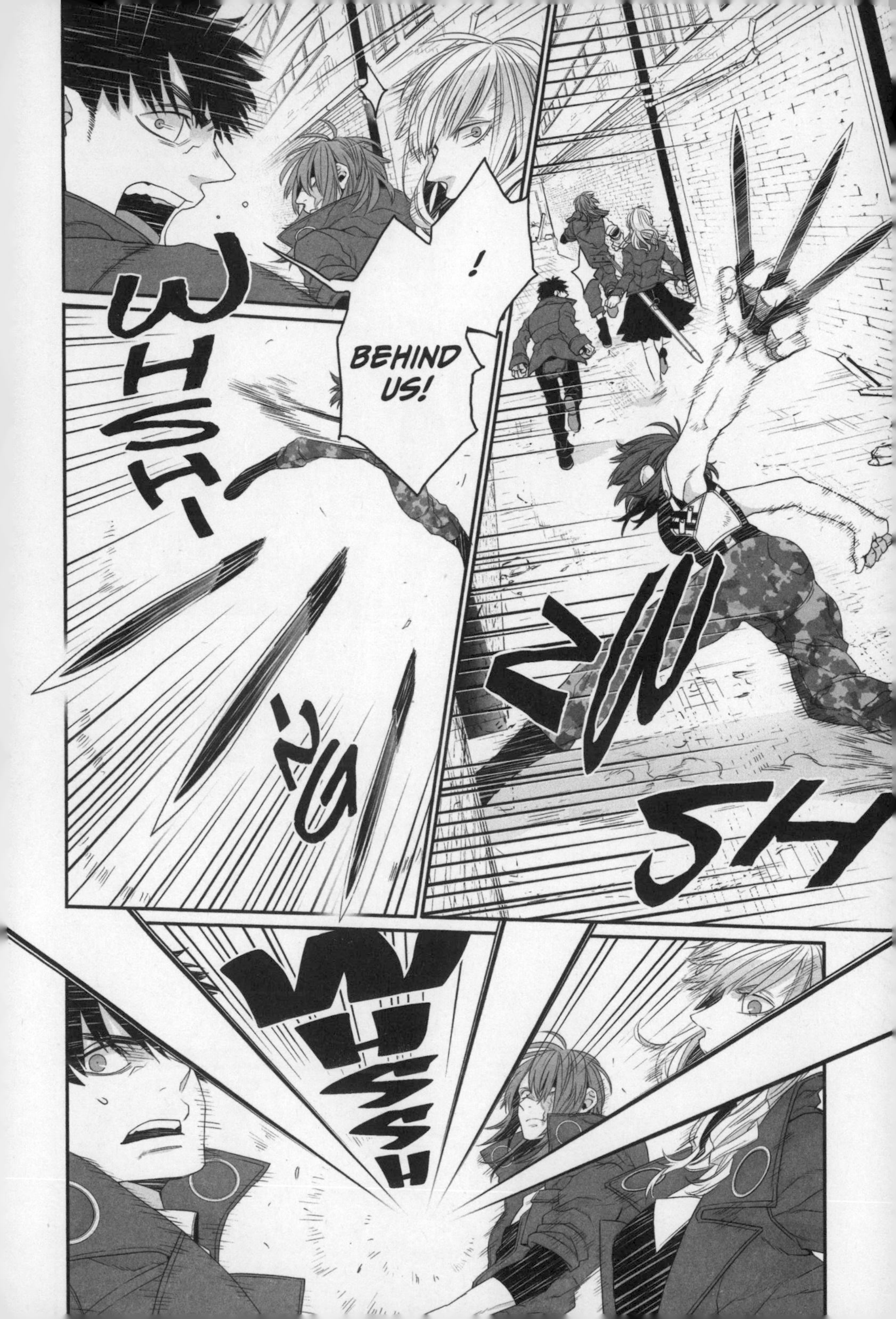
!
BEHIND US!
WHSH!
WHSSH

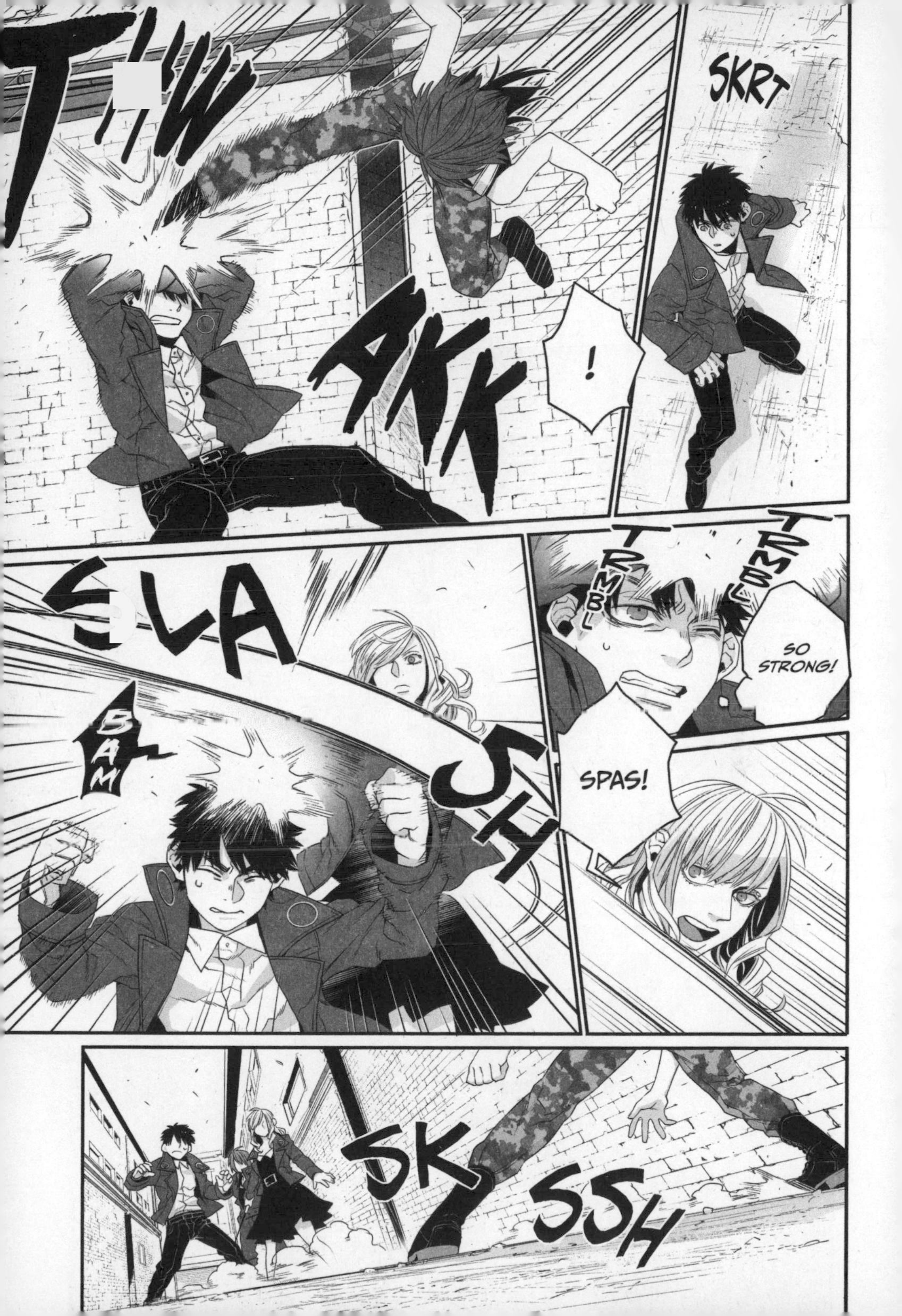
SKRT
T W
AKK
!
TRMBL
TRMBL
SO STRONG!
SPAS!
SLA
SH
BAM
SK
SSH

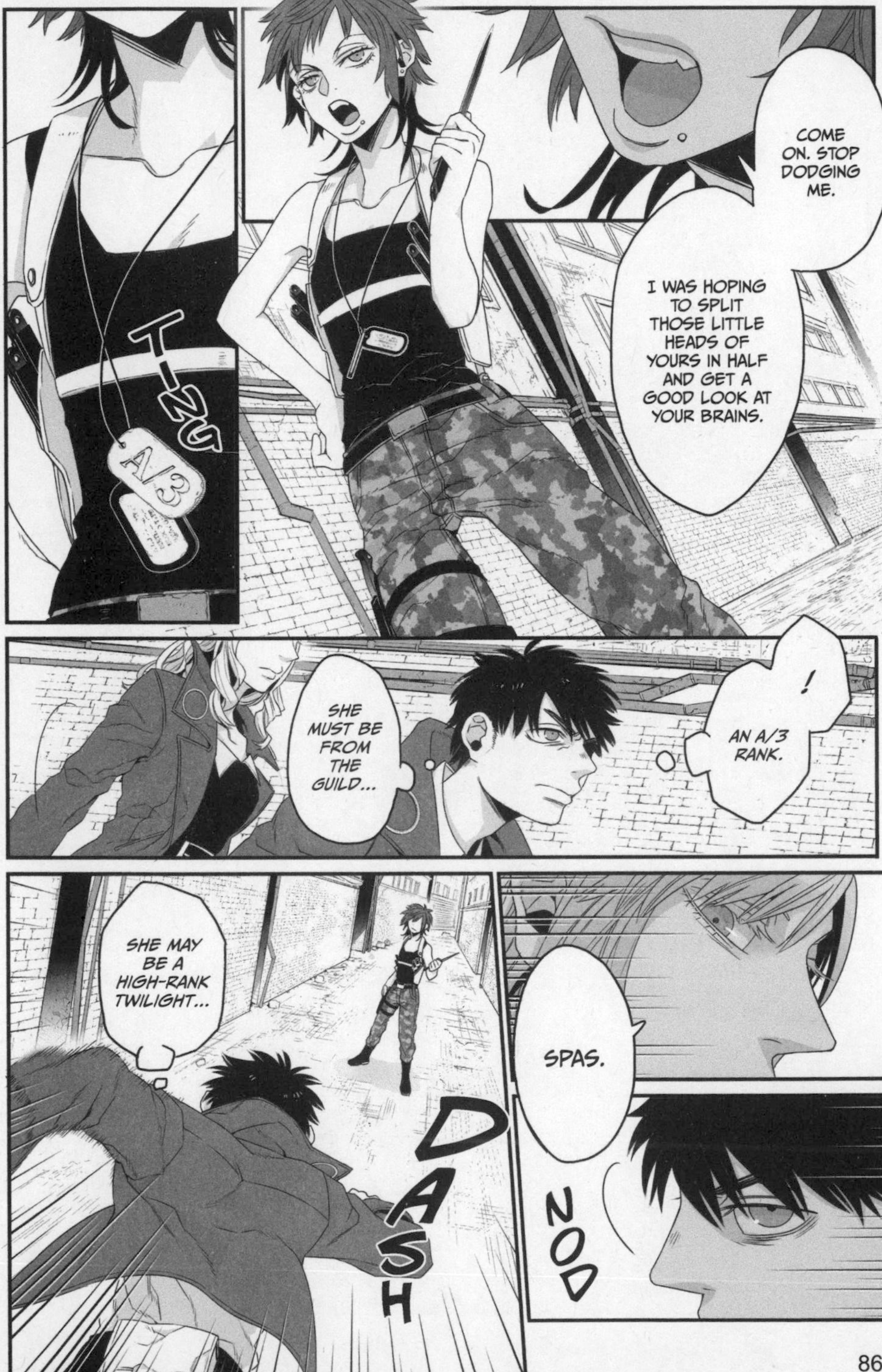
COME ON. STOP DODGING ME.
I WAS HOPING TO SPLIT THOSE LITTLE HEADS OF YOURS IN HALF AND GET A GOOD LOOK AT YOUR BRAINS.
TING
A/3
!
AN A/3 RANK.
SHE MUST BE FROM THE GUILD...
SPAS.
NOD
SHE MAY BE A HIGH-RANK TWILIGHT...
DASH

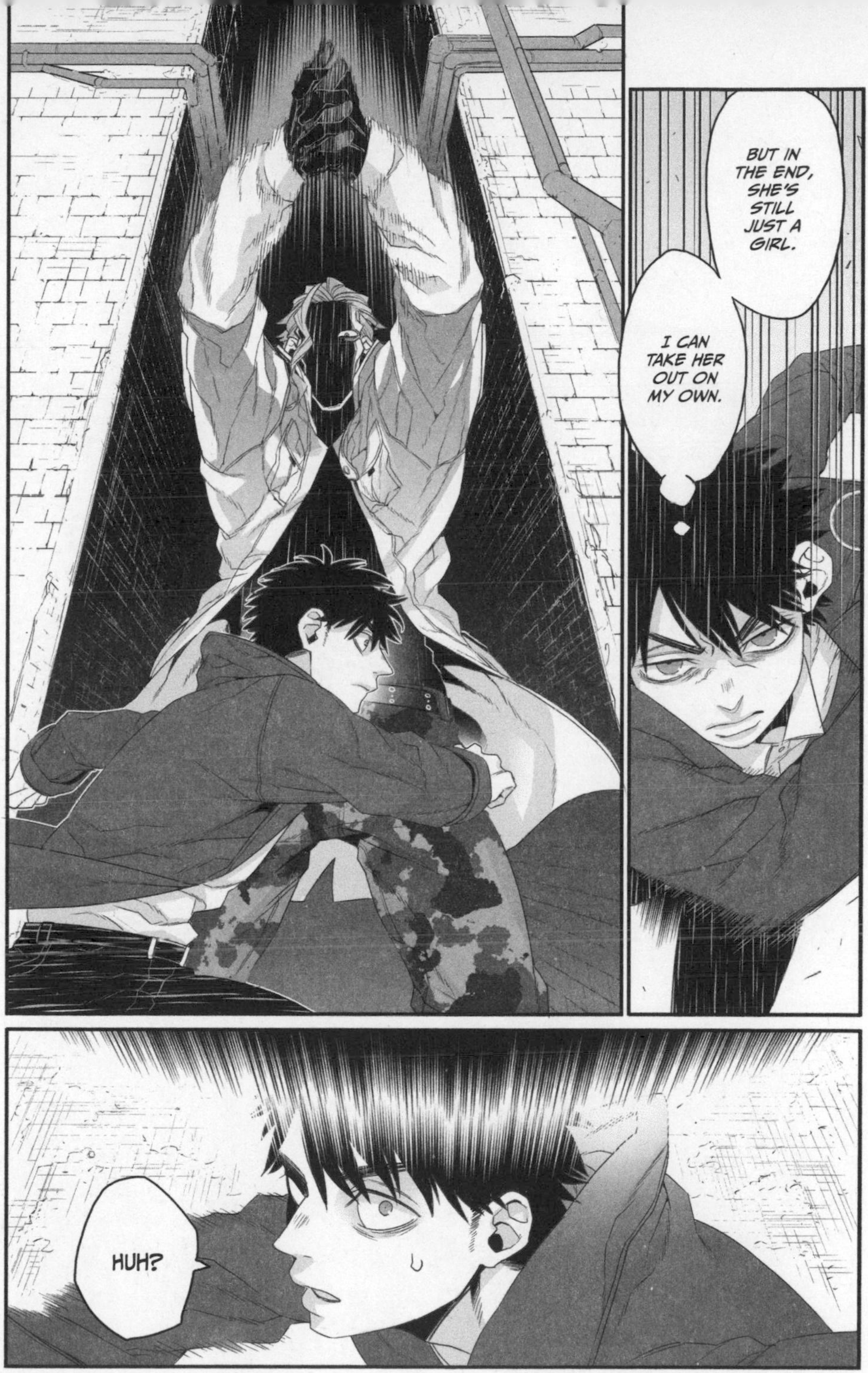
BUT IN THE END, SHE'S STILL JUST A GIRL.
I CAN TAKE HER OUT ON MY OWN.
HUH?

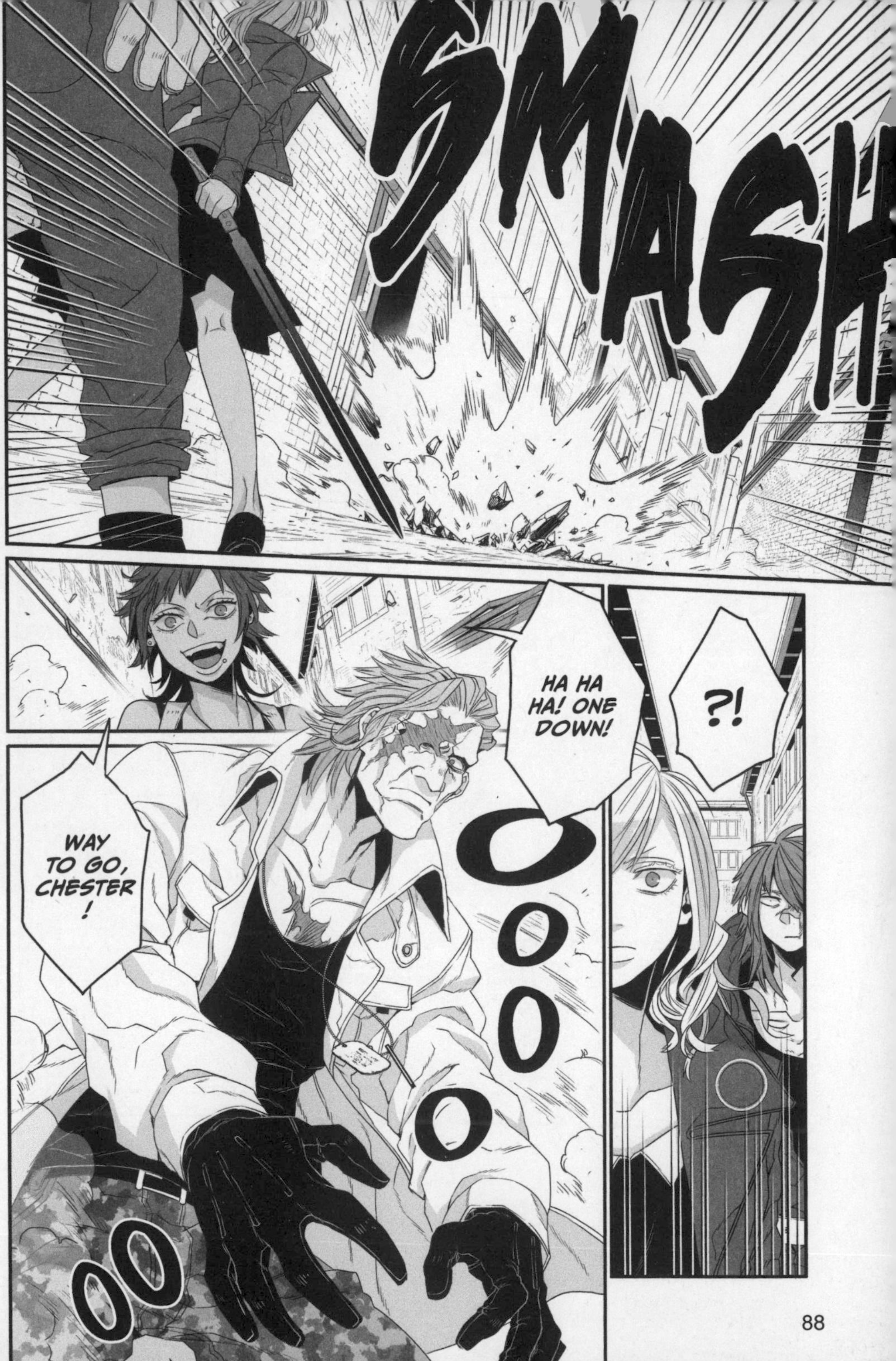
SMASH
?!
HA HA HA! ONE DOWN!
WAY TO GO, CHESTER!
OOOOOO

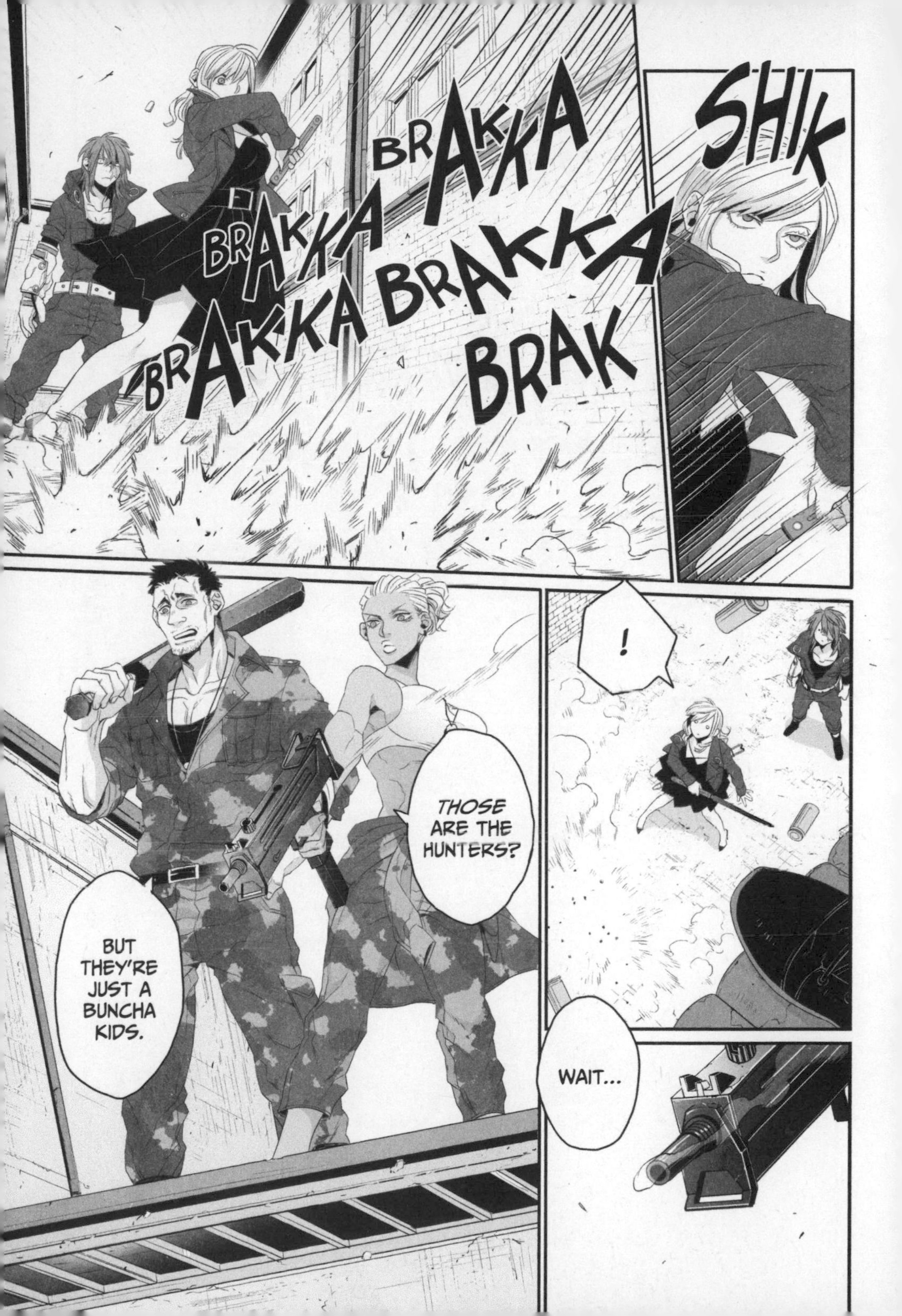
SHIK
BRAKKA
BRAKKA
BRAKKA
BRAKKA
BRAKKA
BRAK
!
WAIT...
THOSE ARE THE HUNTERS?
BUT THEY'RE JUST A BUNCHA KIDS.

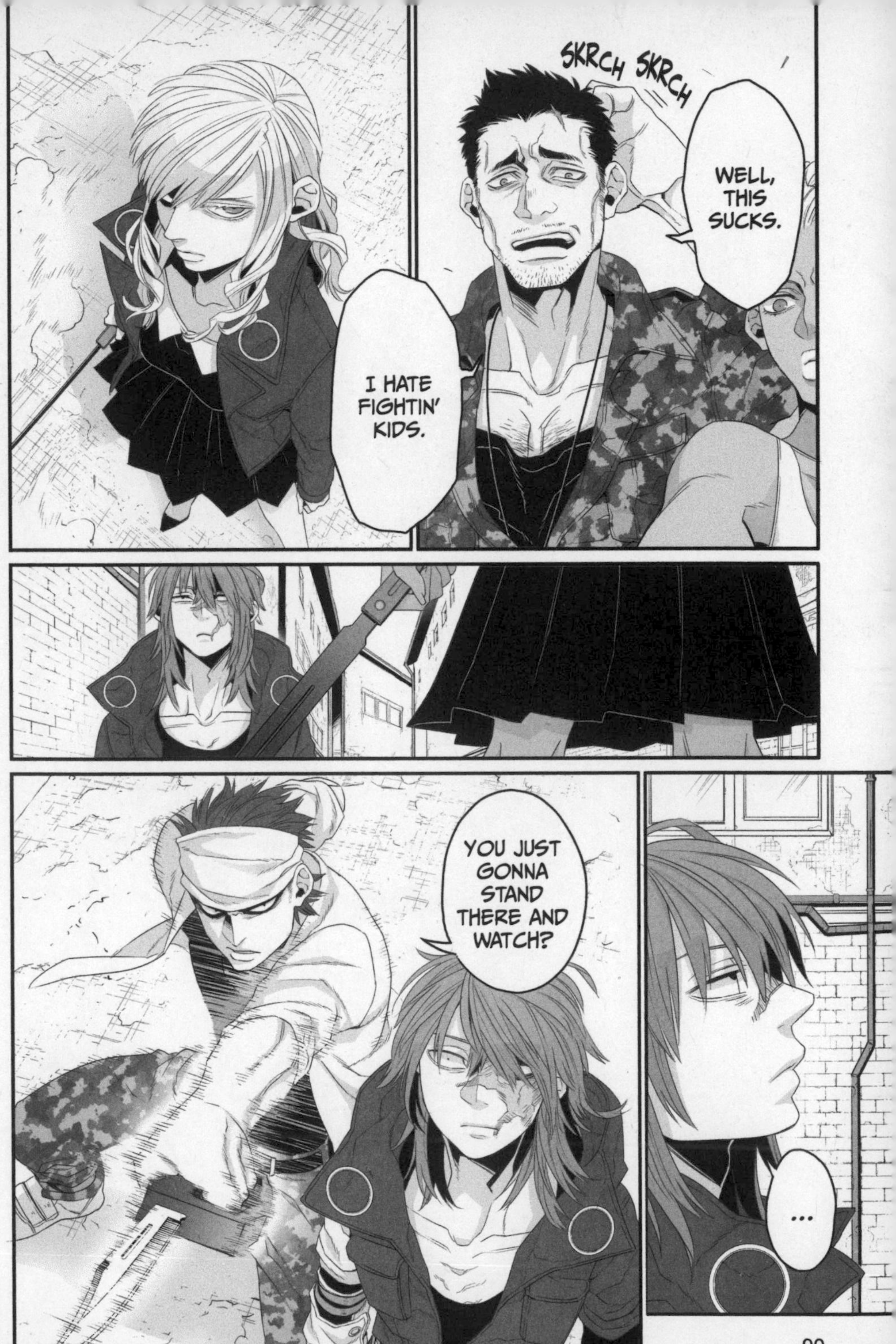
SKRCH SKRCH
WELL, THIS SUCKS.
I HATE FIGHTIN' KIDS.
...
YOU JUST GONNA STAND THERE AND WATCH?

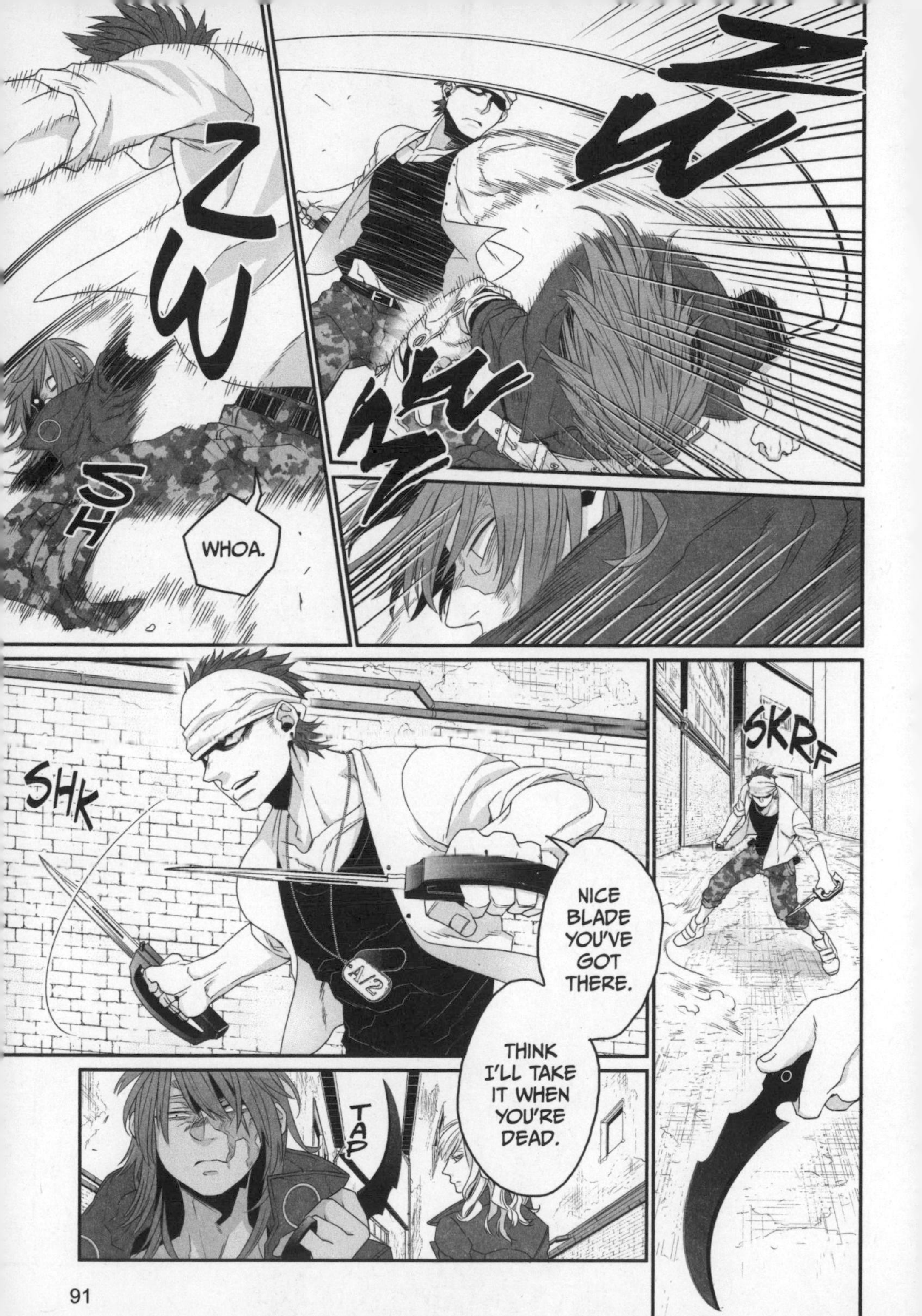
SH
WHOA.
SKRF
SHK
NICE BLADE YOU'VE GOT THERE.
THINK I'LL TAKE IT WHEN YOU'RE DEAD.
TAP

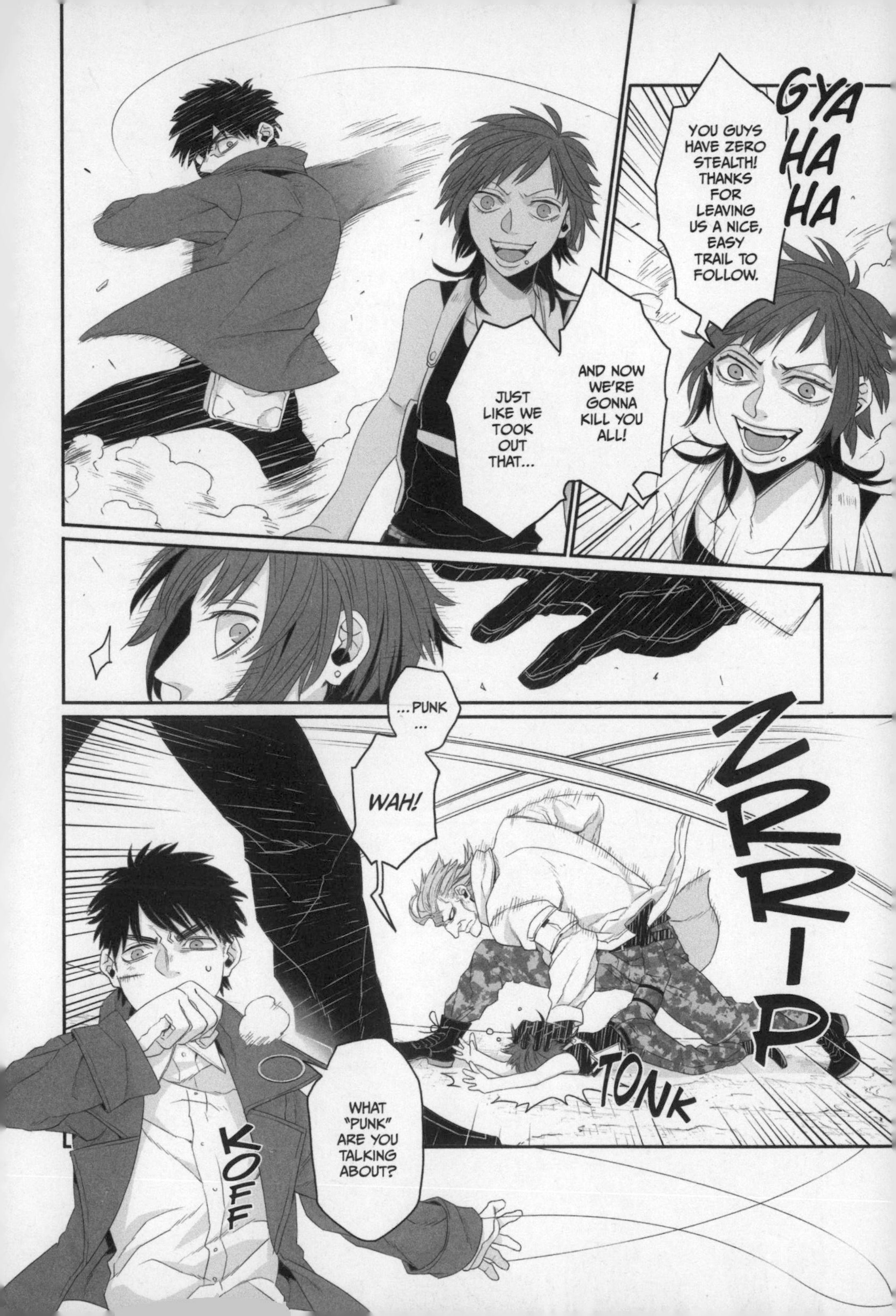
GYA HA HA
YOU GUYS HAVE ZERO STEALTH! THANKS FOR LEAVING US A NICE, EASY TRAIL TO FOLLOW.
AND NOW WE'RE GONNA KILL YOU ALL!
JUST LIKE WE TOOK OUT THAT...
ZRRIP
...PUNK ...
WAH!
TONK
WHAT "PUNK" ARE YOU TALKING ABOUT?
KOFF

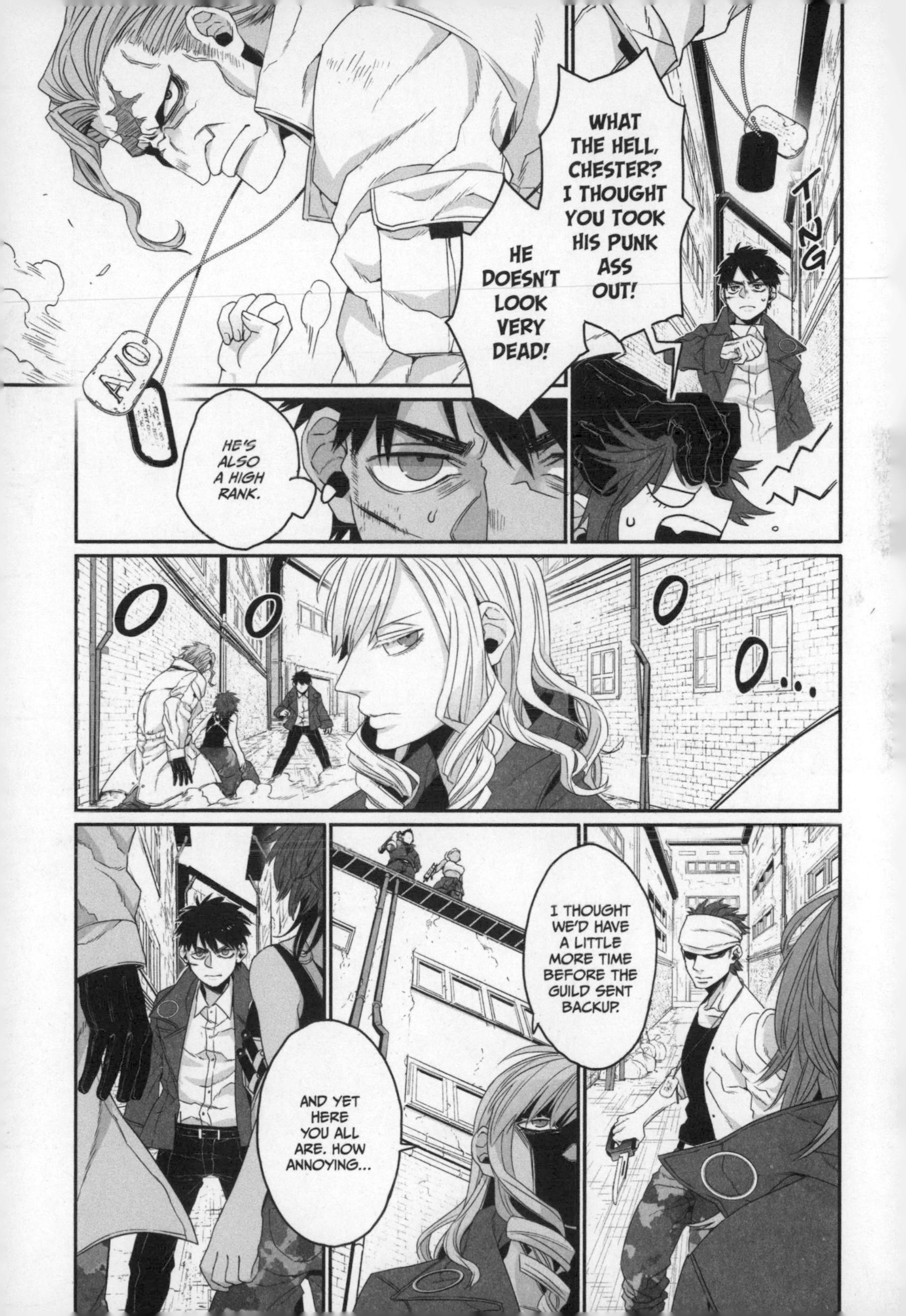
TING
WHAT THE HELL, CHESTER? I THOUGHT YOU TOOK HIS PUNK ASS OUT!
HE DOESN'T LOOK VERY DEAD!
HE'S ALSO A HIGH RANK.
OOOO...
I THOUGHT WE'D HAVE A LITTLE MORE TIME BEFORE THE GUILD SENT BACKUP.
AND YET HERE YOU ALL ARE. HOW ANNOYING...

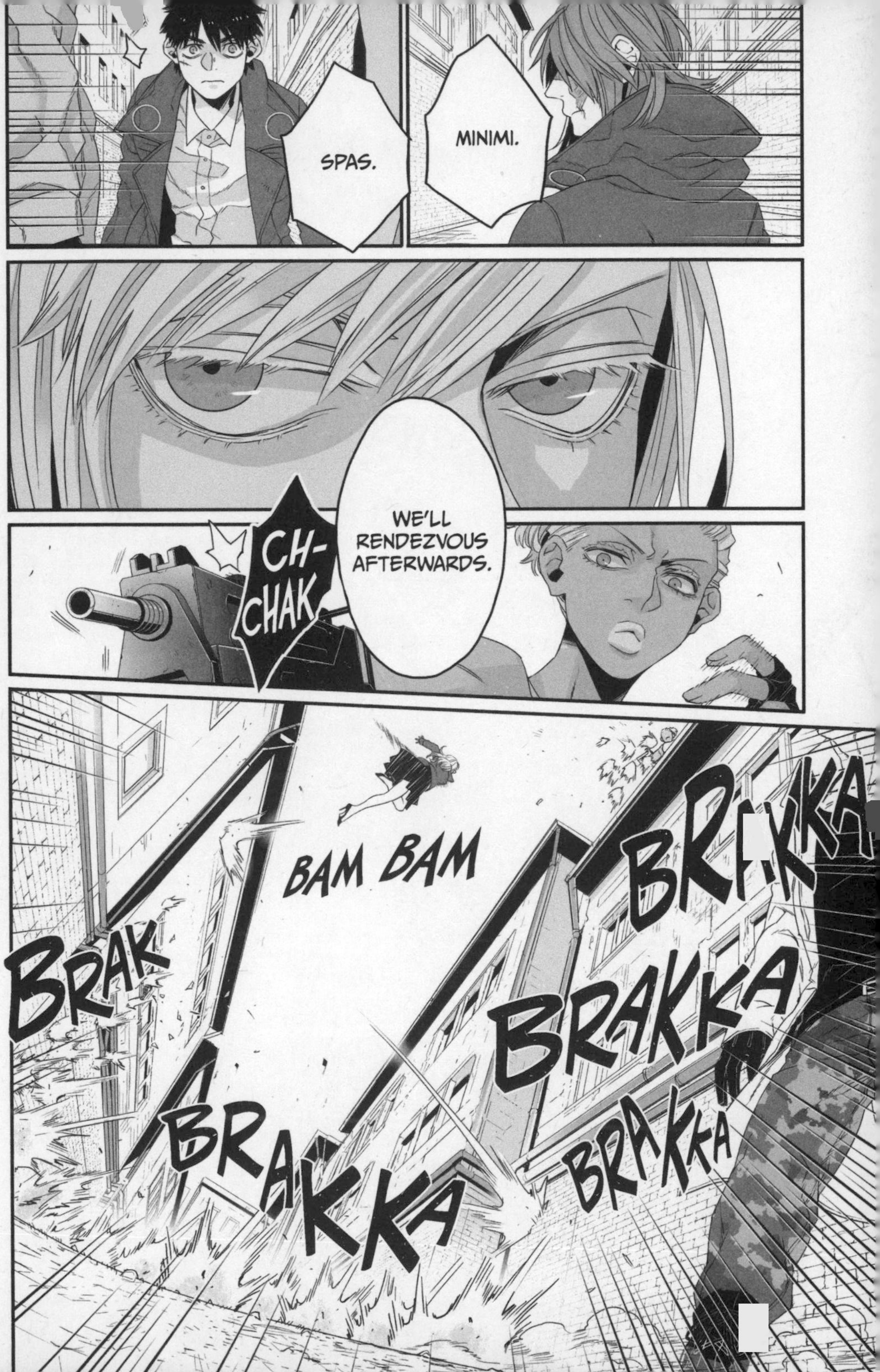
MINIMI.
SPAS.
WE'LL RENDEZVOUS AFTERWARDS.
CH-CHAK
BAM BAM
BRAKKA
BRAK
BRAKKA
BRAKKA

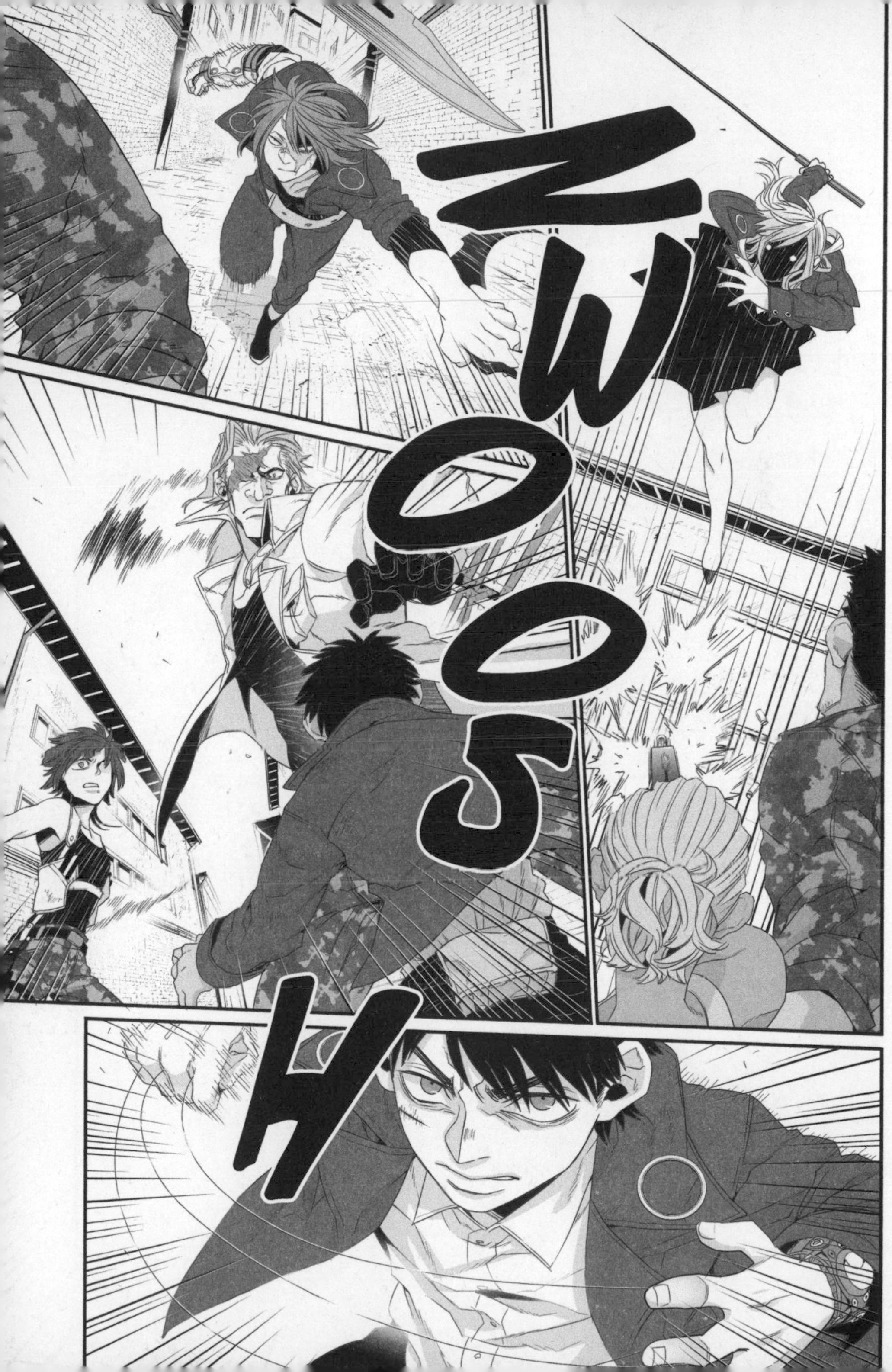
SWOOSH

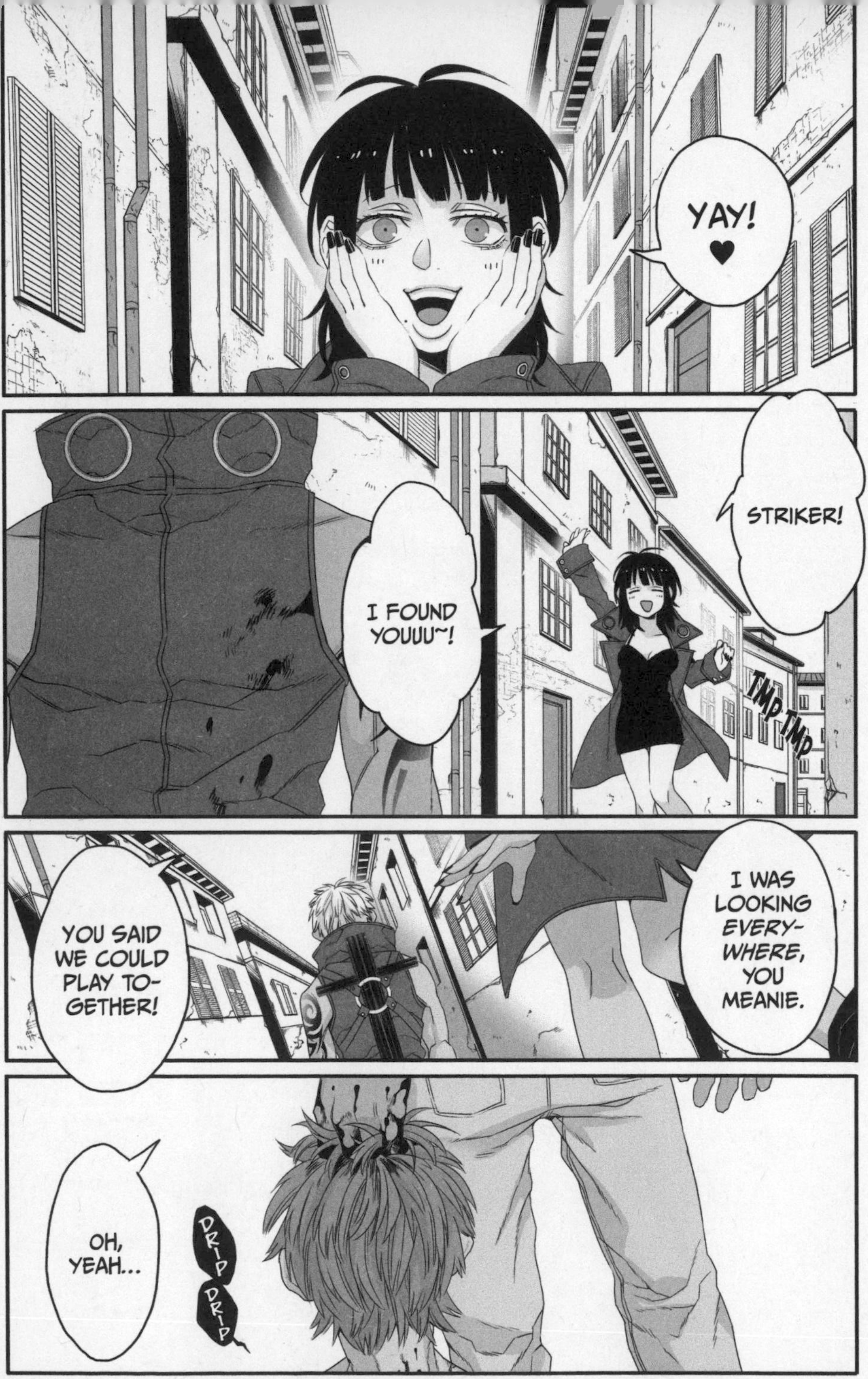
YAY! ♥
STRIKER!
I FOUND YOUUU~!
TMP TMP
I WAS LOOKING EVERY-WHERE, YOU MEANIE.
YOU SAID WE COULD PLAY TO-GETHER!
DRIP DRIP
OH, YEAH...

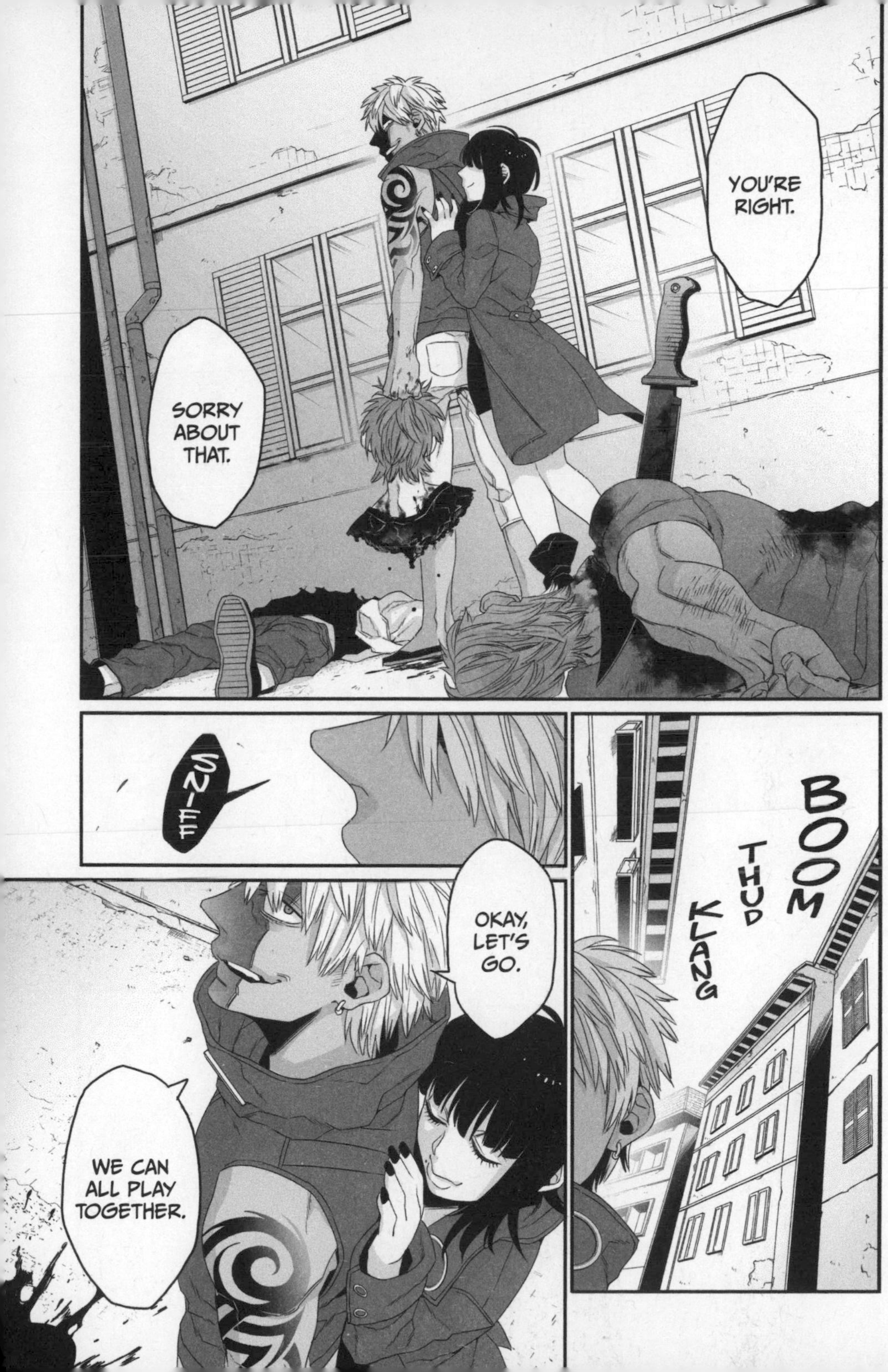
YOU'RE RIGHT.
SORRY ABOUT THAT.
BOOM
THUD
KLANG
SNIFF
OKAY, LET'S GO.
WE CAN ALL PLAY TOGETHER.

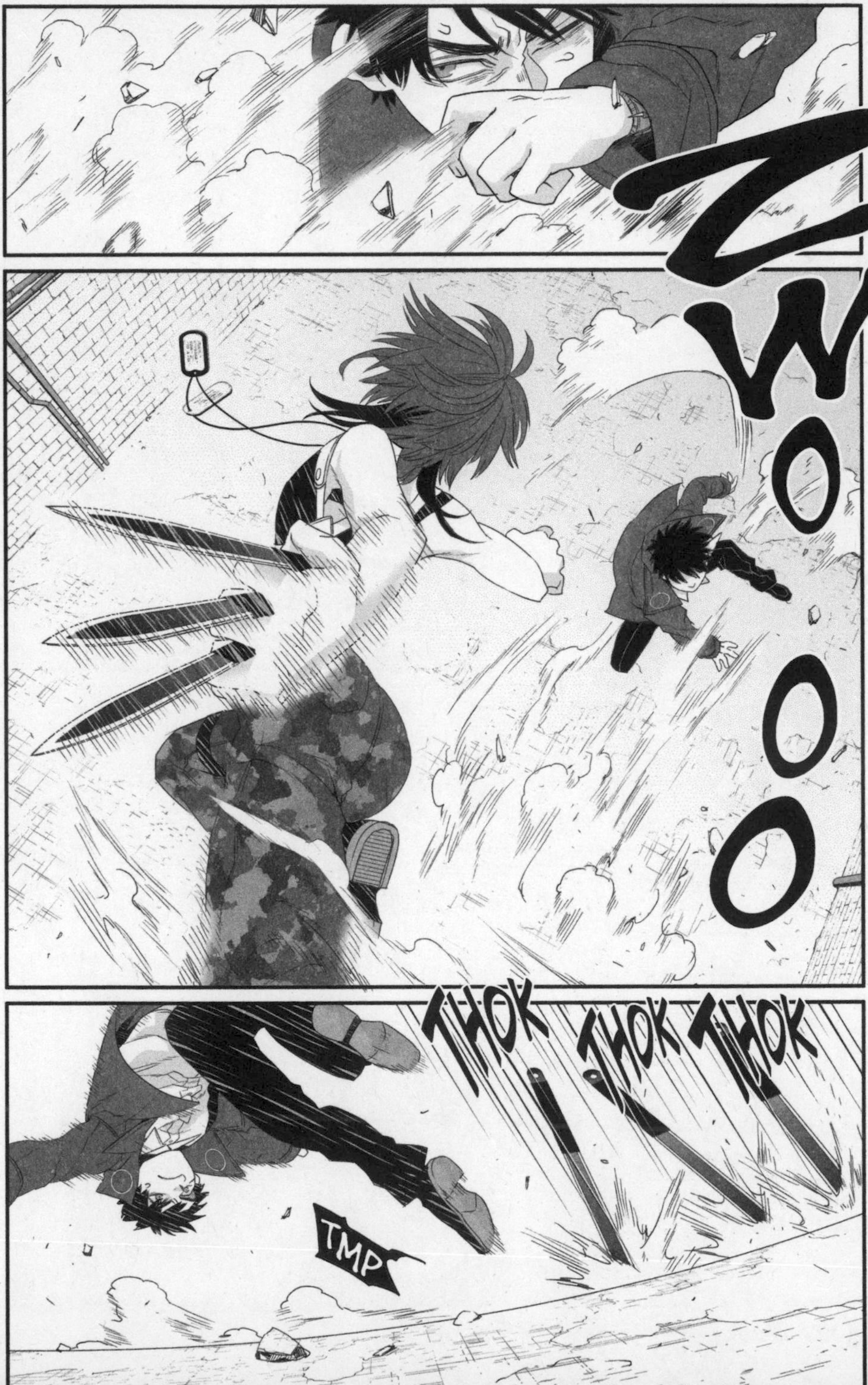
THOK
THOK
THOK
TMP

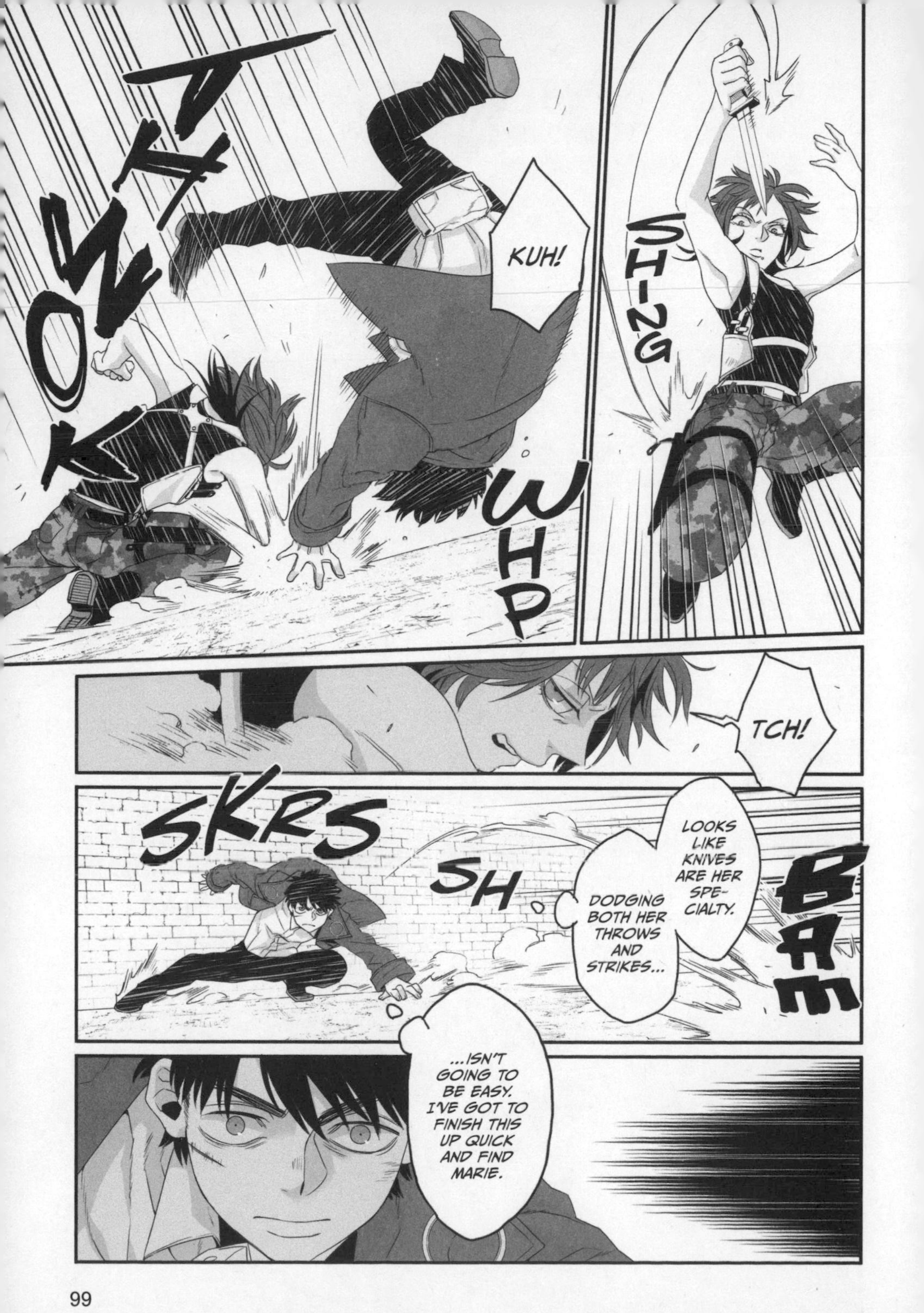
SHING
KUH!
THWOK
WHP
TCH!
BAM
LOOKS LIKE KNIVES ARE HER SPE-CIALTY.
DODGING BOTH HER THROWS AND STRIKES...
SH
SKRS
...ISN'T GOING TO BE EASY. I'VE GOT TO FINISH THIS UP QUICK AND FIND MARIE.

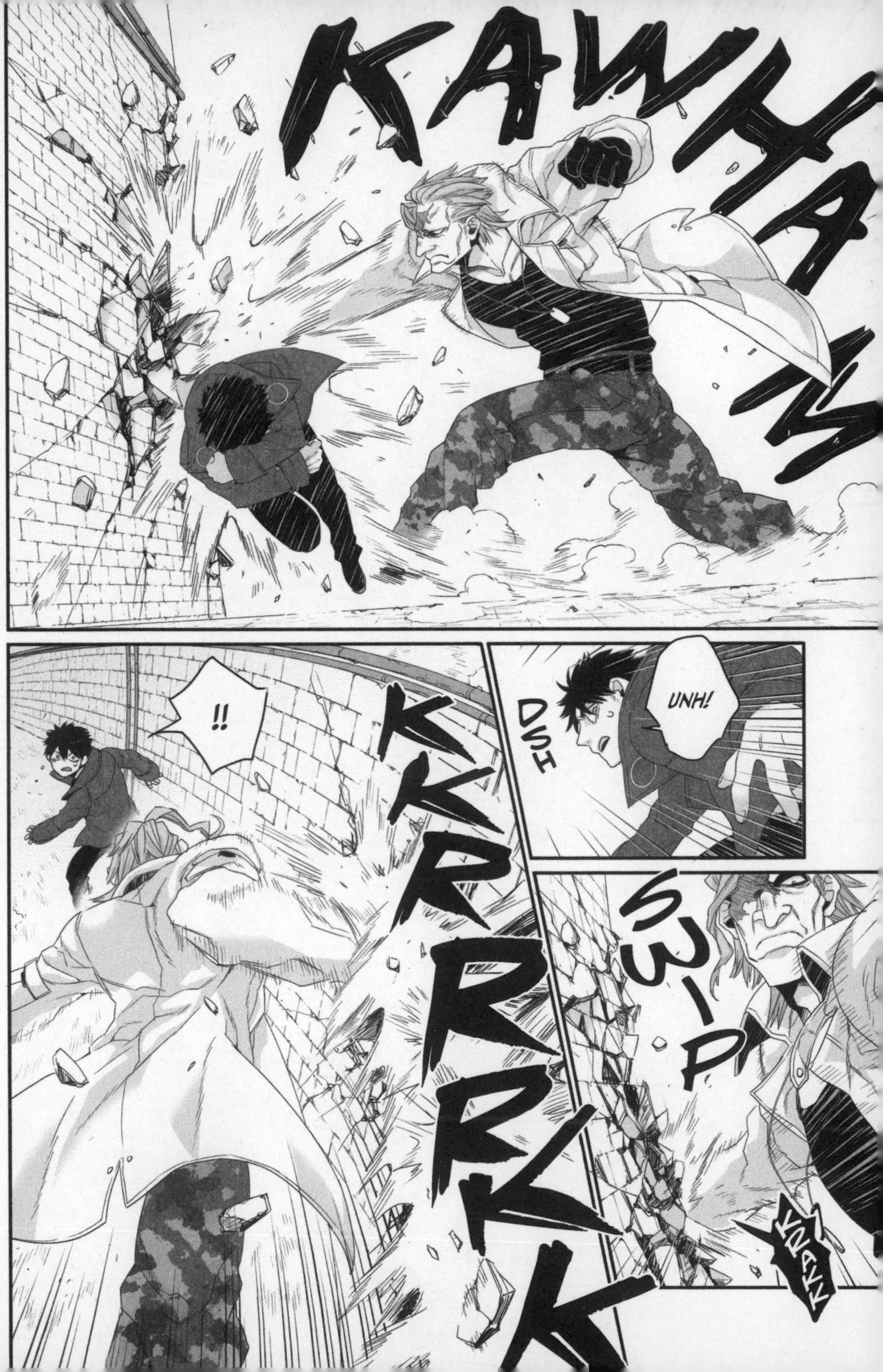
KAWHAM
DSH
UNH!
SWIP
KRAK
!!
KKRRRRK

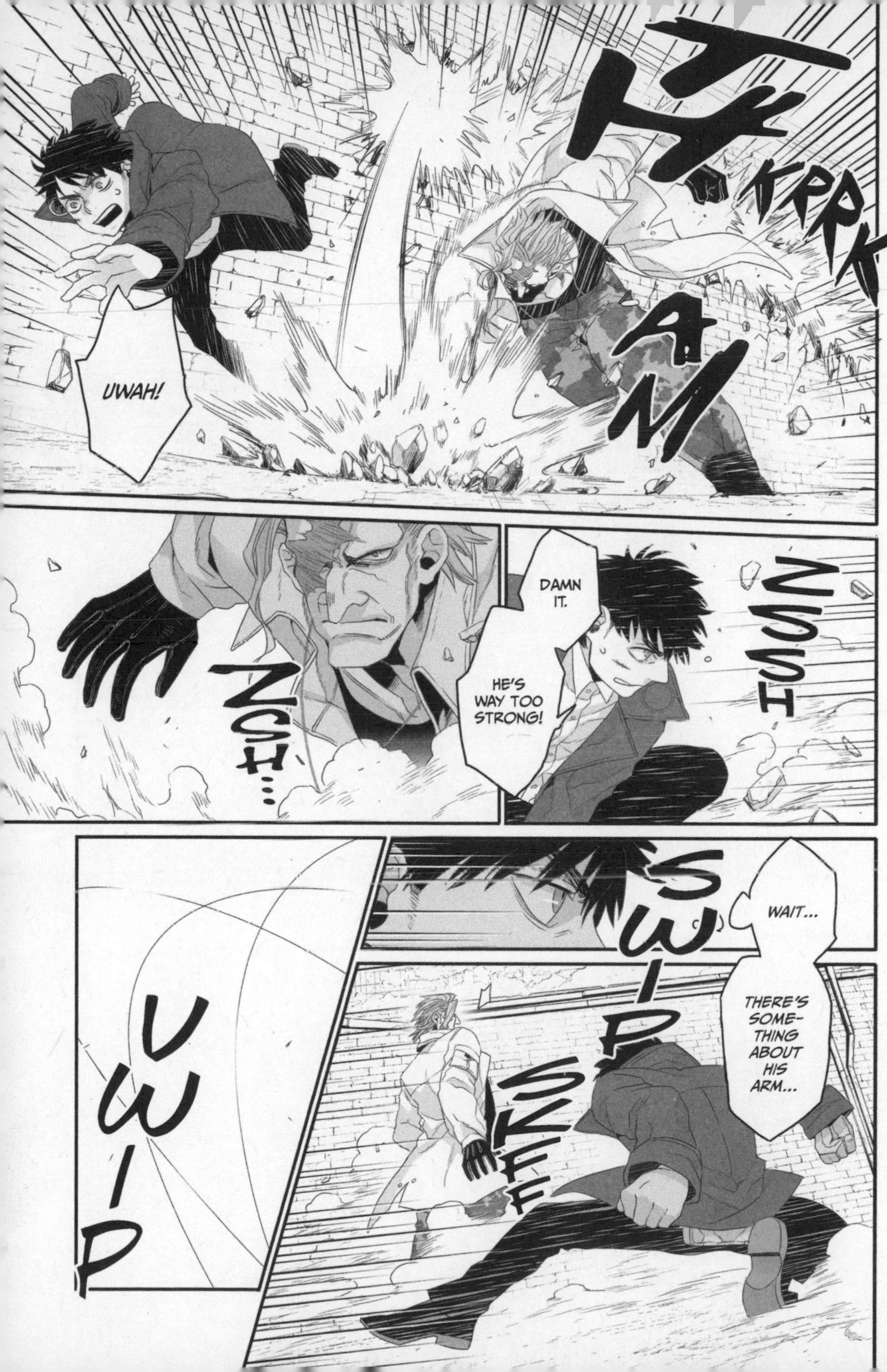
THAM
KRRK
UWAH!
ZSSH
DAMN IT.
HE'S WAY TOO STRONG!
ZSH...
SWIP
WAIT...
THERE'S SOME-THING ABOUT HIS ARM...
SKFF
UWIP

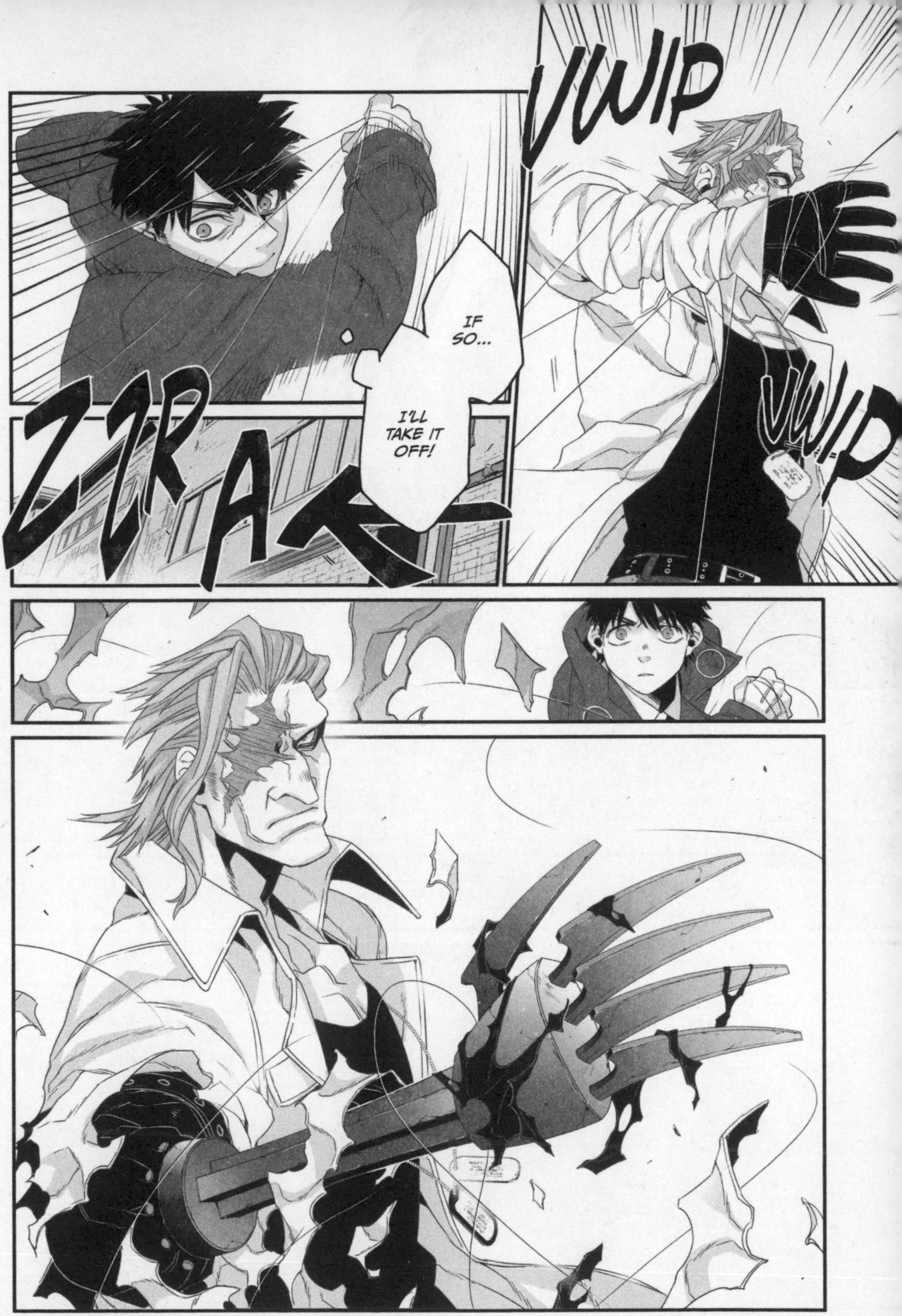
VWIP
VWIP
IF SO...
I'LL TAKE IT OFF!
ZZRAK

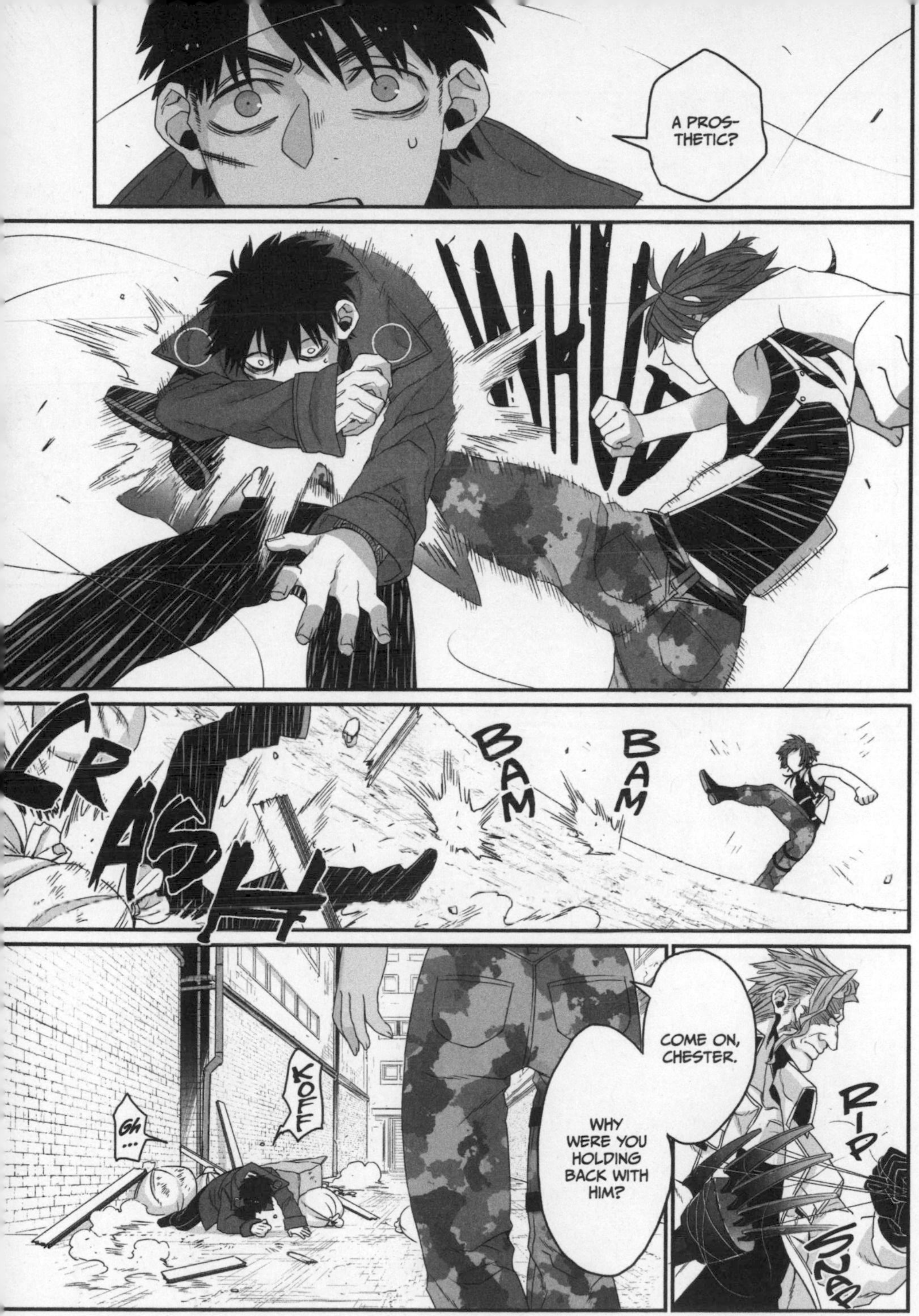
A PROS-
THETIC?
WHUD
BAM
BAM
CRASH
RIP
SNAP
COME ON, CHESTER.
WHY WERE YOU HOLDING BACK WITH HIM?
KOFF
Gh...

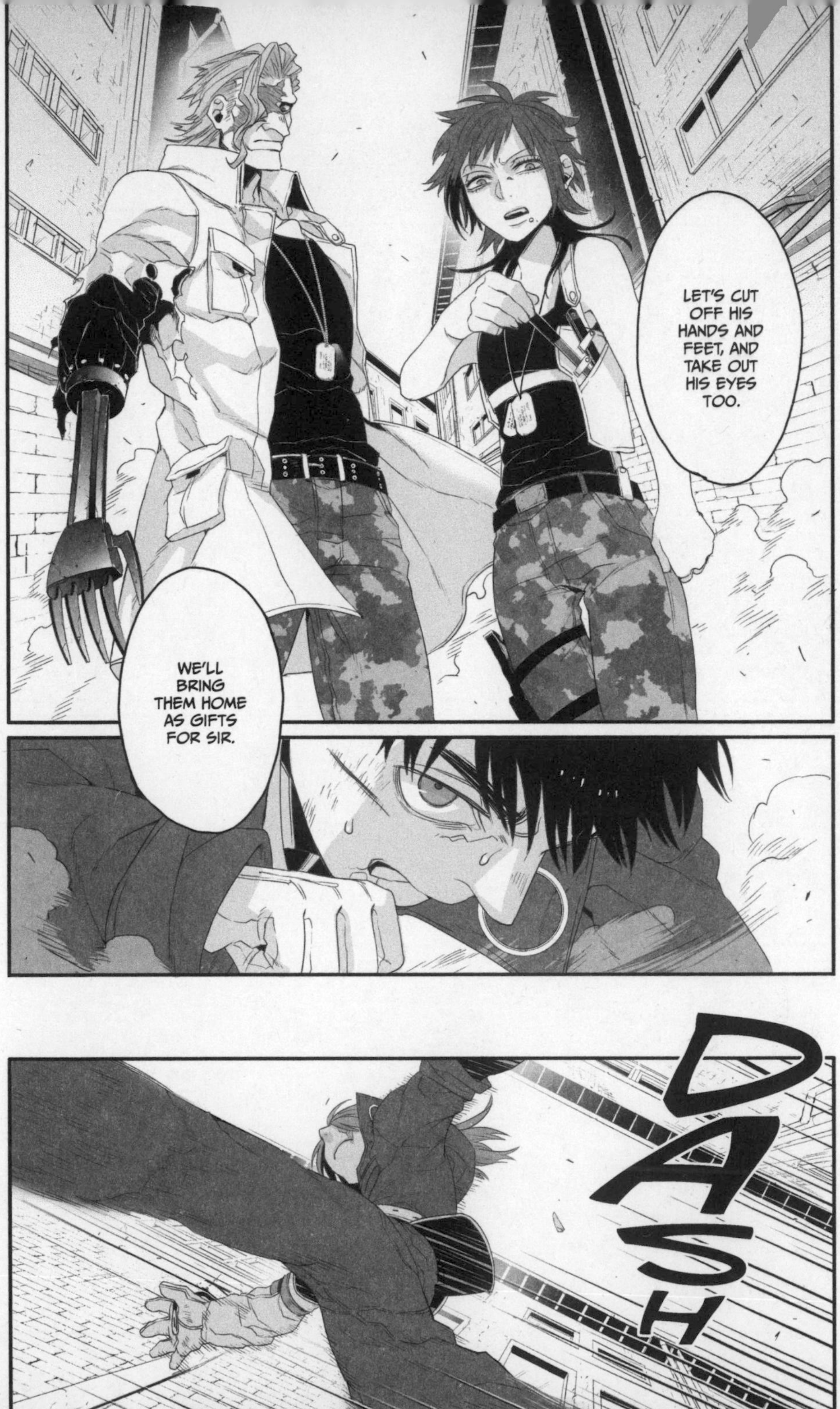
LET'S CUT OFF HIS HANDS AND FEET, AND TAKE OUT HIS EYES TOO.
WE'LL BRING THEM HOME AS GIFTS FOR SIR.
DASH

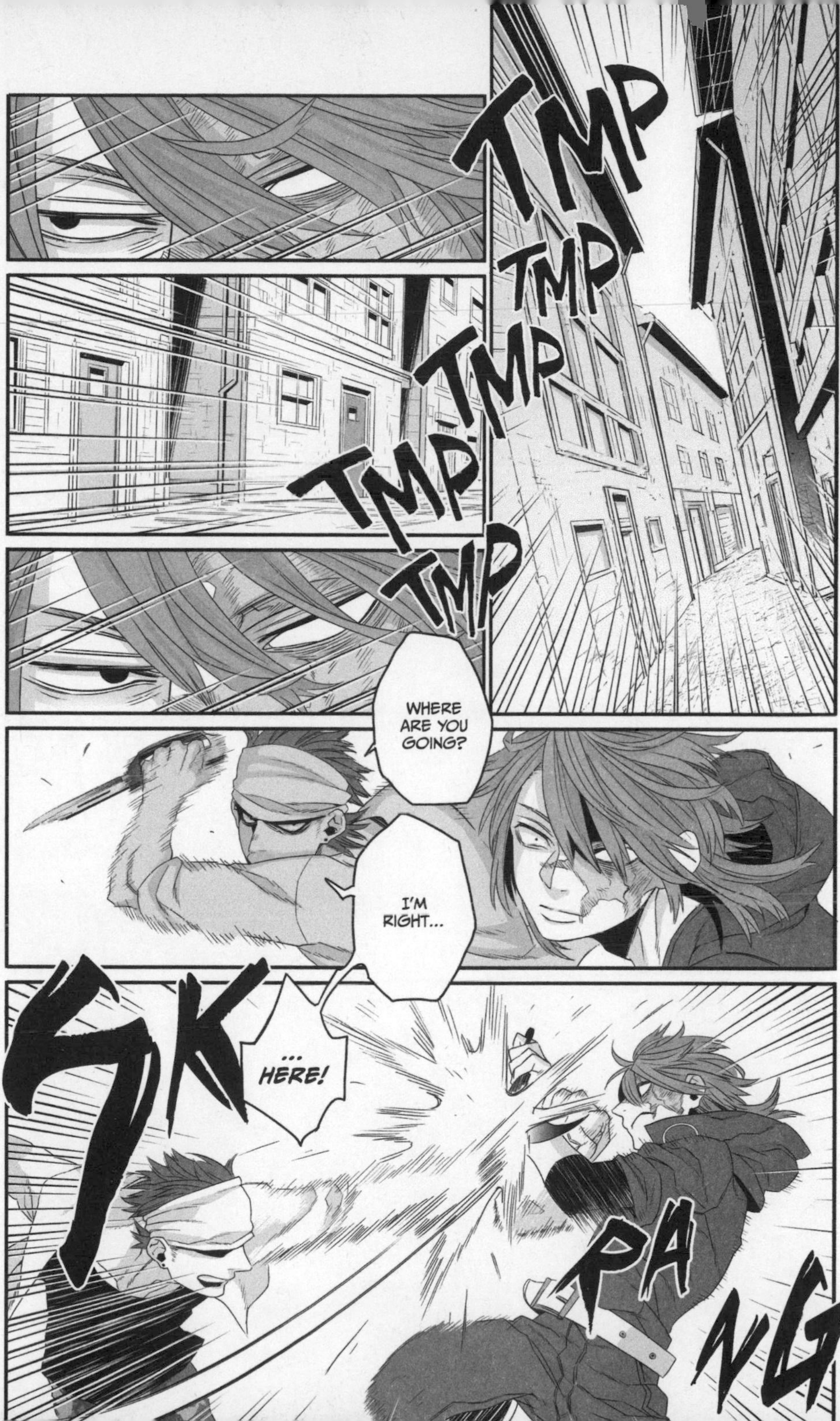
TMP
TMP
TMP
TMP
TMP
TMP
WHERE ARE YOU GOING?
I'M RIGHT...
...HERE!
RANG
SK

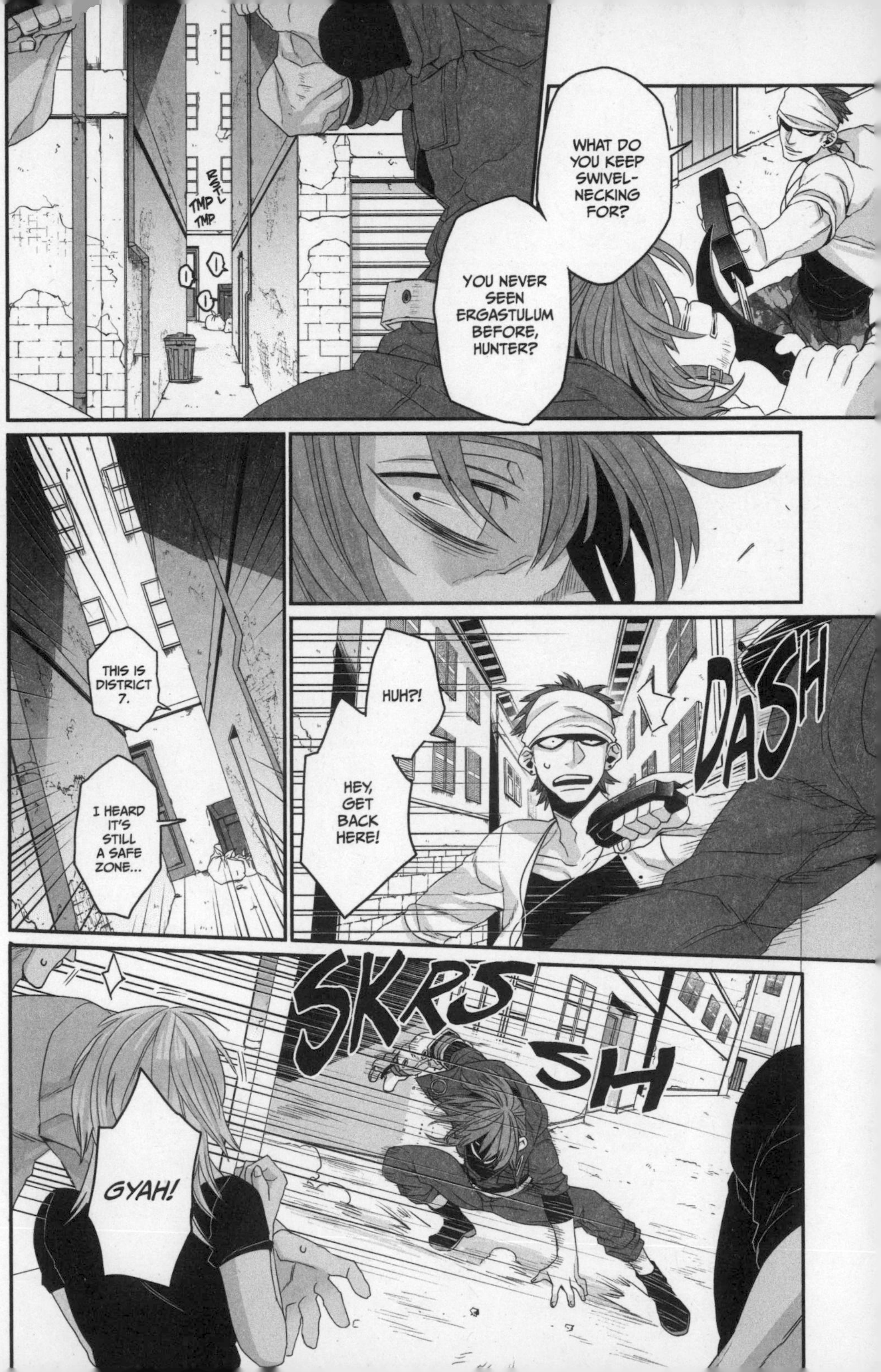
WHAT DO YOU KEEP SWIVEL-NECKING FOR?
YOU NEVER SEEN ERGASTULUM BEFORE, HUNTER?
RSTL
TMP TMP
DASH
HUH?!
HEY, GET BACK HERE!
THIS IS DISTRICT 7.
I HEARD IT'S STILL A SAFE ZONE...
SKRSSH
GYAH!

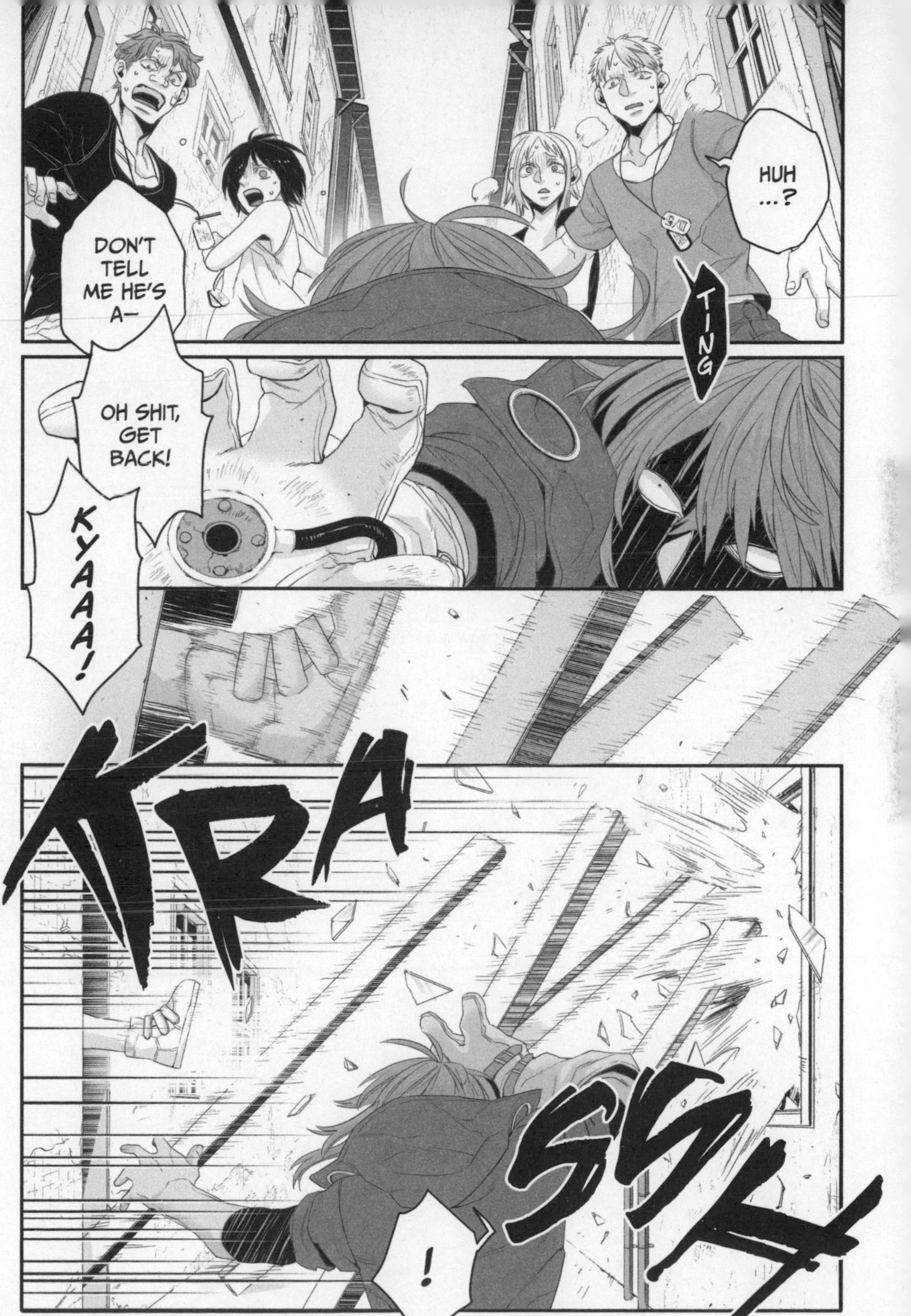
HUH ...?
DON'T TELL ME HE'S A—
TING
OH SHIT, GET BACK!
KYAAAA!
KRASSH
!

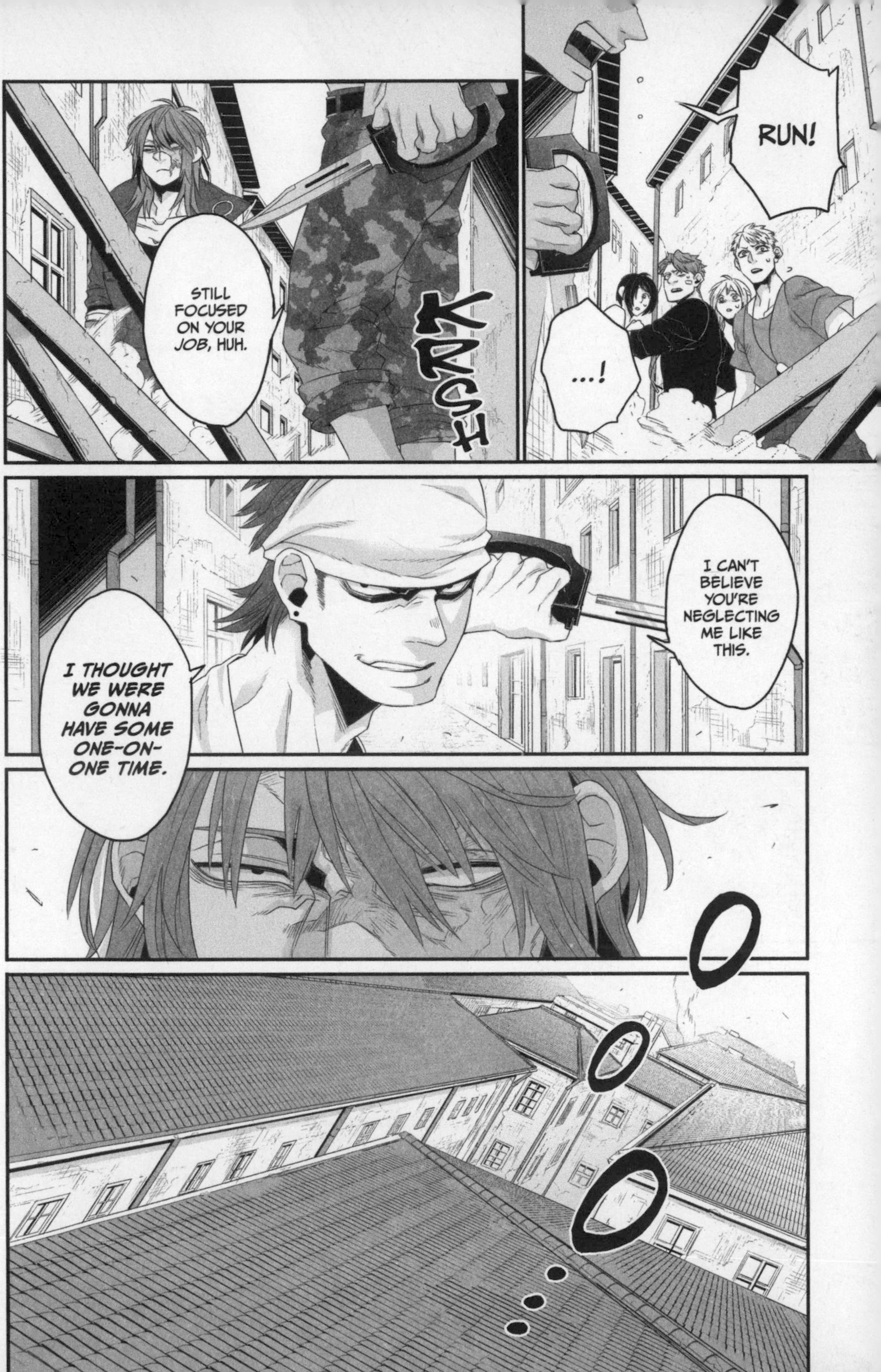
RUN!
...!
STILL FOCUSED ON YOUR JOB, HUH.
KRCH
I CAN'T BELIEVE YOU'RE NEGLECTING ME LIKE THIS.
I THOUGHT WE WERE GONNA HAVE SOME ONE-ON-ONE TIME.

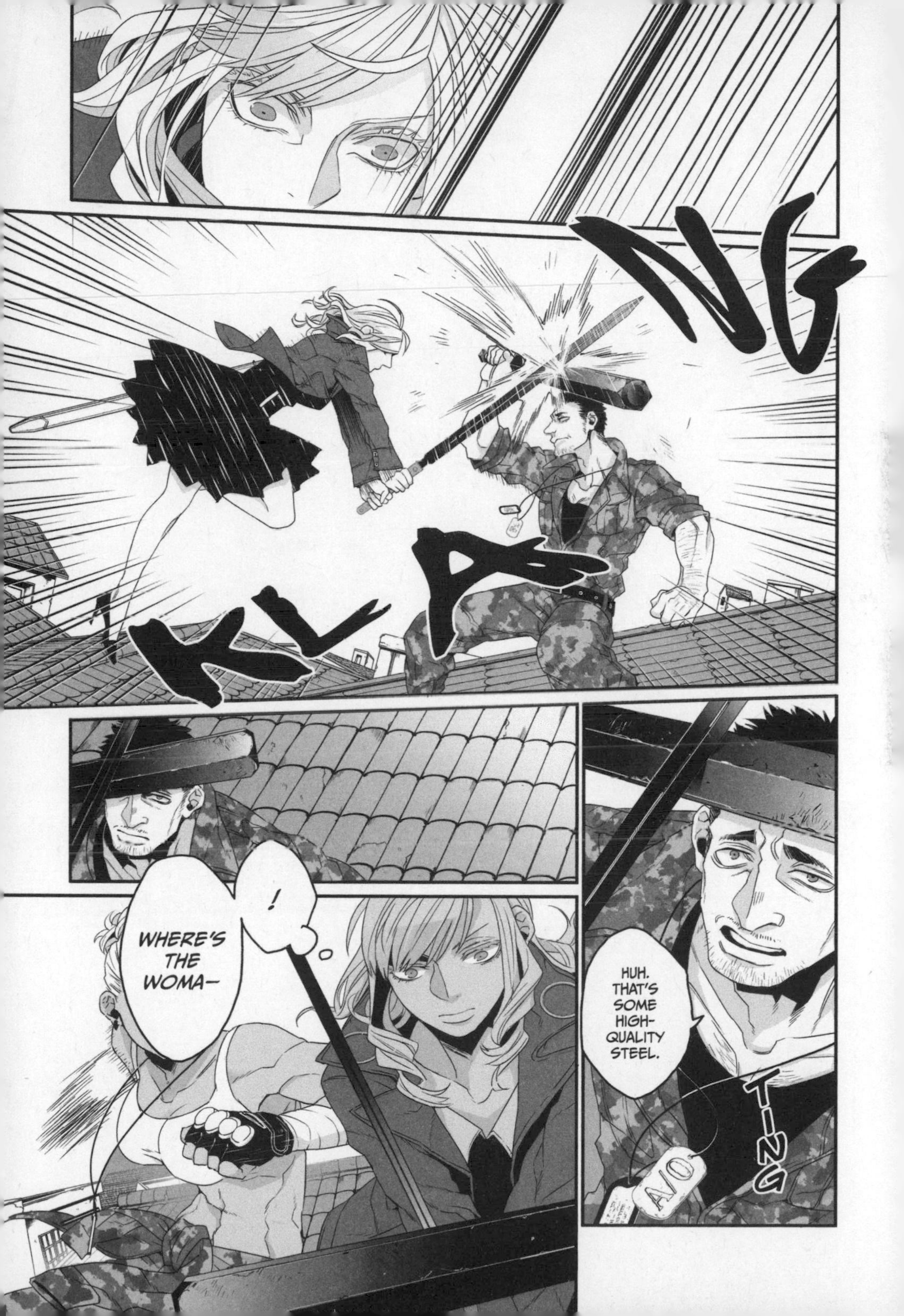
KLA
NG
HUH. THAT'S SOME HIGH-QUALITY STEEL.
TING
A/O
!
WHERE'S THE WOMA-

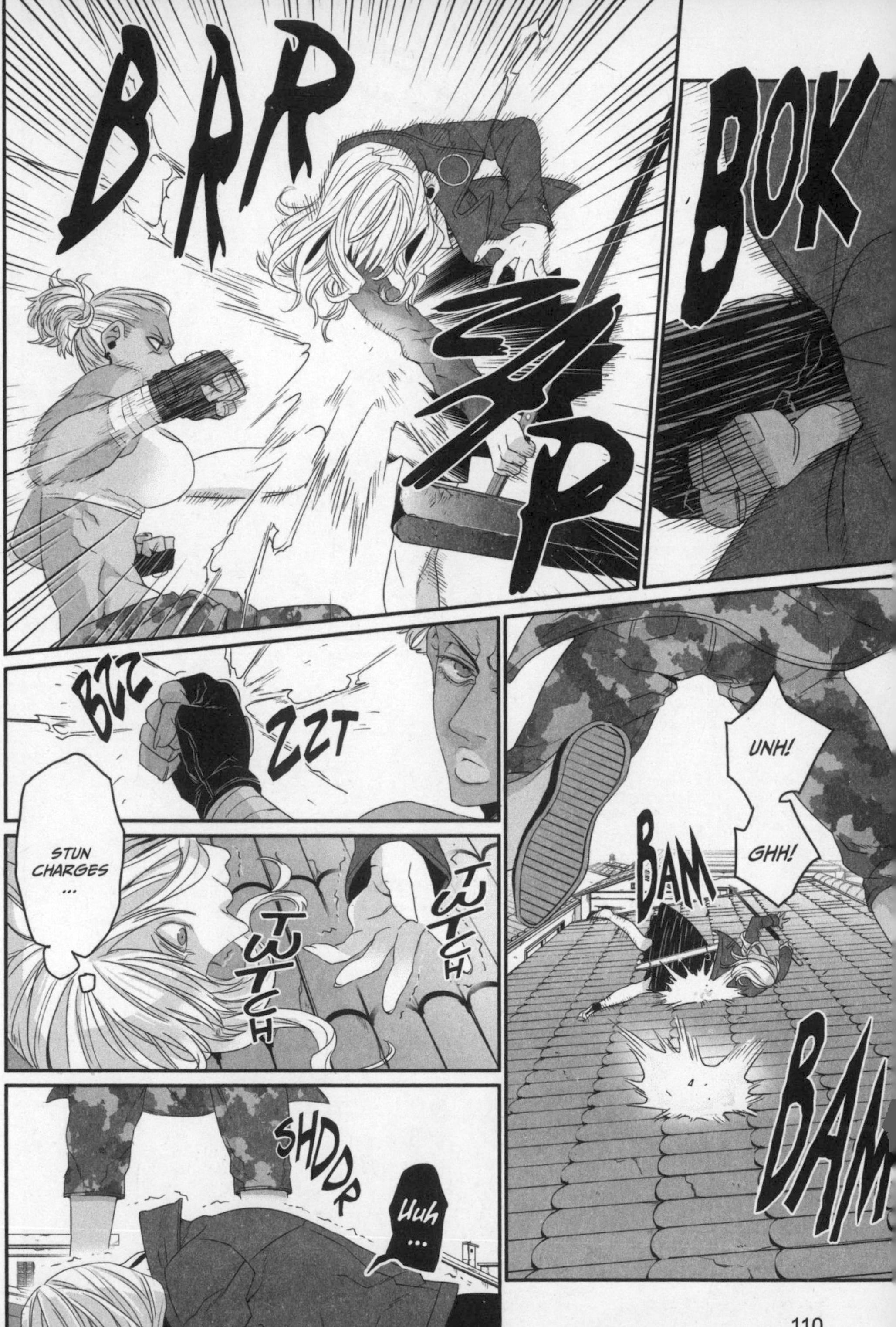
BOK
BRR
ZAP
UNH!
BAM
GHH!
BAM
BZZ
ZZT
STUN CHARGES ...
TWITCH
TWITCH
SHDDR
Uuh ...

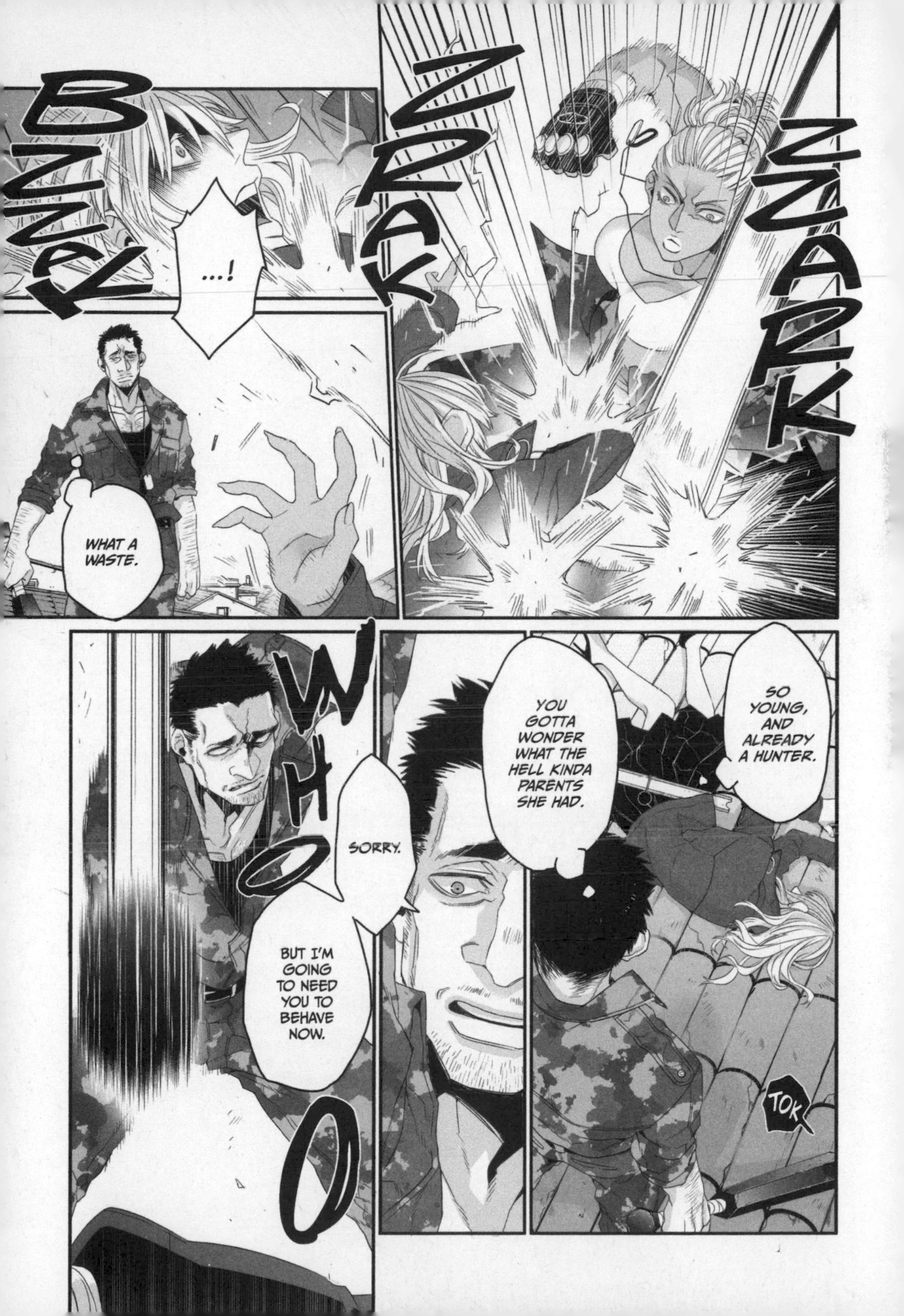
ZZARK
ZZAK
...!
WHAT A WASTE.
SO YOUNG, AND ALREADY A HUNTER.
YOU GOTTA WONDER WHAT THE HELL KINDA PARENTS SHE HAD.
TOK
SORRY.
BUT I'M GOING TO NEED YOU TO BEHAVE NOW.
WHOO

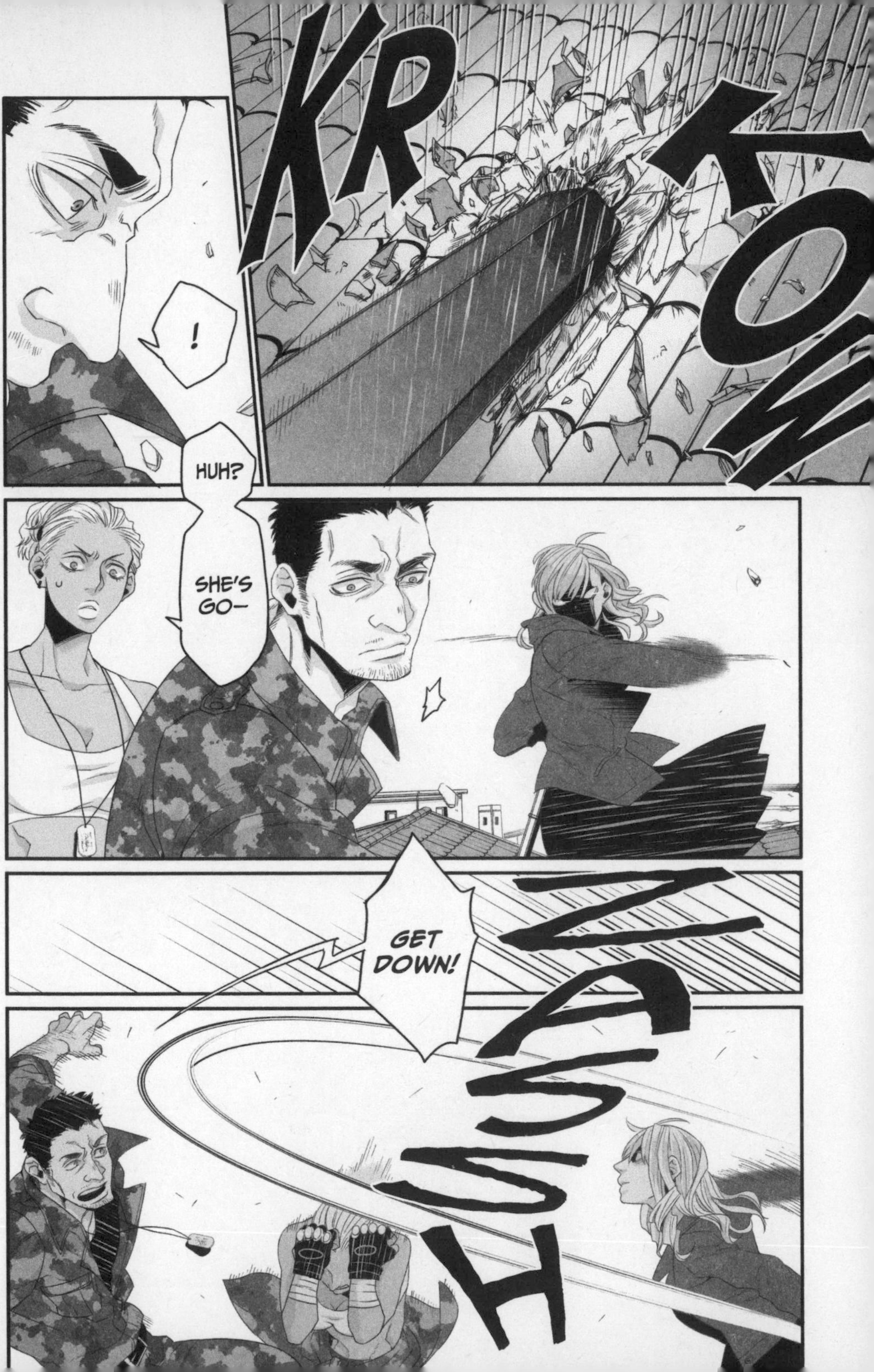
KR
KOW
!
HUH?
SHE'S GO—
GET DOWN!
ZASSH

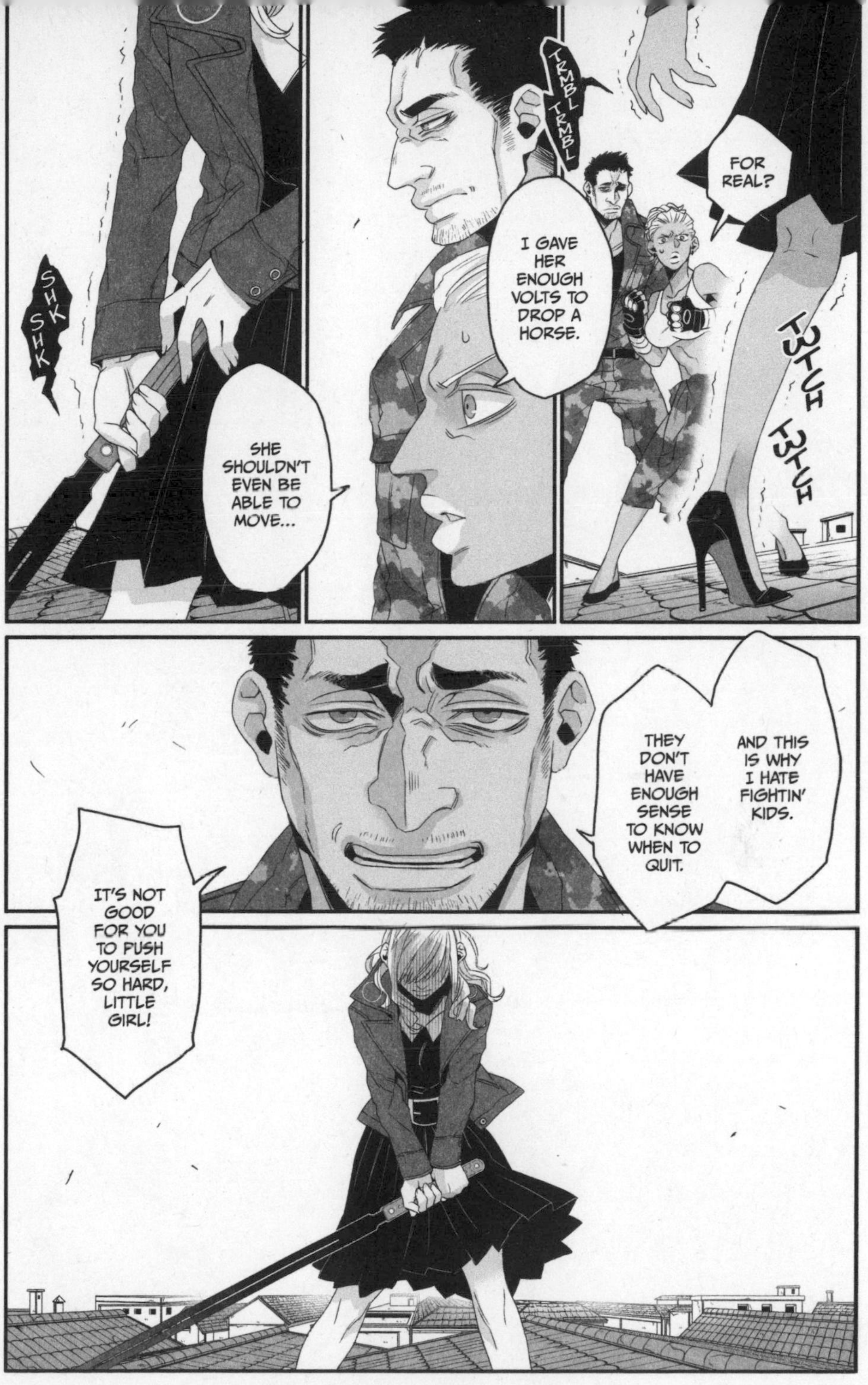
FOR REAL?
TRMBL TRMBL
I GAVE HER ENOUGH VOLTS TO DROP A HORSE.
SHE SHOULDN'T EVEN BE ABLE TO MOVE...
SHK SHK
AND THIS IS WHY I HATE FIGHTIN' KIDS.
THEY DON'T HAVE ENOUGH SENSE TO KNOW WHEN TO QUIT.
IT'S NOT GOOD FOR YOU TO PUSH YOURSELF SO HARD, LITTLE GIRL!

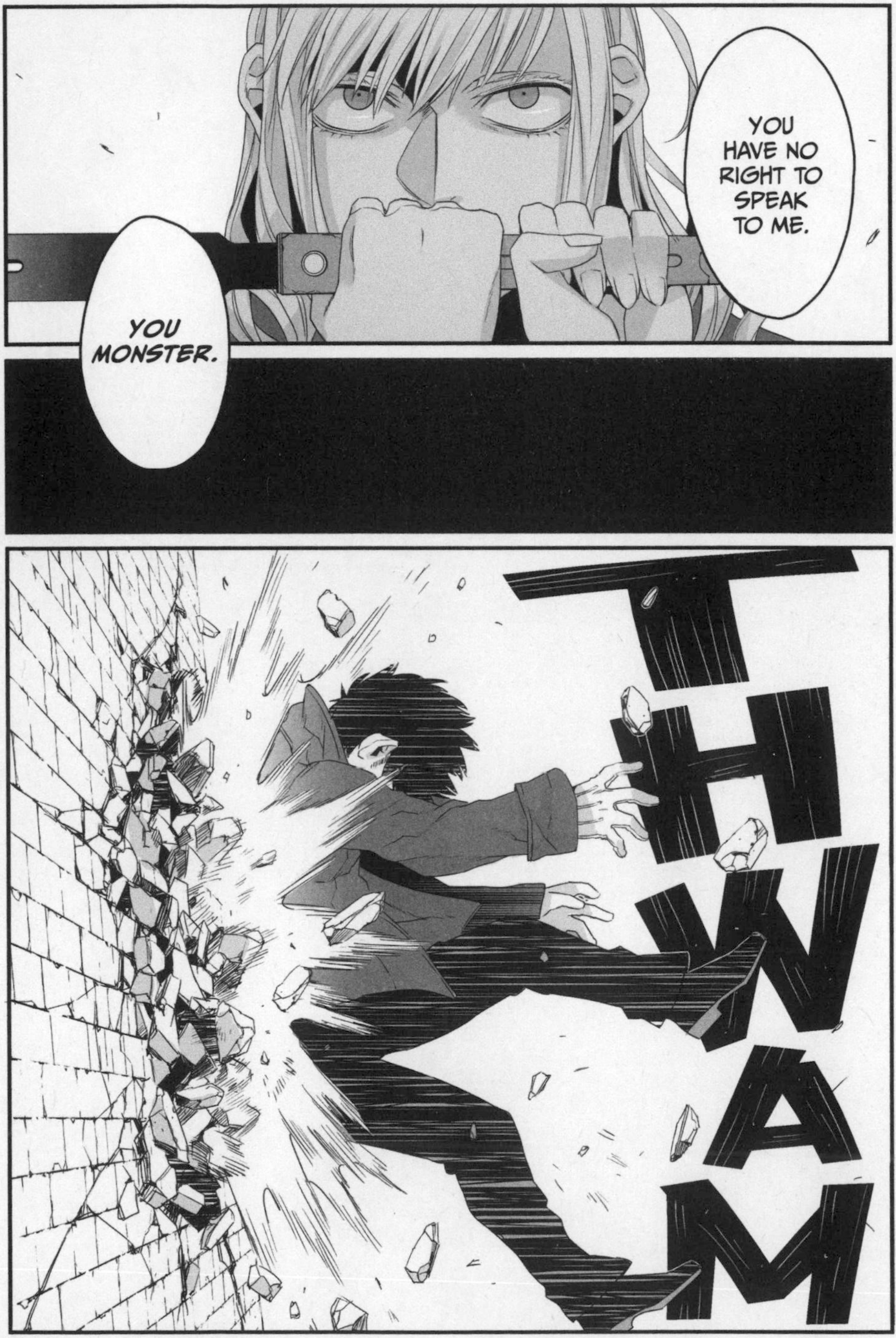
YOU HAVE NO RIGHT TO SPEAK TO ME.
YOU MONSTER.
THWAM

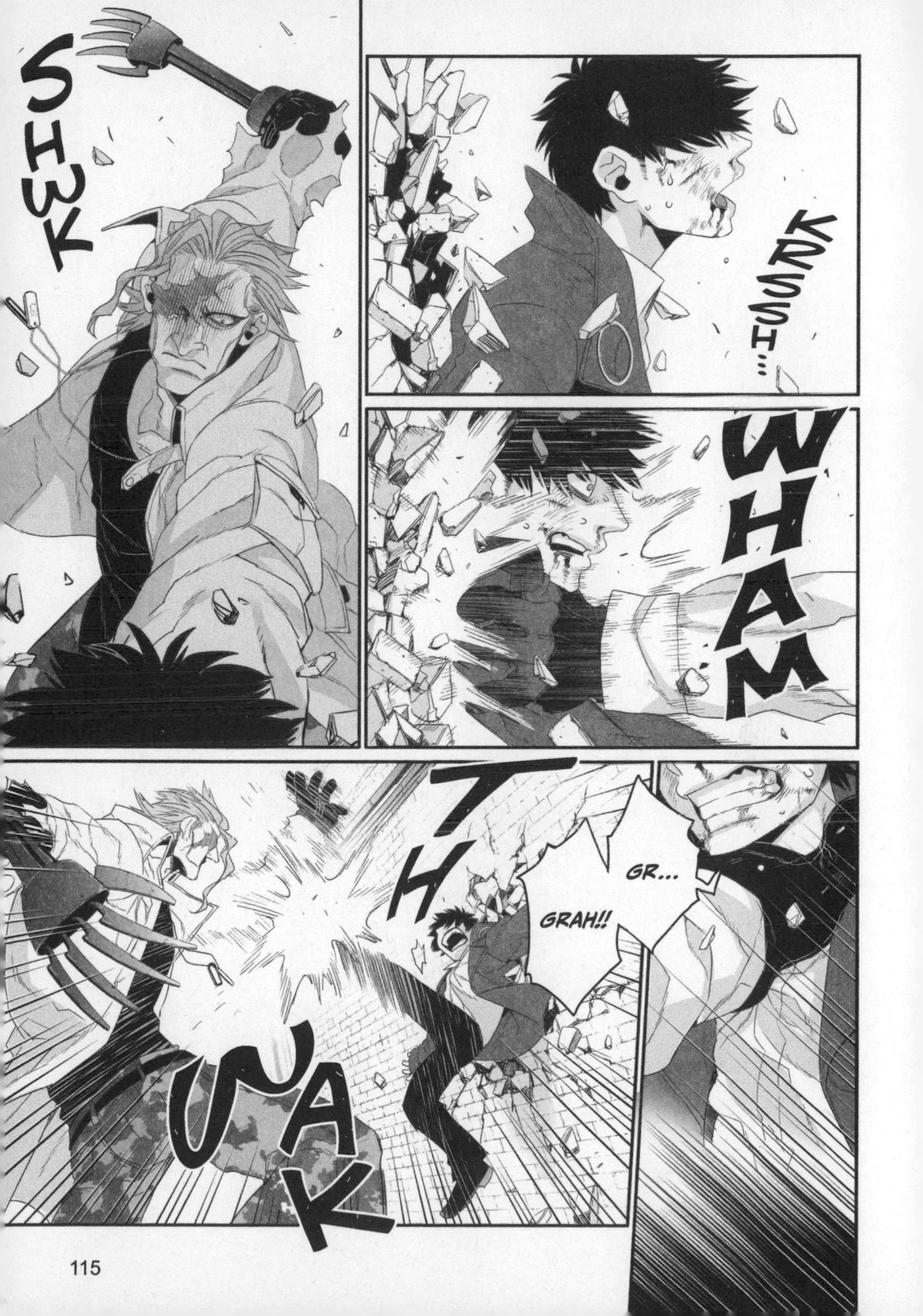
KRSSH...
WHAM
SHWK
GR...
GRAH!!
THWAK

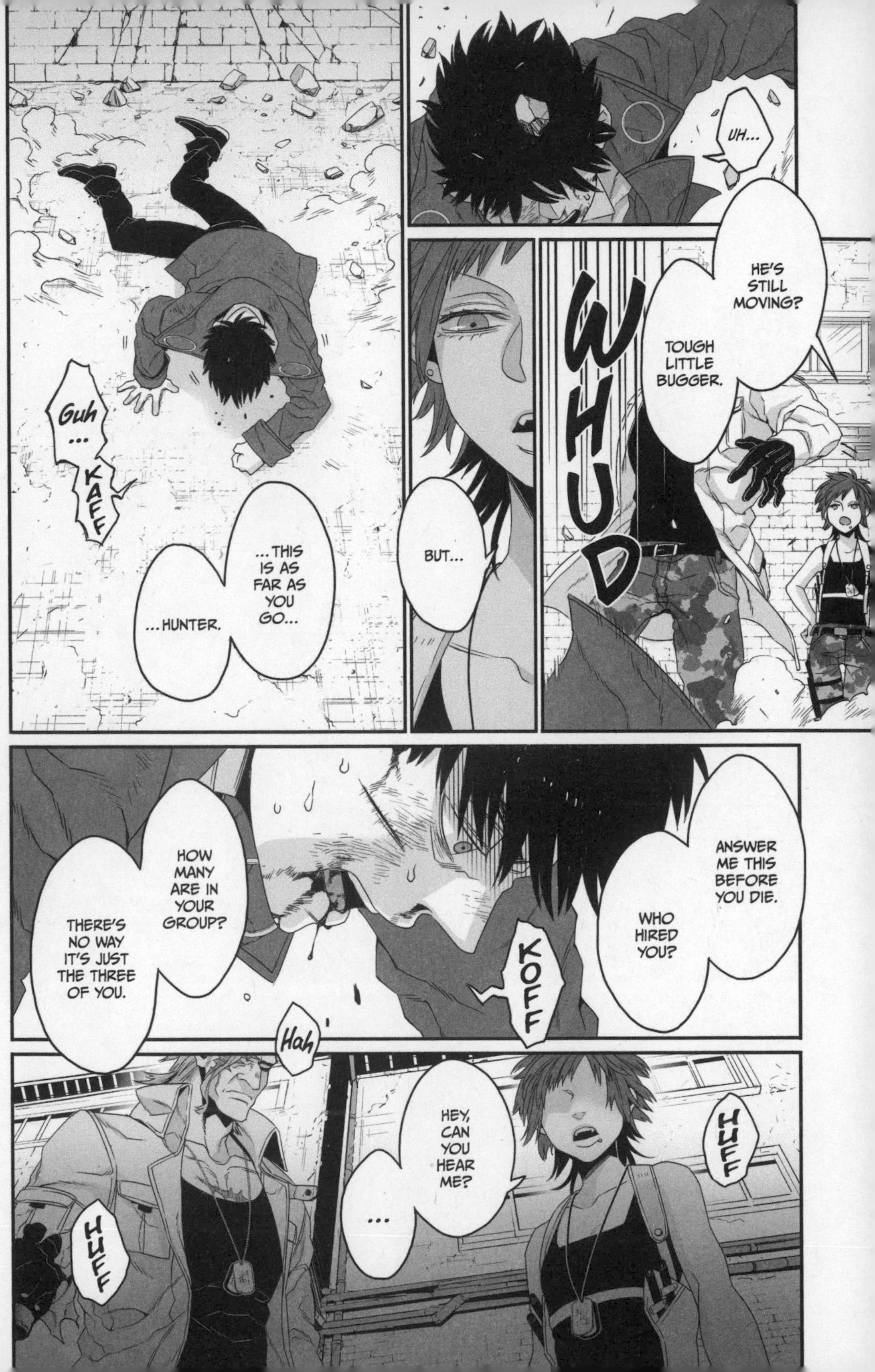
UH...
HE'S STILL MOVING?
TOUGH LITTLE BUGGER.
WHUD
BUT...
...THIS IS AS FAR AS YOU GO...
...HUNTER.
Guh ... KAFF
ANSWER ME THIS BEFORE YOU DIE.
WHO HIRED YOU?
KOFF
HOW MANY ARE IN YOUR GROUP?
THERE'S NO WAY IT'S JUST THE THREE OF YOU.
Hah
HUFF
HEY, CAN YOU HEAR ME?
...
HUFF

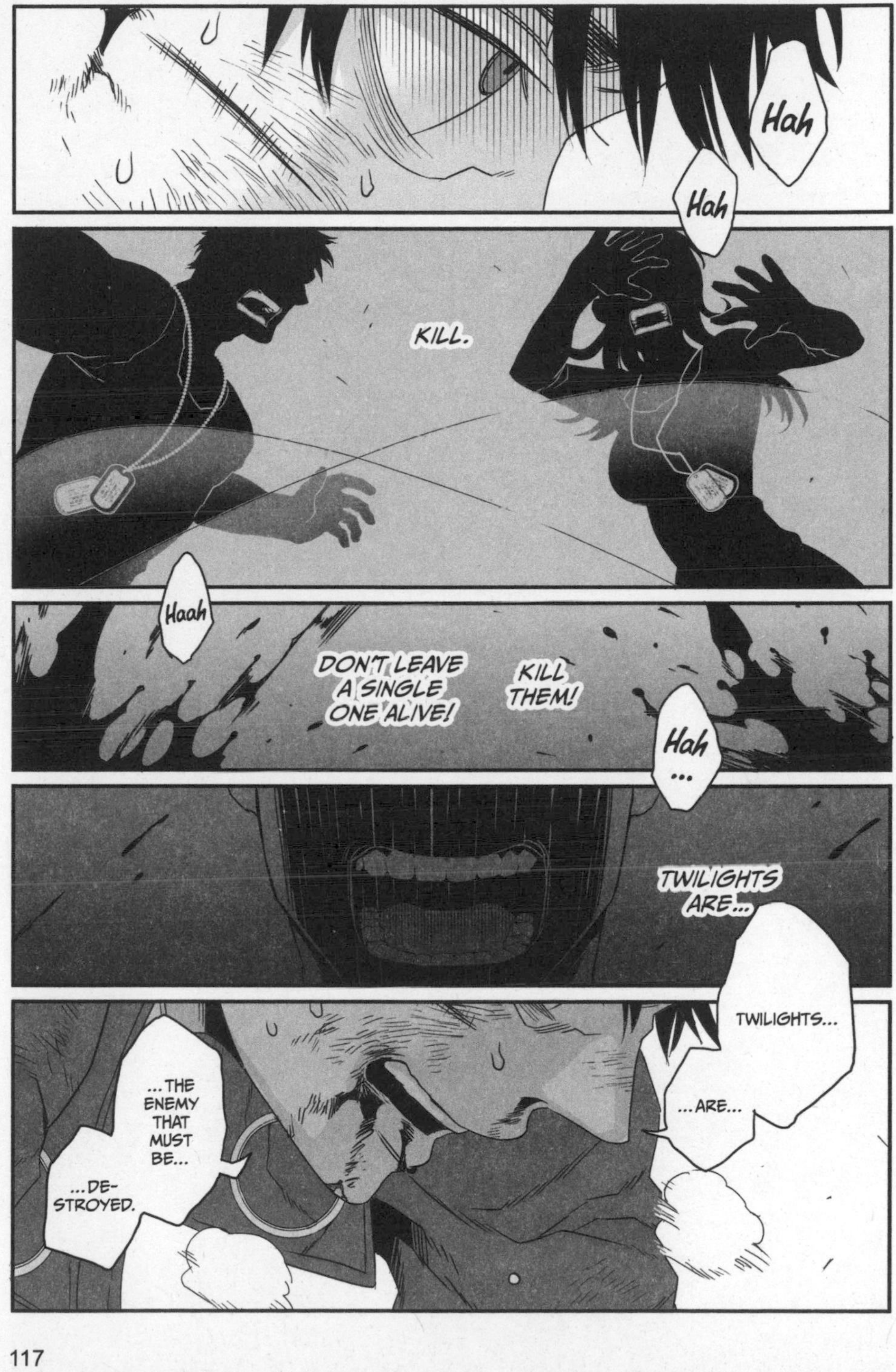
Hah
Hah
KILL.
Hah ...
KILL THEM!
DON'T LEAVE A SINGLE ONE ALIVE!
Haah
TWILIGHTS ARE...
TWILIGHTS...
...ARE...
...THE ENEMY THAT MUST BE...
...DE-STROYED.

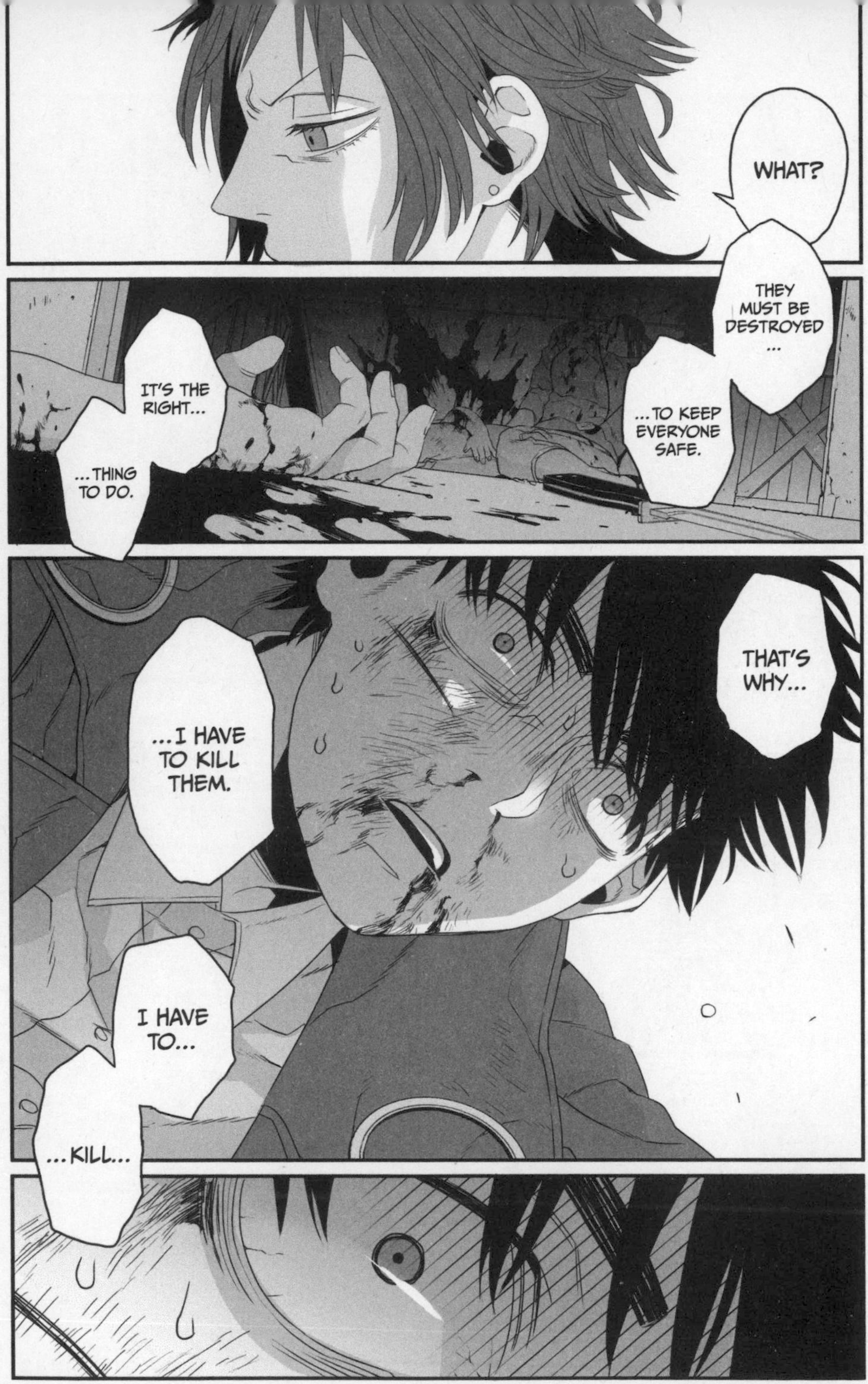
WHAT?
THEY MUST BE DESTROYED ...
...TO KEEP EVERYONE SAFE.
IT'S THE RIGHT...
...THING TO DO.
THAT'S WHY...
...I HAVE TO KILL THEM.
I HAVE TO...
...KILL...

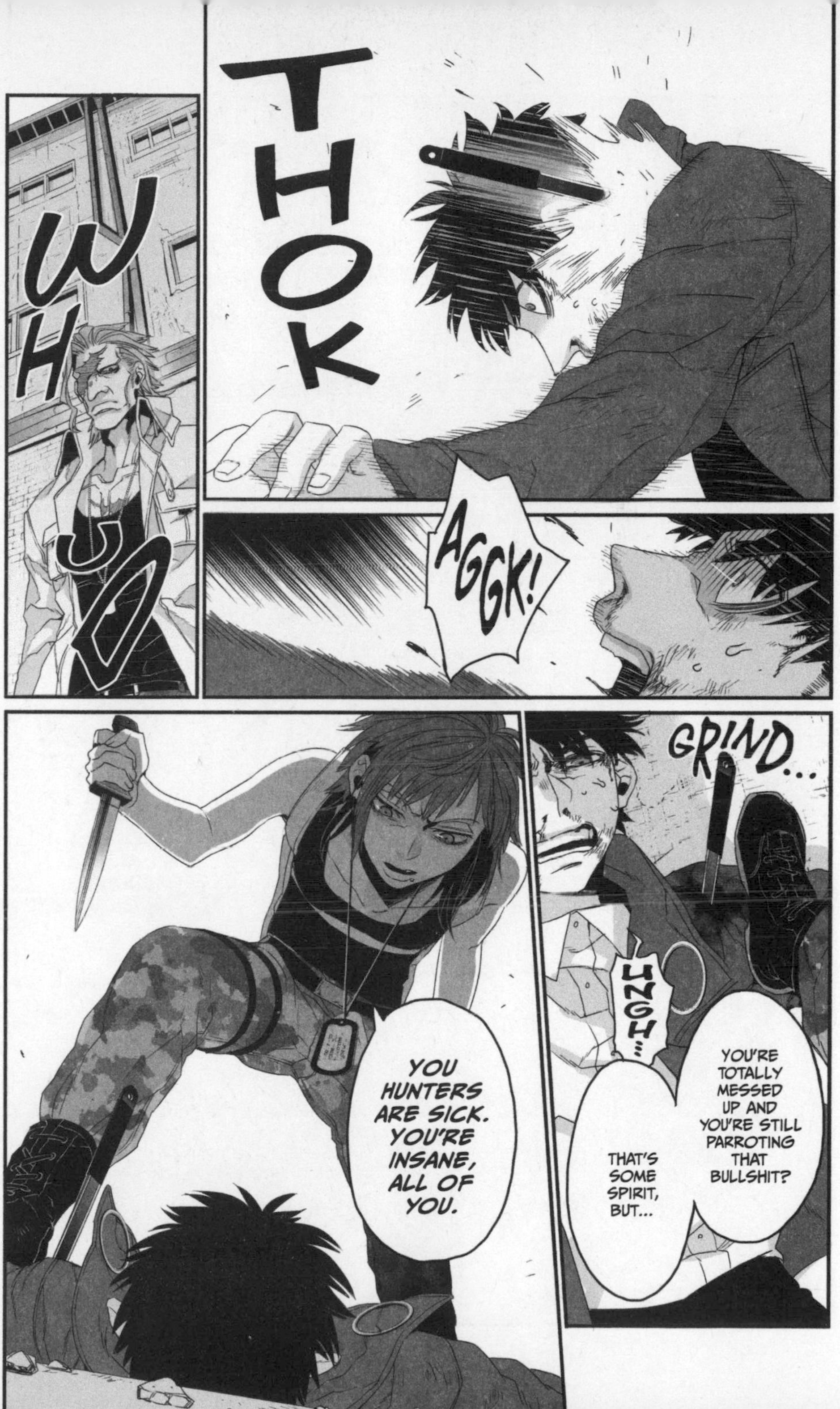
THOK
AGGK!
WHUD
GRIND...
UNGH...
YOU'RE TOTALLY MESSED UP AND YOU'RE STILL PARROTING THAT BULLSHIT?
THAT'S SOME SPIRIT, BUT...
YOU HUNTERS ARE SICK. YOU'RE INSANE, ALL OF YOU.

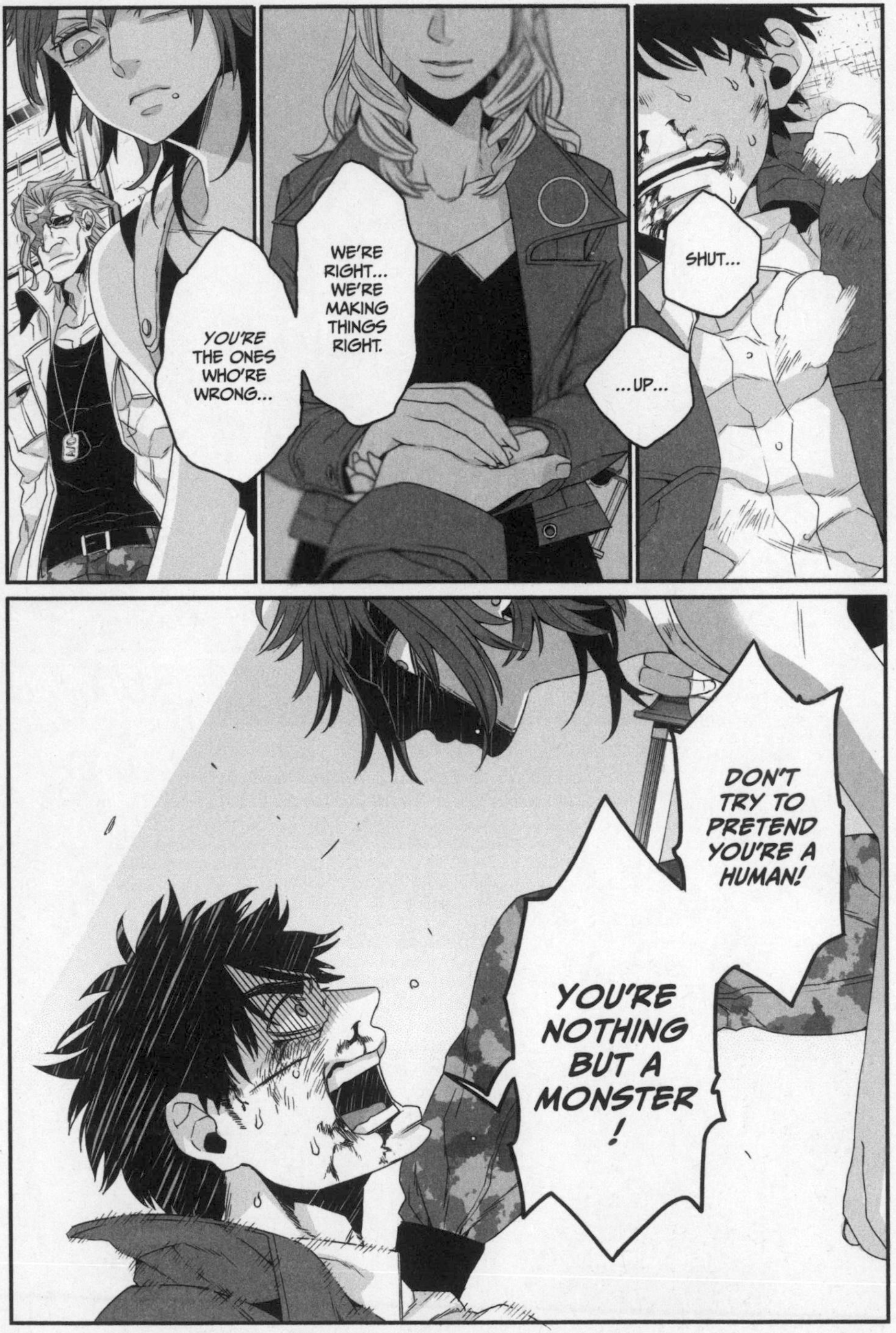
SHUT...
...UP...
WE'RE RIGHT... WE'RE MAKING THINGS RIGHT.
YOU'RE THE ONES WHO'RE WRONG...
DON'T TRY TO PRETEND YOU'RE A HUMAN!
YOU'RE NOTHING BUT A MONSTER!

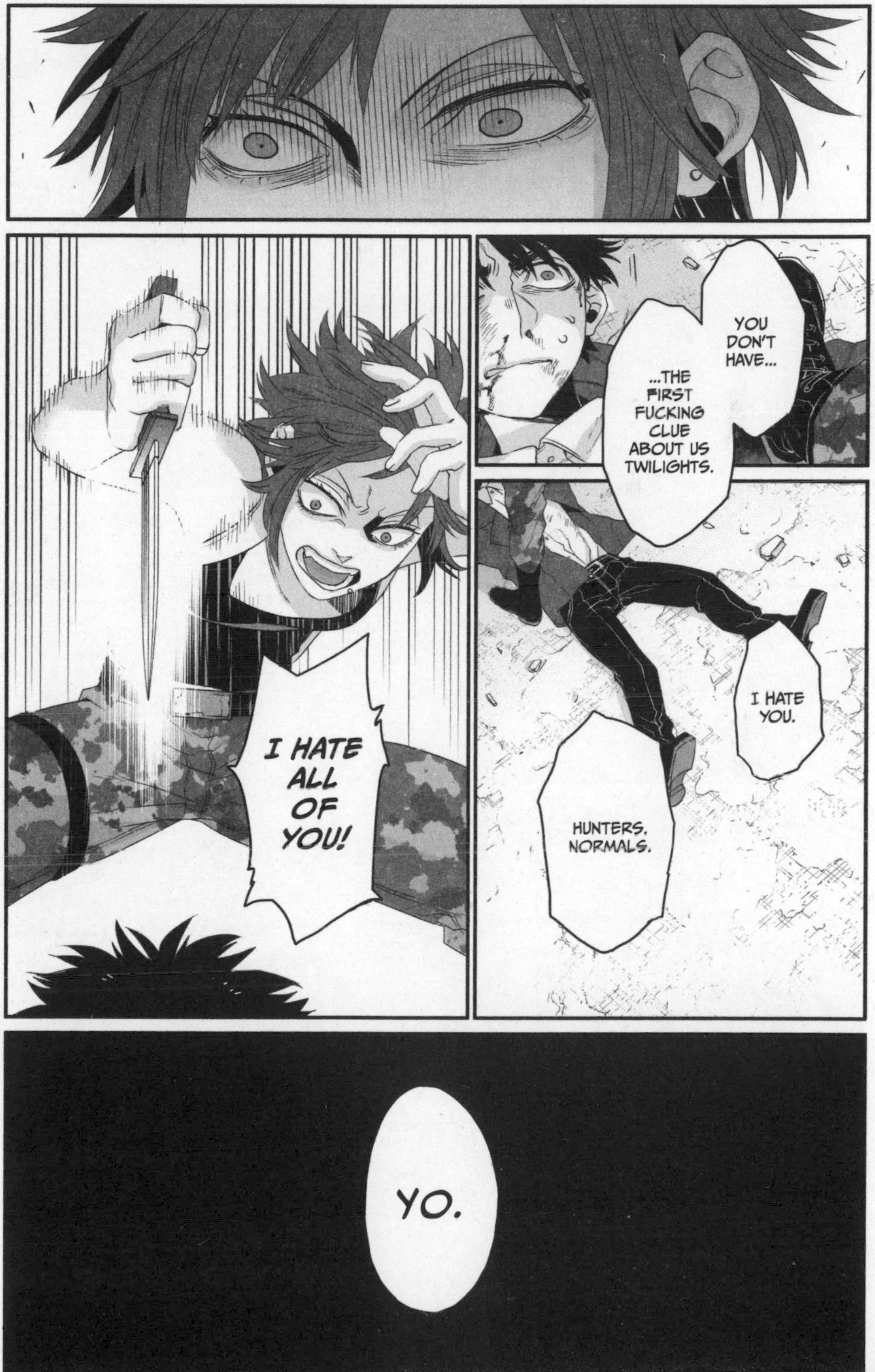
YOU DON'T HAVE...
...THE FIRST FUCKING CLUE ABOUT US TWILIGHTS.
I HATE YOU.
HUNTERS. NORMALS.
I HATE ALL OF YOU!
YO.

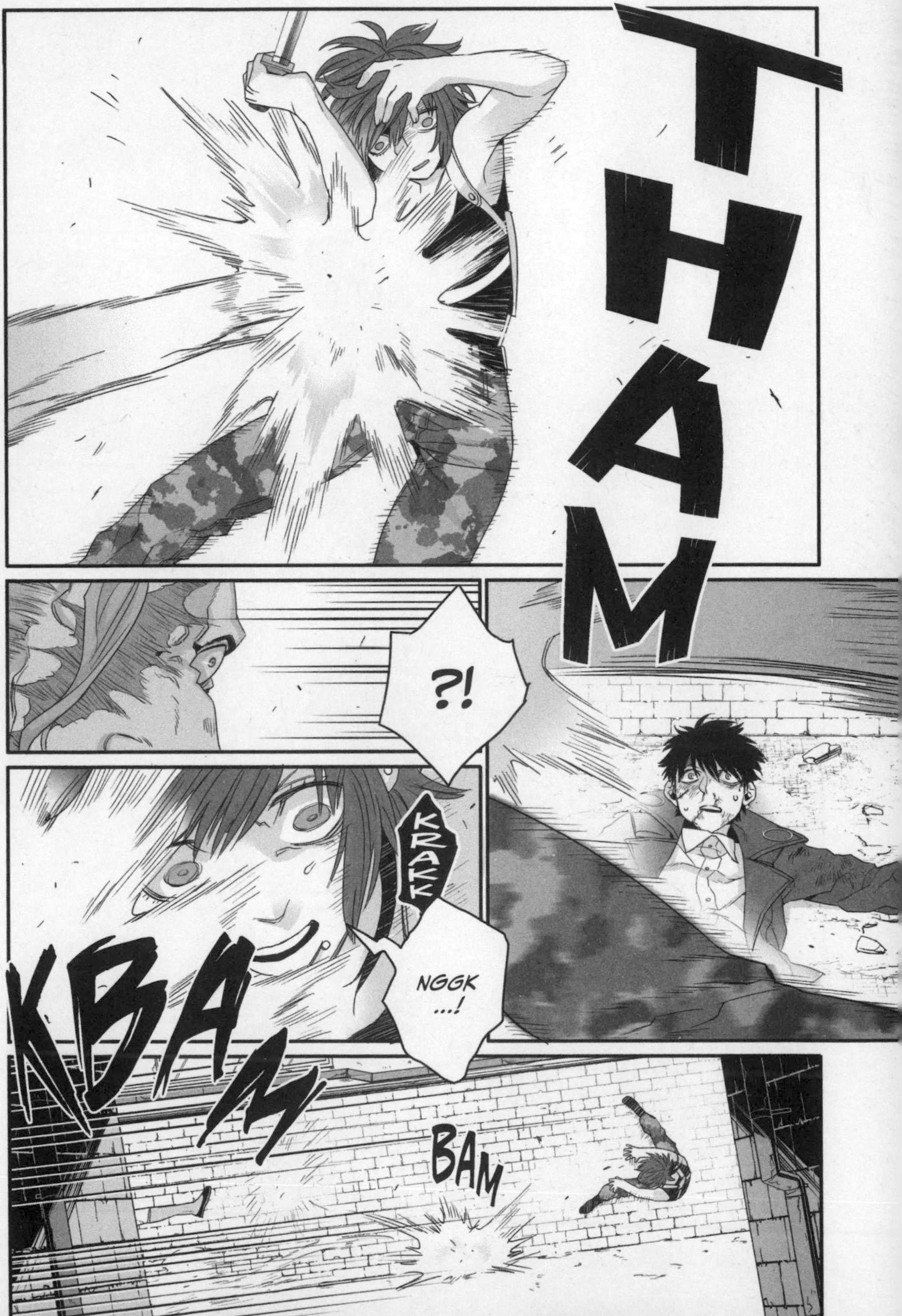
THAM
?!
KRAKK
NGGK ...!
KBAM
BAM

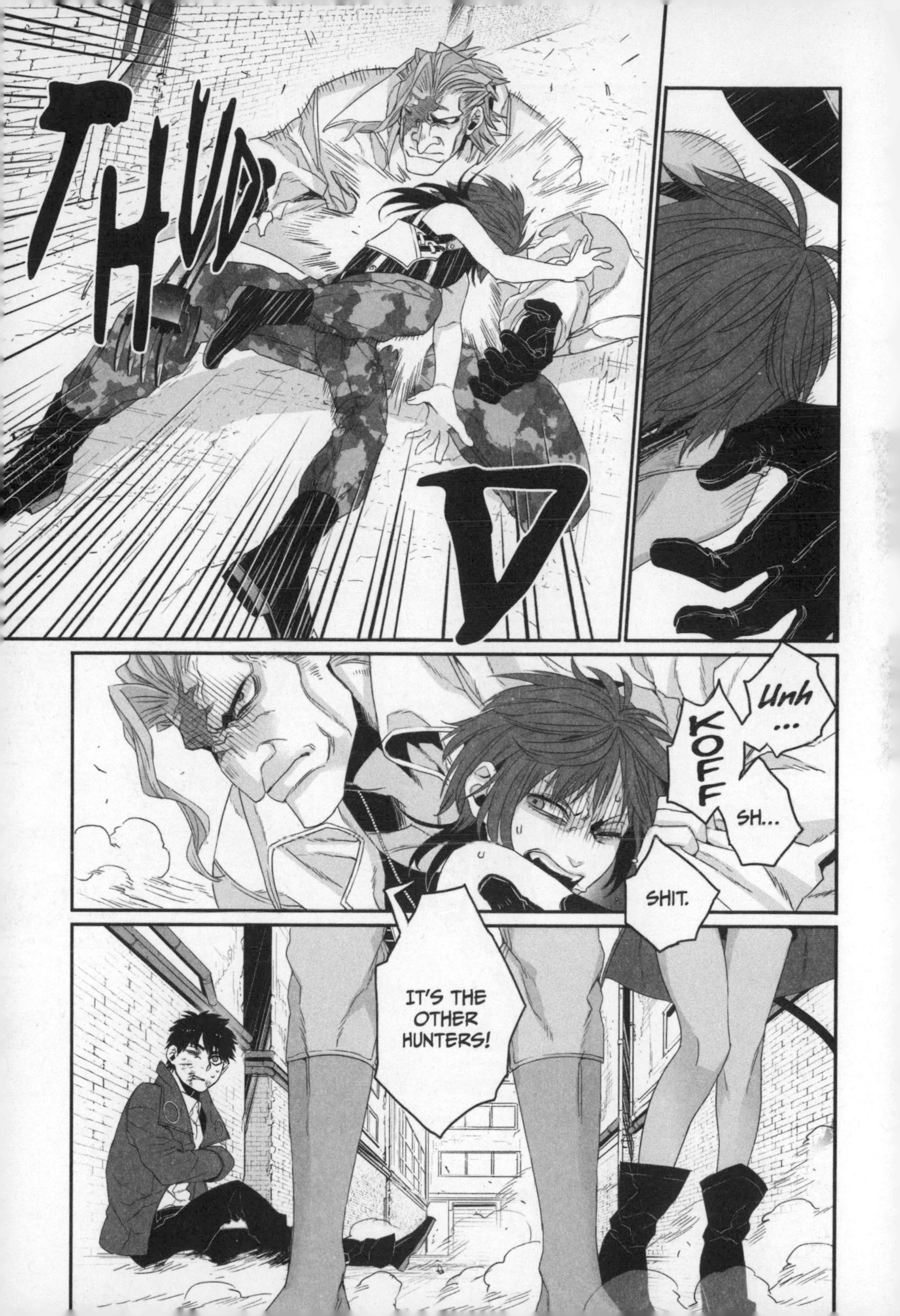
THUD
Unh ...
KOFF
SH...
SHIT.
IT'S THE OTHER HUNTERS!

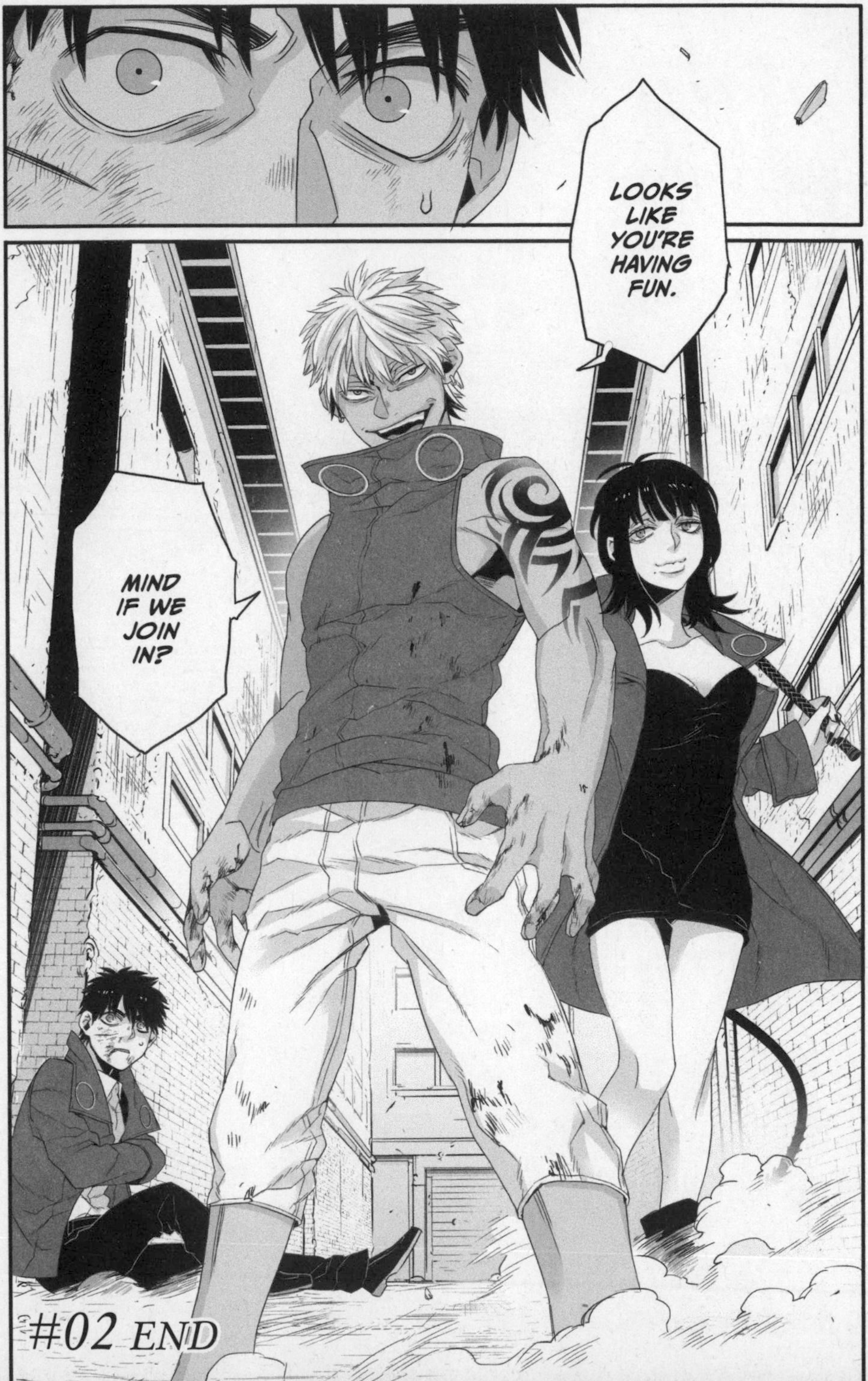
LOOKS LIKE YOU'RE HAVING FUN.
MIND IF WE JOIN IN?
#02 END

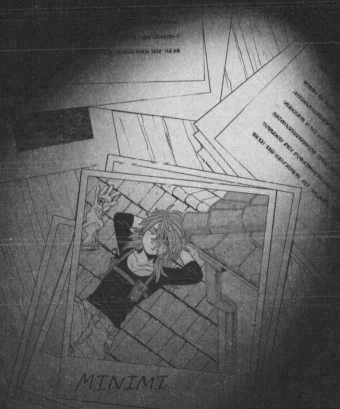

MINIMI

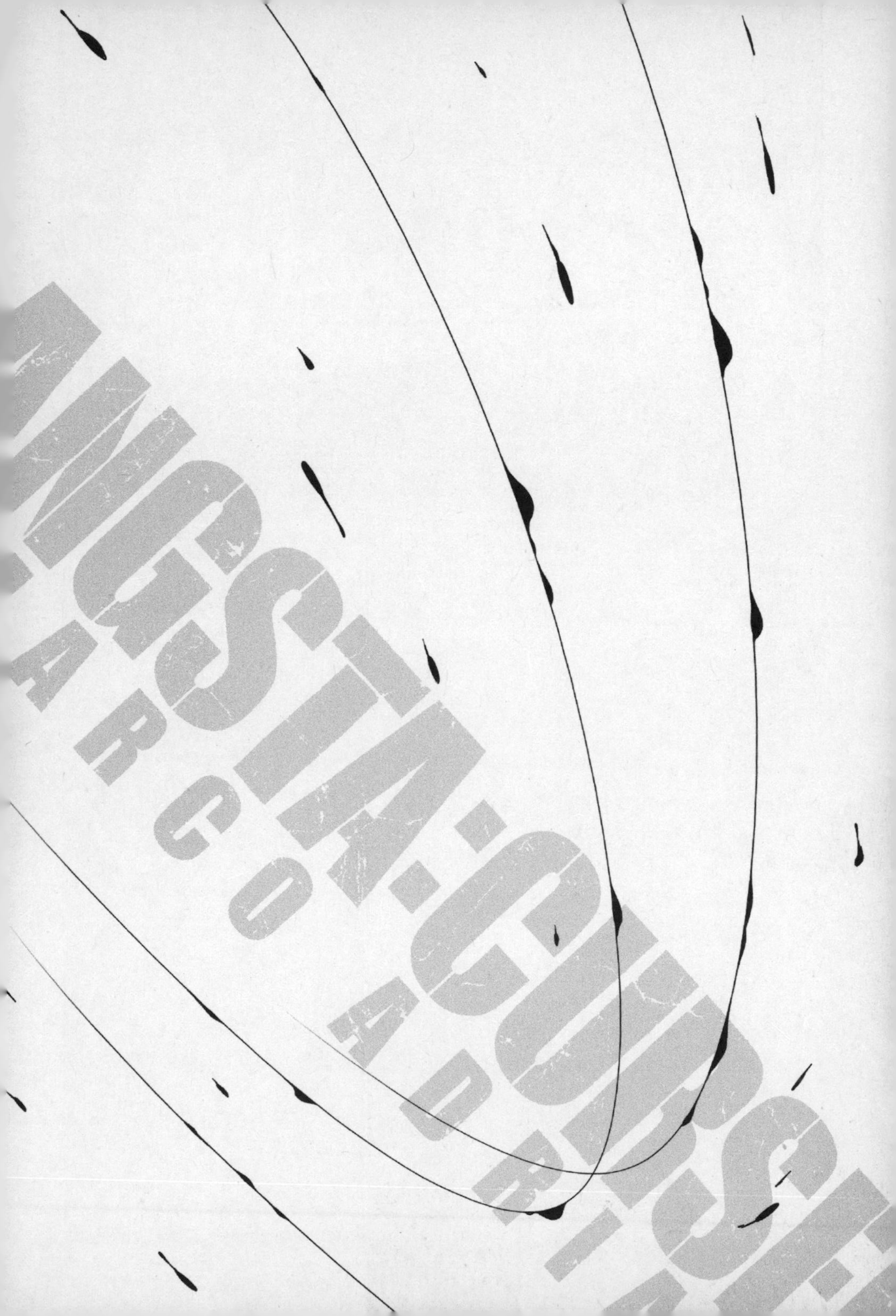

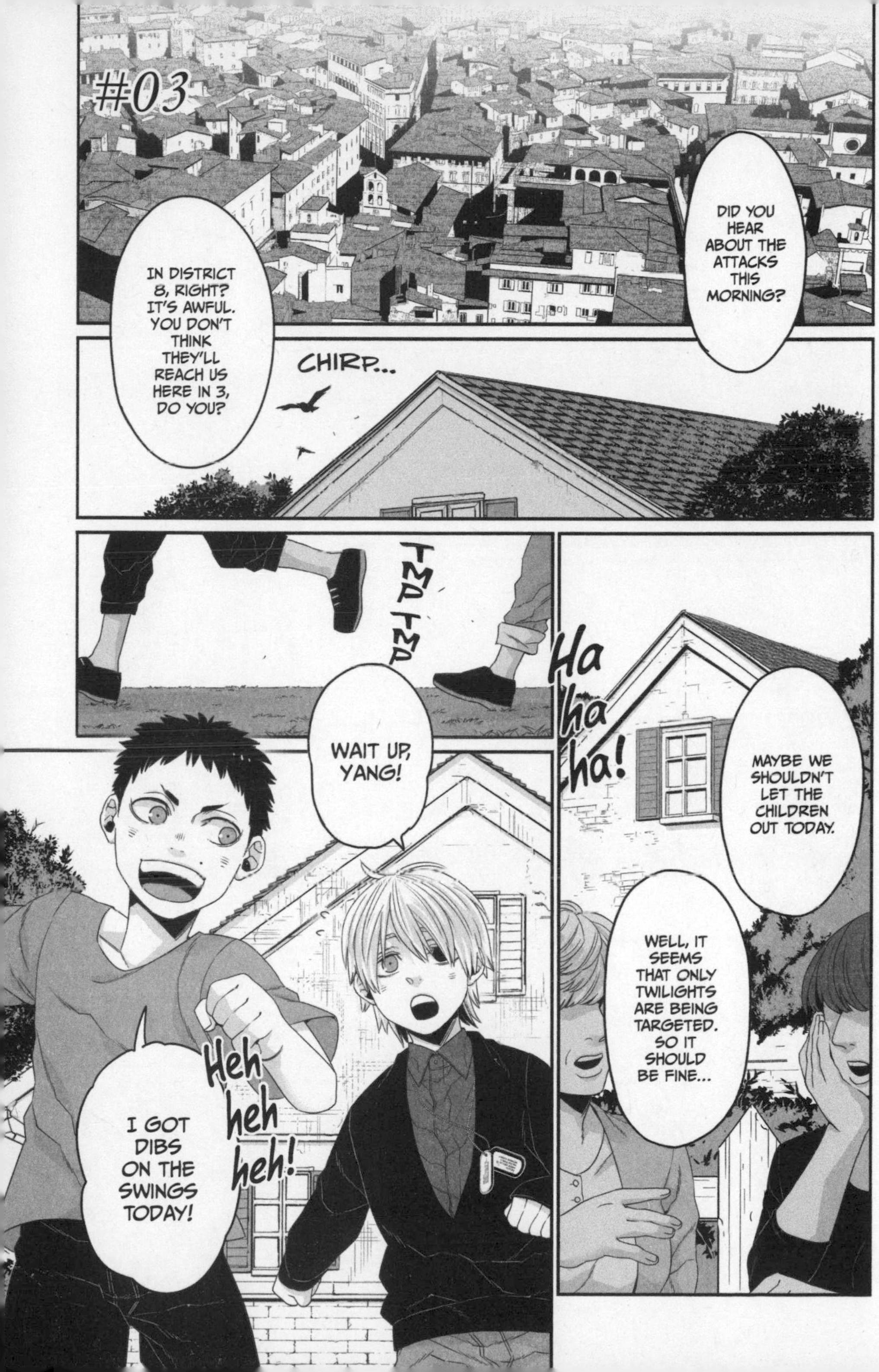

#03
DID YOU HEAR ABOUT THE ATTACKS THIS MORNING?
IN DISTRICT 8, RIGHT? IT'S AWFUL. YOU DON'T THINK THEY'LL REACH US HERE IN 3, DO YOU?
CHIRP...
Ha ha ha!
MAYBE WE SHOULDN'T LET THE CHILDREN OUT TODAY.
WELL, IT SEEMS THAT ONLY TWILIGHTS ARE BEING TARGETED. SO IT SHOULD BE FINE...
TMP TMP
WAIT UP, YANG!
Heh heh heh!
I GOT DIBS ON THE SWINGS TODAY!

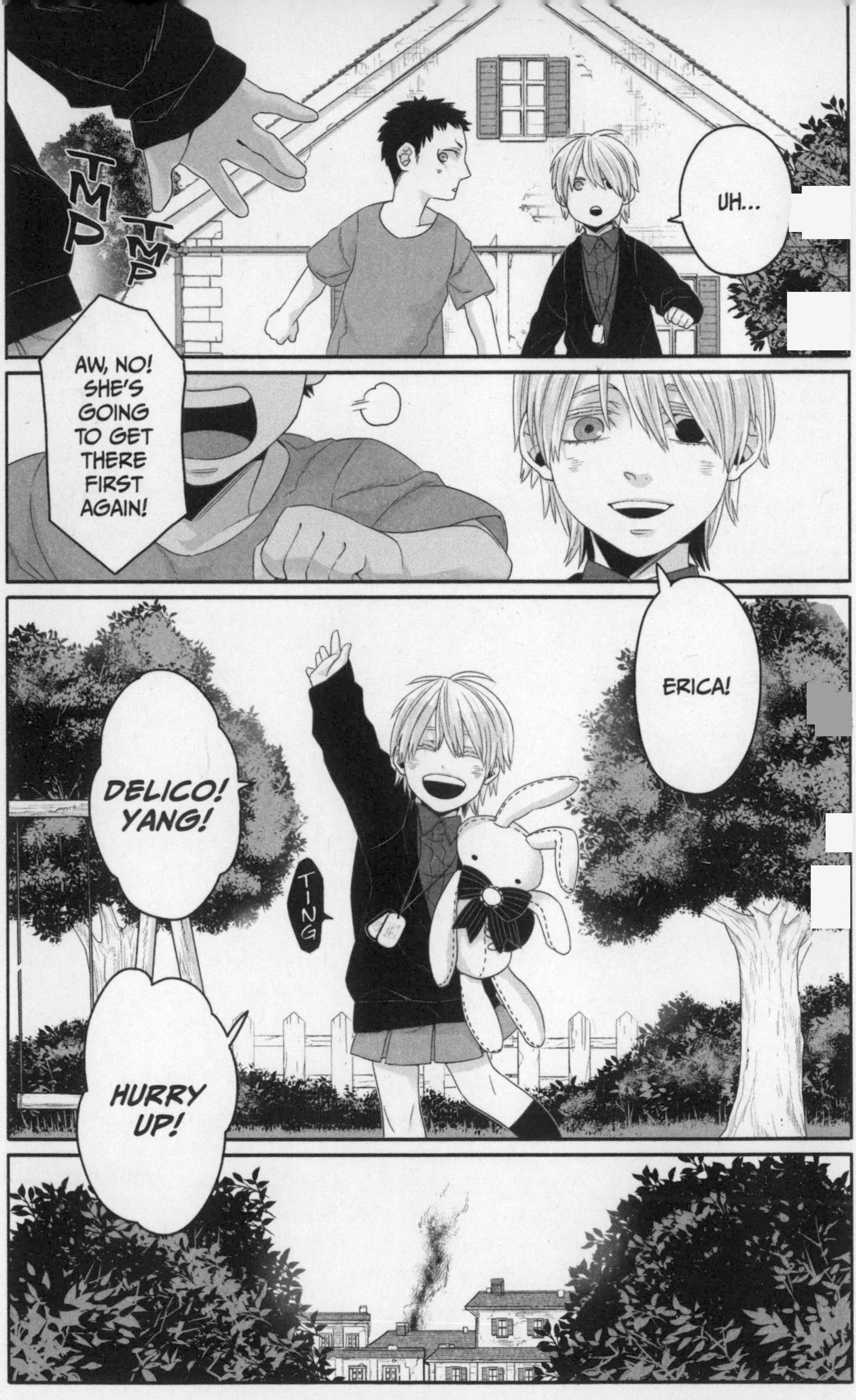
UH...
TMP
TMP
AW, NO! SHE'S GOING TO GET THERE FIRST AGAIN!
ERICA!
DELICO! YANG!
TING
HURRY UP!

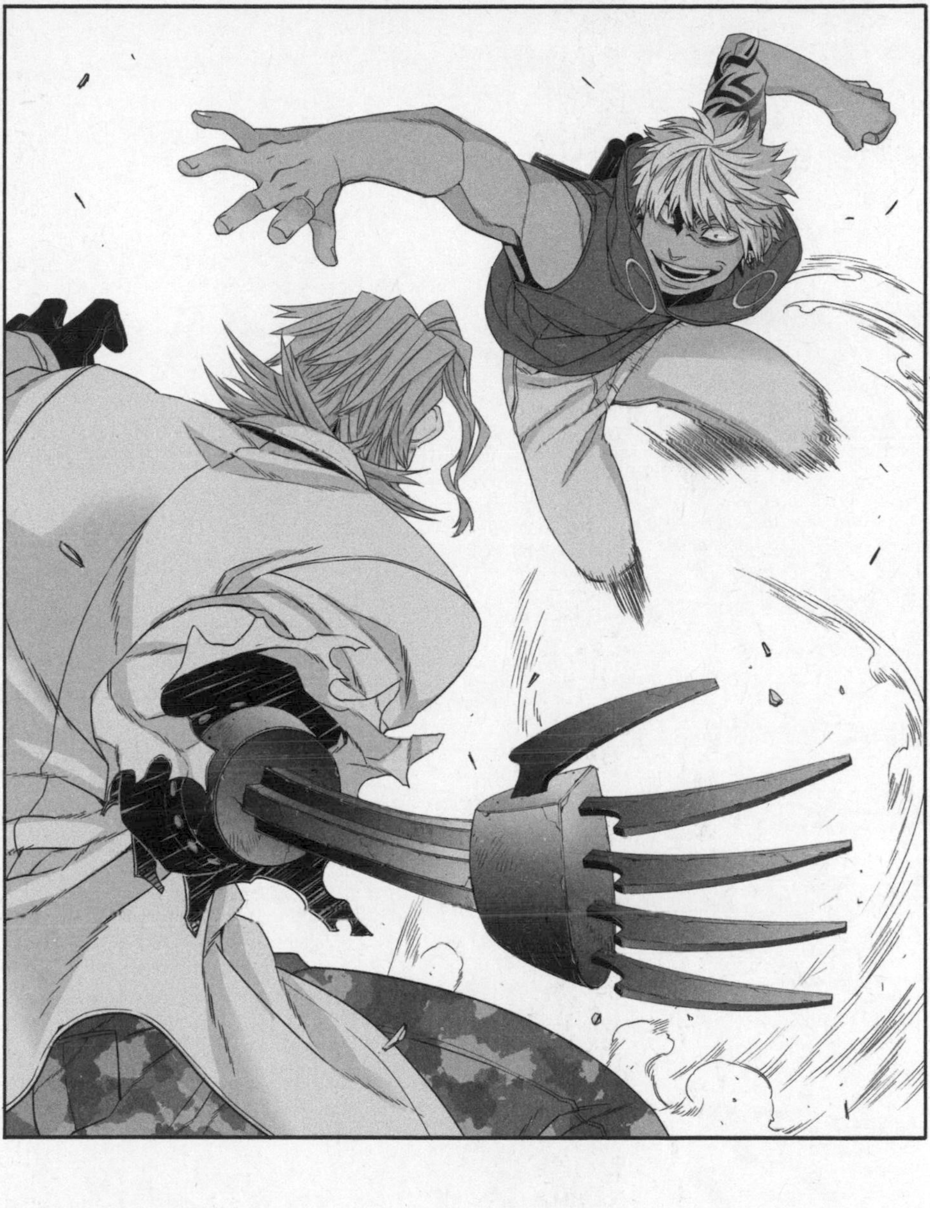

#03

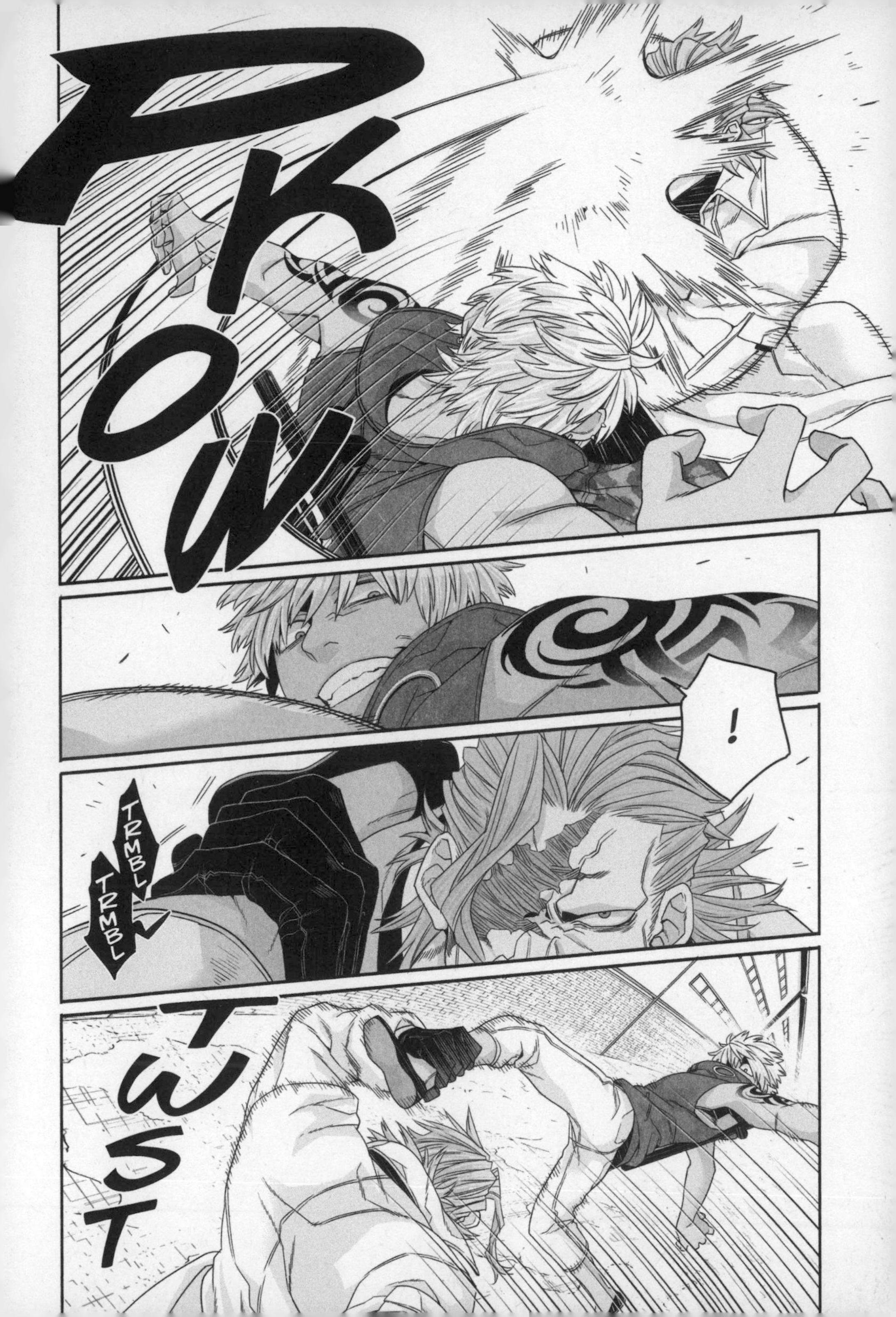
POW
!
TRMBL TRMBL
TWST

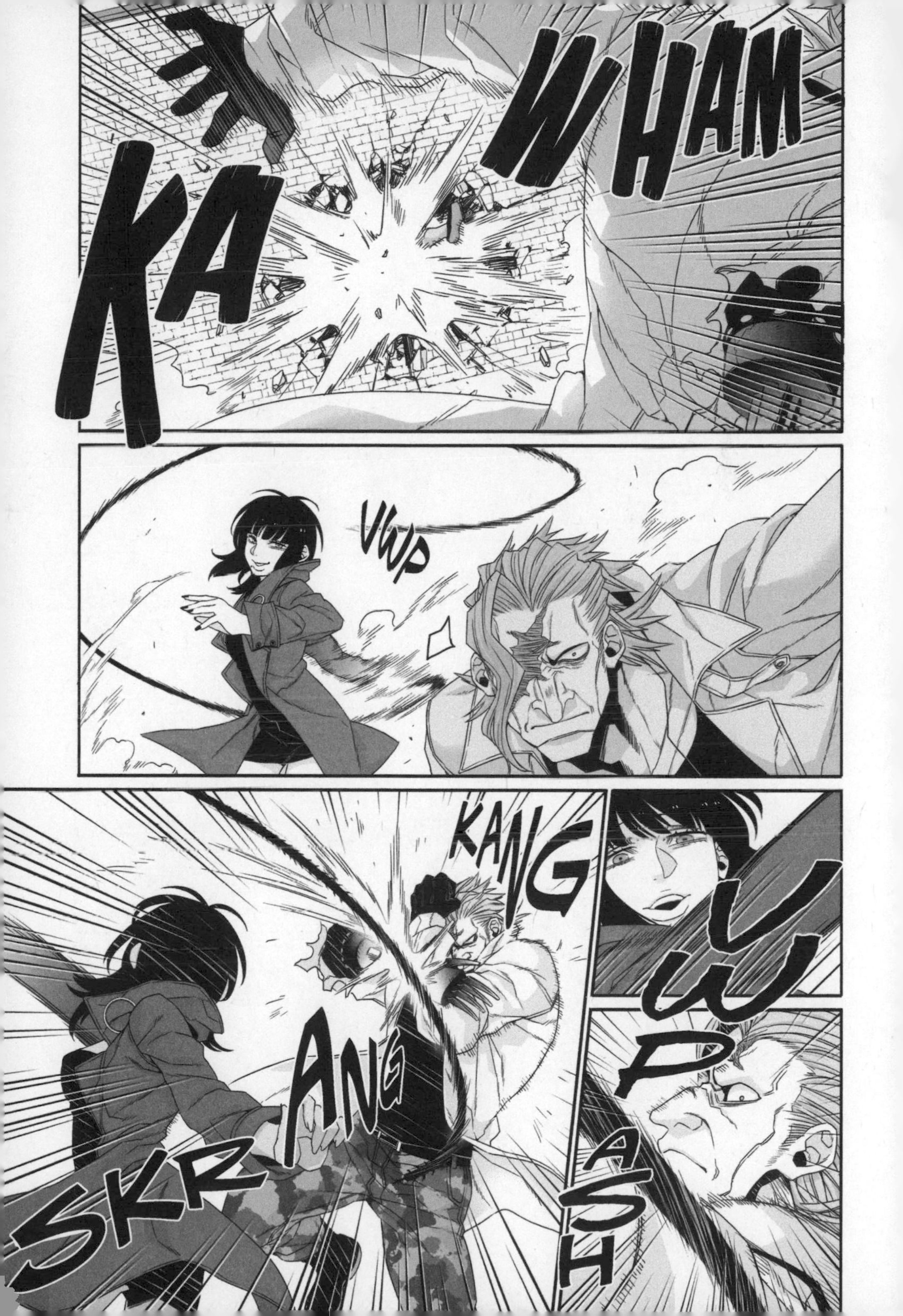
WHAM
KA
VWP
VWP
ASH
KANG
SKRANG

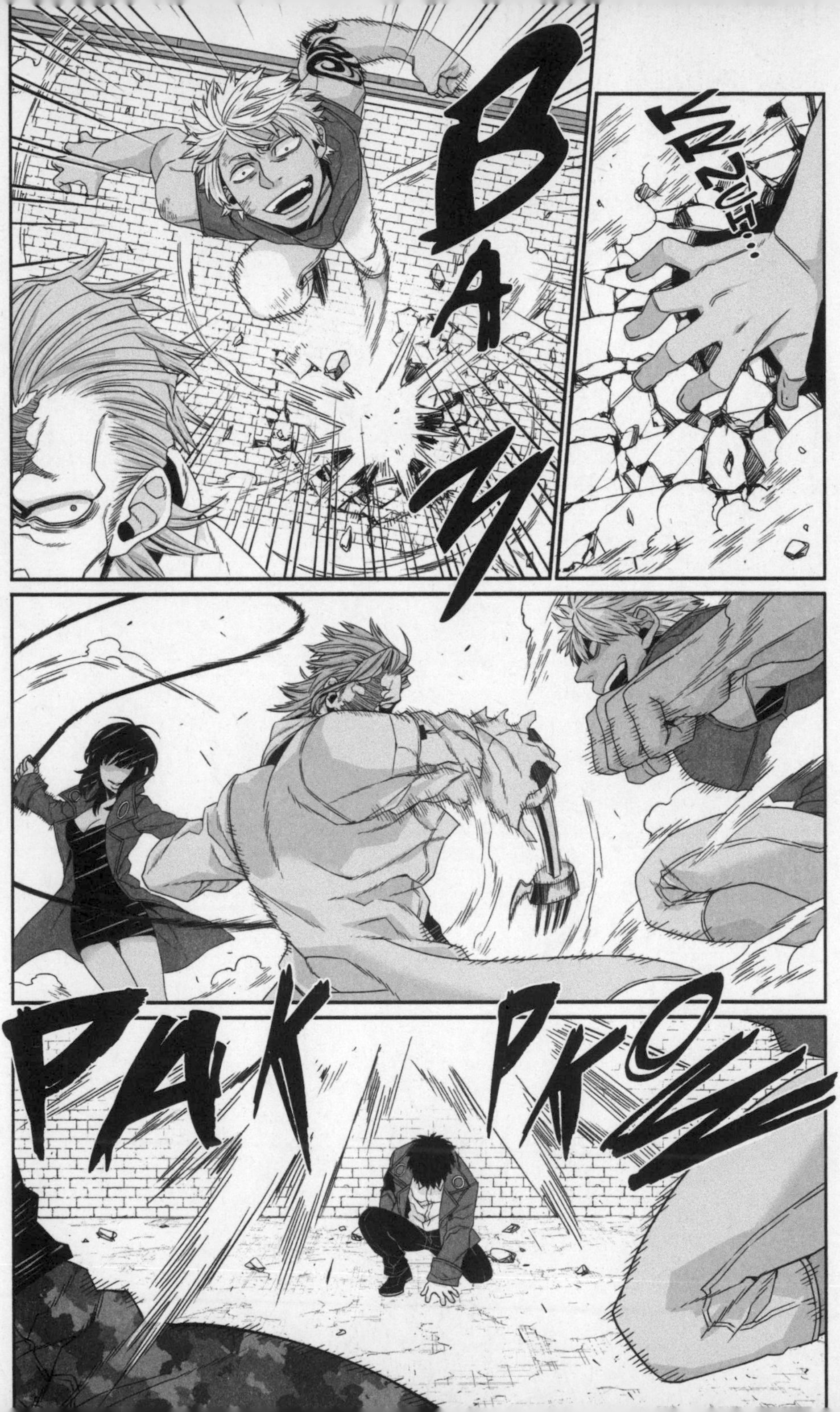
KRZUH...
BAM
PAK PKOW

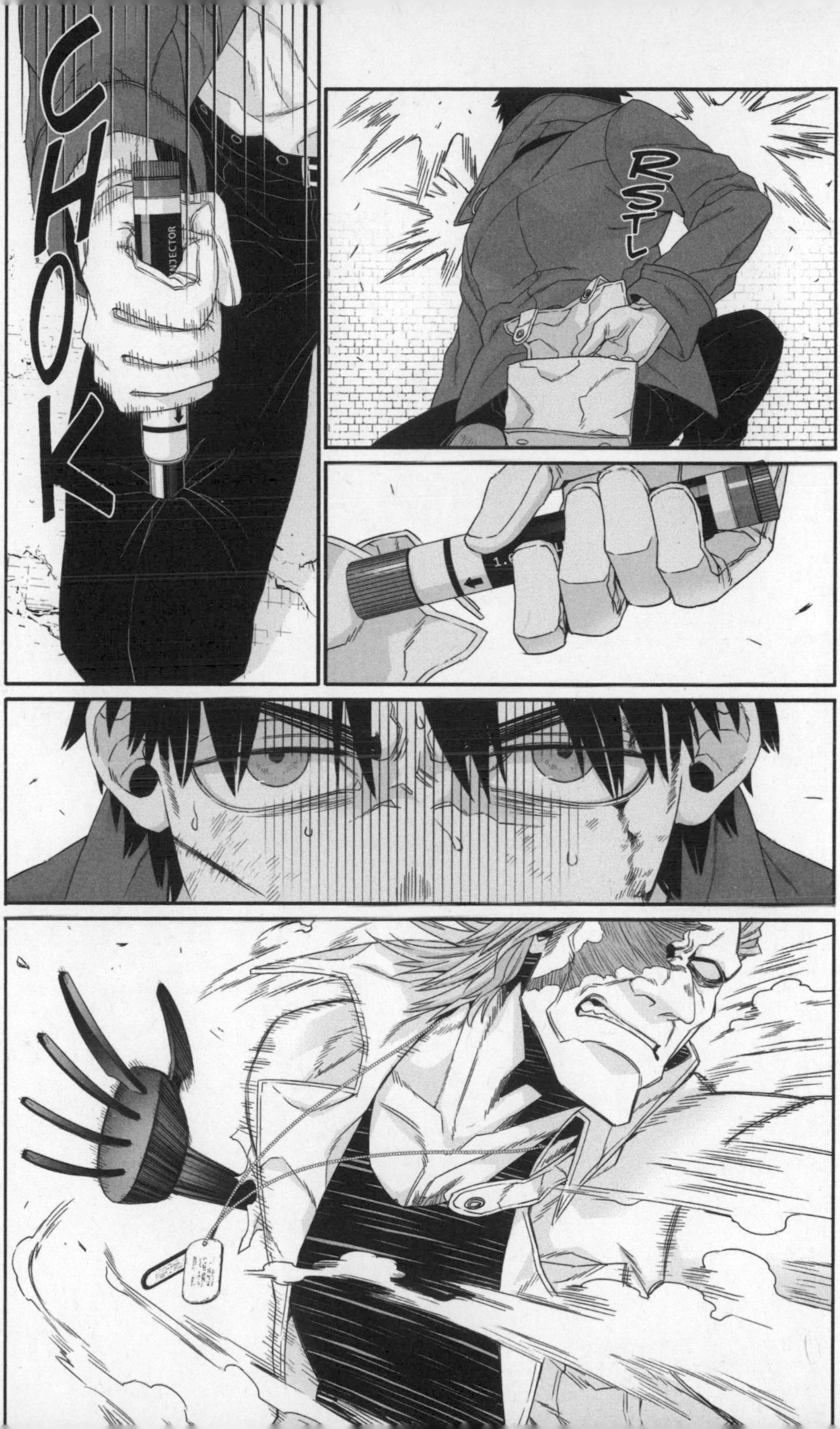
RSTL
CHOK

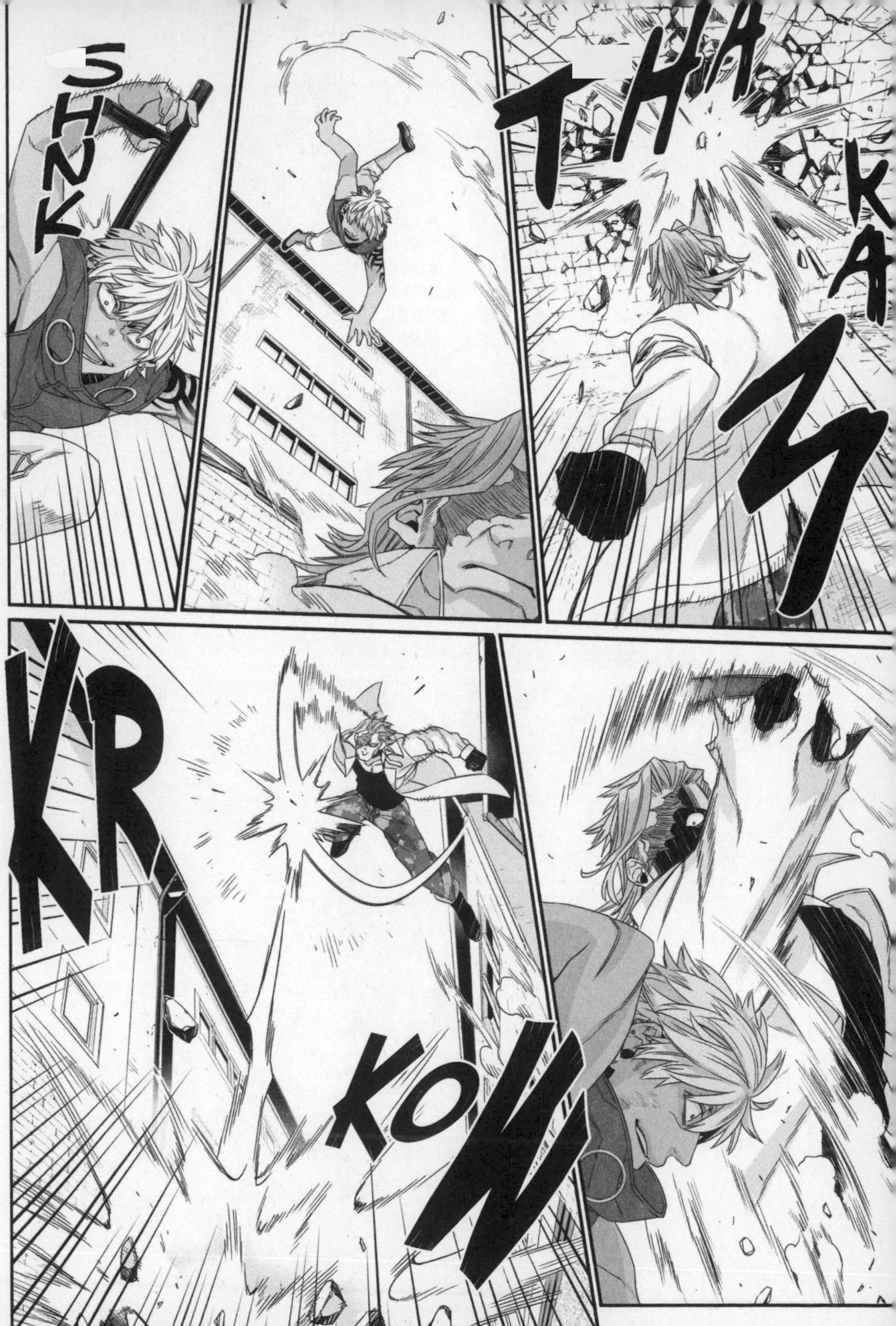
THA
KA
SHNK
KR
KO

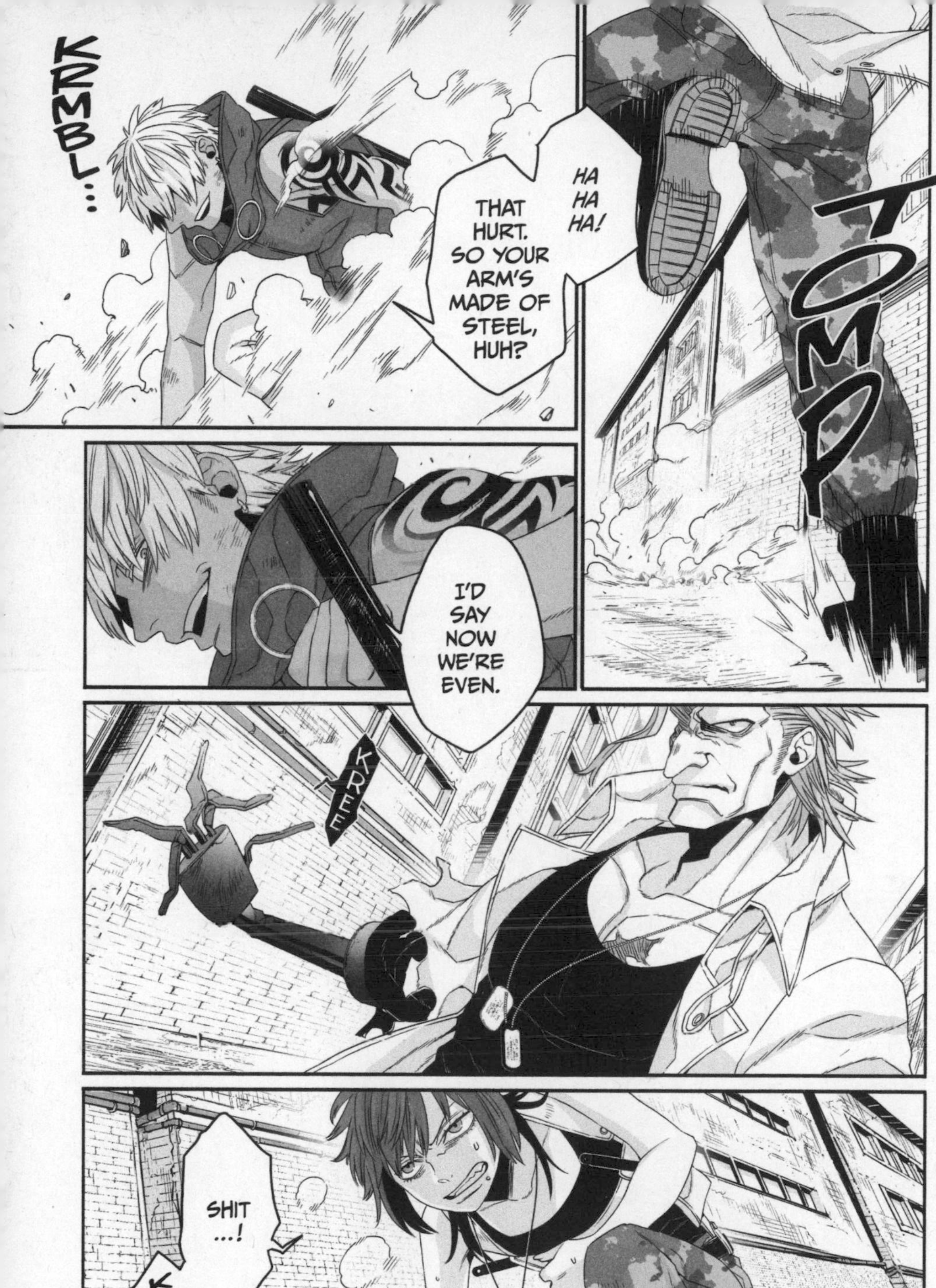
TOMP
HA HA HA!
THAT HURT. SO YOUR ARM'S MADE OF STEEL, HUH?
KRMBL...
I'D SAY NOW WE'RE EVEN.
KREE
SHIT ...!
KOFF

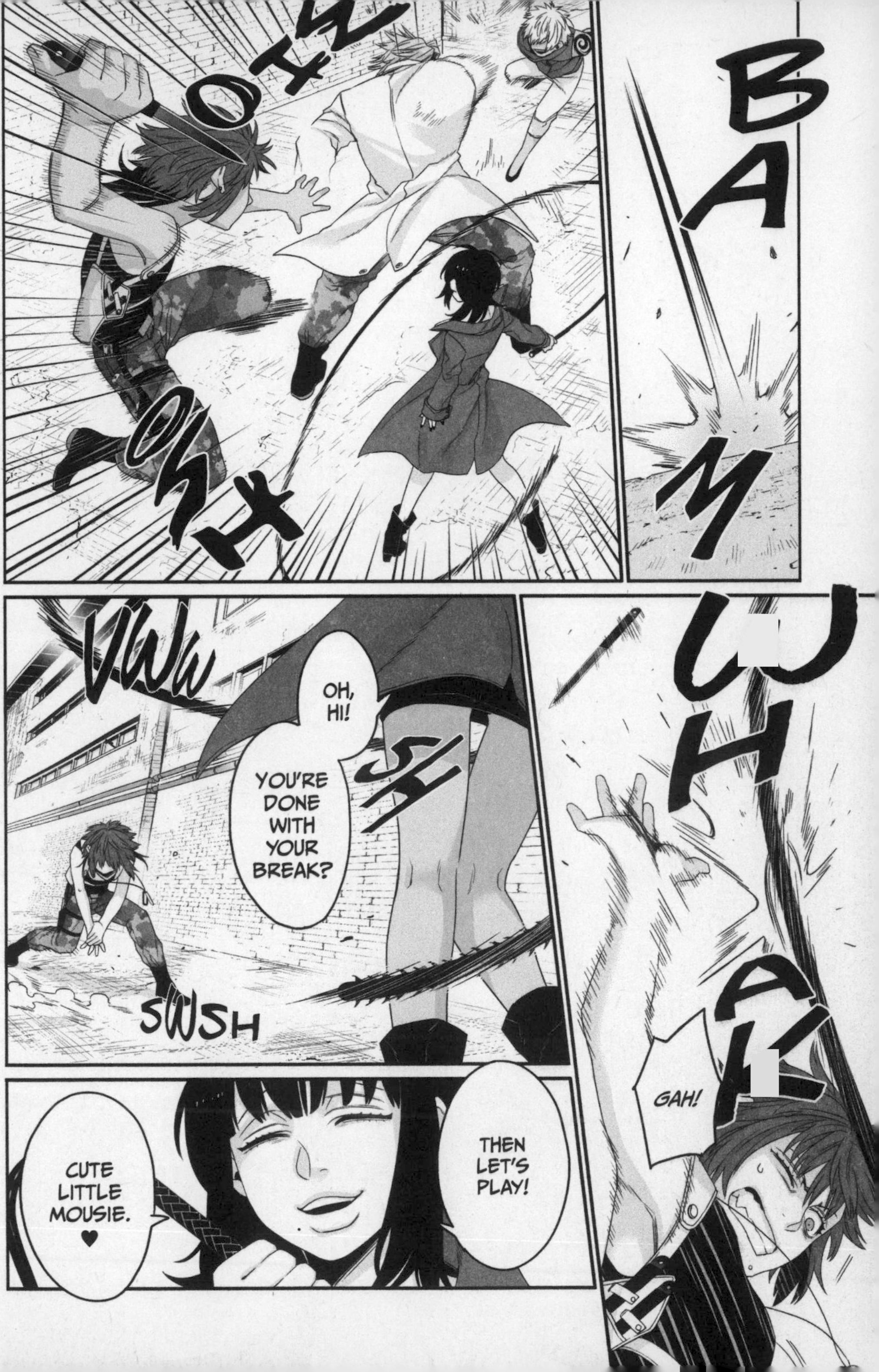
BAM
WHAK
GAH!
VWW
OH, HI!
YOU'RE DONE WITH YOUR BREAK?
SH
SWSH
THEN LET'S PLAY!
CUTE LITTLE MOUSIE. ♥

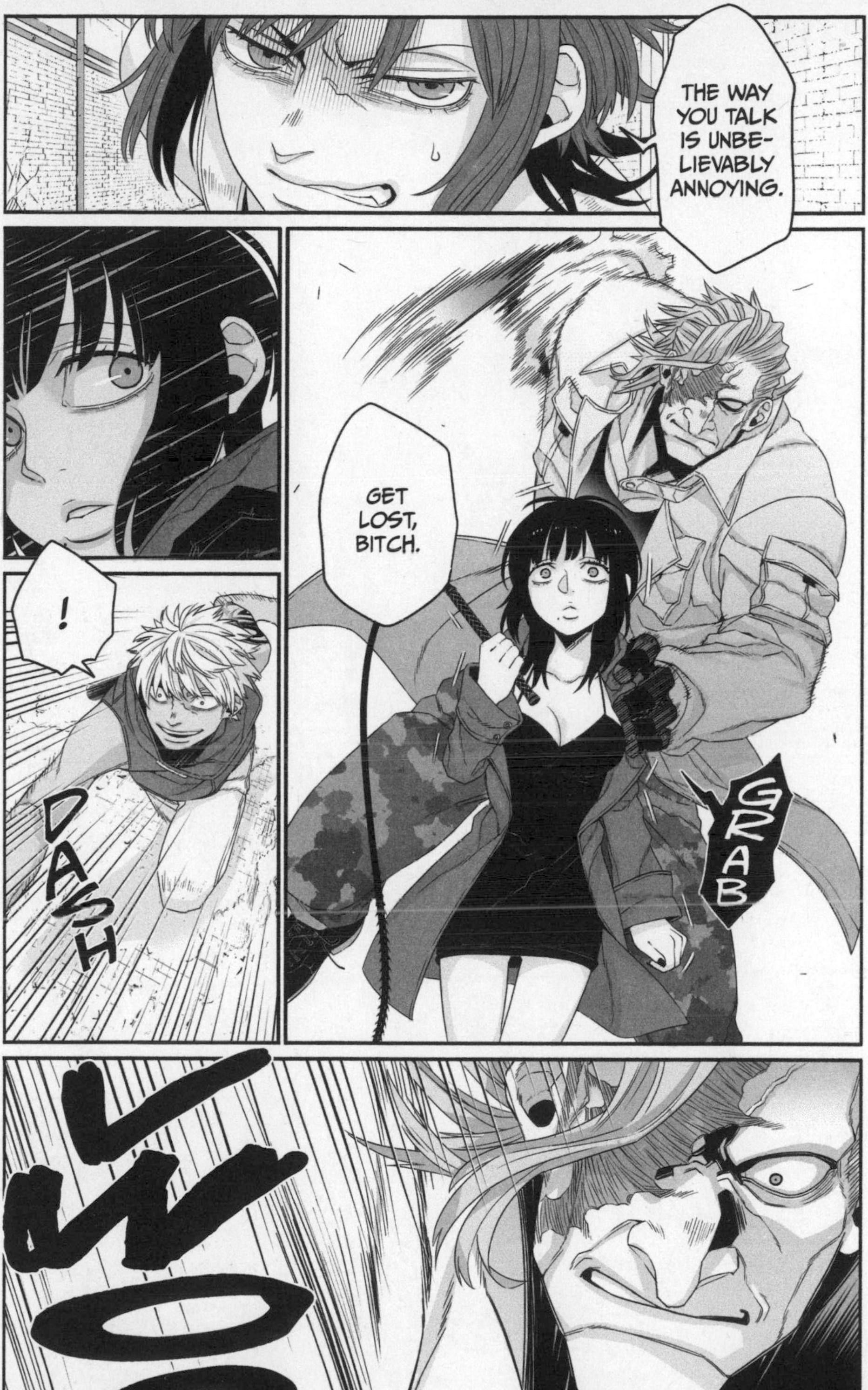
THE WAY YOU TALK IS UNBE-LIEVABLY ANNOYING.
GET LOST, BITCH.
GRAB
!
DASH

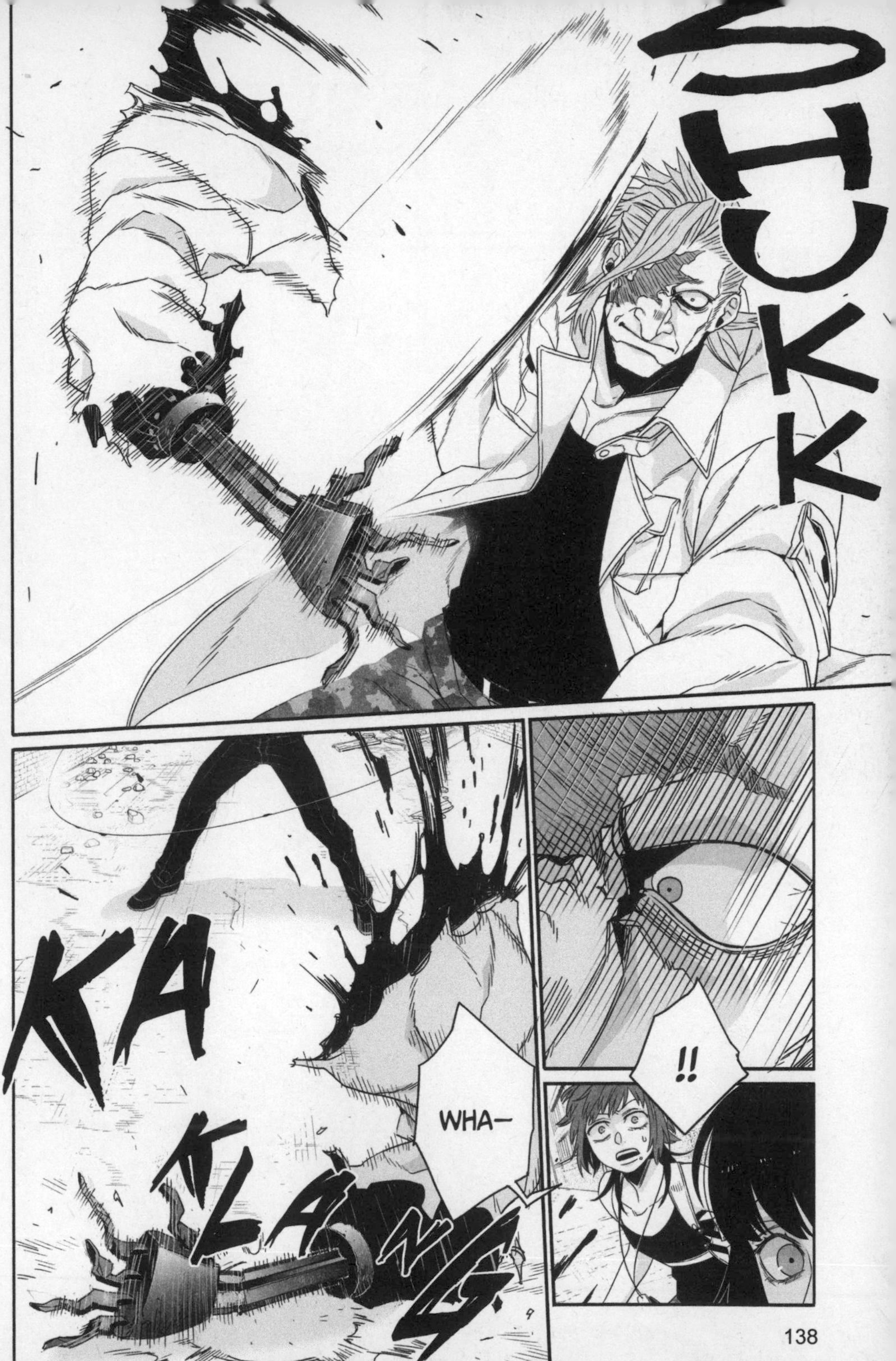
CHUKK
!!
WHA-
KA KLANG

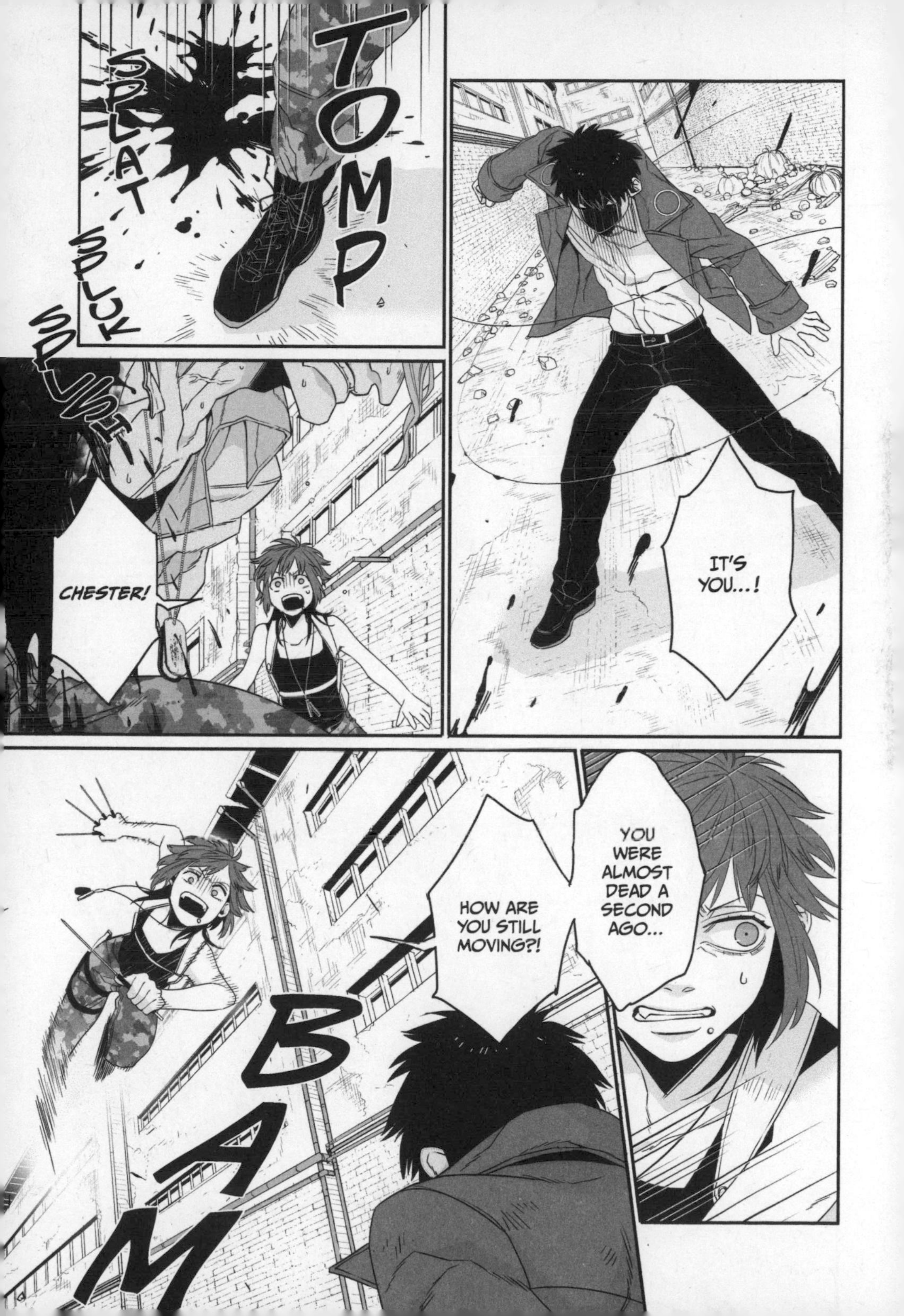
IT'S YOU...!
TOMP
SPLAT
SPLUK
SPLUSH
CHESTER!
YOU WERE ALMOST DEAD A SECOND AGO...
HOW ARE YOU STILL MOVING?!
BAM

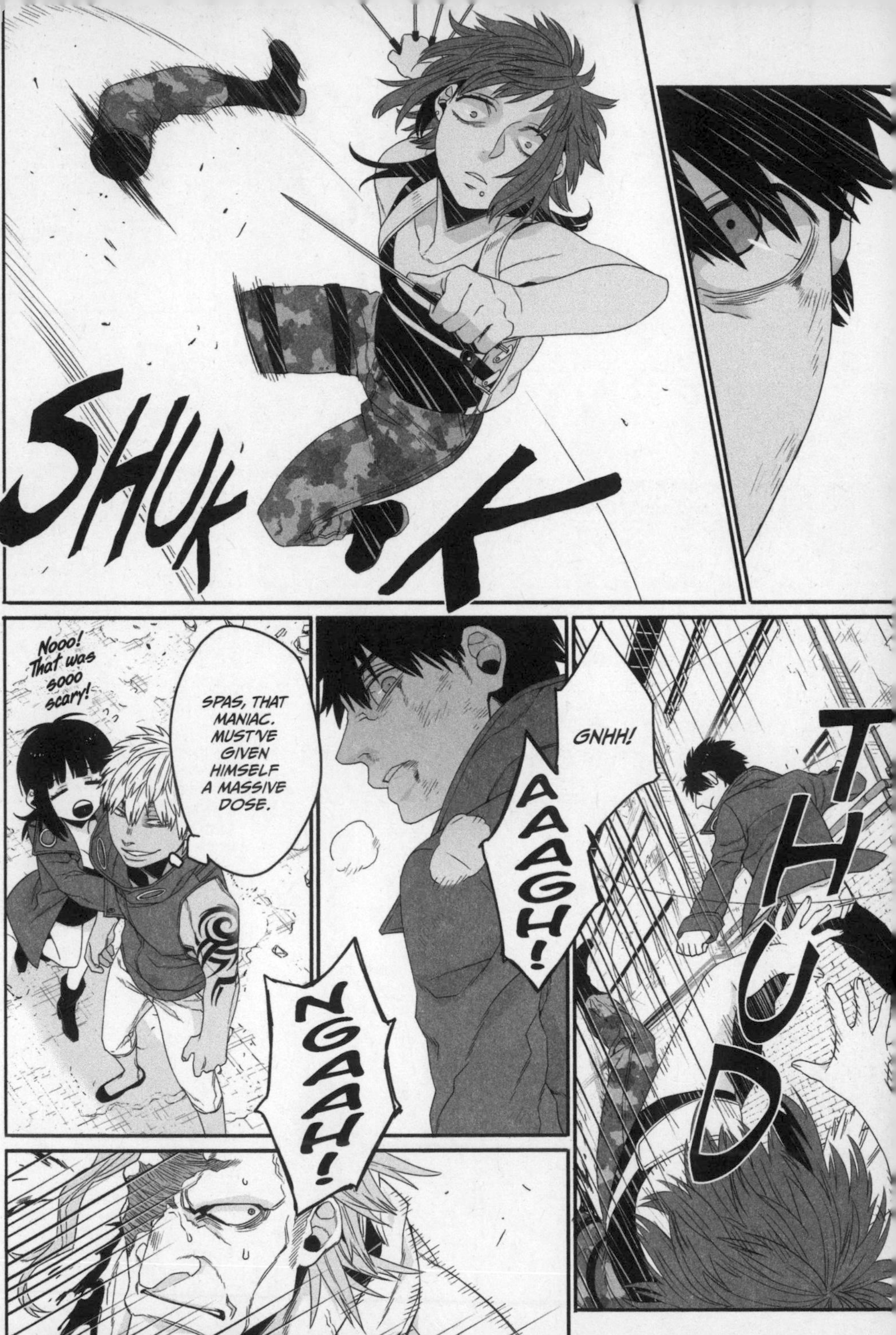
SHUK K
GNHH!
AAAGH!
THUD
SPAS, THAT MANIAC. MUST'VE GIVEN HIMSELF A MASSIVE DOSE.
Nooo! That was sooo scary!
NGAAH!

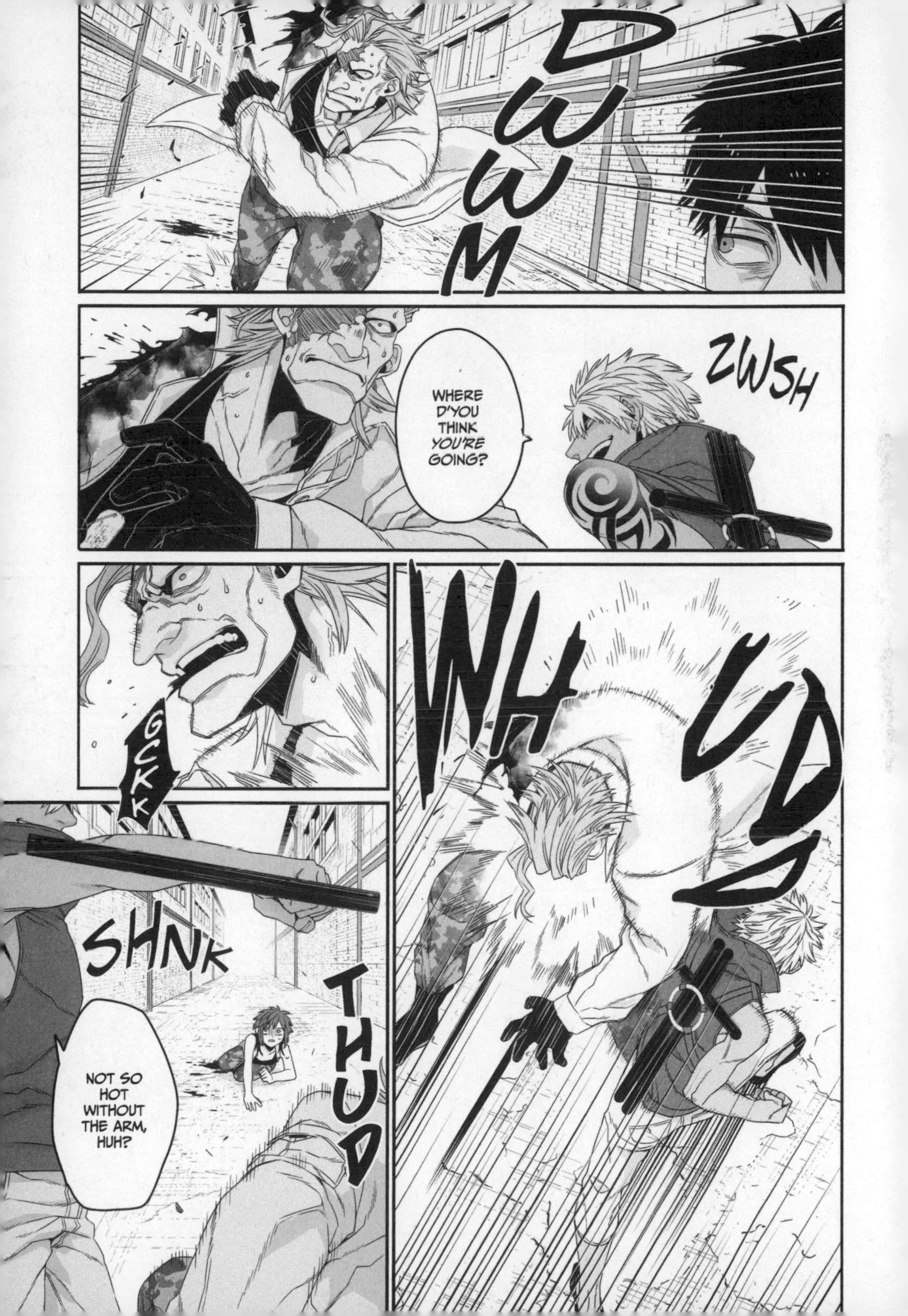
DWWM
ZWSH
WHERE D'YOU THINK *YOU'RE* GOING?
WHUD
GCKK
SHNK
THUD
NOT SO HOT WITHOUT THE ARM, HUH?

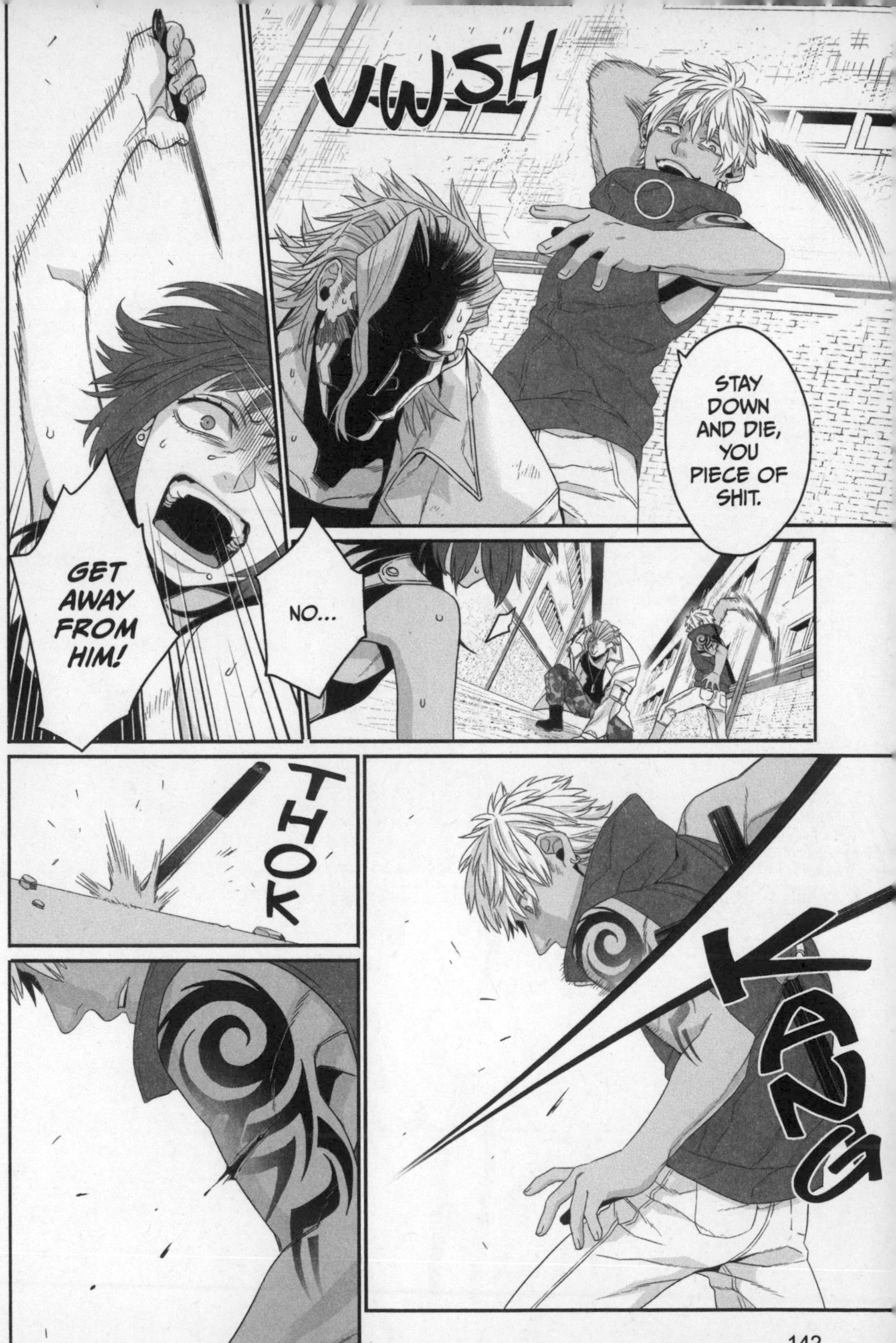
VWSH
STAY DOWN AND DIE, YOU PIECE OF SHIT.
NO...
GET AWAY FROM HIM!
KANG
THOK

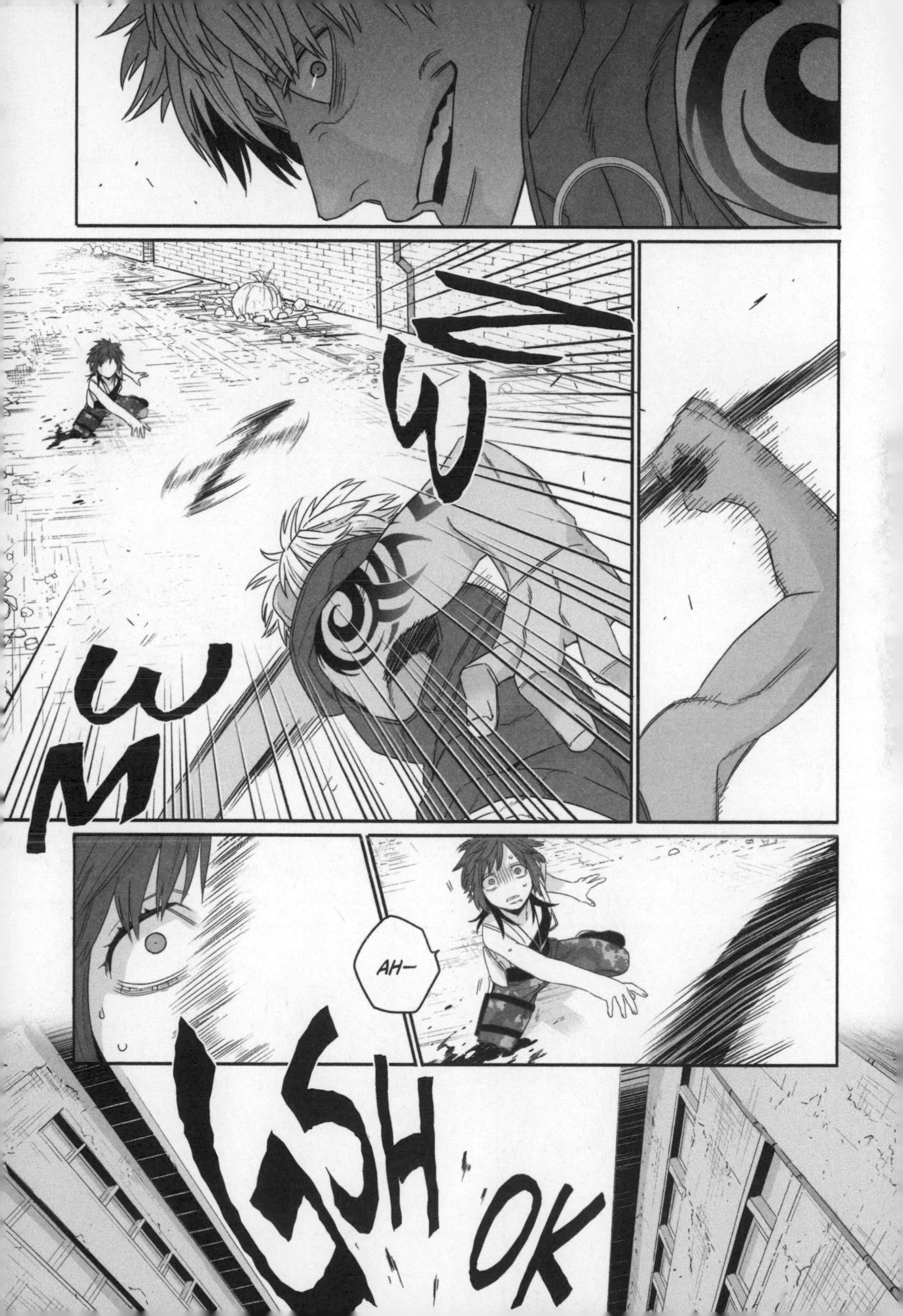
AH—

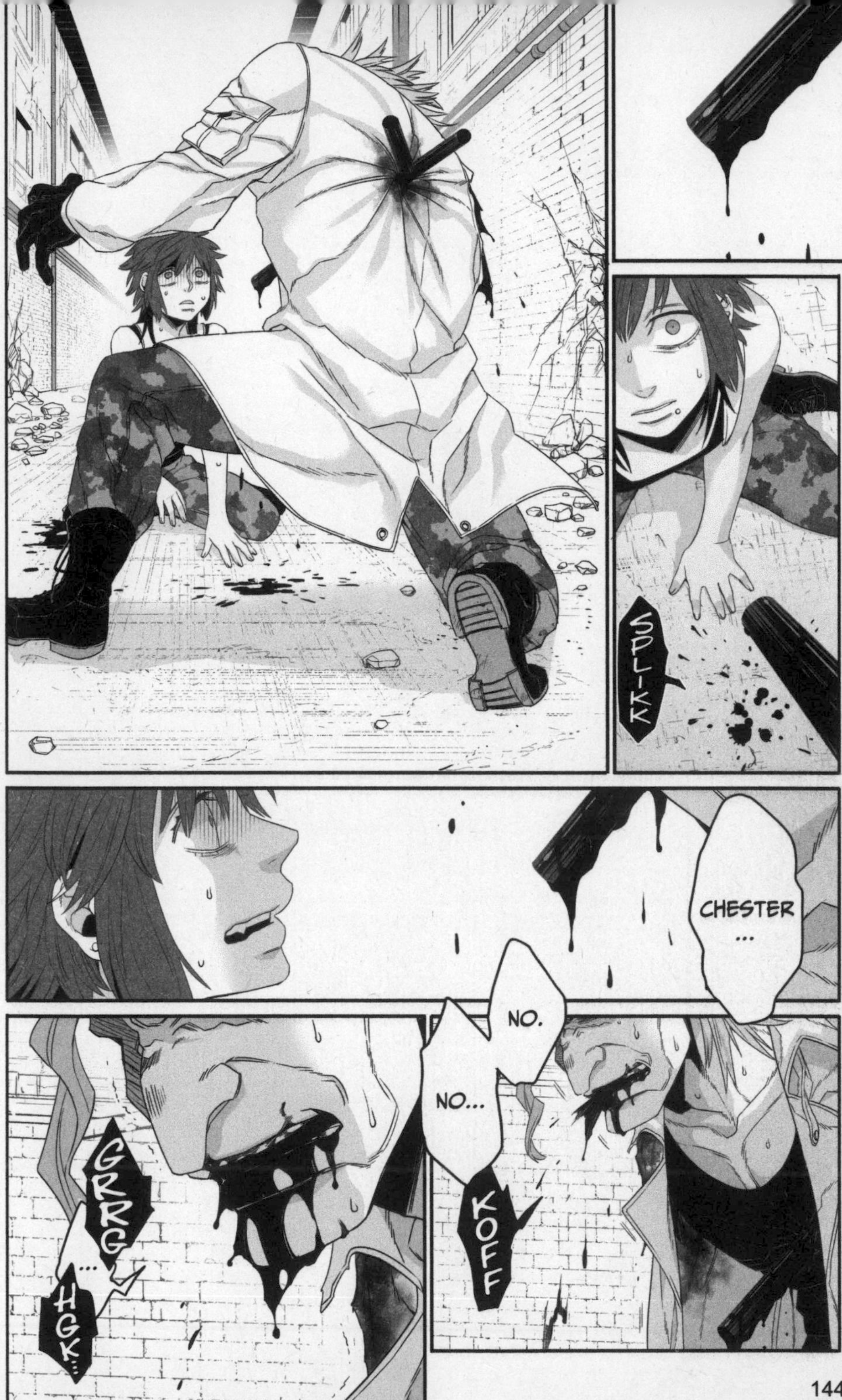
SPLIKK
CHESTER...
NO.
NO...
KOFF
GRRG...
HGK...

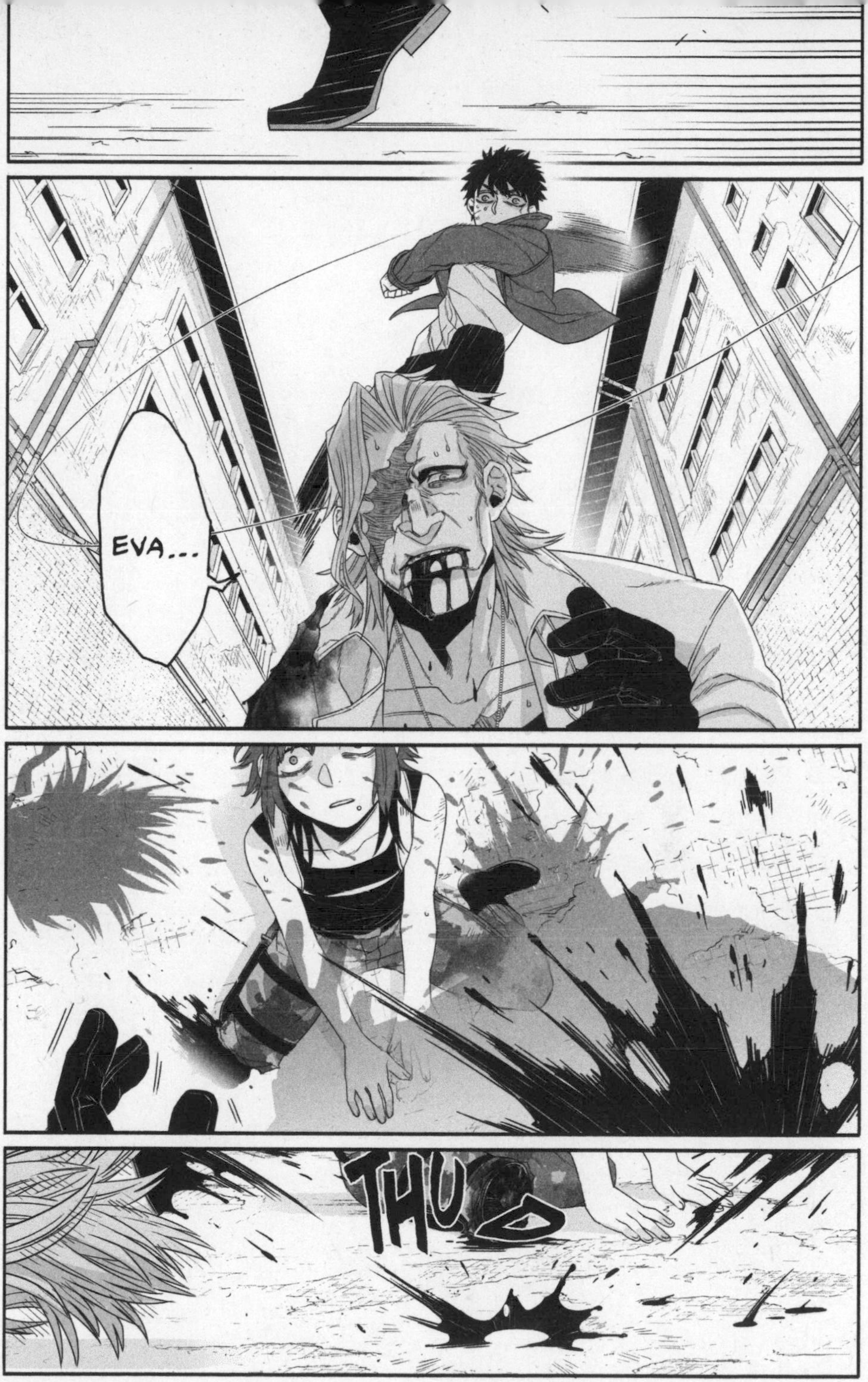
EVA...
THUD

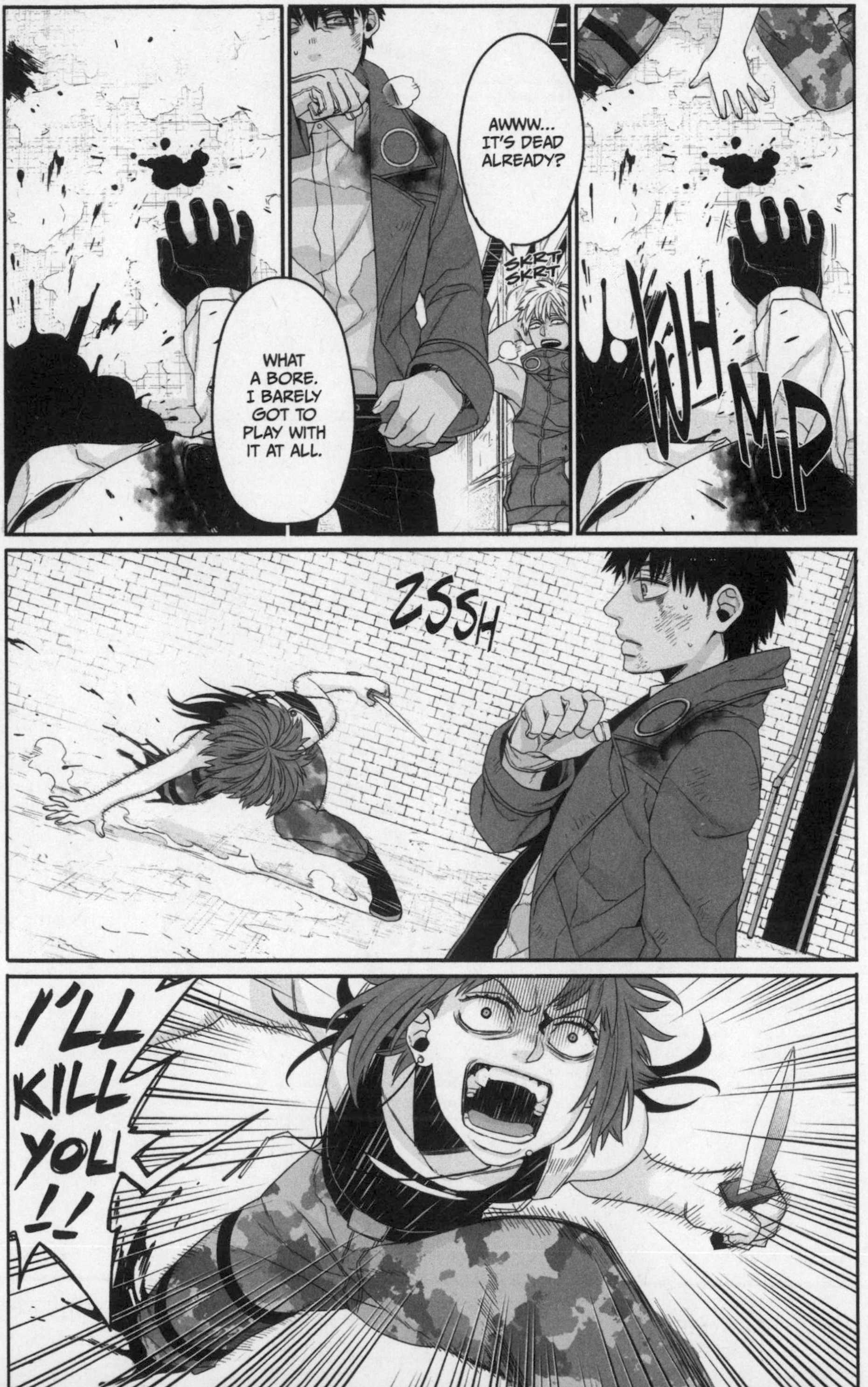
WHUMP
AWWW... IT'S DEAD ALREADY?
SKRT SKRT
WHAT A BORE. I BARELY GOT TO PLAY WITH IT AT ALL.
ZSSH
I'LL KILL YOU!!

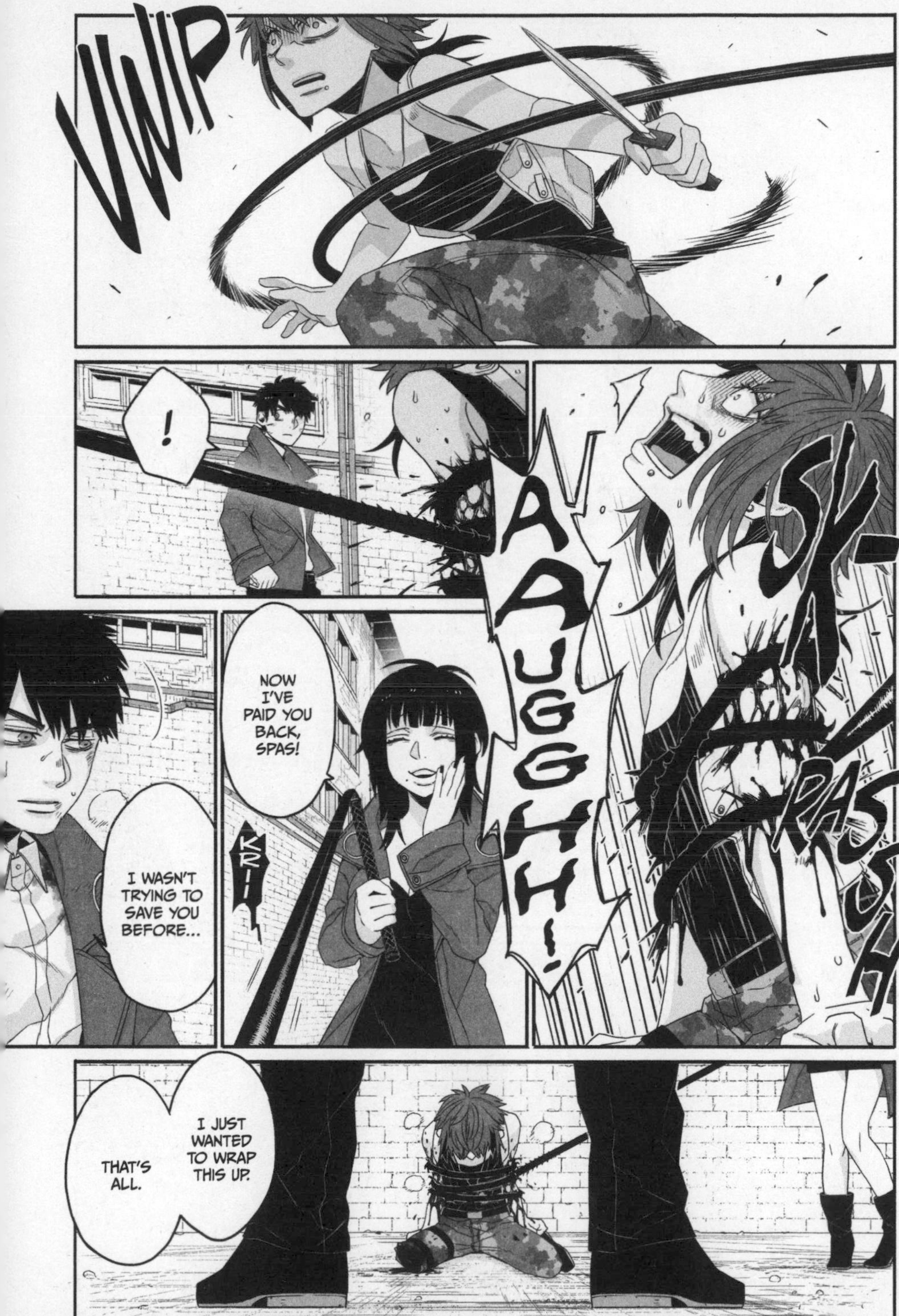

VWIP
AAUGGHH!
SK-
PASSH
!
NOW I'VE PAID YOU BACK, SPAS!
KRI
I WASN'T TRYING TO SAVE YOU BEFORE...
I JUST WANTED TO WRAP THIS UP.
THAT'S ALL.

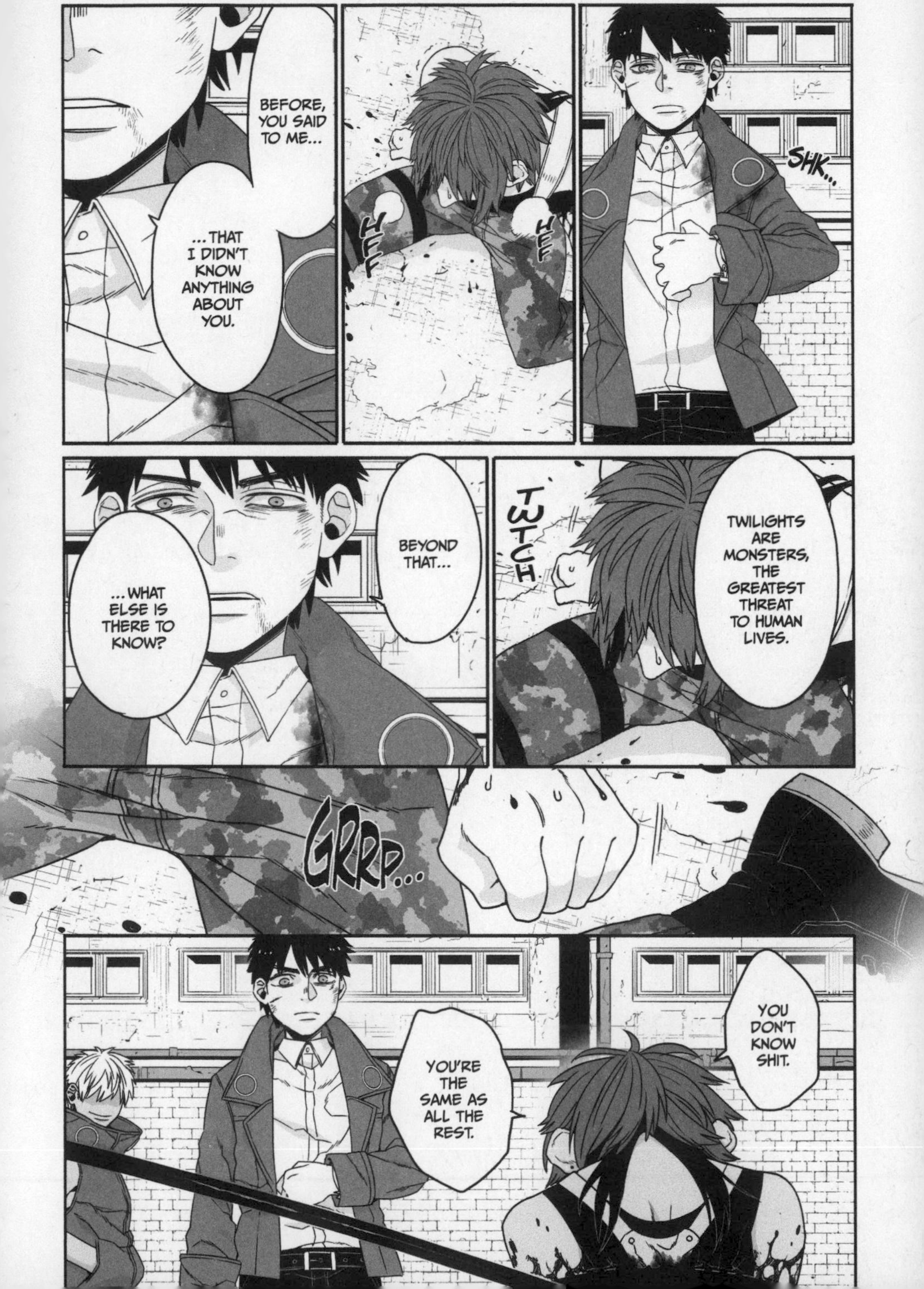
SHK...
HEFF
HEFF
BEFORE, YOU SAID TO ME...
...THAT I DIDN'T KNOW ANYTHING ABOUT YOU.
TWILIGHTS ARE MONSTERS, THE GREATEST THREAT TO HUMAN LIVES.
TWTCH
BEYOND THAT...
...WHAT ELSE IS THERE TO KNOW?
GRRP...
YOU DON'T KNOW SHIT.
YOU'RE THE SAME AS ALL THE REST.

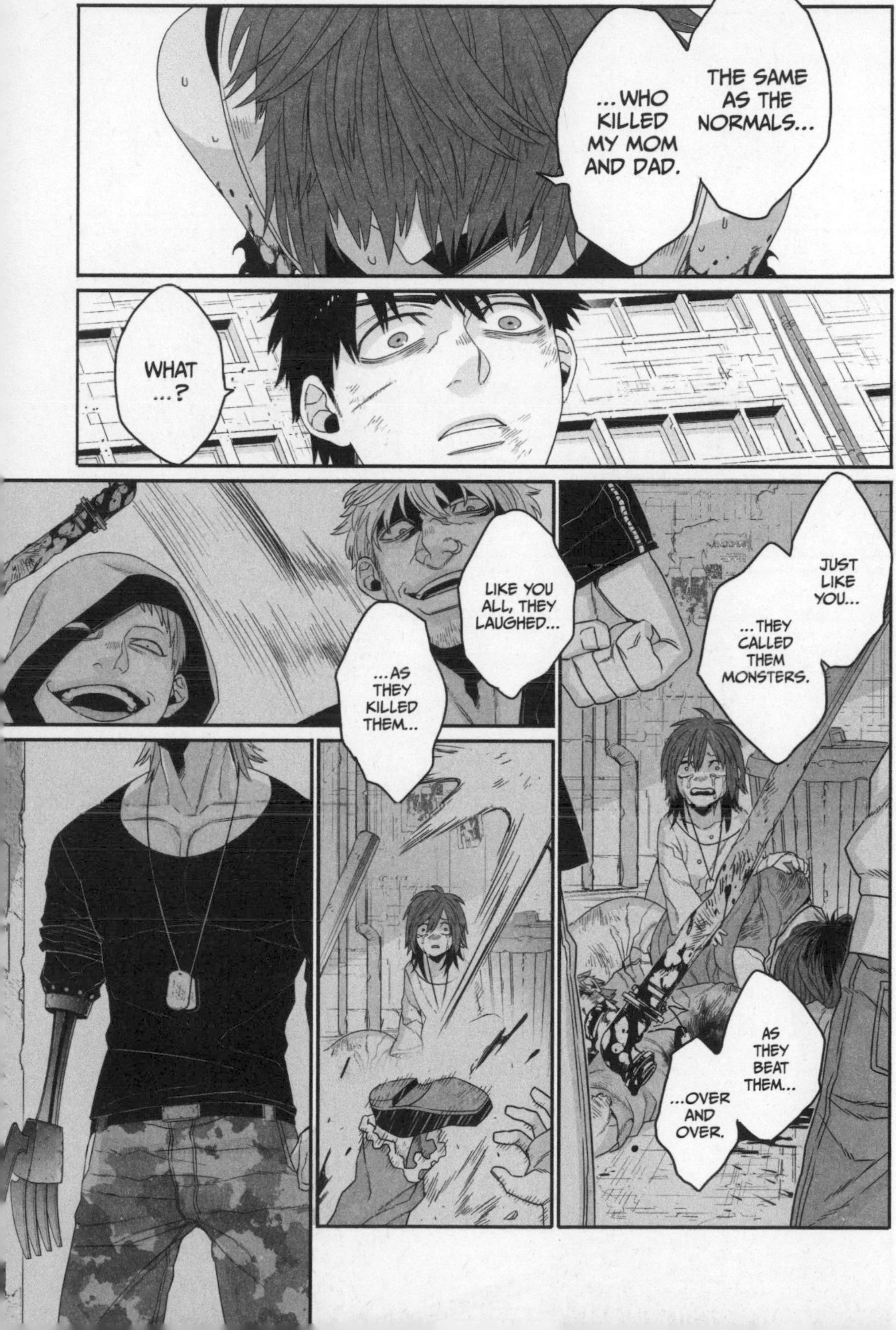
THE SAME AS THE NORMALS...
...WHO KILLED MY MOM AND DAD.
WHAT ...?
JUST LIKE YOU...
...THEY CALLED THEM MONSTERS.
LIKE YOU ALL, THEY LAUGHED...
...AS THEY KILLED THEM...
AS THEY BEAT THEM...
...OVER AND OVER.

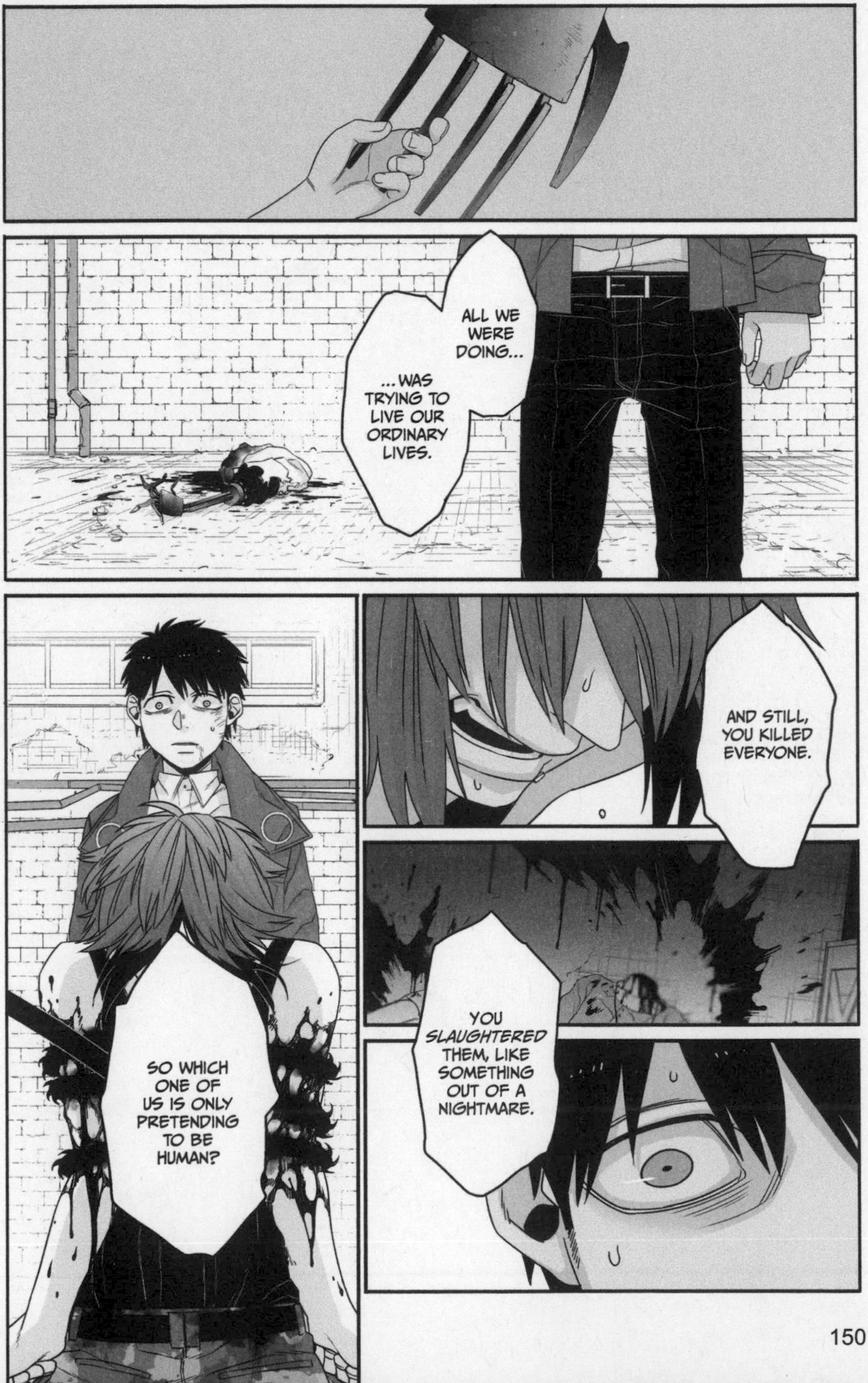
ALL WE WERE DOING...
...WAS TRYING TO LIVE OUR ORDINARY LIVES.
AND STILL, YOU KILLED EVERYONE.
YOU SLAUGHTERED THEM, LIKE SOMETHING OUT OF A NIGHTMARE.
SO WHICH ONE OF US IS ONLY PRETENDING TO BE HUMAN?

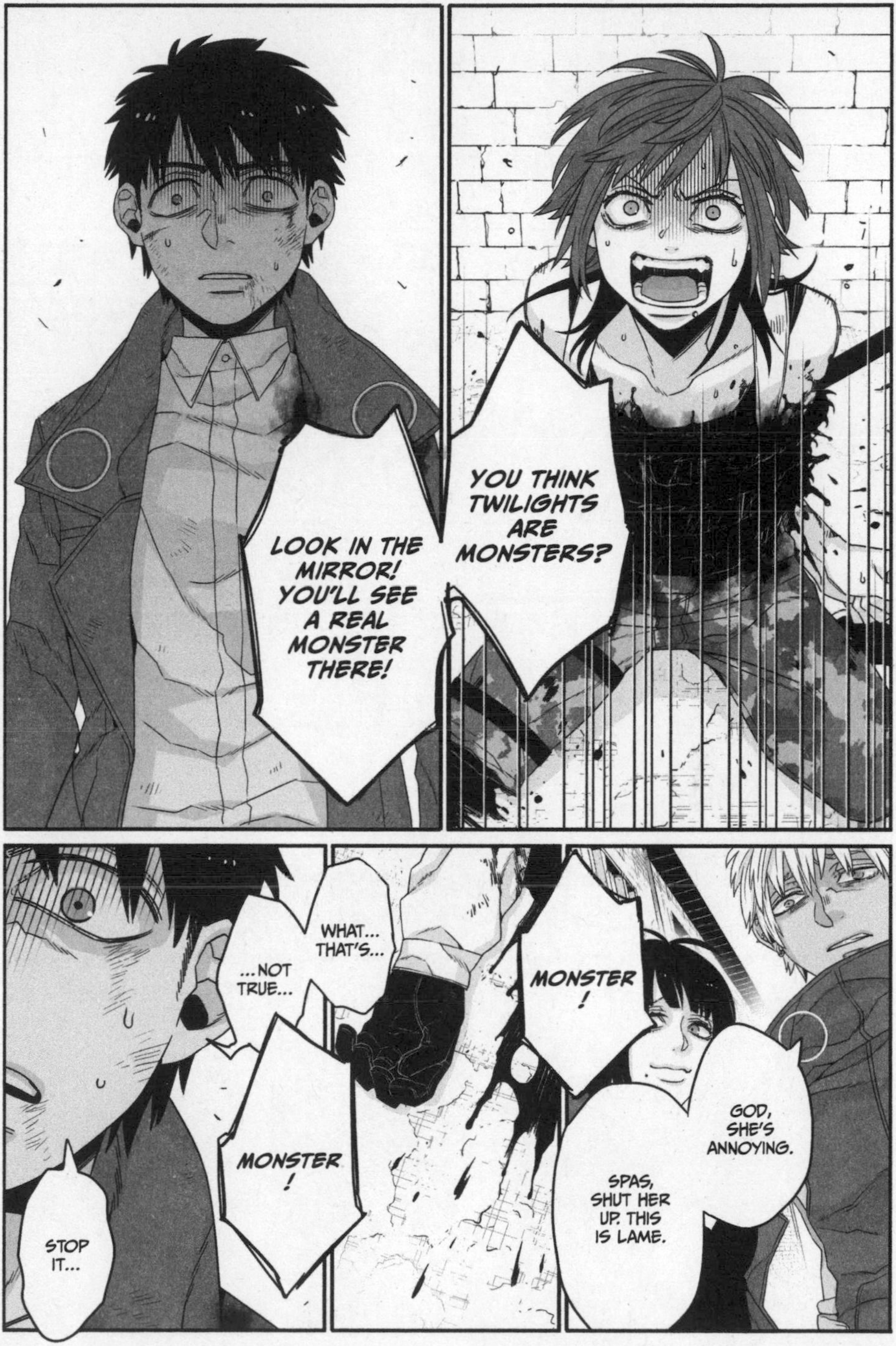
YOU THINK TWILIGHTS ARE MONSTERS?
LOOK IN THE MIRROR! YOU'LL SEE A REAL MONSTER THERE!
MONSTER!
GOD, SHE'S ANNOYING.
SPAS, SHUT HER UP. THIS IS LAME.
WHAT... THAT'S...
MONSTER!
...NOT TRUE...
STOP IT...

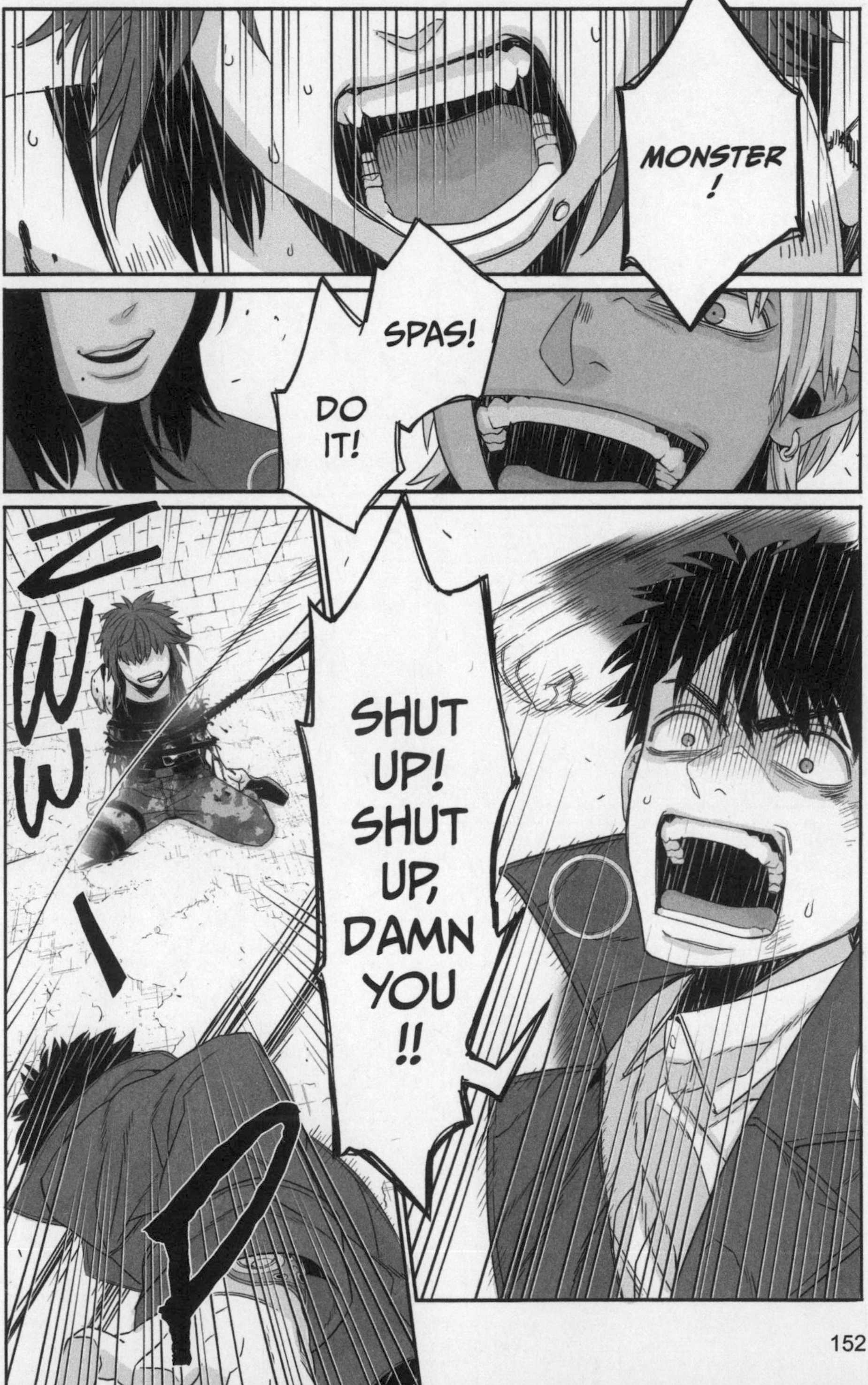
MONSTER!
SPAS!
DO IT!
SHUT UP! SHUT UP, SHUT UP, DAMN YOU!!

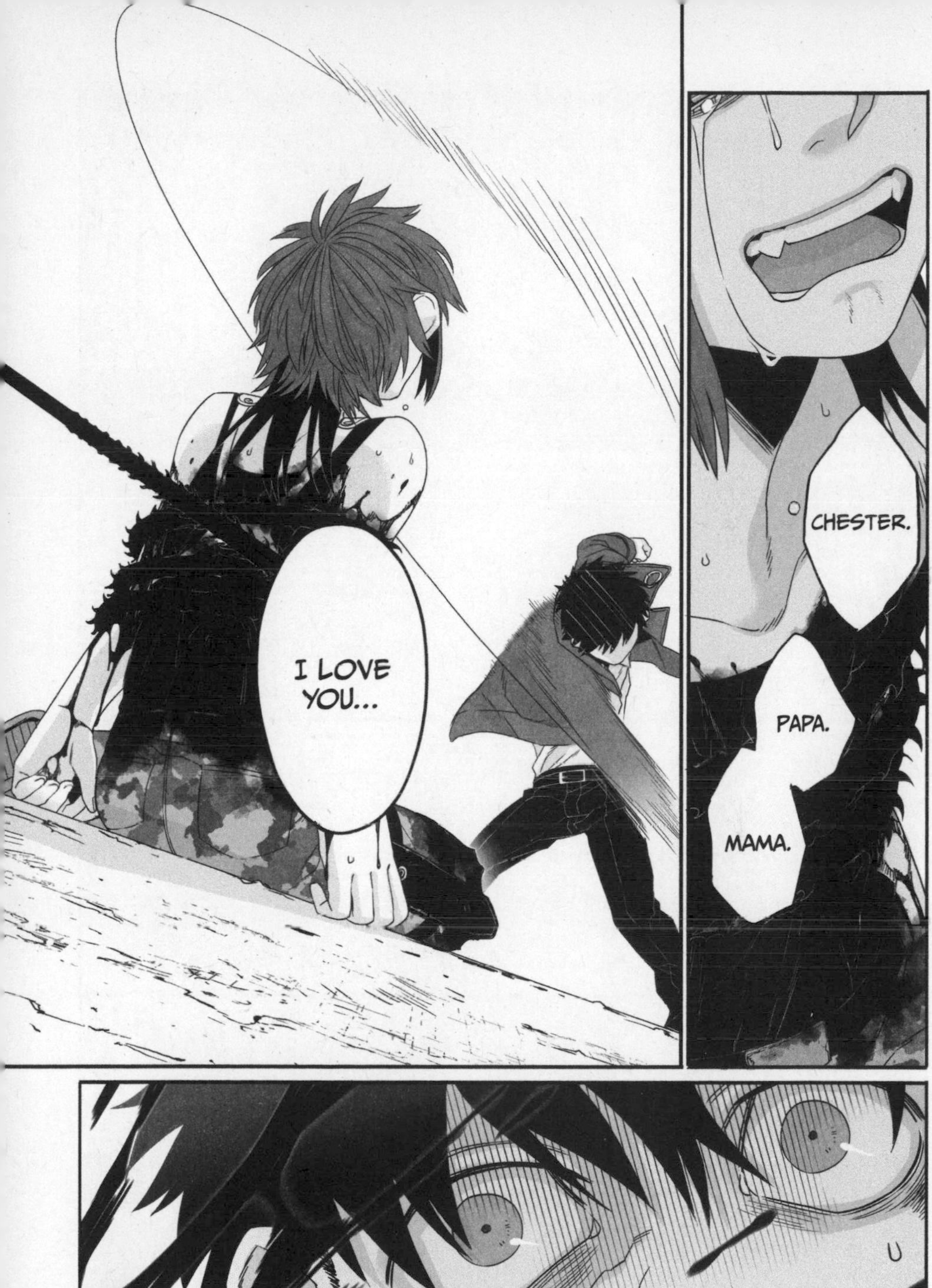
CHESTER.
PAPA.
MAMA.
I LOVE YOU...

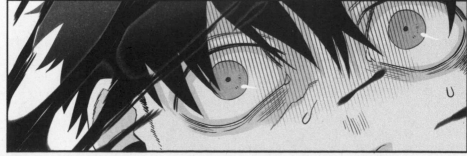

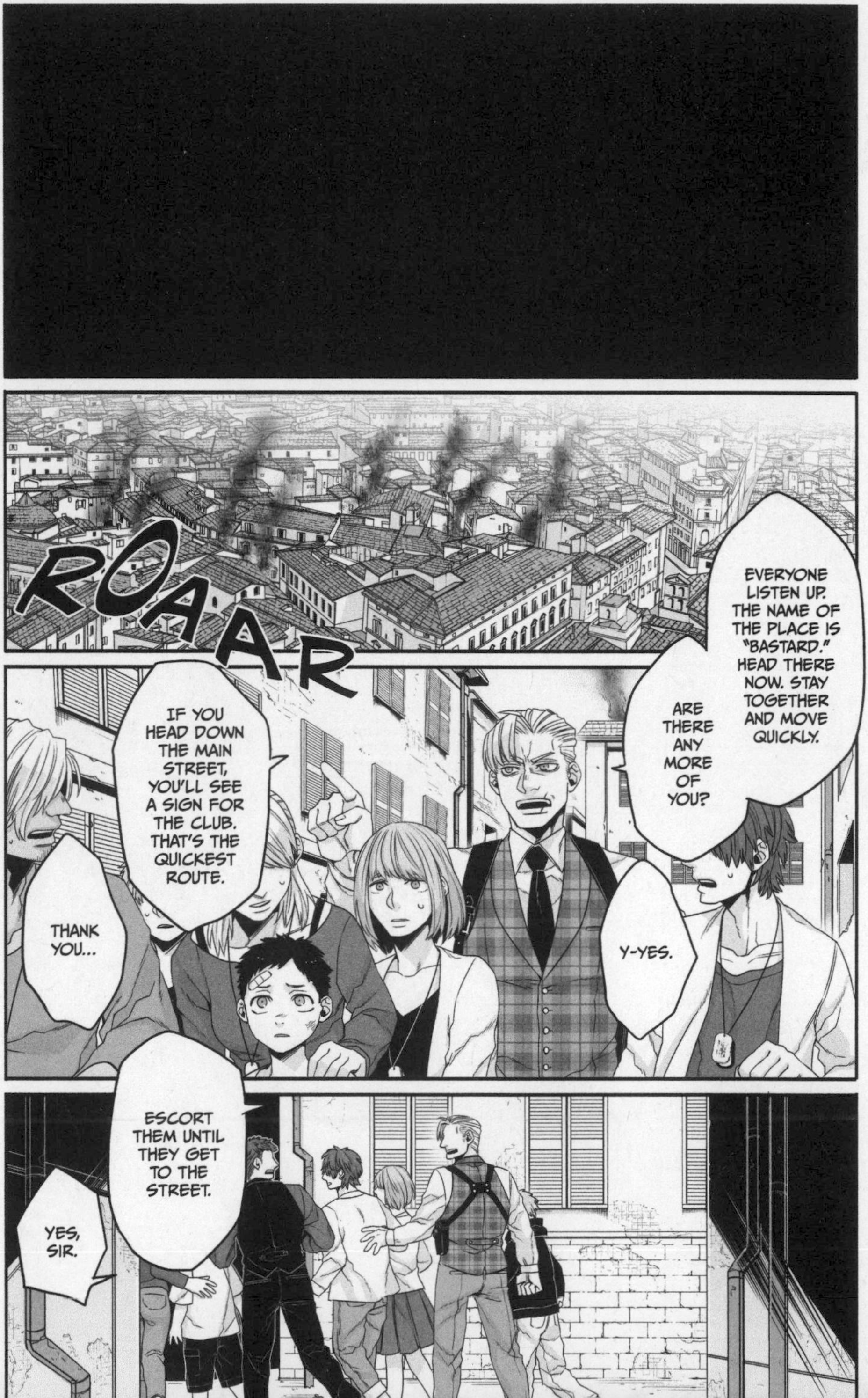
ROAAR
EVERYONE LISTEN UP. THE NAME OF THE PLACE IS "BASTARD." HEAD THERE NOW. STAY TOGETHER AND MOVE QUICKLY.
ARE THERE ANY MORE OF YOU?
IF YOU HEAD DOWN THE MAIN STREET, YOU'LL SEE A SIGN FOR THE CLUB. THAT'S THE QUICKEST ROUTE.
Y-YES.
THANK YOU...
ESCORT THEM UNTIL THEY GET TO THE STREET.
YES, SIR.

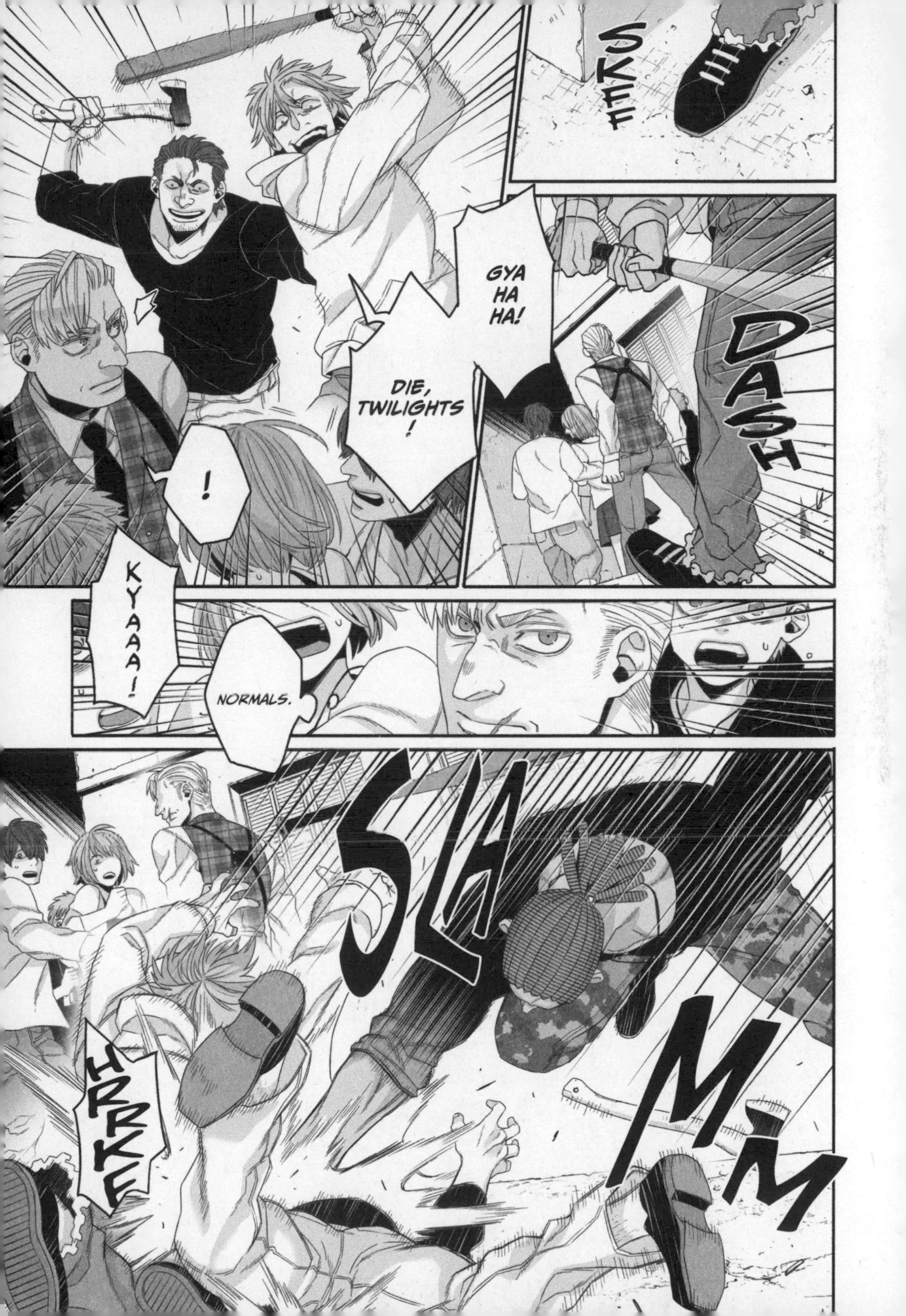
SKFF
DASH
GYA HA HA!
DIE, TWILIGHTS!
!
KYAAA!
NORMALS.
SLAMM
HRRKF

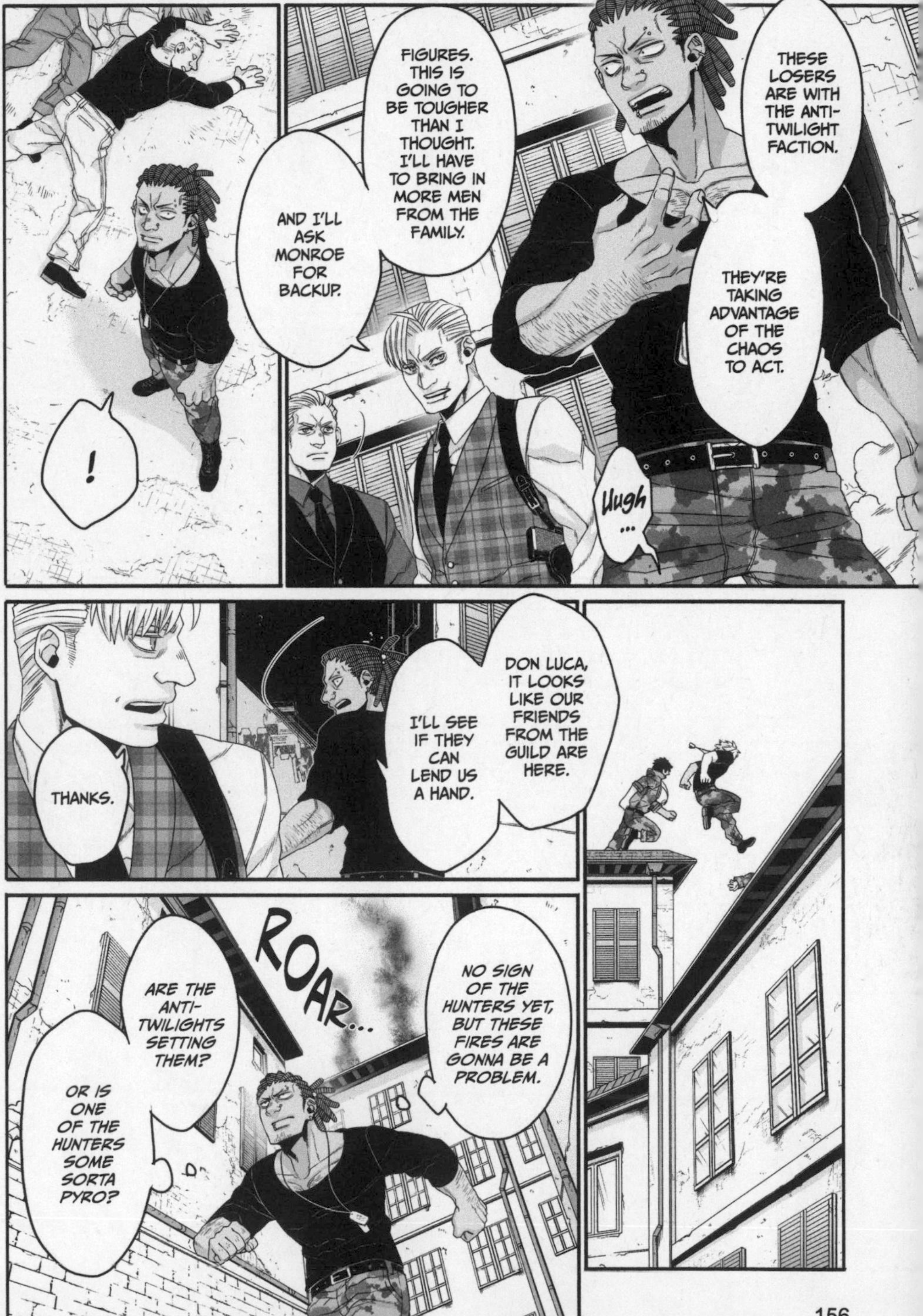
THESE LOSERS ARE WITH THE ANTI-TWILIGHT FACTION.
THEY'RE TAKING ADVANTAGE OF THE CHAOS TO ACT.
Ugh...
FIGURES. THIS IS GOING TO BE TOUGHER THAN I THOUGHT. I'LL HAVE TO BRING IN MORE MEN FROM THE FAMILY.
AND I'LL ASK MONROE FOR BACKUP.
!
DON LUCA, IT LOOKS LIKE OUR FRIENDS FROM THE GUILD ARE HERE.
I'LL SEE IF THEY CAN LEND US A HAND.
THANKS.
NO SIGN OF THE HUNTERS YET, BUT THESE FIRES ARE GONNA BE A PROBLEM.
ROAR...
ARE THE ANTI-TWILIGHTS SETTING THEM?
OR IS ONE OF THE HUNTERS SOME SORTA PYRO?

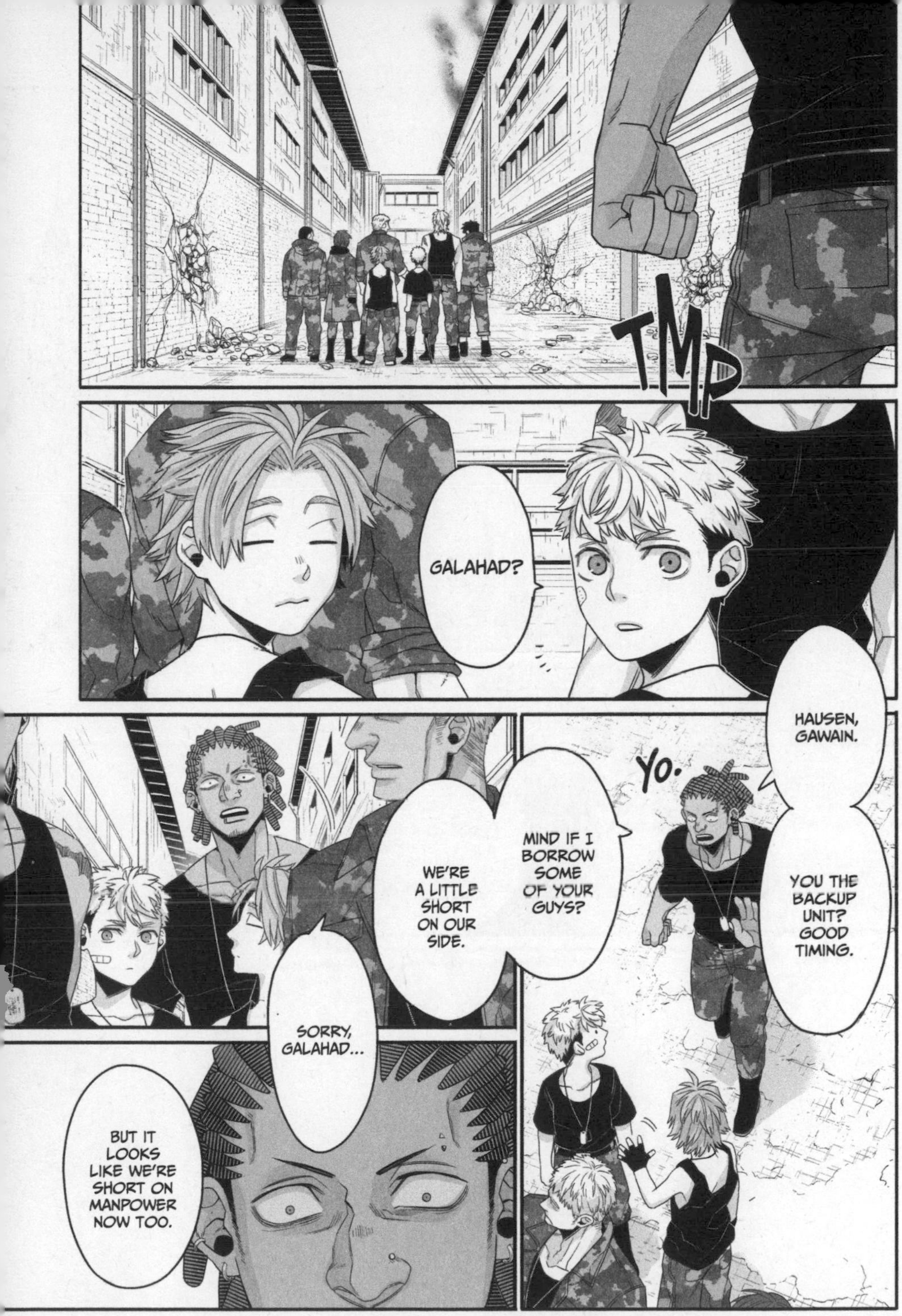
TMP
GALAHAD?
HAUSEN, GAWAIN.
YO.
YOU THE BACKUP UNIT? GOOD TIMING.
MIND IF I BORROW SOME OF YOUR GUYS?
WE'RE A LITTLE SHORT ON OUR SIDE.
SORRY, GALAHAD...
BUT IT LOOKS LIKE WE'RE SHORT ON MANPOWER NOW TOO.

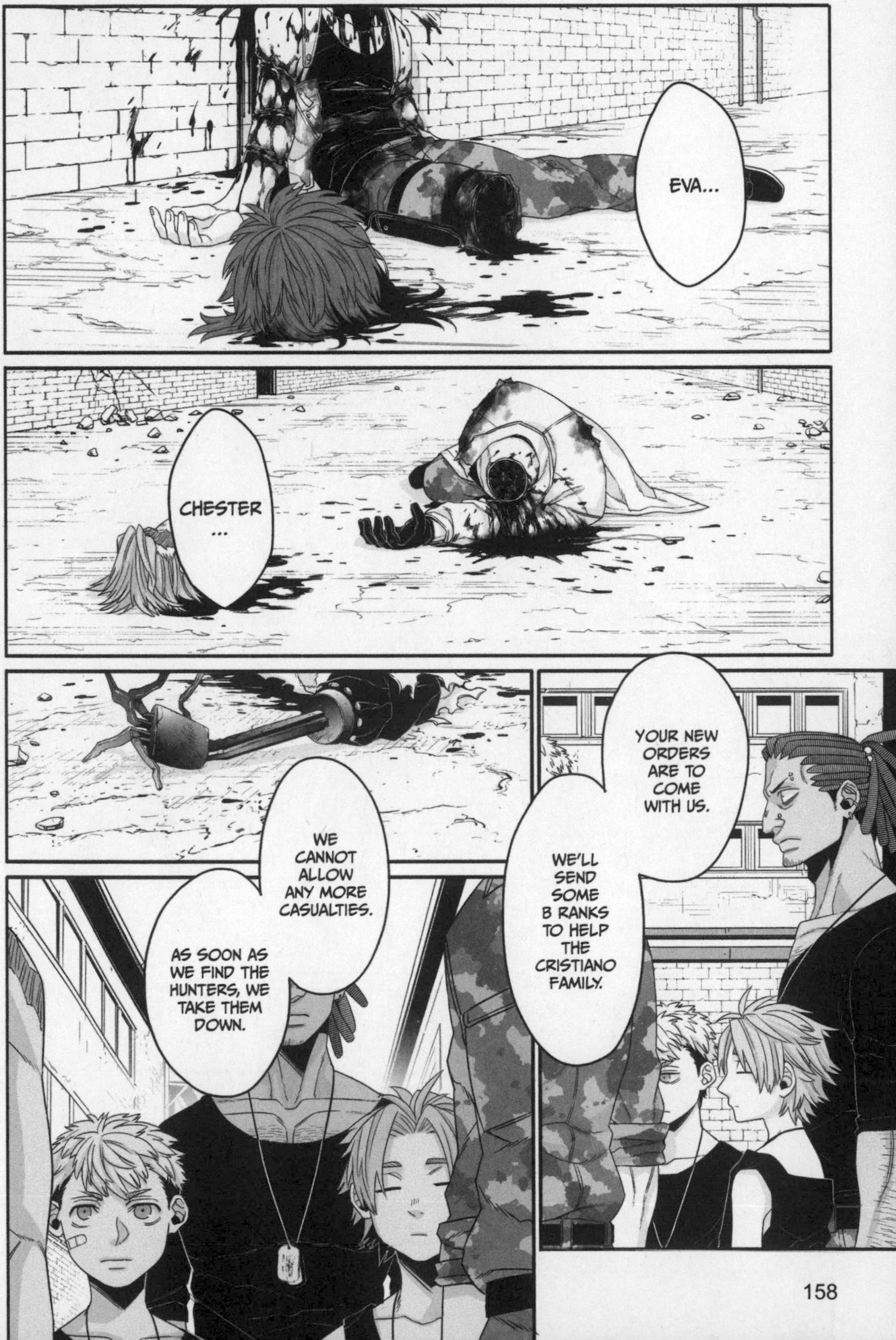
EVA...
CHESTER ...
YOUR NEW ORDERS ARE TO COME WITH US.
WE'LL SEND SOME B RANKS TO HELP THE CRISTIANO FAMILY.
WE CANNOT ALLOW ANY MORE CASUALTIES.
AS SOON AS WE FIND THE HUNTERS, WE TAKE THEM DOWN.

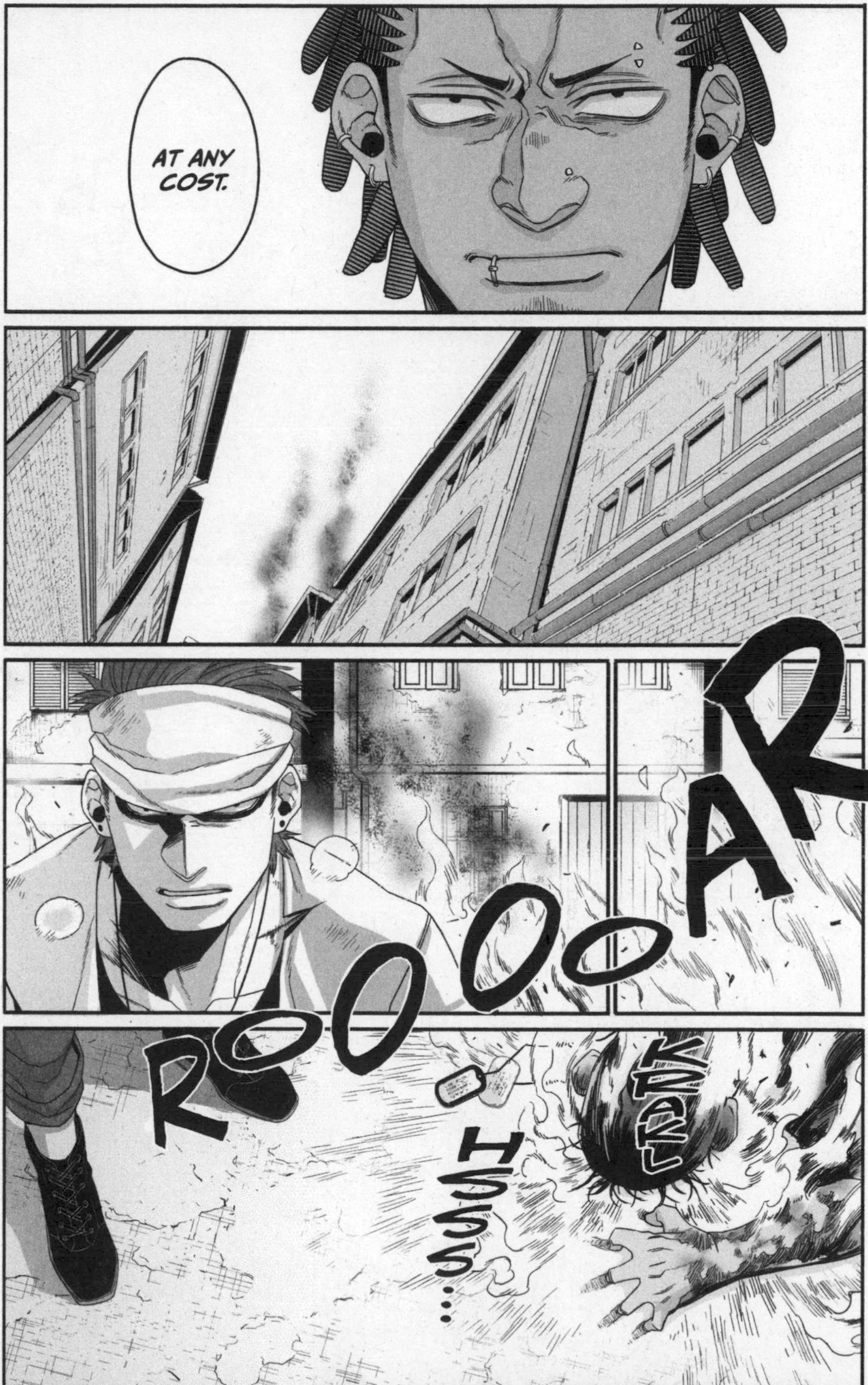
AT ANY COST.
ROOOOOOAR
KRRL
HSSS...

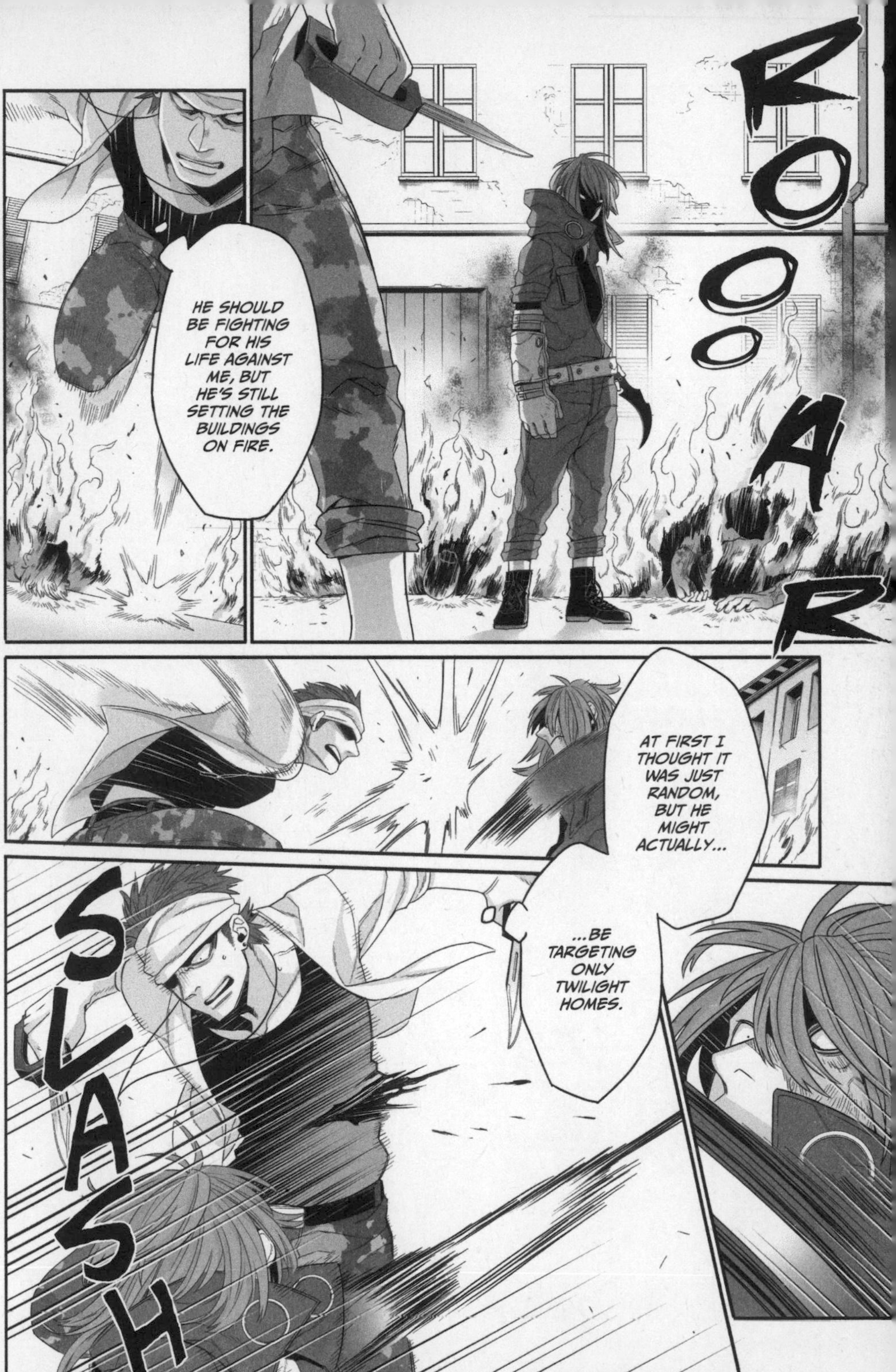
ROOOAR
HE SHOULD BE FIGHTING FOR HIS LIFE AGAINST ME, BUT HE'S STILL SETTING THE BUILDINGS ON FIRE.
AT FIRST I THOUGHT IT WAS JUST RANDOM, BUT HE MIGHT ACTUALLY...
...BE TARGETING ONLY TWILIGHT HOMES.
SLASH

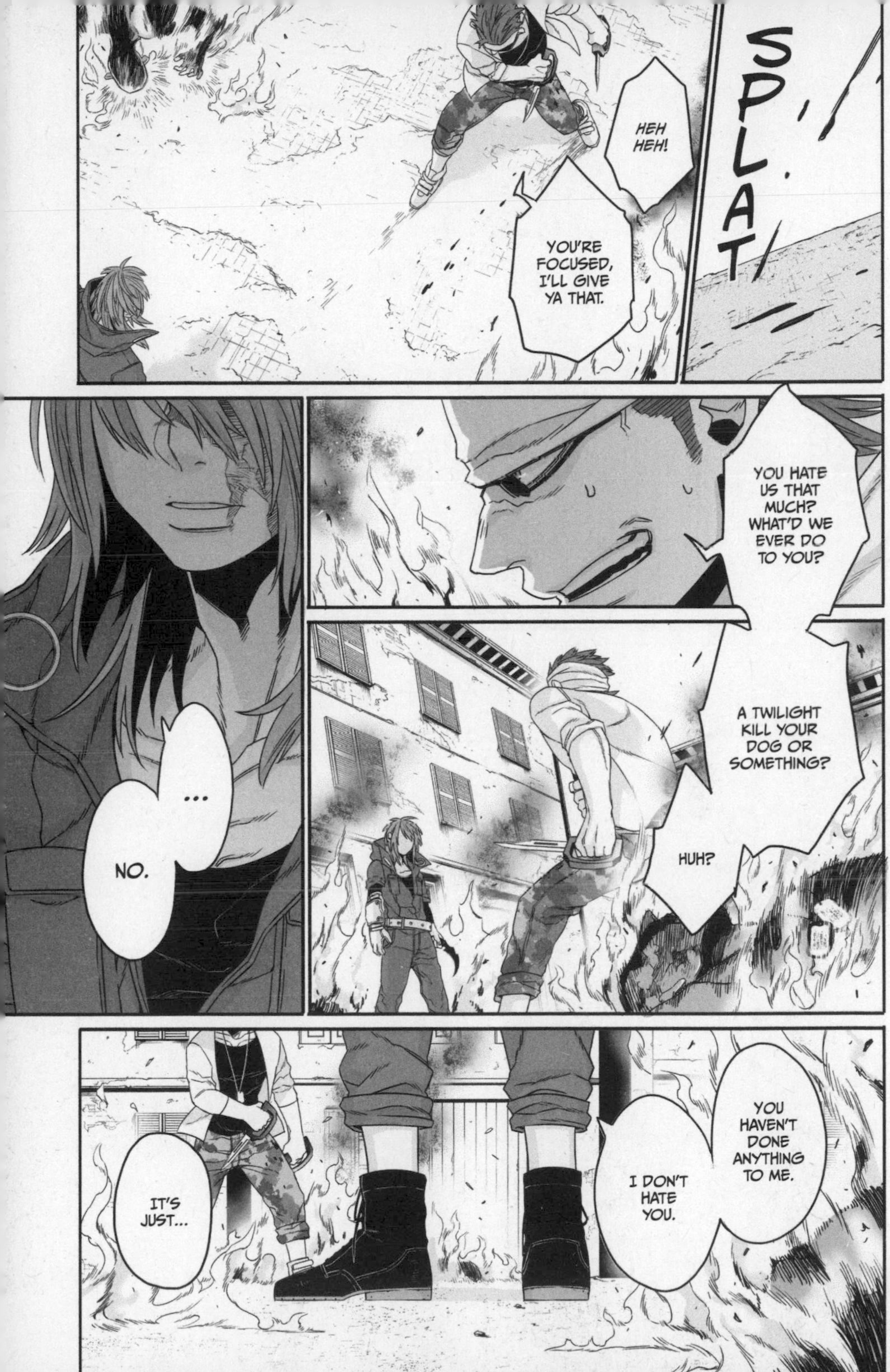
SPLAT
HEH HEH!
YOU'RE FOCUSED, I'LL GIVE YA THAT.
YOU HATE US THAT MUCH? WHAT'D WE EVER DO TO YOU?
A TWILIGHT KILL YOUR DOG OR SOMETHING?
HUH?
...
NO.
YOU HAVEN'T DONE ANYTHING TO ME.
I DON'T HATE YOU.
IT'S JUST...

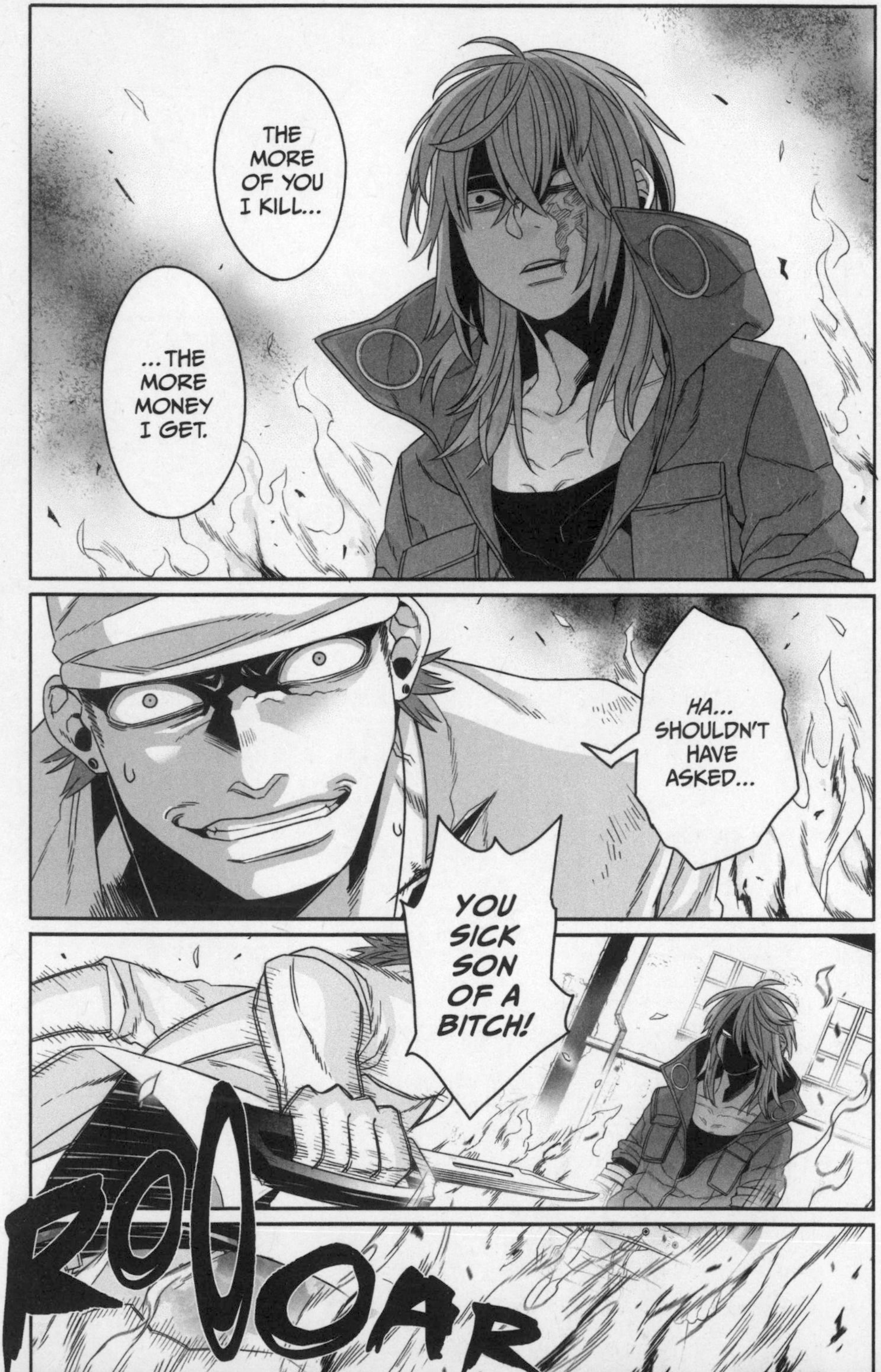
THE MORE OF YOU I KILL...
...THE MORE MONEY I GET.
HA... SHOULDN'T HAVE ASKED...
YOU SICK SON OF A BITCH!
ROOOAR

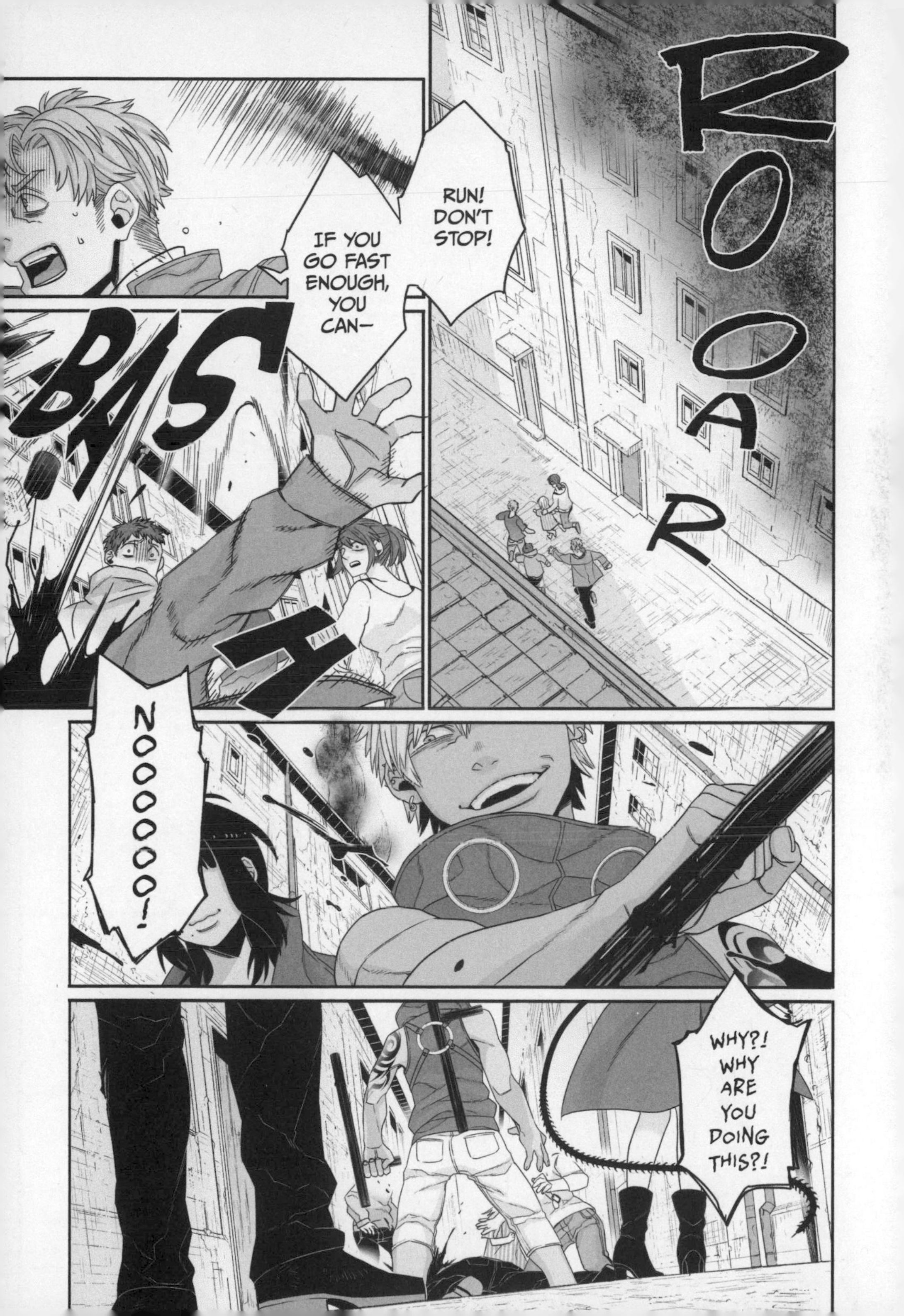
ROOAR
RUN! DON'T STOP!
IF YOU GO FAST ENOUGH, YOU CAN—
BASH
NOOOOOOO!
WHY?! WHY ARE YOU DOING THIS?!

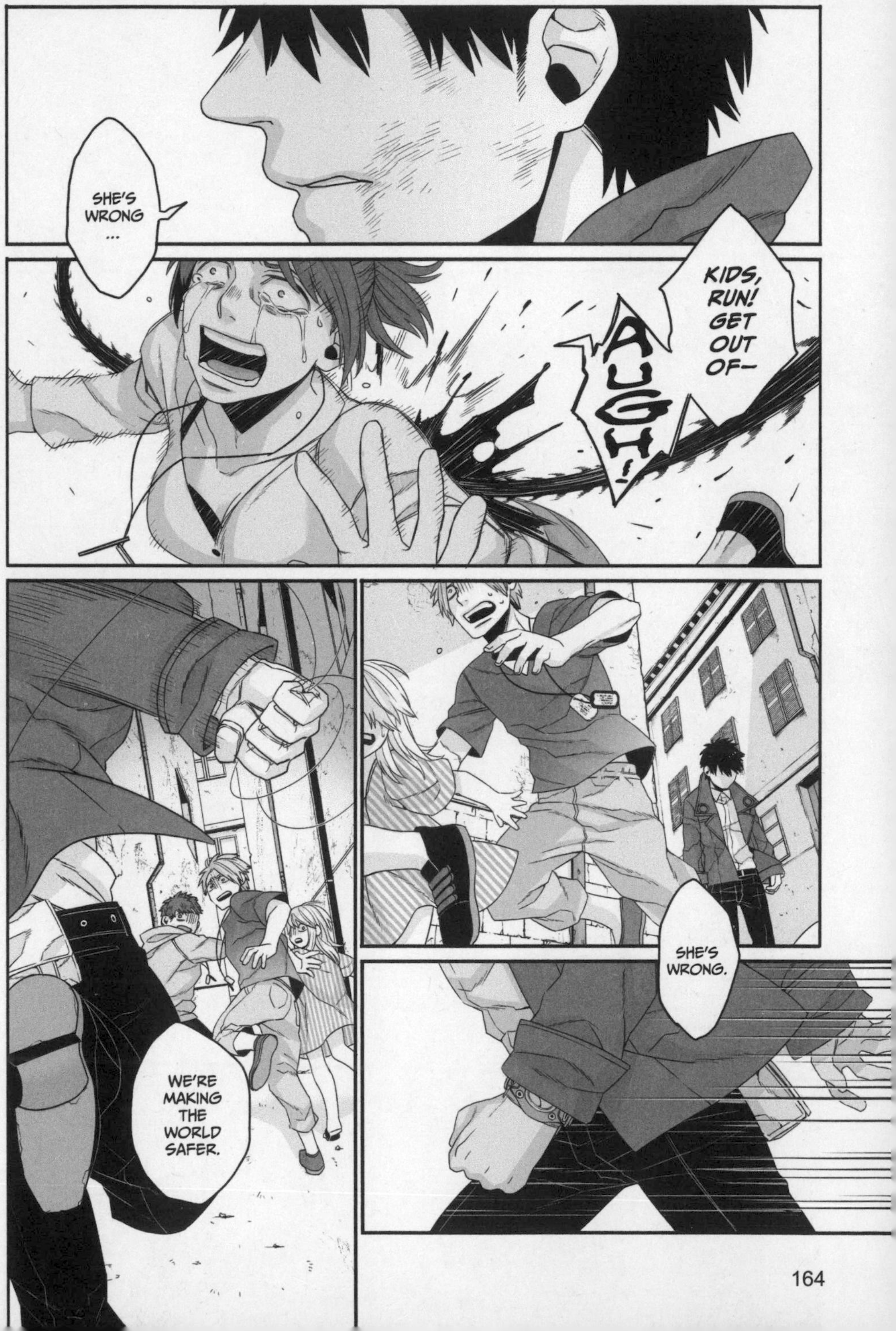
SHE'S WRONG ...
KIDS, RUN! GET OUT OF—
AUGH!
SHE'S WRONG.
WE'RE MAKING THE WORLD SAFER.

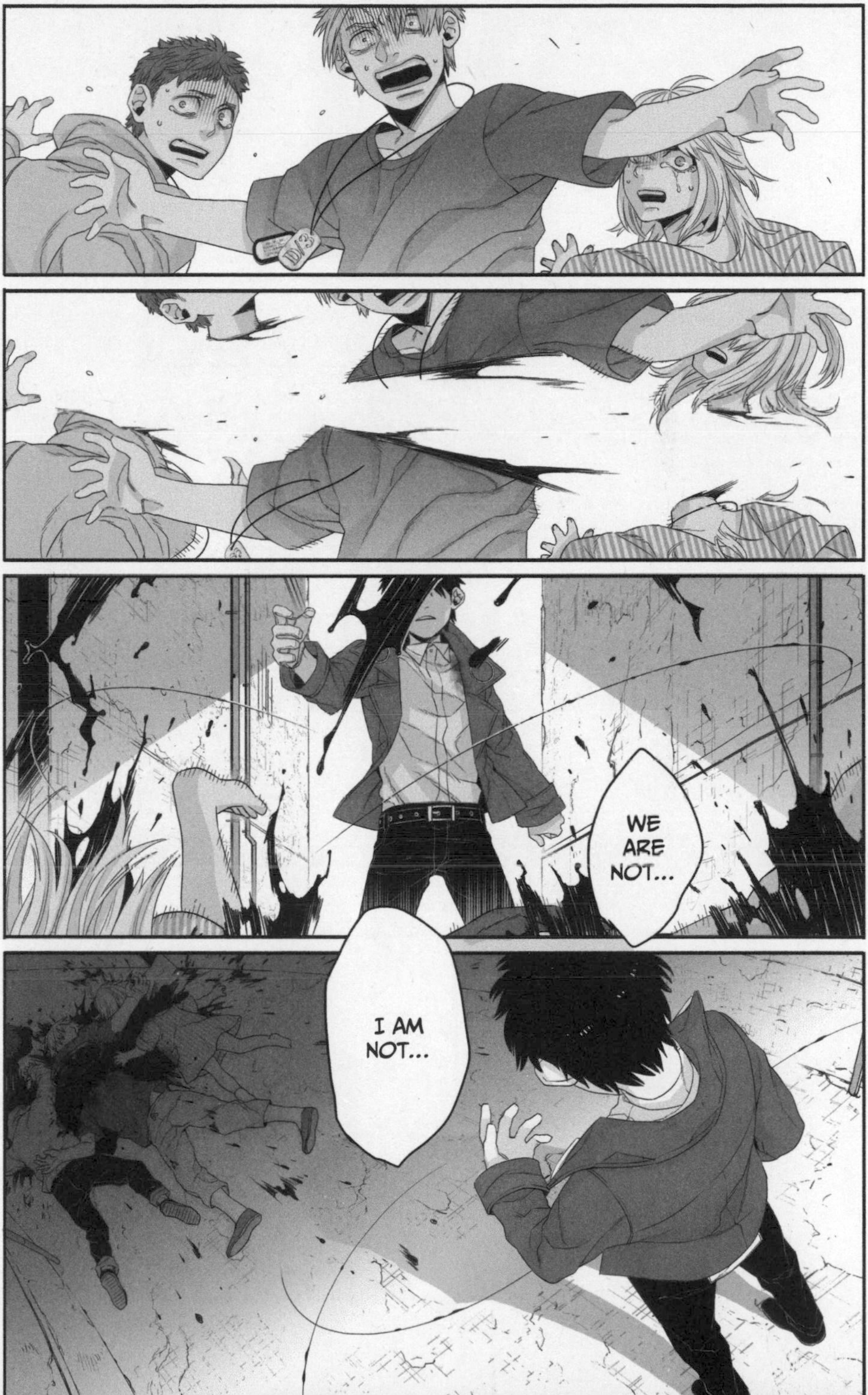
WE ARE NOT...
I AM NOT...

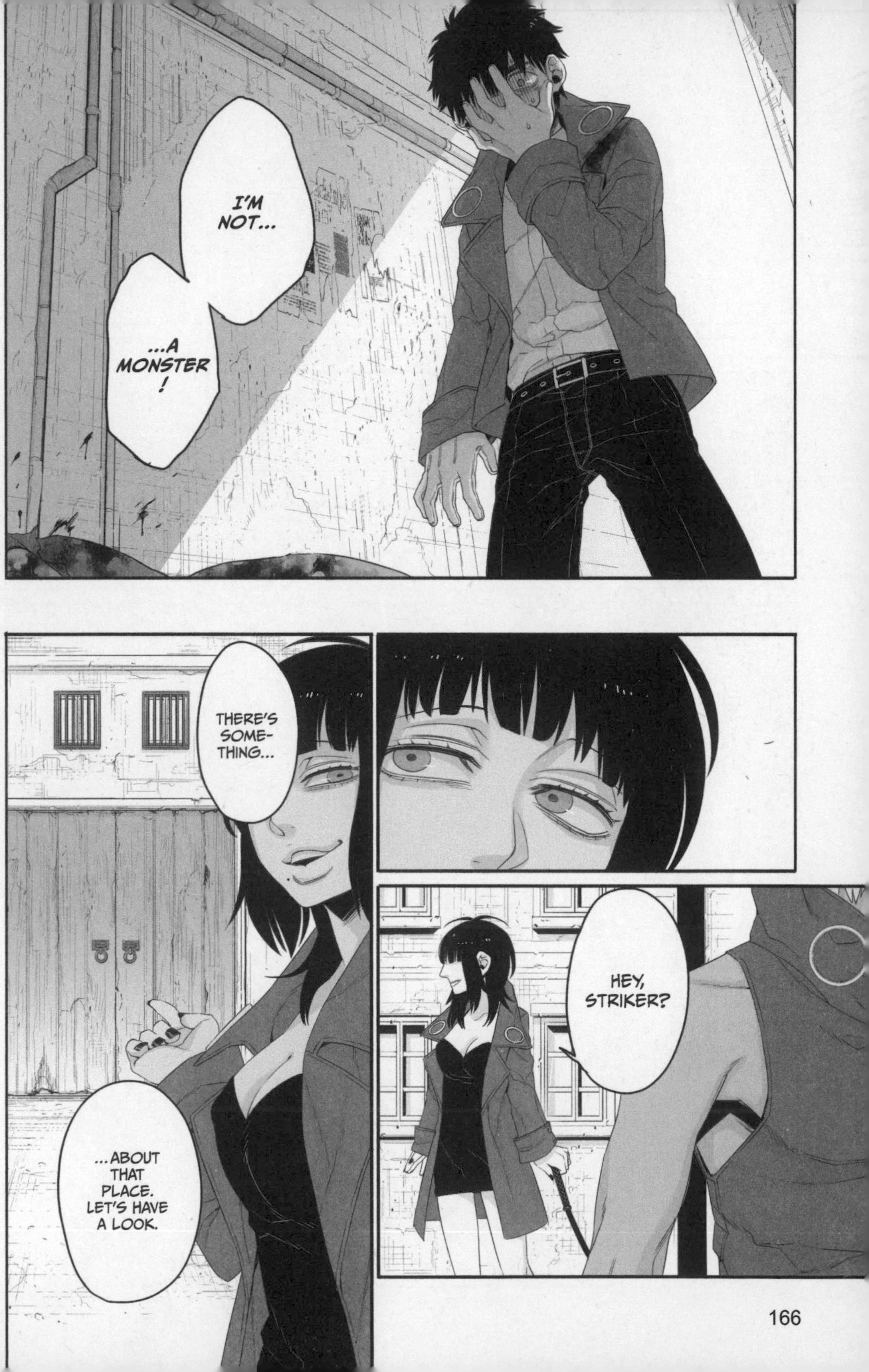
I'M NOT...
...A MONSTER!
HEY, STRIKER?
THERE'S SOME-THING...
...ABOUT THAT PLACE. LET'S HAVE A LOOK.

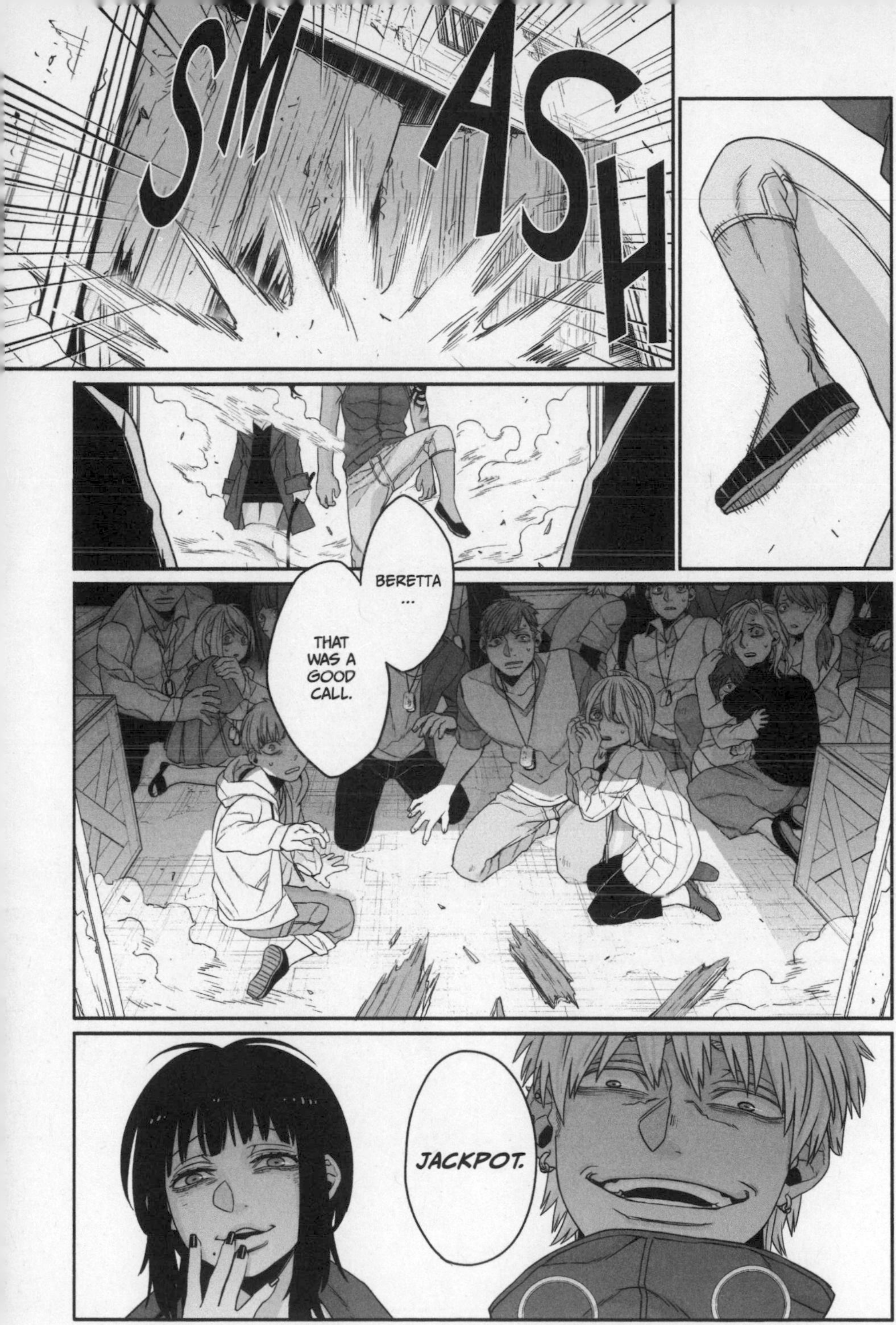
SMASH
BERETTA ...
THAT WAS A GOOD CALL.
JACKPOT.

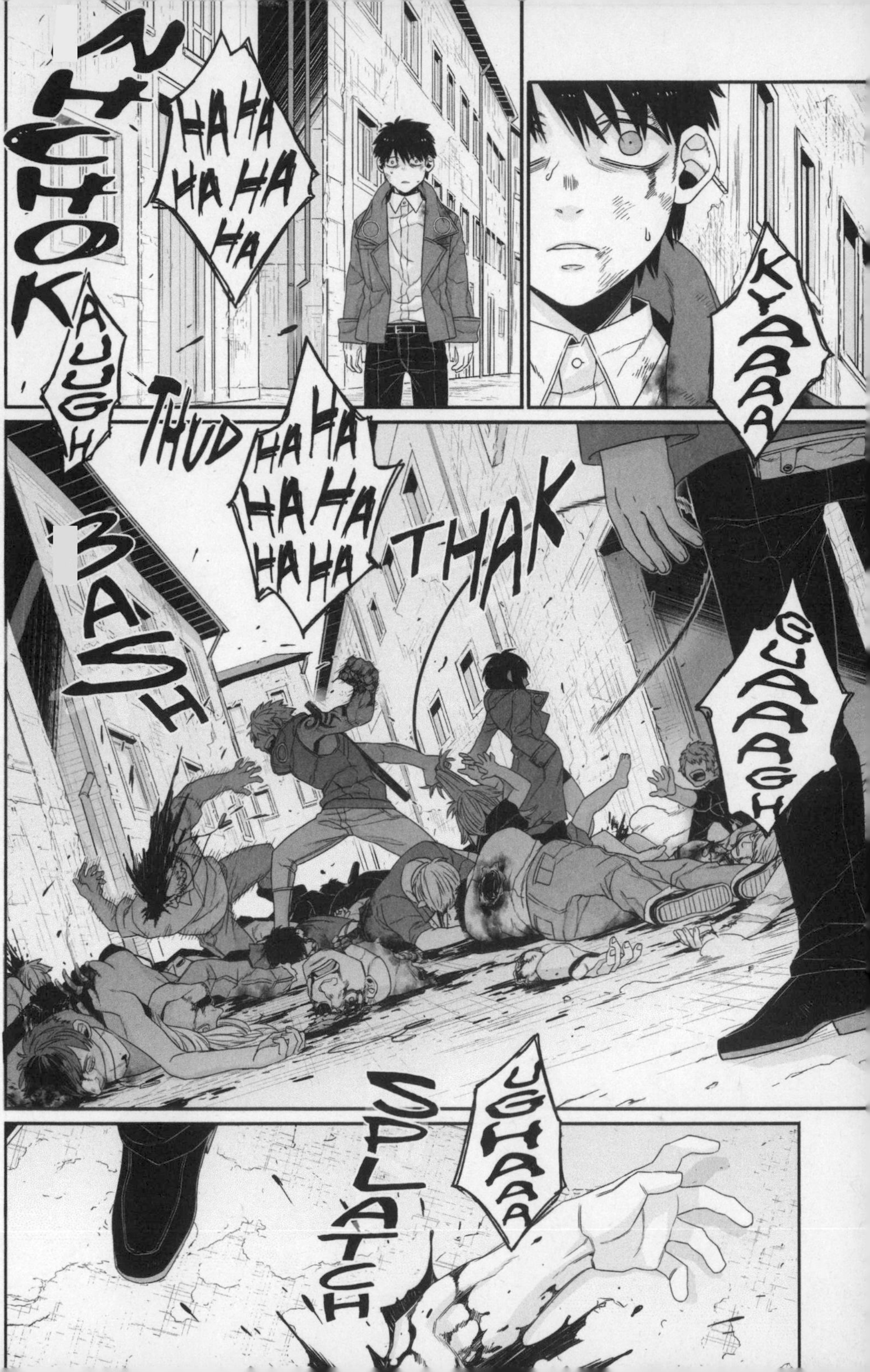
KYAAAA
HA HA
HA HA
HA
AAUUGH
THUD
HA HA
HA HA
HA HA
THAK
GUAAAAGH
BASH
UGHAAA
SPLATCH

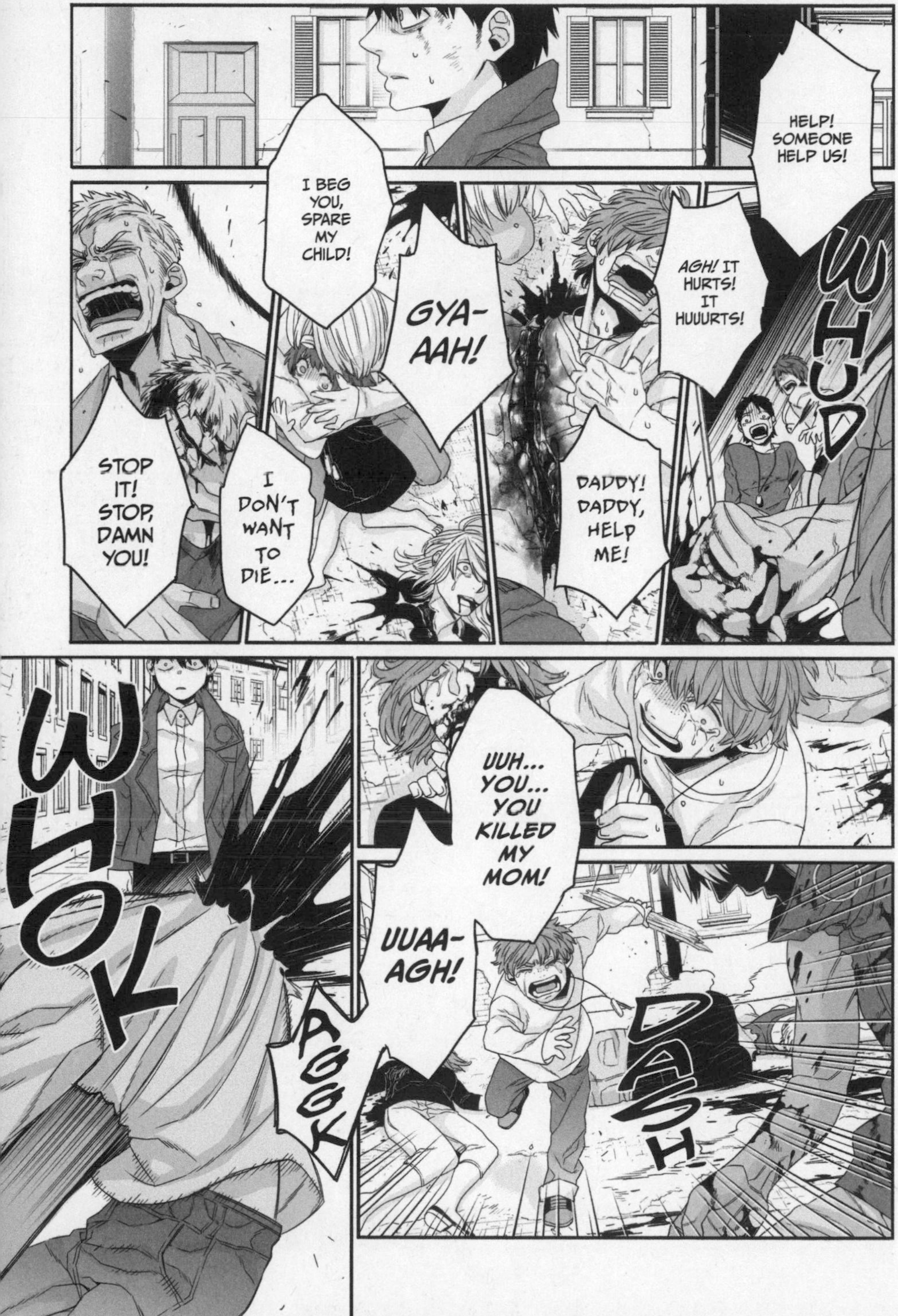
HELP! SOMEONE HELP US!
I BEG YOU, SPARE MY CHILD!
WHUD
AGH! IT HURTS! IT HUUURTS!
DADDY! DADDY, HELP ME!
GYA-AAH!
I DON'T WANT TO DIE...
STOP IT! STOP, DAMN YOU!
UUH... YOU... YOU KILLED MY MOM!
UUAA-AGH!
DASH
WHOK
AGOOK

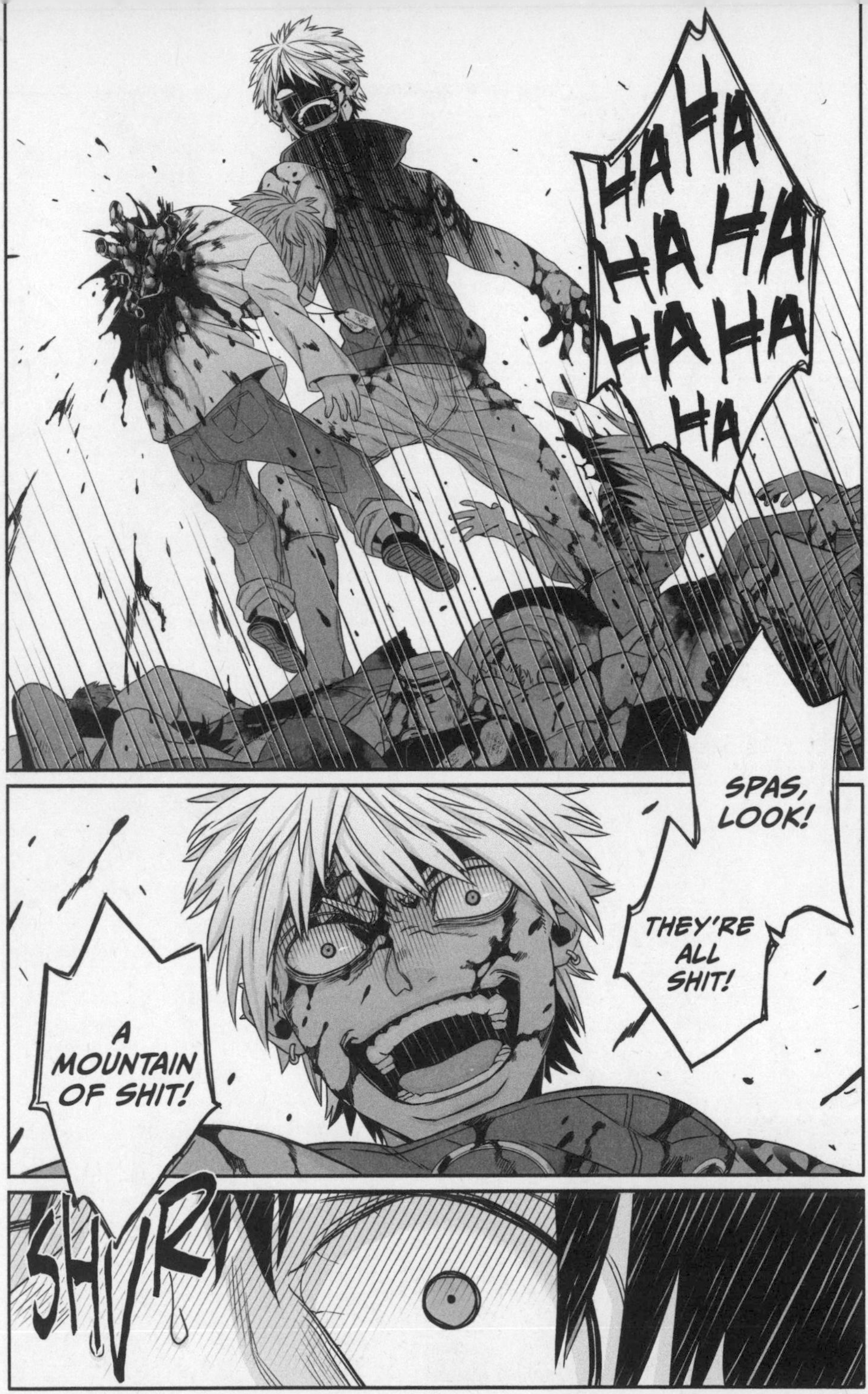
HAHA HAHA HAHA HAHA HA
SPAS, LOOK!
THEY'RE ALL SHIT!
A MOUNTAIN OF SHIT!
SHIVR

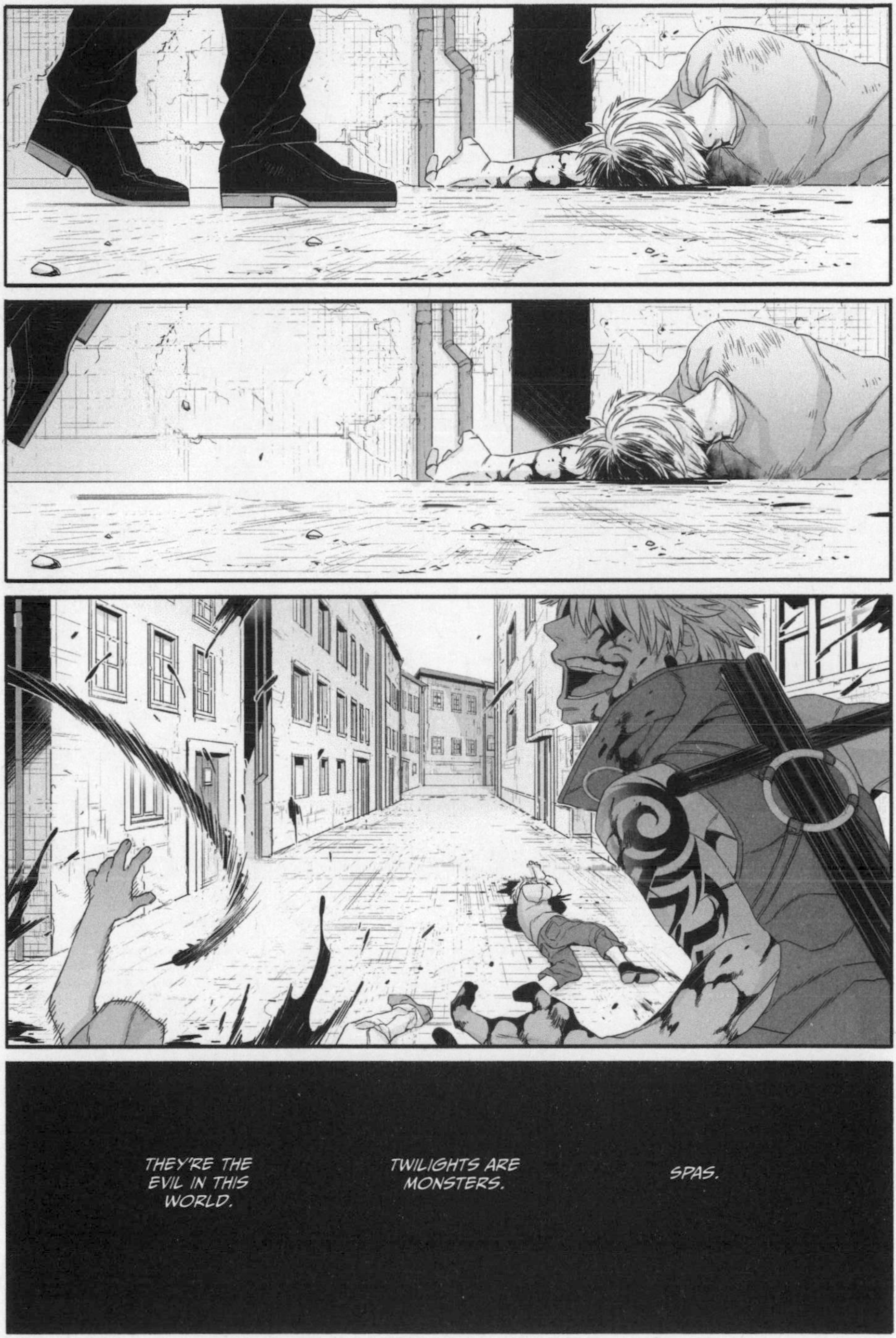
SPAS.
TWILIGHTS ARE MONSTERS.
THEY'RE THE EVIL IN THIS WORLD.

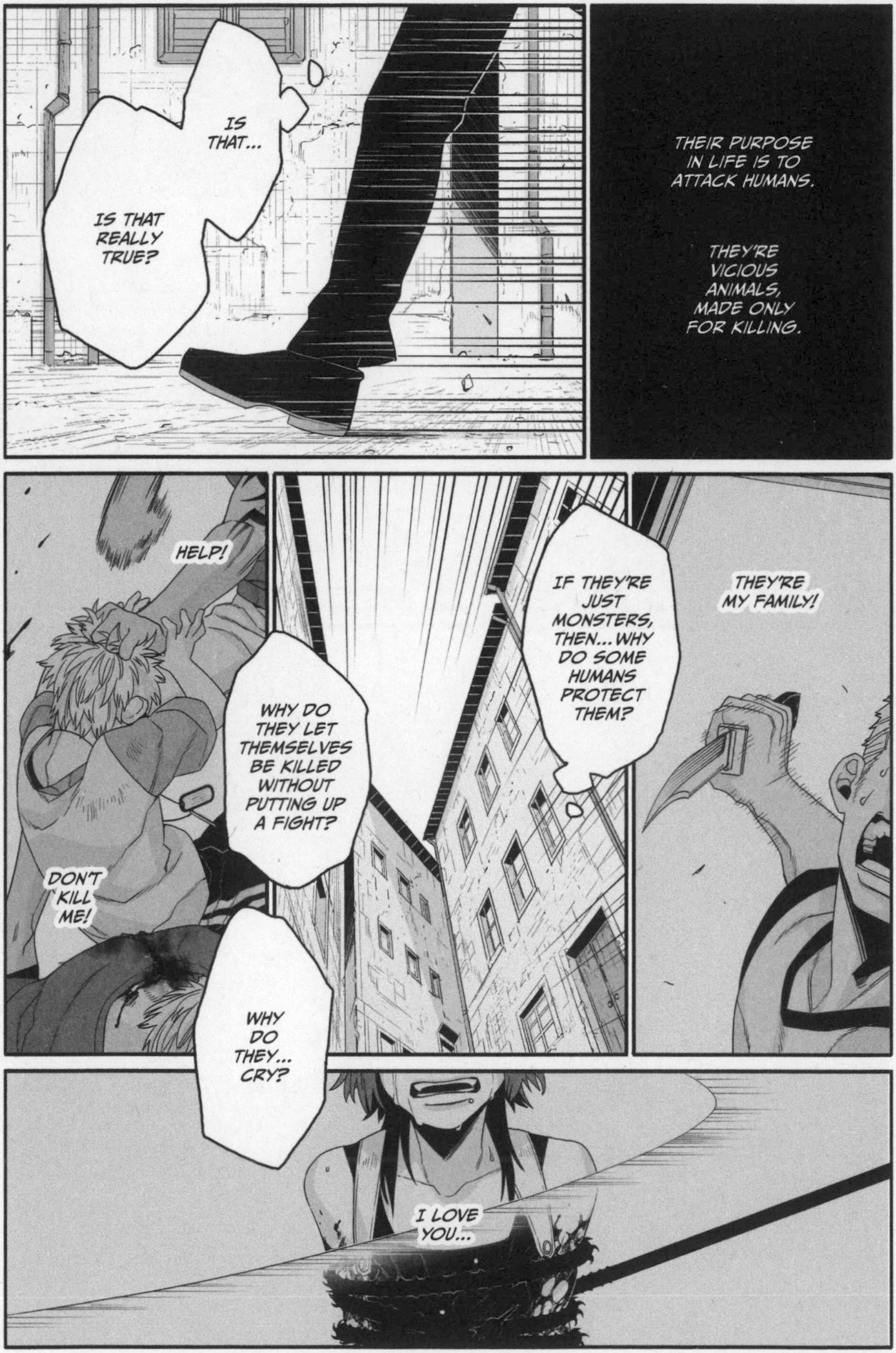
THEIR PURPOSE IN LIFE IS TO ATTACK HUMANS.
THEY'RE VICIOUS ANIMALS, MADE ONLY FOR KILLING.
IS THAT...
IS THAT REALLY TRUE?
THEY'RE MY FAMILY!
IF THEY'RE JUST MONSTERS, THEN... WHY DO SOME HUMANS PROTECT THEM?
HELP!
WHY DO THEY LET THEMSELVES BE KILLED WITHOUT PUTTING UP A FIGHT?
DON'T KILL ME!
WHY DO THEY... CRY?
I LOVE YOU...

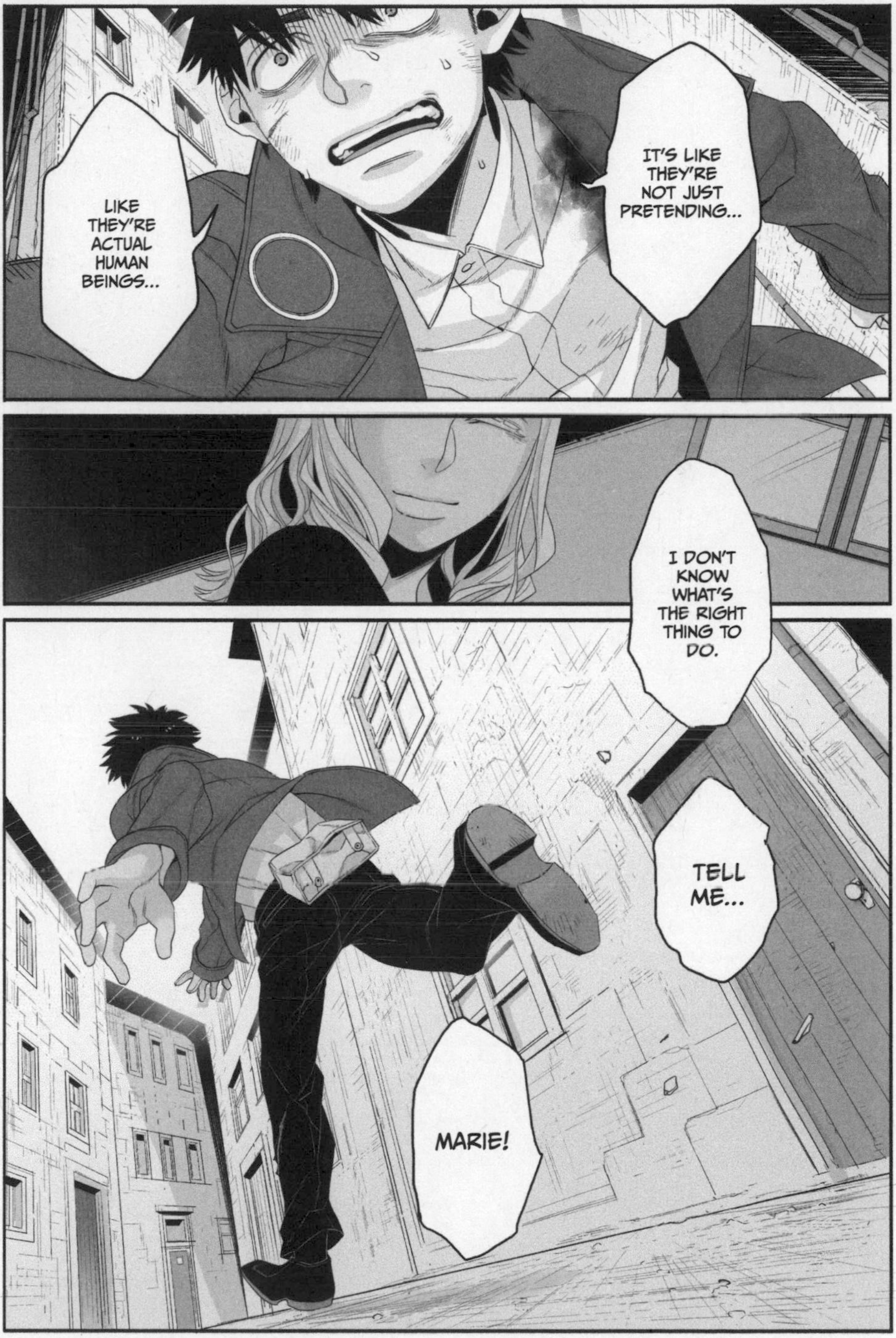
IT'S LIKE THEY'RE NOT JUST PRETENDING...
LIKE THEY'RE ACTUAL HUMAN BEINGS...
I DON'T KNOW WHAT'S THE RIGHT THING TO DO.
TELL ME...
MARIE!

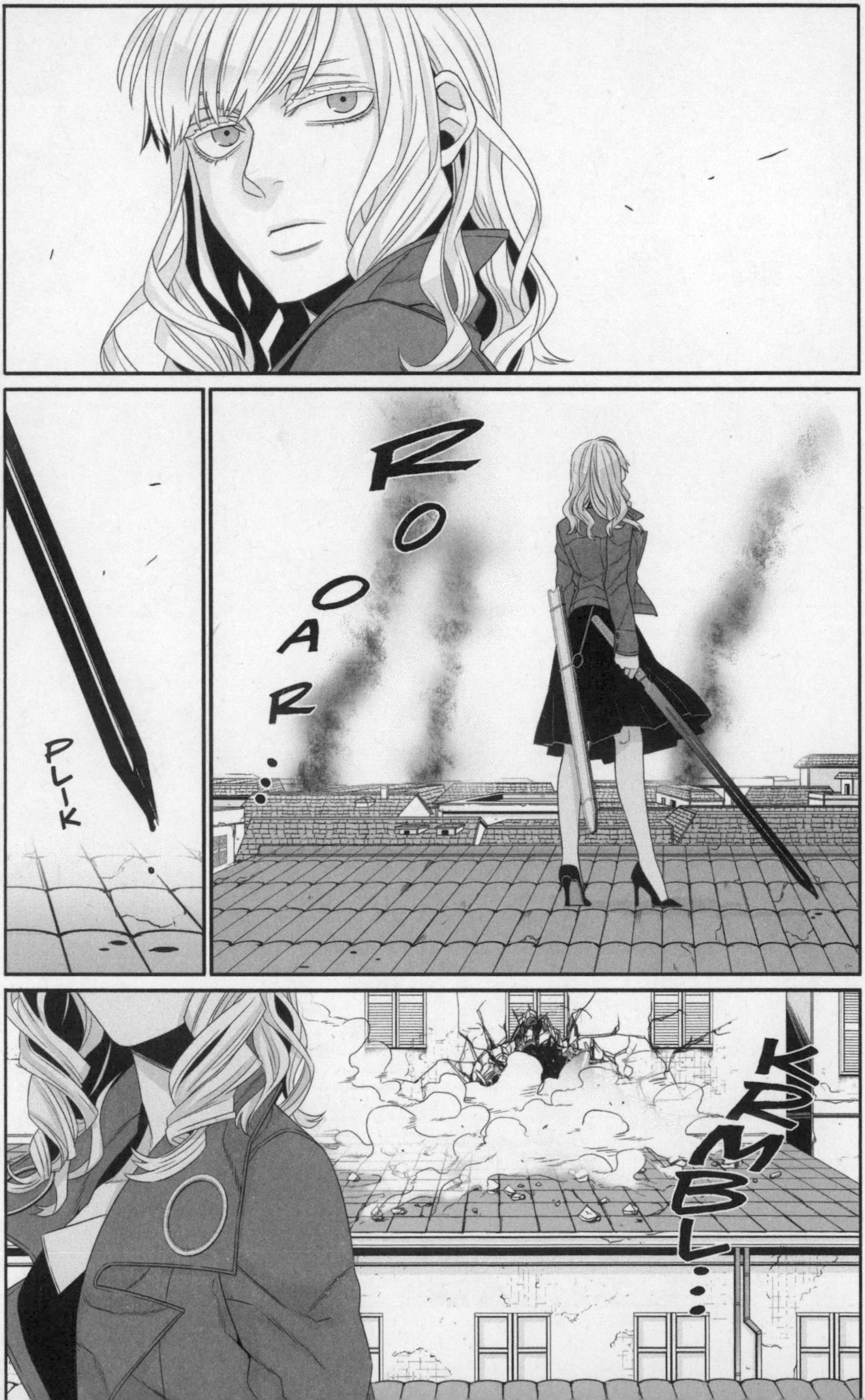
ROOOAR...
PLIK
KRMBL...

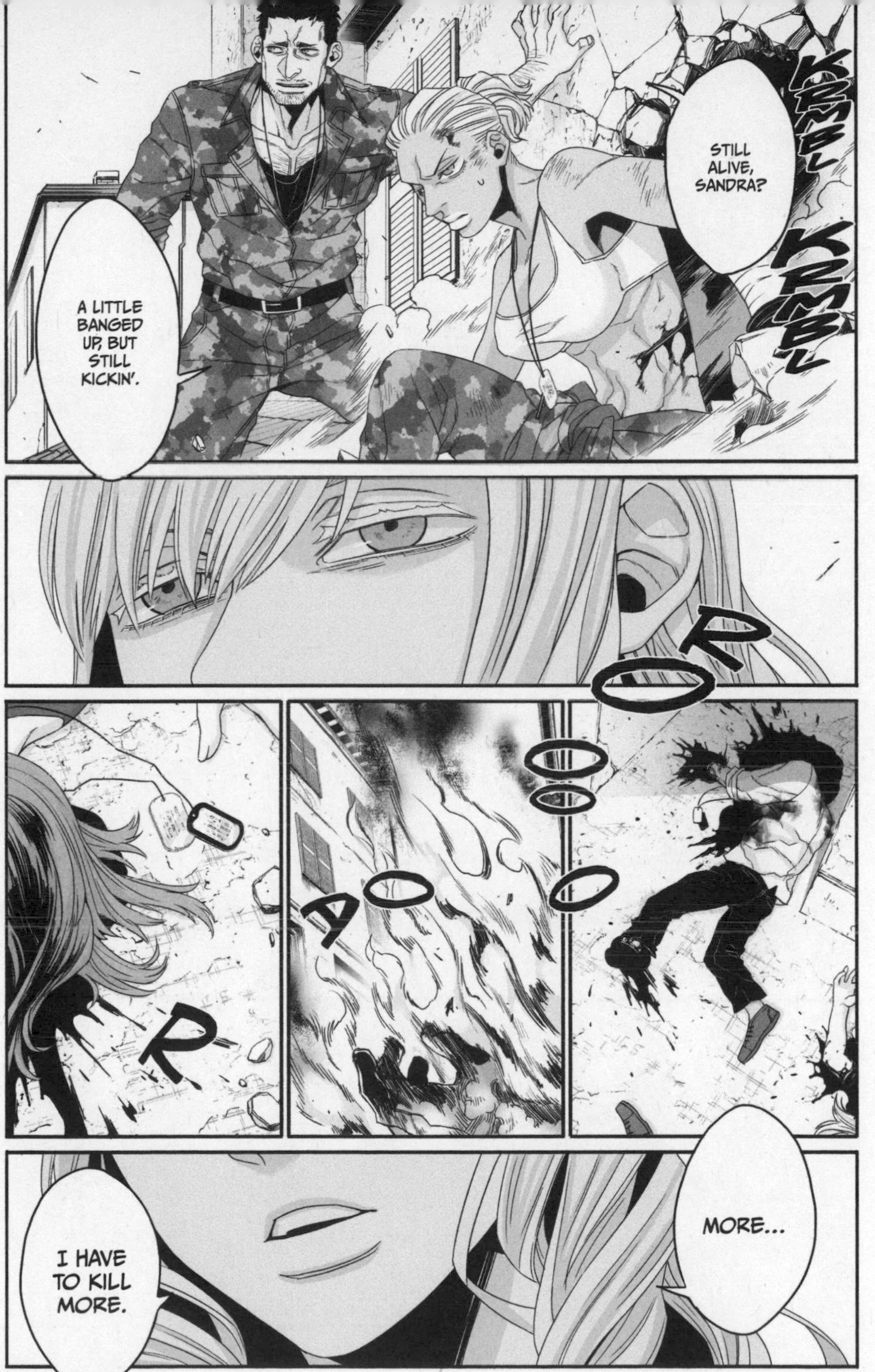
KRMBL
KRMBL
STILL ALIVE, SANDRA?
A LITTLE BANGED UP, BUT STILL KICKIN'.
ROOOOOAR
MORE...
I HAVE TO KILL MORE.

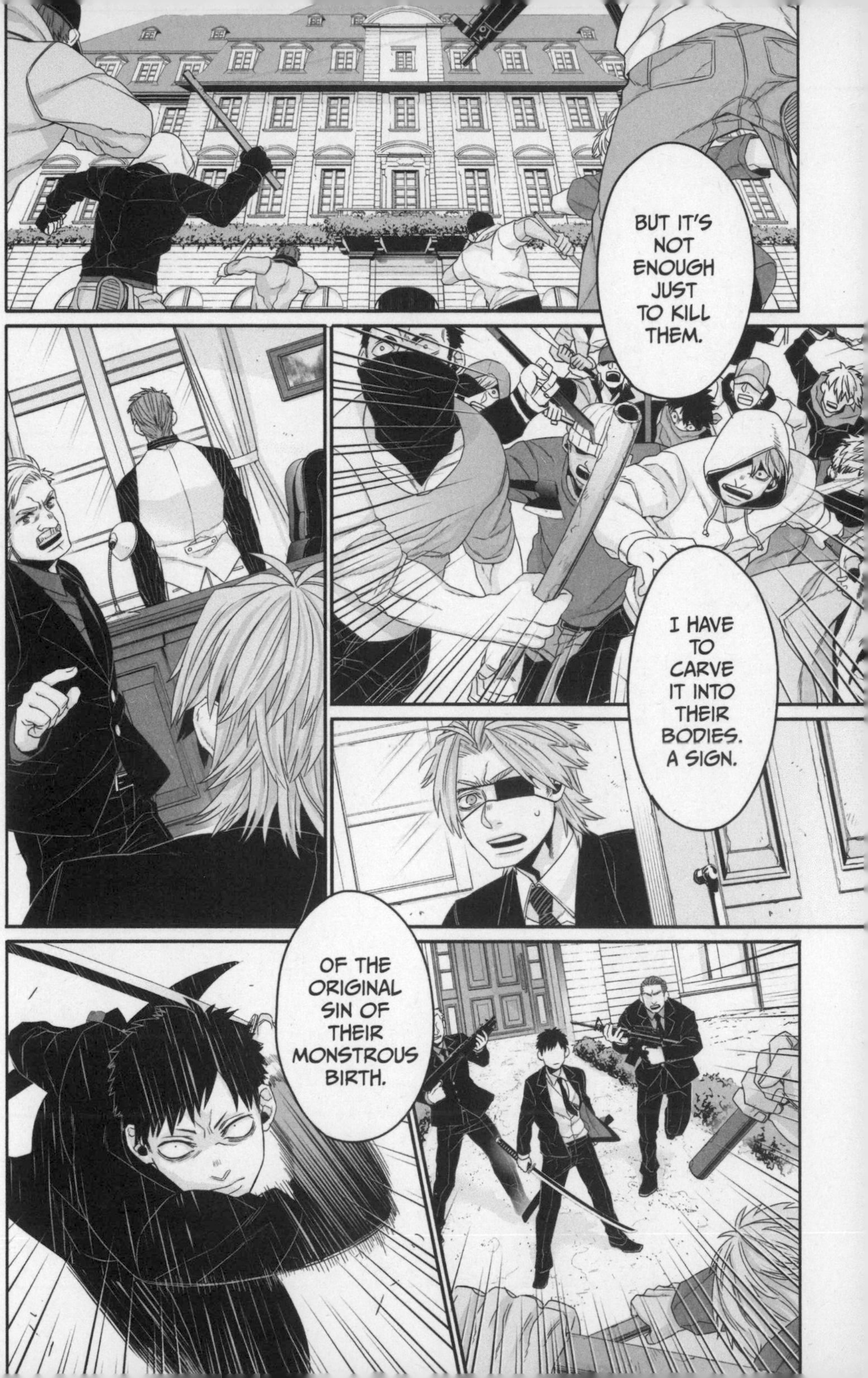
BUT IT'S NOT ENOUGH JUST TO KILL THEM.
I HAVE TO CARVE IT INTO THEIR BODIES. A SIGN.
OF THE ORIGINAL SIN OF THEIR MONSTROUS BIRTH.

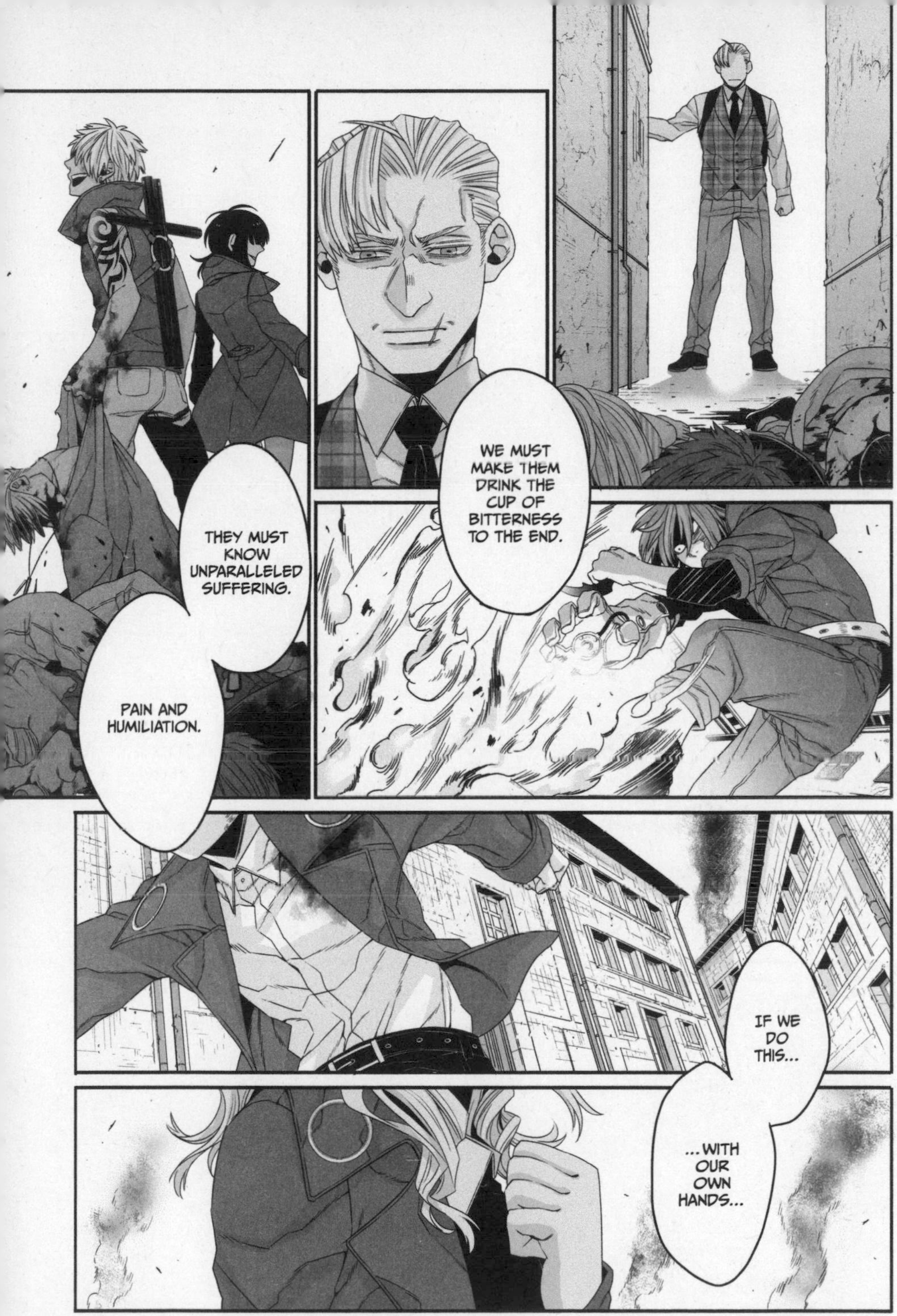
WE MUST MAKE THEM DRINK THE CUP OF BITTERNESS TO THE END.
THEY MUST KNOW UNPARALLELED SUFFERING.
PAIN AND HUMILIATION.
IF WE DO THIS...
...WITH OUR OWN HANDS...

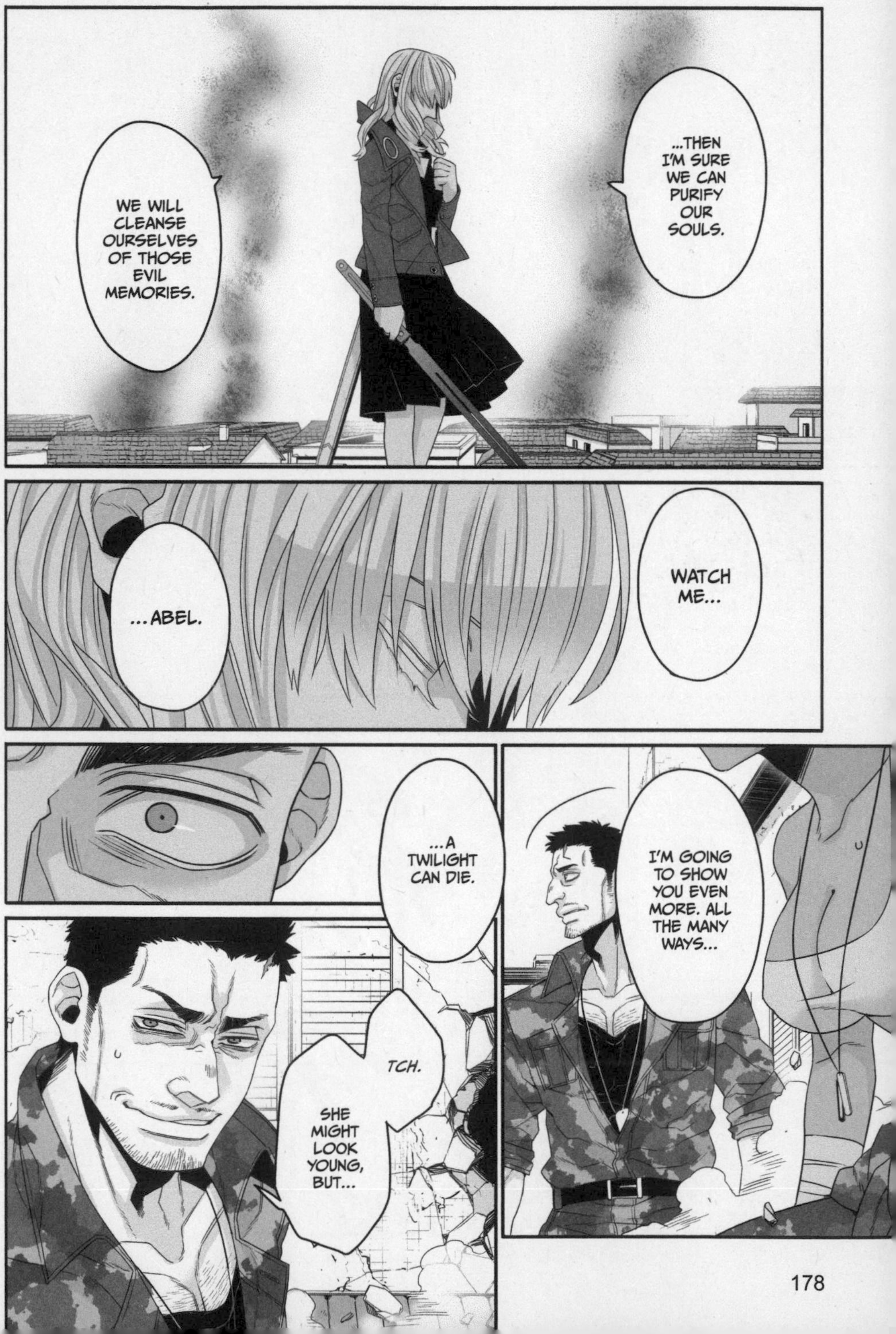
...THEN I'M SURE WE CAN PURIFY OUR SOULS.
WE WILL CLEANSE OURSELVES OF THOSE EVIL MEMORIES.
WATCH ME...
...ABEL.
I'M GOING TO SHOW YOU EVEN MORE. ALL THE MANY WAYS...
...A TWILIGHT CAN DIE.
TCH.
SHE MIGHT LOOK YOUNG, BUT...

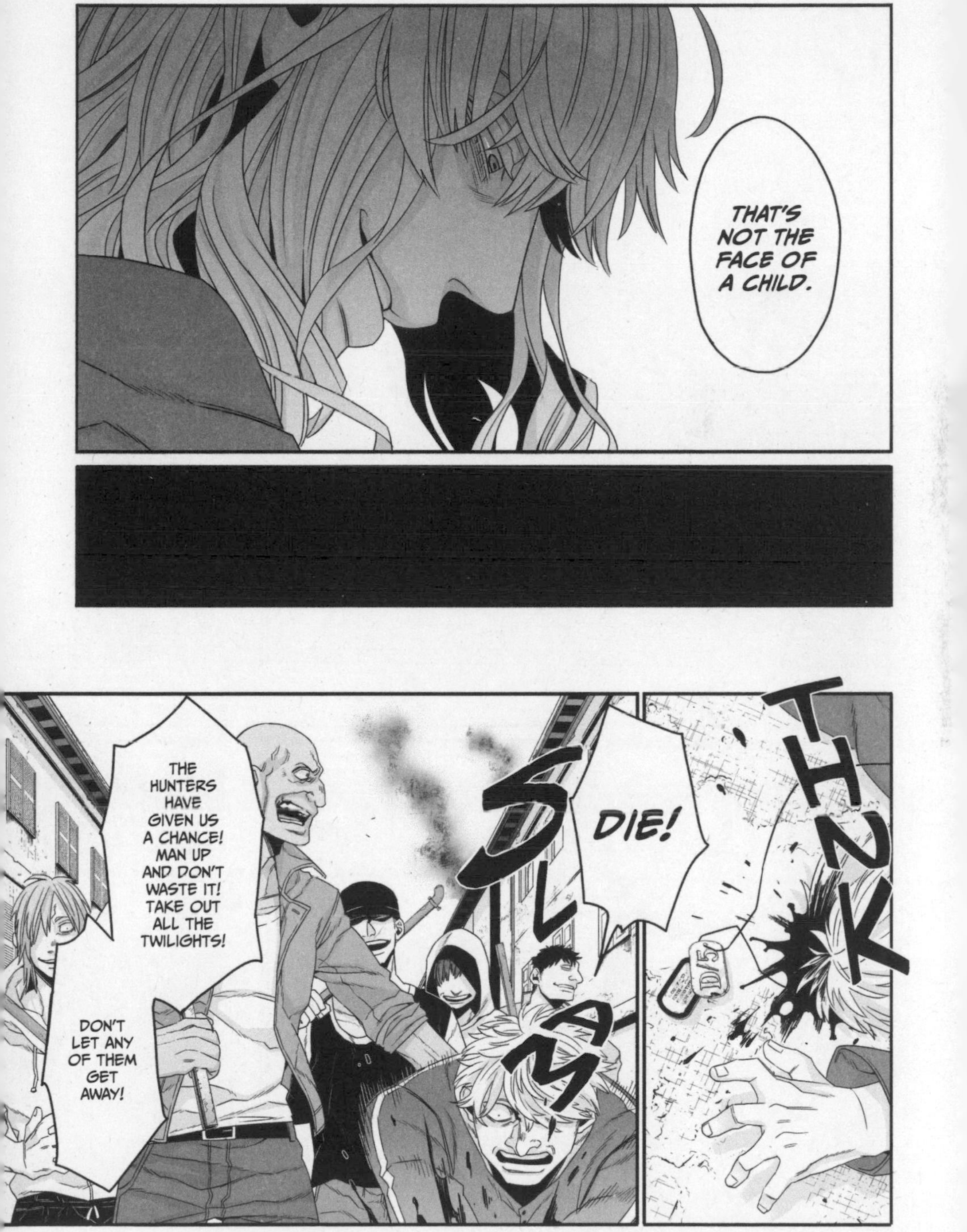
THAT'S NOT THE FACE OF A CHILD.
THNK
DIE!
SLAM
THE HUNTERS HAVE GIVEN US A CHANCE! MAN UP AND DON'T WASTE IT! TAKE OUT ALL THE TWILIGHTS!
DON'T LET ANY OF THEM GET AWAY!

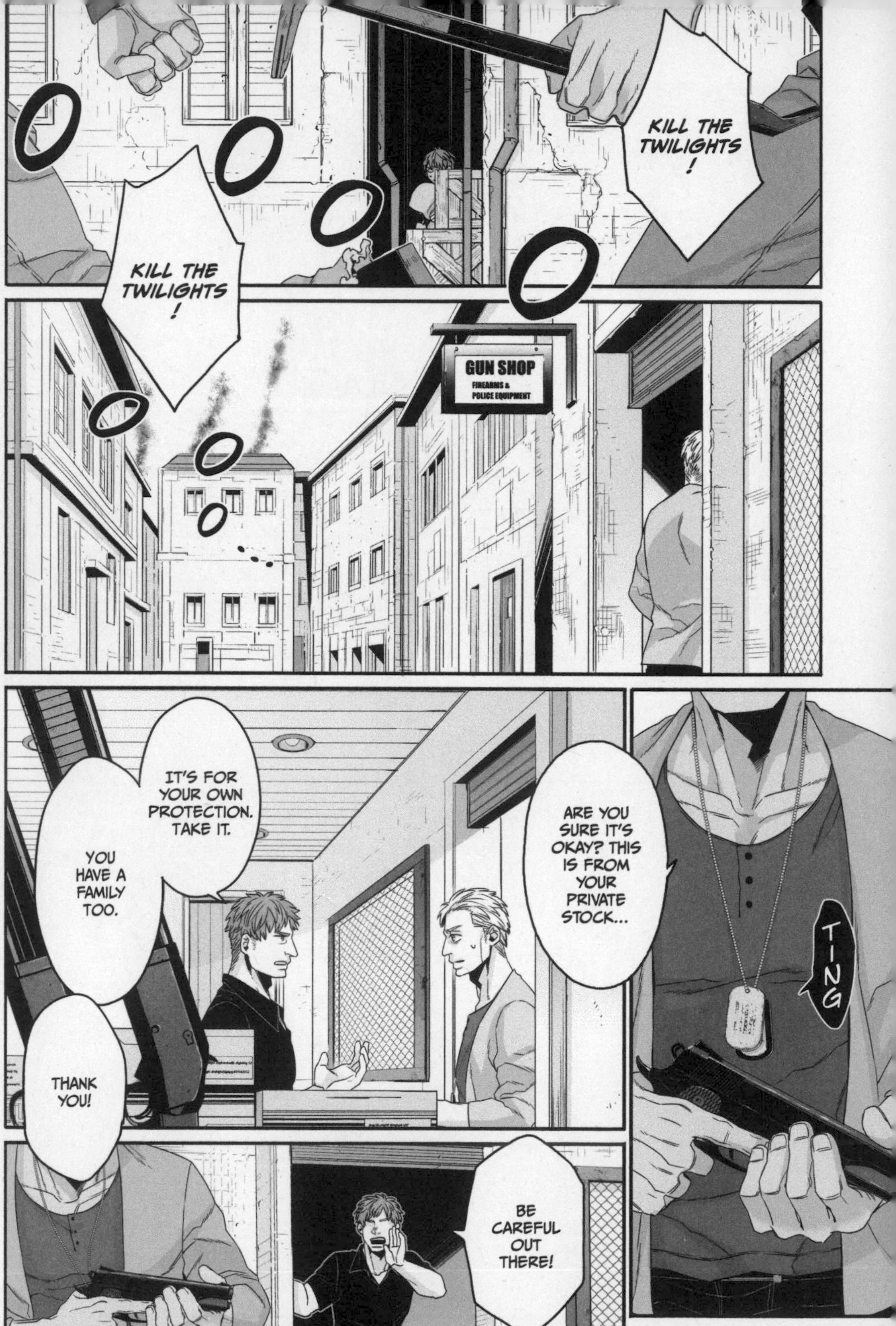
KILL THE TWILIGHTS!
KILL THE TWILIGHTS!
GUN SHOP
FIREARMS & POLICE EQUIPMENT
TING
ARE YOU SURE IT'S OKAY? THIS IS FROM YOUR PRIVATE STOCK...
IT'S FOR YOUR OWN PROTECTION. TAKE IT.
YOU HAVE A FAMILY TOO.
THANK YOU!
BE CAREFUL OUT THERE!

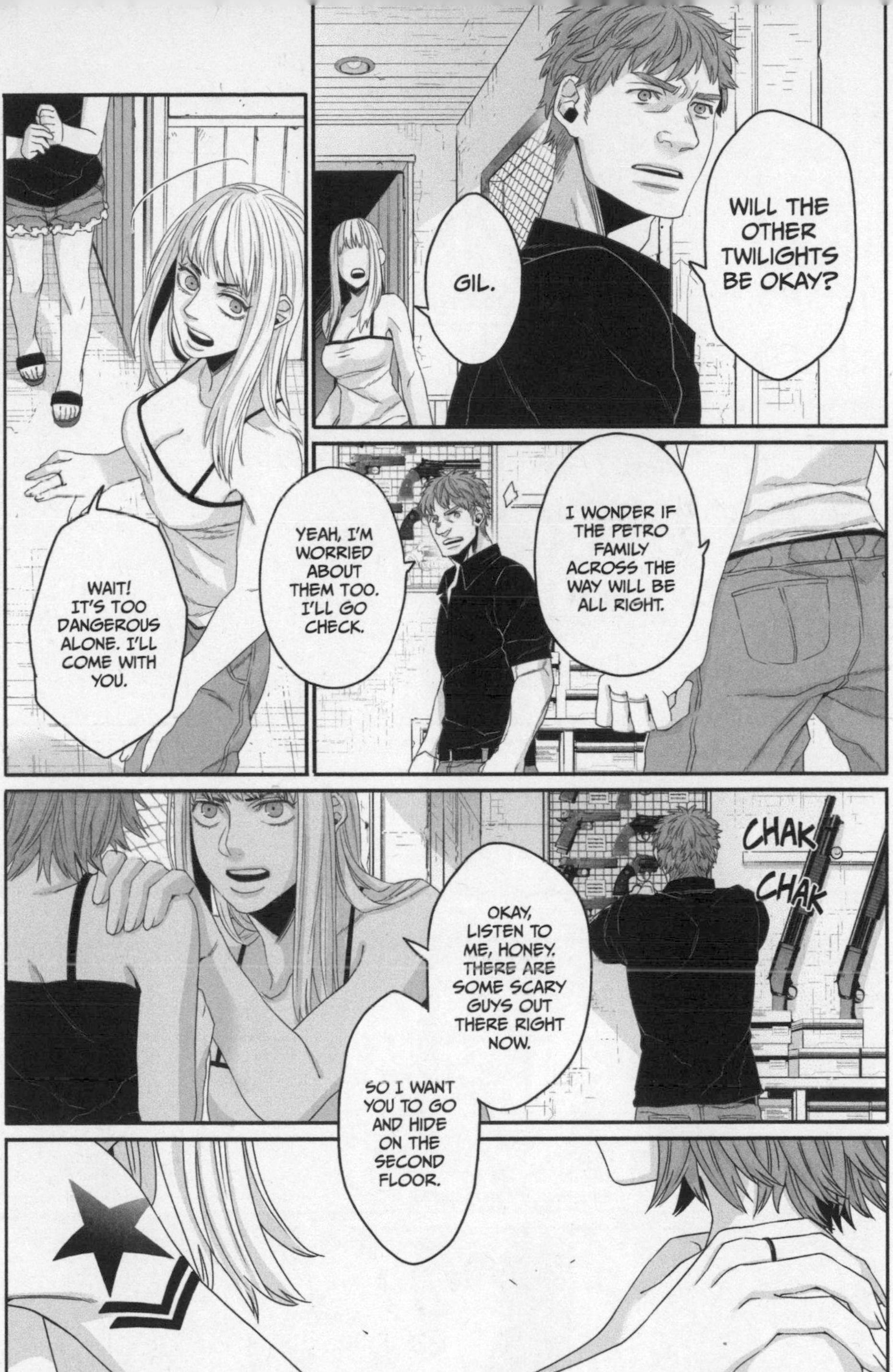
WILL THE OTHER TWILIGHTS BE OKAY?
GIL.
I WONDER IF THE PETRO FAMILY ACROSS THE WAY WILL BE ALL RIGHT.
YEAH, I'M WORRIED ABOUT THEM TOO. I'LL GO CHECK.
WAIT! IT'S TOO DANGEROUS ALONE. I'LL COME WITH YOU.
CHAK
CHAK
OKAY, LISTEN TO ME, HONEY. THERE ARE SOME SCARY GUYS OUT THERE RIGHT NOW.
SO I WANT YOU TO GO AND HIDE ON THE SECOND FLOOR.

YOU NEED TO STAY THERE AND STAY QUIET UNTIL WE GET BACK.
DO YOU UNDERSTAND, CONNIE?
DADDY?
MOMMY?
DON'T LEAVE ME...

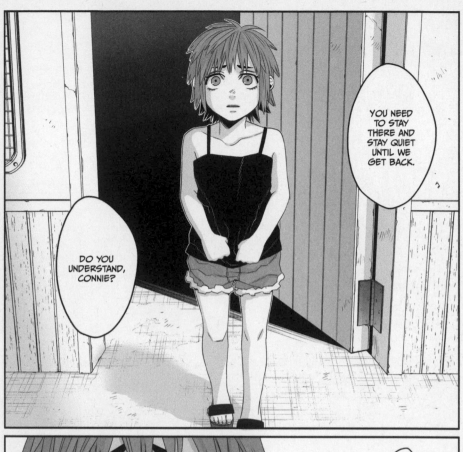

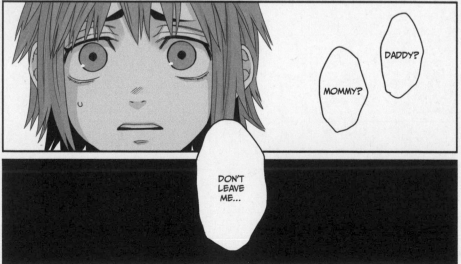

#03 END

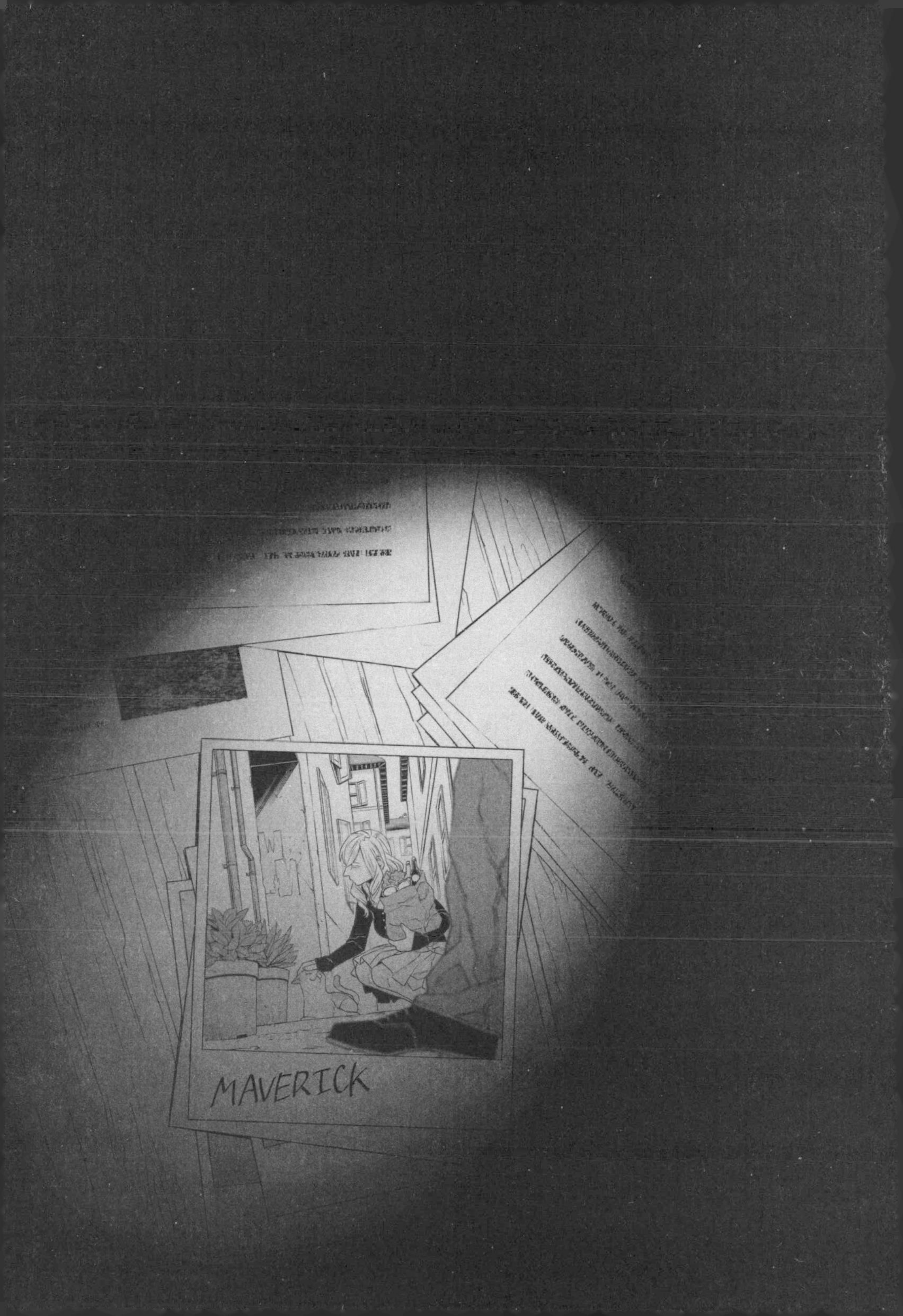
MAVERICK

Destroyer Daily Life

Collection

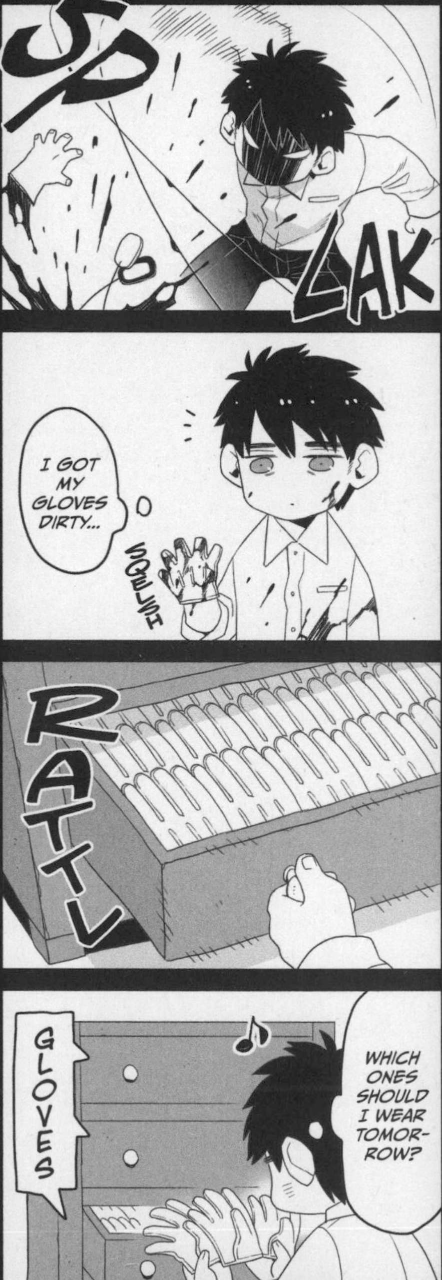
SP
LAK
I GOT MY GLOVES DIRTY...
SQELSH
RATTL
WHICH ONES SHOULD I WEAR TOMORROW?
GLOVES

Interest

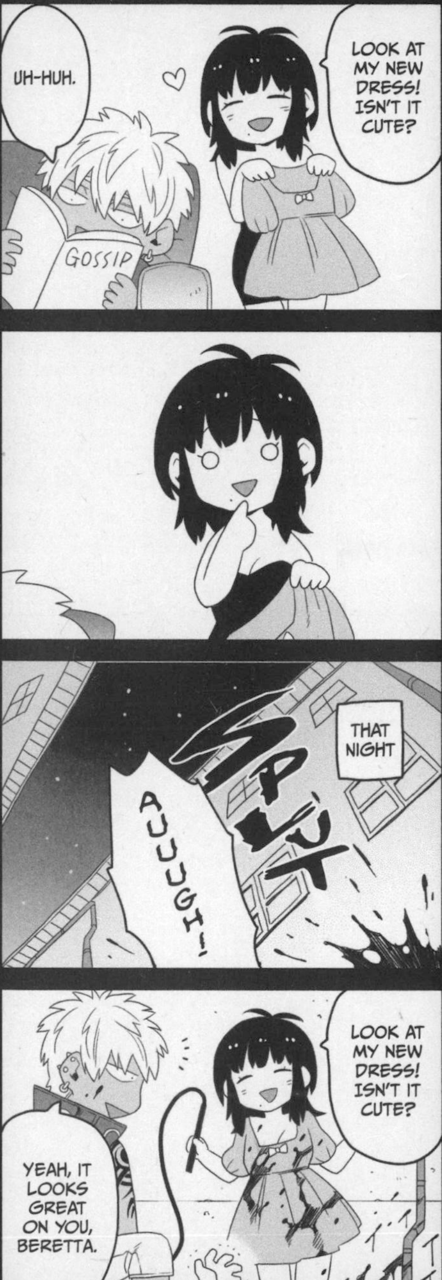
LOOK AT MY NEW DRESS! ISN'T IT CUTE?
UH-HUH.
GOSSIP
THAT NIGHT
SPLUT
AUUUGH!
LOOK AT MY NEW DRESS! ISN'T IT CUTE?
YEAH, IT LOOKS GREAT ON YOU, BERETTA.

Destroyer Daily Life

Chimney

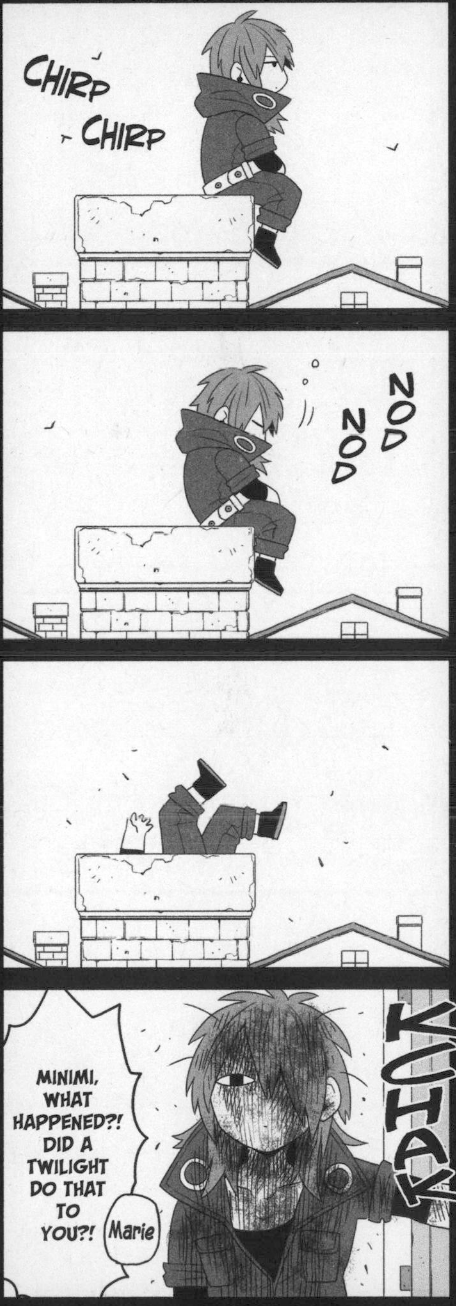
CHIRP
CHIRP
NOD NOD
KCHAK
MINIMI, WHAT HAPPENED?! DID A TWILIGHT DO THAT TO YOU?!
Marie

Medicine

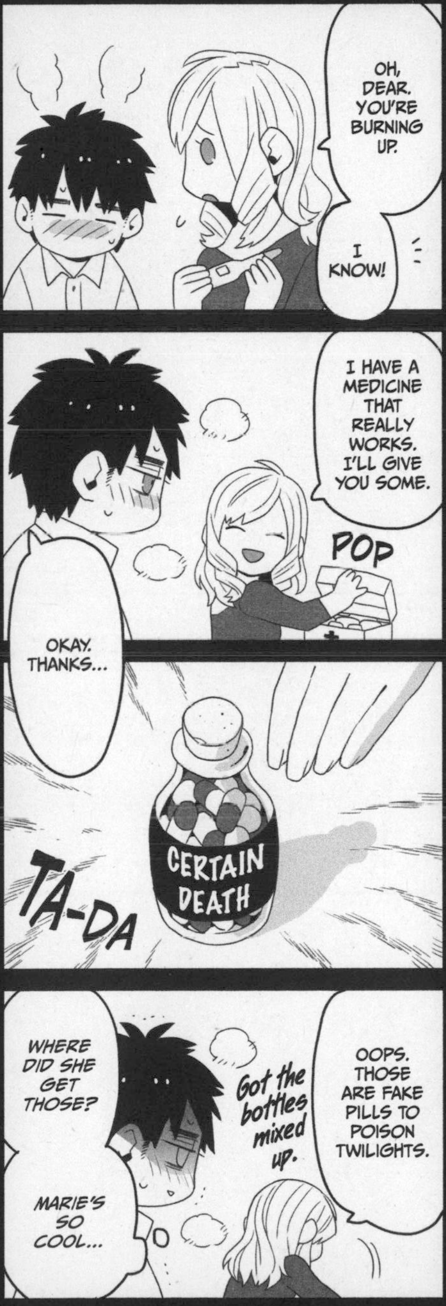
OH, DEAR. YOU'RE BURNING UP.
I KNOW!
I HAVE A MEDICINE THAT REALLY WORKS. I'LL GIVE YOU SOME.
POP
OKAY. THANKS...
CERTAIN DEATH
TA-DA
OOPS. THOSE ARE FAKE PILLS TO POISON TWILIGHTS.
Got the bottles mixed up.
WHERE DID SHE GET THOSE?
MARIE'S SO COOL...

This is Kamo

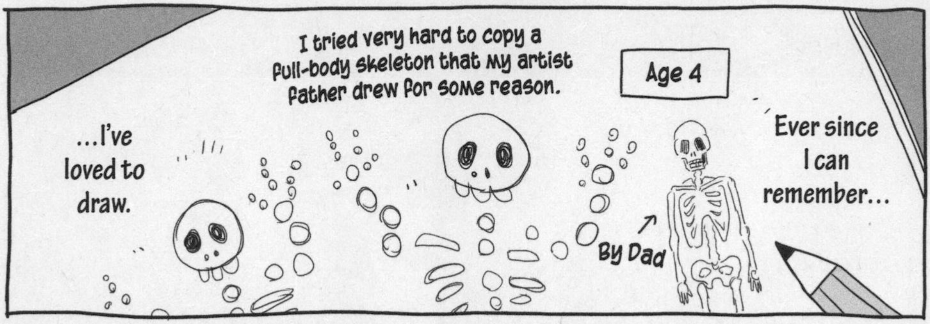
Ever since I can remember...
Age 4
I tried very hard to copy a full-body skeleton that my artist father drew for some reason.
By Dad
...I've loved to draw.

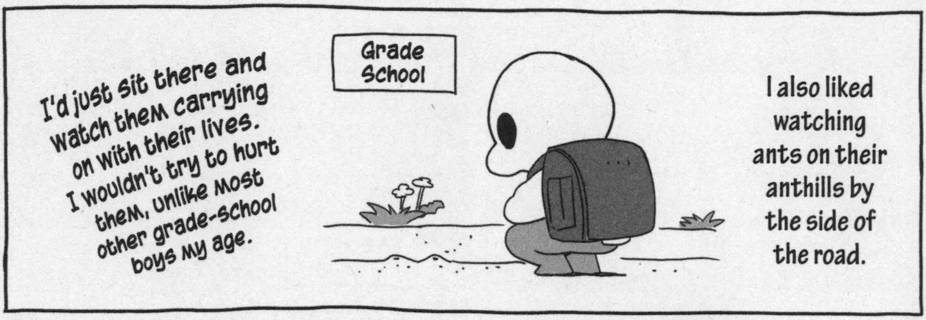
I also liked watching ants on their anthills by the side of the road.
Grade School
I'd just sit there and watch them carrying on with their lives. I wouldn't try to hurt them, unlike most other grade-school boys my age.

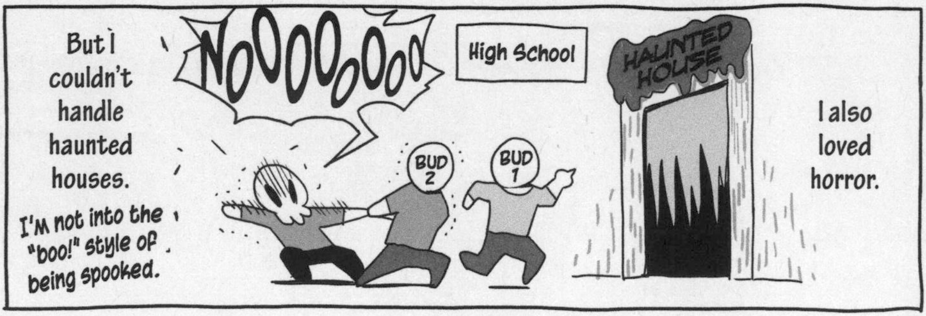
I also loved horror.
HAUNTED HOUSE
High School
BUD 1
BUD 2
NOOOOOOOO
But I couldn't handle haunted houses.
I'm not into the "boo!" style of being spooked.

Nice to meet you.

My name is Syuhei Kamo, and I drew this story.

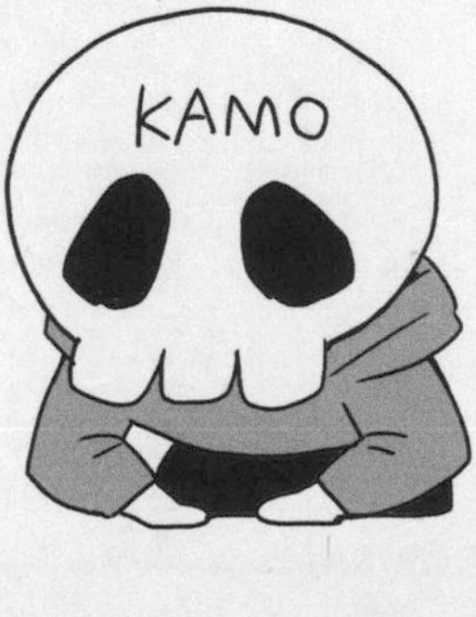
KAMO

I very much appreciate you buying this book.

About Kohske

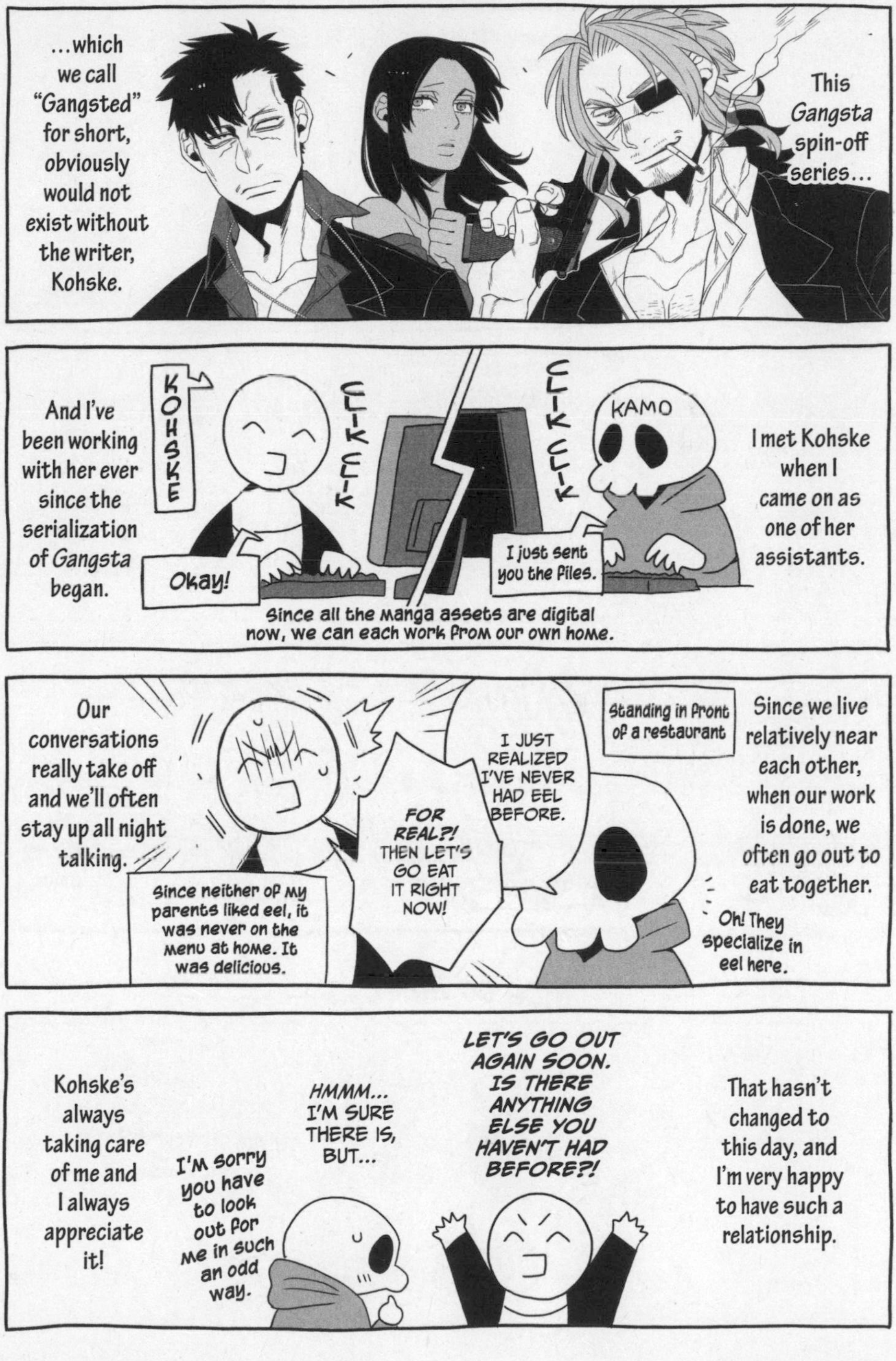
This Gangsta spin-off series…
…which we call "Gangsted" for short, obviously would not exist without the writer, Kohske.
I met Kohske when I came on as one of her assistants.
KAMO
CLIK CLIK
I just sent you the files.
CLIK CLIK
KOHSKE
Okay!
And I've been working with her ever since the serialization of Gangsta began.
Since all the manga assets are digital now, we can each work from our own home.
Since we live relatively near each other, when our work is done, we often go out to eat together.
Standing in front of a restaurant
I JUST REALIZED I'VE NEVER HAD EEL BEFORE.
Oh! They specialize in eel here.
FOR REAL?! THEN LET'S GO EAT IT RIGHT NOW!
Our conversations really take off and we'll often stay up all night talking.
Since neither of my parents liked eel, it was never on the menu at home. It was delicious.
That hasn't changed to this day, and I'm very happy to have such a relationship.
LET'S GO OUT AGAIN SOON. IS THERE ANYTHING ELSE YOU HAVEN'T HAD BEFORE?!
HMMM… I'M SURE THERE IS, BUT…
I'm sorry you have to look out for me in such an odd way.
Kohske's always taking care of me and I always appreciate it!

Cursed

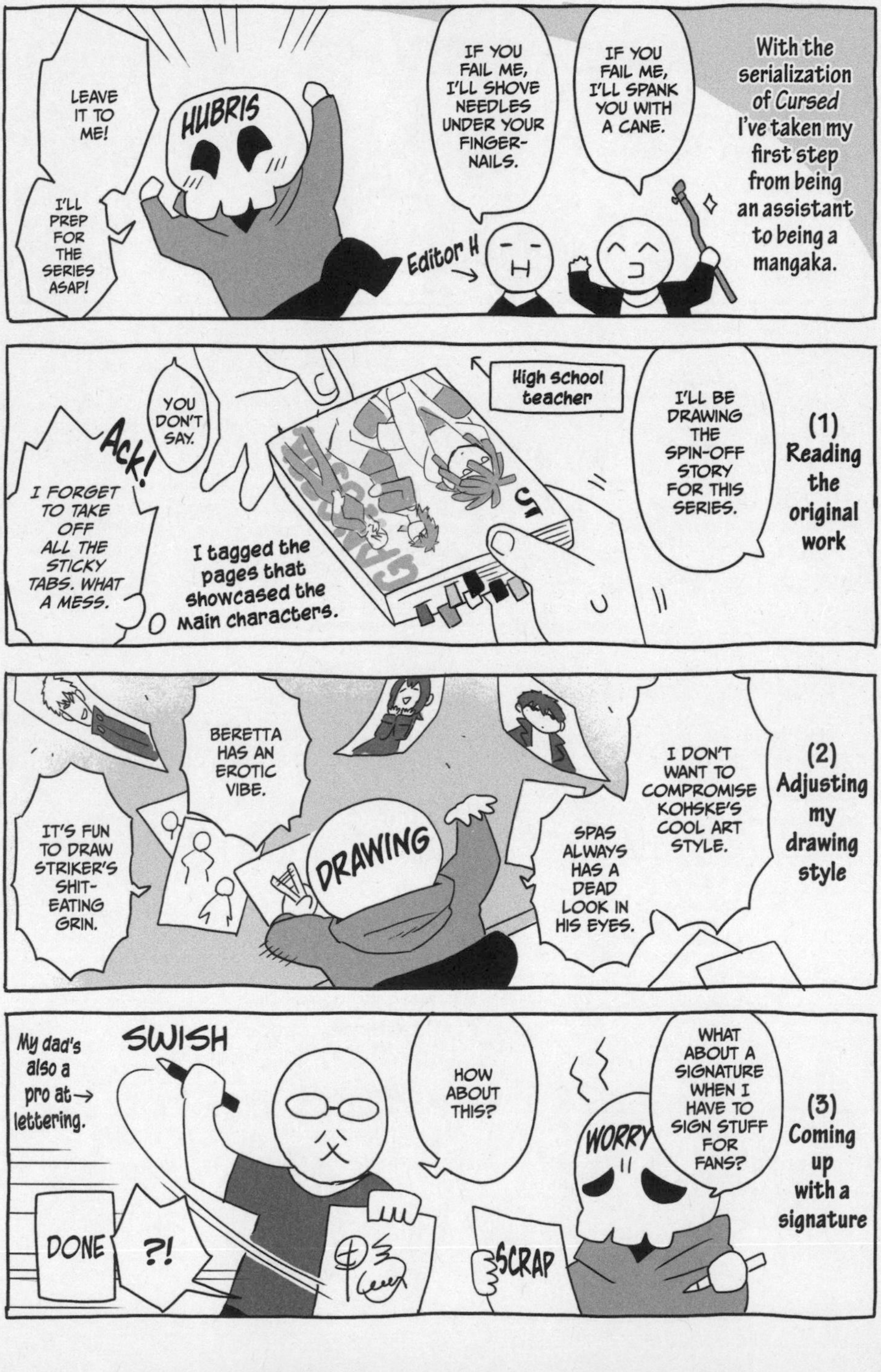
With the serialization of Cursed I've taken my first step from being an assistant to being a mangaka.
IF YOU FAIL ME, I'LL SPANK YOU WITH A CANE.
IF YOU FAIL ME, I'LL SHOVE NEEDLES UNDER YOUR FINGER-NAILS.
Editor H
HUBRIS
LEAVE IT TO ME!
I'LL PREP FOR THE SERIES ASAP!
(1) Reading the original work
I'LL BE DRAWING THE SPIN-OFF STORY FOR THIS SERIES.
High school teacher
YOU DON'T SAY.
Ack!
I tagged the pages that showcased the main characters.
I FORGET TO TAKE OFF ALL THE STICKY TABS. WHAT A MESS.
(2) Adjusting my drawing style
I DON'T WANT TO COMPROMISE KOHSKE'S COOL ART STYLE.
SPAS ALWAYS HAS A DEAD LOOK IN HIS EYES.
BERETTA HAS AN EROTIC VIBE.
DRAWING
IT'S FUN TO DRAW STRIKER'S SHIT-EATING GRIN.
(3) Coming up with a signature
WHAT ABOUT A SIGNATURE WHEN I HAVE TO SIGN STUFF FOR FANS?
WORRY
SCRAP
HOW ABOUT THIS?
SWISH
My dad's also a pro at lettering.
?!
DONE

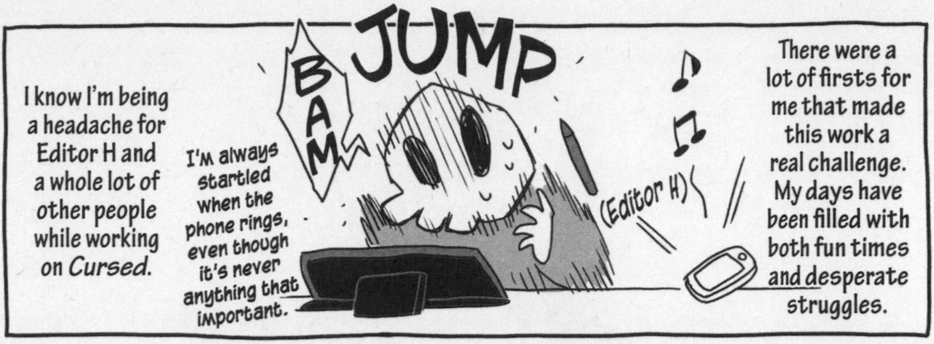
There were a lot of firsts for me that made this work a real challenge. My days have been filled with both fun times and desperate struggles.
JUMP
(Editor H)
BAM
I'm always startled when the phone rings, even though it's never anything that important.
I know I'm being a headache for Editor H and a whole lot of other people while working on *Cursed*.

GANGSTA: CURSED IS MY DEBUT WORK. TO THINK THAT IT'S ALREADY BEEN COMPILED INTO A WHOLE VOLUME AND IS IN NOW BOOKSTORES... EVEN AS I TYPE THIS SENTENCE, PART OF ME WONDERS IF ANY OF THIS IS REAL.

FUELED BY CEREBRET (OKAY, FRISK MINT CANDY), I'M GOING TO WORK EXTRA HARD TO SHOW EVERYONE ANOTHER SIDE OF THE *GANGSTA* WORLD. SO I APPRECIATE YOUR SUPPORT AND GOOD WILL.

SEE YOU AGAIN IN THE NEXT VOLUME!

KOHSKE
ASSISTANT K / ASSISTANT M / ASSISTANT H
EDITOR H / DESIGNER ISHIKAWA
DAD / MOM / LITTLE BRO / MY DOG
AND TO EVERYONE WHO'S TAKEN SUCH GOOD CARE OF ME.

THANK YOU VERY MUCH!

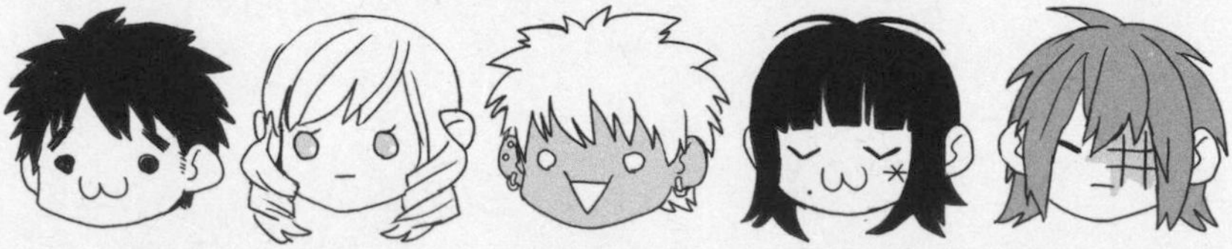

In the Next Volume

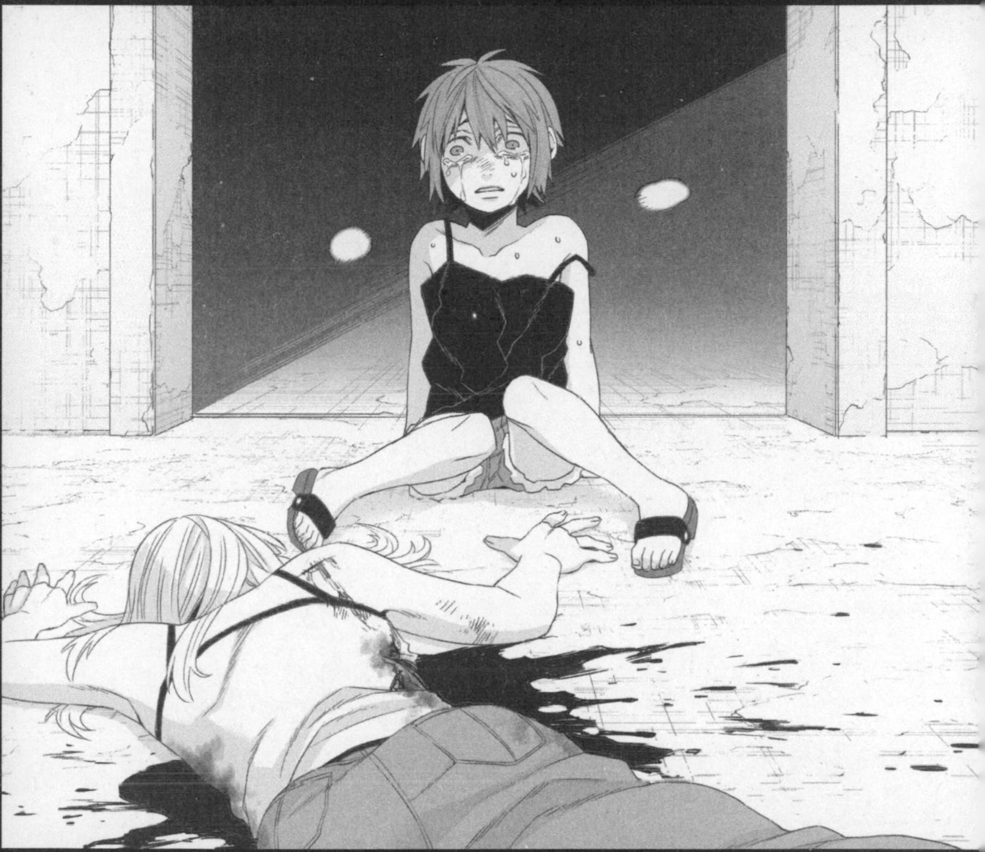

As Spas and the rest of the Hunters carry out their gruesome duty, his indoctrinated belief that eliminating all Twilights is the only way to guarantee the safety of the Normal population begins to erode. Unable to reconcile the high-minded teachings of his past with the brutal realities of his present, he stands on the brink of a decision that will change his life—and the lives of those he loves—forever.

GANGSTA-CURSED.
EP_MARCO ADRIANO

Gangsta:Cursed. Ep_Marco Adriano
Volume 1

VIZ Signature Edition

Story by Kohske
Art by Syuhei Kamo

Translation & Adaptation/Christine Schilling
Touch-up Art & Lettering/Eric Erbes
Cover & Graphic Design/Sam Elzway
Editor/Leyla Aker

GANGSTA:CURSED.EP_MARCO ADRIANO
© Kohske 2015.
© Syuhei Kamo 2015. All rights reserved.
English translation rights arranged with SHINCHOSHA PUBLISHING CO.
through Tuttle-Mori Agency, Inc., Tokyo.

The stories, characters and incidents mentioned in this
publication are entirely fictional.

Printed in the U.S.A.

Published by VIZ Media, LLC
P.O. Box 77010
San Francisco, CA 94107

10 9 8 7 6 5 4 3 2 1
First printing, December 2016

www.viz.com

RATED M FOR MATURE
PARENTAL ADVISORY
GANGSTA:CURSED. is rated M for Mature and is
recommended for mature readers. This volume
contains graphic violence and mature themes.
ratings.viz.com

VIZ SIGNATURE